T0368352

Seek Ye First

A Daily Devotional

GAIL GLEATON BELL

WESTBOW
PRESS®
A DIVISION OF THOMAS NELSON
& ZONDERVAN

WestBow Press books may be ordered through booksellers or by contacting:

WestBow Press
A Division of Thomas Nelson & Zondervan
1663 Liberty Drive
Bloomington, IN 47403
www.westbowpress.com
1 (866) 928-1240

ISBN: 978-1-9736-8196-0 (sc)
ISBN: 978-1-9736-8197-7 (hc)
ISBN: 978-1-9736-8195-3 (e)

Library of Congress Control Number: 2019920675

Print information available on the last page.

WestBow Press rev. date: 07/29/2020

... the kingdom of God and His righteousness, and all these things shall be added unto you. (Matt. 6:33)

The morning steals upon the night, melting the darkness.
(Shakespeare, *The Tempest*, Act 5, Scene 1, Line 65)

The fear of the Lord is the beginning of wisdom, and the
knowledge of the Holy One is understanding. (Prov. 9:10)

Dedication

I have included sayings at the beginning of each devotional because my dear mother raised my siblings and me on little sayings and quotes that she felt would help us to remember the life lessons that she wanted to impress upon our thinking and actions. I have embraced these little jewels as precious treasures because they tend to come to mind at just the right time. My own children have reaped the benefit of many of them as I have passed them along for the same reason. Not all 365 that I have used here were in her collection of words, but many were.

While sayings are catchy and thought provoking, Scripture is much more precious. "The word of God is living and active and sharper than any two edged sword, and piercing as far as the division of soul and spirit, of both joints and marrow, and able to judge the thoughts and intentions of the heart" (Heb. 4:12). Since the Bible is such a powerful tool for life and living, Mother and Daddy always made sure that we were exposed to God's Word at home and that we were in church for all activities to learn and grow spiritually. It is easy to hide God's Word in your heart when you make it a habit to read it as we were encouraged to do.

My devotional book is dedicated to my wonderful and loving parents, Fred and LaVerne Gleaton, who I love dearly still. They rest together in their heavenly home, but one day I will see them again when I see Jesus. I never doubted that I was loved unconditionally. Such a love gave me a clear and present picture of God's love, the One who guided their lives. I count it a blessing to be their child and His.

Contents

January

February

March

April

May

June

July

August

September

October

November

December

Introduction

I am humbled by the fact that my mighty and glorious heavenly Father could ever even imagine that I could pen His words into a devotional book. Please know that I could never have done this on my own. Because He placed this undertaking on my heart and because He has encouraged me and inspired me through the years, it has come to pass. I have constantly questioned Him concerning this matter, not ever doubting His adequacy but constantly questioning mine. Always He assured me that His grace is sufficient for all my needs and that His power is made perfect in my weakness and inability. As the apostle Peter admonished us to do, I humbled myself, therefore, under the mighty hand of God (1 Peter 5:6).

We limit God only by our disobedience and our failure to believe that He can do what He says He will do. He never points us in a direction unless He has prepared the way. I am reminded of King David's last words to his son, Solomon, who would succeed his father as king: "As for you, my son Solomon, know the God of your father, and serve Him with a whole heart and a willing mind; for the Lord searches all hearts, and understands every intent of the thoughts. If you seek Him, He will let you find Him; but if you forsake Him, He will reject you forever" (1Chron. 28:9).

I am His and He is mine. My desire is to serve Him with a willing heart, to know Him more each day, and to share the fruits of His Spirit. I am abundantly grateful for the confidence He has shown in me and that He has given to me such an opportunity as this. No reward is mine except that it glorify my heavenly Father.

I challenge you, the reader, to hear Him as He speaks to you and enjoy the victory as He leads you through the project that He has for you to do as you are obedient to Him. The blessings are in the study of His Word as you seek Him first.

January

O God, Thou art my God; I shall seek Thee earnestly;
my soul thirsts for Thee, my flesh yearns for Thee, in
a dry and weary land where there is no water.

—Psalm 63:1

January 1
All things are possible to him who believes. –Mark 9:23

As you seek God first today, have you dressed in His armor? We cannot truly be ready for our day until we dress appropriately for the battle. "For our struggle is not against flesh and blood, but against rulers, against the powers, against the world forces of this darkness, against the spiritual forces of wickedness in the heavenly places" (Eph. 6:12).

The devil is our enemy. He prowls about like a roaring lion seeking someone to devour (Peter 5:8). It is important for us to be strong in our faith. In order to do that, we must put on the full armor of God so that we can resist the temptations and deception of the evil one. Our armor consists of truth, righteousness, the gospel of peace, faith, salvation, and the Holy Spirit. Suiting ourselves in this armor each day equips us for the battles that we face in life. We are called to believe and trust that Jesus has made a way for us to do all things through Him. The word *believe,* according to the dictionary, means "to accept as true or real; have confidence in; trust." Is your confidence in Jesus? Do you trust Him, knowing that His way is the best way and the only way?

As we begin a new year, we need to establish within ourselves exactly in whom we believe. It is important to believe in oneself. However, we in ourselves are limited. Many times our decisions and efforts fall through. Even our most sincere attempts fall short. Our hope lies in Jesus Christ. When we put our confidence and trust in Him, there is nothing that we cannot accomplish. All things are possible. We can look ahead with assurance that He will lead and He will guide. *Isn't that exciting?* Our load is lifted already. What a year this will be if we, at its beginning, lay all our burdens at the foot of the cross, confessing that we are sinners, asking for forgiveness, inviting Him into the sanctuary of our hearts, and seeking Him and His will each day.

**But seek first His kingdom and His righteousness and
all these things shall be added to you. (Matt. 6:33)**

January 2
To have a friend, be one!

I was eating in a restaurant once, surrounded by three friends treating me to lunch on my birthday. It was one of the restaurants where the young waiters and waitresses bring in a small dessert with a lighted candle on the top and all stand around the honoree to sing "Happy Birthday" if so arranged. My friends had so arranged it, and I was thrilled and totally surprised. It was a special time.

As we were leaving the restaurant after our celebration, a lady at the next table said to me, "I can look at you and tell you are rich."

I was taken aback for a moment. I was not dripping in diamonds or furs. What did she mean? "You have such nice friends around you," she said.

Jesus was a friend of sinners when He came to earth, and He still is. When God became flesh and dwelt among us, He came not for the saved but so that sinners might come to know Him, trust in Him, and be saved from eternal doom. Jesus said, "It is not those who are well who need a physician, but those who are sick. I have not come to call the righteous but sinners to repentance" (Luke 5:31–32). This should give us a clue as to what a true friend is. Jesus was criticized more than once for fraternizing with sinners. We should in no way ever compromise our values or integrity in order to reach someone, but we should be to the struggling sinner a lighthouse of God's grace and truth.

What a treasure we have in our friends—just one of those precious gems that our heavenly Father blesses us with in this life. We can be glad that our heavenly Father loved us enough to call us to repentance and call us friend before we knew Him.

Take time today to call a friend or two. Tell them how much they mean to you. Then reach out to a weaker brother or sister who needs to know the friend of sinners. They might not know that He came for them too.

I am the good shepherd; and I know My own, and My own know Me…. And I have other sheep, which are not of this fold; I must bring them also, and they shall hear My voice; and they shall become one flock *with* one shepherd. (John 10:14, 16)

January 3
I believe in the sun even when it is not shining. I believe in love even when not feeling it. I believe in God even when He is silent.

After researching to find out where these amazing words came from, I discovered that they had been found scratched out on a wall in a cellar in Cologne, Germany. It seems that Jews had hidden in that cellar during World War II, and some optimistic soul had recorded his or her thoughts to be discovered later. Such faith and trust are what God calls His children to, if we want to please Him. It is impossible for us to please God without faith.

What is faith? How can we trust someone we have never seen? That is what faith is. It is standing on His promises and believing that He will do what He says He will do. His Word, the Bible, is filled with marvelous accounts of His faithfulness. We have only to read from Genesis to Revelation and know that He is the God who never changes. Every prophetic word, every covenant, every ordinance, and every word that proceeded from the mouth of God has come to pass. Even today we are seeing signs of the end times that Jesus spoke of when He walked on this earth. We can believe without fear or hesitation that the truth of God's Word is without error or deviation.

Has God called you to believe and trust Him lately? Noah believed God when He told him to build an ark on dry land. It took years to accomplish this, but Noah believed God when He said that He would bring a flood to the earth, although it had never before rained. God told Moses to lift his staff over the Red Sea because He was about to part the waters and let them cross over. The Israelite people would have never known deliverance had Moses refused to obey God, trusting that God would do what He said He would do. A young Jewish girl named Mary listened and believed as an angel gave her a message from God that she would give birth to the promised Messiah. Faith means that we do not have to do anything but choose to obey the One who asks us to trust Him, believing that He will do what He said He would do.

Now faith is the assurance of things hoped for, the conviction of things not seen. (Heb. 11:1)

January 4
The one thing worse than a quitter is a man who is afraid to begin.

Life is filled with adventures, challenges, and new horizons that we all have equal opportunity to reach. Setting goals for oneself and striving through hard work and a positive attitude can move you forward in this new year to accomplish more than you ever dreamed you could. Look ahead. Don't look back and think of what you should have done. Look forward and think of what you will do. Beginnings are great because we have a clean canvas before us. The sky is the limit. Believe in your own abilities as a person created by God who wants to bless you. Give God the reins. Let Him guide you.

There is a cause greater than yourself, and that is God's purpose for your life. Are there goals that you feel helpless and overwhelmed by? God has a purpose for each of our lives. Until you find it, you haven't lived, and until you fulfill it, you're not ready to die.

At twelve years of age, Jesus said, "I must be about my Father's business." Just twenty-one years later, He announced, "It is finished." The work He had come to do on this earth was completed. Mission accomplished! He had a cause greater than Himself, and He was faithful to allow God to do wonders through Him.

We face giants every day that sometimes overwhelm us. Young David stepped forward because God's people were being threatened by a giant. Everybody around him was afraid to tackle the problem. When you are confronted with a situation that needs to be changed, what is it that makes you rise up and say, "I'm going to do something about it"? Could it be that you see a cause greater than yourself? David did. Paul wrote in Philippians 1:21, "For to me to live is Christ." Paul desired to exalt the name of Christ and promote His kingdom. Paul is very much responsible for the Gentiles' being grafted into the covenant promises. That was a cause greater than himself. Joshua had watched the Israelites' failures and rebellions as God's man, Moses, led them toward the promised land. When the baton was passed to him, he could have easily said, "No, thank you. I don't think I want the job." But instead, he told the people, "Consecrate yourself, for tomorrow the Lord will do wonders among you" (Joshua 3:5).

Don't let the enemy rob you of the purpose God has for you. Satan is the great discourager. God calls you to prepare yourself so that you can bless Him and He can bless you. Consecrate yourself; the Lord will do wonders! Your blank canvas can be a masterpiece if God is at the center of it. Begin today, and don't quit!

Forgetting what lies behind and reaching forward to what lies ahead, I press on toward the goal for the prize of the upward call of God in Christ Jesus. (Phil. 3:13–14)

January 5
Procrastination is a thief of time.

God has allotted to each of us a lifetime. For some, a lifetime is just a few years. For others, a lifetime is one hundred years and more. What we do with our allotted time is up to each of us. I knew a lady once who set a daily goal to live each day as if it were her last. What a great philosophy! Time would become very valuable if we knew we only had a little of it left. Yet we never know, and we rob ourselves of so much time by not filling each moment.

No one made an impact on this world like our Savior, Jesus Christ. He was in this world only thirty-three years. He was a humble yet powerful man. Jesus came into the world to redefine power. He even left His power source, the Holy Spirit, for all who would accept Him.

What does God expect of us in a changing world in the time we have left? We don't know our time line; only He does. That doesn't matter. We are only responsible for making the most of the time that He gives us. "Let us also lay aside every encumbrance, and the sin which so easily entangles us, and let us run with endurance the race that is set before us, fixing our eyes on Jesus" (Heb. 12:1b–2a). Jesus said to his disciples as He healed a man who was born blind, "We must work the works of Him who sent Me, as long as it is day; night is coming, when no man can work" (John 9:4). Now is the time to work the work of Him who sent us. When we put off doing what God calls us to do, when we procrastinate, we miss many blessings along the way. I know that firsthand. My mother wanted so badly for me to finish this devotional book before she died. I have regretted so many times that I didn't make it a priority in my life and in her time.

Life is not how much time we have but how we spend that time. Plan your work and work your plan. Move forward and don't put things off. We all have the same twenty-four hours. Make yours count!

**He who began a good work in you will perfect it
until the day of Christ Jesus. (Phil. 1:6)**

January 6
People who fail didn't plan to fail. They failed to plan.

Directions are essential in our daily lives. We need to know where we are going and how we will get there. Starting out on a long trip would be disastrous without a map or GPS. If you had never been to your planned destination, you might set out in the wrong direction. How can we know God's direction for us in this life? How can we know what is right and what is wrong? There is only one place to find absolutes, pure truth, and that is in God's Word to us, the Bible. He tells us that His word is a lamp unto our feet and a light unto our path (Ps. 119:105). In it we find our directions and instructions on how to live while passing through this life on earth.

If you ever get into God's Word to His people, you will be amazed at how His plan unfolds. He uses ordinary people to accomplish His extraordinary purpose. He calls out prophets and priests and kings by His own choosing, and disciples follow after Him without hesitation. God has an amazing plan that was ordained before the beginning of time. He is the Alpha and the Omega, the beginning and the end.

An inventor or creator of something knows better than anyone else just how to operate his invention or creation. He writes down explicit instructions so that those who acquire his design will know how to operate it to its full potential. Without those directions or instructions, it could be a worthless hunk of metal or a completely useless product. So it is with the human race. How can we ever expect to function properly without reading the instruction manual provided for us on how best to live? God, our Creator, provided distinct and yet simple instructions for us in His instruction book, the Bible. A person can go through his or her entire life without ever reading those instructions, hence missing out on all the wonderful promises meant just for him or her. How we do limit God! How we do deprive ourselves! Read your Bible daily. Know what your Creator says about how you best operate. Trust Him with your life. He made you. He knows. Don't miss out on God's plan..

The words of the Lord are pure words; as silver tried in a furnace on the earth, refined seven times. (Ps. 12:6)

January 7
A positive mental attitude is an irresistible force that knows no such thing as an immovable body.

Along with all the other choices we have in life is the choice of having a positive outlook and approach or a negative one. I heard a successful woman speak on this one time. She explained that until she rid herself of her negative attitude, she was at a standstill in her career and just spinning her wheels. She went on to say that people with negative approaches to life have to first realize that they have such outlooks, and only then can they do something about it. She explained that people with negative attitudes tell themselves that they are being realistic and everyone else is just living in a dreamworld.

Being positive about yourself and about life can make a difference in how you view everything around you. Positive people look at their families and see beautiful joys, while negative people see financial burdens. Positive people look at roses and see the beautiful blooms and smell the sweet aroma, while negative people see and feel only the thorns. Positive people look at life as a challenge and an adventure, but negative people see life as a struggle, as laboring day in and day out to make a go of it. What is your outlook? Positive or negative? The difference could be between just existing or truly living. Don't go through life only existing when you could be living life to its fullest.

Corrie ten Boom is one of those precious people who went through horrible situations and with God's grace made the best of it. She and her entire Christian family were arrested for hiding Jews in their home to escape the Nazi Holocaust during World War II. After her release from prison due to a clerical error, she set out to open homes for victims of the Holocaust. She shared her story wherever she was asked to speak, always giving a message of hope to people who were desperate for hope.

Christians are without excuse. If you know Jesus, you know the light of the world. Our hope is built on nothing less than Jesus's blood and righteousness. He is what positive is all about!

The thief comes only to steal, and kill and destroy; I came that they might have life, and might have it abundantly. (John 10:10)

January 8
Actions speak louder than words!

This was one of my mother's most-used sayings as I remember. It is amazing how, even as a child, I understood the meaning behind little gems of wisdom such as this. My siblings and I soon realized that we could try to talk our way out of things, but what we were doing would far override anything we could say or excuse we could give.

It is so easy to *say* words—that is simple enough. However, what purpose do empty words serve? "I love you" is a beautiful, power-packed statement, but only if it is from the heart and the issuer of the statement shows that love in his or her actions. Sometimes it is hard to hear what is being said because we see what is being done. It is hypocrisy to say one thing and do quite another. Always let your deeds correspond to all you say. This builds truth and integrity.

Recently, an e-mail came to me with part of a story that I was totally unaware of, although it happened many years ago. More than fifty years ago, two astronauts, Buzz Aldrin and Neil Armstrong, did something that no human being had done before. Yes, they walked on the moon, and the whole world knew about it when it happened. However, there was one part of that mission that the media never reported: Buzz Aldrin took communion on the moon's surface. He later wrote an article for *Guidepost* in which he described in detail how he opened the small packages of the bread and wine that his minister had prepared for him. He read scripture from the Gospel of John, and he took communion. "I gave thanks for the intelligence and spirit that had brought two young pilots to the Sea of Tranquility," he wrote. He went on to say that it was interesting to him that the first liquid and first food consumed on the moon were the communion elements and that the first words spoken were the words of Jesus Christ, who made the earth and the moon. Buzz Aldrin's actions blessed God that day. He had planned this ahead of time, and his actions showed his gratitude to God and his priorities for worship.

Little children, let us not love with word or with tongue, but in deed and truth. (1John 3:18)

January 9
The nicest place to be is in someone's thoughts, the safest place to be is in someone's prayers, and the very best place to be is in the hands of God.

The disciples thought so. Jesus brought them His peace, His provision, and His promise. As He sat at the table with His disciples for the last time before His departure toward the cross, He sought to comfort them with these words: "Let not your heart be troubled" (John 14:1). I imagine that an atmosphere of sadness filled the upper room as Jesus related to them that He would be leaving them. They had no idea of the suffering that He was facing. Jesus, thinking of only them, gave them words of peace, assuring them that because they believed, there were better days ahead for them. He let them know that by going, He was making provisions for their coming, preparing a place for them where they could dwell with Him for eternity. In His last words to His followers, Jesus also left a promise. The promise was that He would come again and that one day they would be with Him forever in this prepared place. These words must have brought much comfort to this room full of men who had followed after Him for three years. They had observed Him as no one else at that time had. They had seen His prayer life, witnessed His miracles, and heard His profound teaching. They also knew that His promises to them would never be broken because they had observed His faithfulness.

Jesus left us His peace, His provision, and His promise, as well. Let us today be comforted in the wonderful assurance that we can believe and rely on all the words that He has given us. Do not be troubled today. If you are a child of God, if you have chosen to follow Him, you too can live today in peace, looking forward to the day when He will come again and receive you to Himself for eternity.

Look around you. Who can you share with today? Who will benefit from your peace? Tell them of God's provision, His Son, and the promise of heaven, if they will only trust Him.

If anyone loves Me, he will keep My word; and My Father will love him, and We will come to him, and make our abode with him. (John 14:23)

January 10
Be sincere—it secures respect.

What is sincerity? The dictionary says "presenting no false appearance; not hypocritical; honest."

To be sincere, one must be genuine, not false in any way, and holding fast to truth. Not saying one thing and doing another but truly living an honest life is a picture of sincerity. We human beings can spot insincerity a mile away. Don't you just love to be around someone who is the same every time you see them—a person who is his or her own self and doesn't put on a different mask for a different group?

We have the greatest example of genuine sincerity in Jesus. He showed humility and sincerity as He walked on the earth and dwelt among humankind. Those closest to Him respected Him; however, it took His horrible death and His miraculous resurrection for the world to recognize the One who came in all sincerity and power for the purpose of redeeming humankind. A suffering servant who presented no false appearance or hypocrisy became the exalted One, and He sits today at the right hand of His Father. Now, centuries later, the impact of His life continues to be felt.

It is amazing that Jesus would ever want to be raised again, to come back into the midst of evil men who had been so brutal to Him. Many had rejected the truth that He taught and despised His very presence. With His mission accomplished, why would He even want to go further? Why not go directly from the grave back to the Father? Because His finished work was to give us—yes, us, anyone who would come to Him in repentance and acceptance—eternal life. His resurrection made it possible that we, too, will one day be raised and go to the Father. His sincere love for us won the victory over death for believers. "O death, where is your victory? O death, where is your sting?" (1 Cor. 15:55). Only our perfect Savior could accomplish that for all who come to Him. Thank you, Jesus, for loving us enough to come again into this cruel world and give us victory over the grave.

Do nothing from selfishness or empty conceit, but with humility of mind let each of you regard one another as more important than himself. (Phil. 2:3 NAS)

January 11
Inside every human being there are treasures to unlock. —Mike Huckabee

Be yourself. God made each of us an individual and special. Be proud. You are an original. No one is exactly like you. Have you ever stopped to think what a miracle that is in itself? Of the billions of people in the entire world, no two are exactly alike. Even twins are different in one way or another. Not only do people look different, but each person's personality is different. Sometimes I just get overwhelmed when I think about the miraculous creations of God. He gave to each of us our own special talents and abilities. Each person's potential is so great. We alone limit ourselves.

We can go back to the beginning of creation to find our origin and know that we are the offspring of the Trinity: "Then God said, 'Let us make man in Our image, according to Our likeness'" (Gen. 1:26). I find myself on shouting ground when I read these words. The thought that humankind is a replica of Holy God is beyond comprehension. In his sermon on Mars Hill in the book of Acts, the apostle Paul reminded the people of Athens that in God "we live and move and exist ... being then the offspring of God, we ought not to think that the Divine Nature is like gold or silver or stone, an image formed by the art and thought of man" (17:28, 29). Without God we would not exist. He is our source for life and our hope in death.

Strike out today to be all that you can be. Know first that you have a heavenly Father who loves you and wants only the best for you. God does not make any junk! He makes only quality gems. You are one sparkling treasure in His beautiful creation. Paul again reminds us that we can do all things through Him who strengthens us (Phil. 4:13). Unlock the treasures that are yours alone. Share your knowledge, your talents, and your gifts with those around you. Mother Teresa once said, "The Father loves me, He wants me, He needs me."

Every good thing bestowed and every perfect gift is from above, coming down from the Father of lights, with whom there is no variation, or shifting shadow. (James 1:17 NAS)

January 12
Habits are first cobwebs, then cables.

Have you ever tried to break a bad habit? It's not easy, is it? I can hear my mother's words now: "Don't start bad habits and you won't have to worry about breaking them." Good advice, right? She would always tell us to run from alcohol like it was a rattlesnake. I believed her, and I am glad I listened. I have seen the destruction it causes in the lives of many.

I've always wondered why it's so much easier to break a good habit than it is a bad one. Have you noticed that? Family devotionals are a good habit that the average family can't seem to keep going. You start out really well and remain faithful for a while into the New Year, but it soon falls by the wayside and eventually is forgotten about. It's funny—we never miss that favorite television show, always remembering when and what time it comes on. Early-morning quiet time does not always happen either, but we never miss that cup of coffee in the morning. We are certainly creatures of habit, but we do exactly what we want to do. We start habits and, therefore, it has to be a willing decision of our minds to break one. It hurts us to think that we would choose to hang onto bad habits while good ones slide away. But we are products of our choices, so we have to be intentional about hanging onto the good ones and eliminating the bad ones. Bad habits can become a yoke or bondage that we would never desire for ourselves if we could see the end at the onset. That is why God tries with every precept in His Word to steer us toward the narrow path that leads to life. When we allow our old sinful nature to have preeminence over our choices, we set ourselves on the wide road that leads to destruction. Before I was old enough to listen to God, I listened to my mother and daddy, who listened to God and set my feet on the right path. No one wants to be a slave to a bad habit. Flee before that snake bites. God has a better way for you. Rick Warren said it this way: "Every time you defeat a temptation, you become more like Jesus."

Do not be deceived, God is not mocked; for whatever a man sows, this he will also reap. (Gal. 6:7 NAS)

January 13
Good health makes for power-packed living.

How blessed we are if we continue in good health throughout our lifetimes. So often we take good health for granted. I immediately think of the apostle Paul. We don't know what Paul's affliction was. He referred to it only as "a thorn in the flesh" (2 Cor. 12:7). However, no man was ever more devoted to carrying the message of Jesus than Paul. He looked above his circumstances and kept his eyes on Jesus, running the race with every ounce of his energy. I have come to realize more and more through the years how much the condition of the mind and heart has to do with how we work through our physical infirmities. Attitude plays an important part in our physical condition. We can give in to physical problems, letting them consume us with pity and depression, or we can keep a positive outlook and with determination work through them.

My morning walks have gotten to be a routine I look forward to. I meet three neighbors each morning, and we spend thirty minutes together walking, discussing the news of the day, sharing prayer requests, and solving the problems of the world (if anybody would listen). We walk through the cold in the winter and the heat in the summer. We have even walked in the rain with umbrellas. Some of us have fallen headlong, thankfully without any debilitating injuries. The older we get, the more we appreciate the fact that we can still get out and walk.

Daily walking with Jesus is much like my morning strolls. There are many blessings along the way, but there are also many obstacles to contend with. Just as my friends hold me accountable to walk each morning just by being there, Jesus encourages us to never give up and never give in to life's distractions, hindrances, and nuisances. He promises that He will always be there for us and will remain with us to the end of the age. We must stay close to the path our Maker has put us on if we want to know the benefits of a healthy Christian life. And I must continue my daily walks if I want to reap the rewards of a healthy physical life.

Like Paul, we must realize that there are earthly things that we have to deal with now. The ultimate goal is the prize of eternity with our Creator and sustainer. That's living!

I, therefore, entreat you to walk in a manner worthy of the calling with which you have been called. (Eph. 4:1)

January 14
Some people make the world brighter just by being in it.

When I think of physical suffering, I immediately think of my dear, sweet mother, whose sweet spirit and positive attitude have always been an inspiration to me. Rheumatoid arthritis came to take up permanent residence in her strong and active body when she was about forty years old. She was square in the middle of raising four children and being the best farmer's wife a woman could be. We saw this dreaded disease take hold of her healthy body and try to pull her down. Through all the pain and suffering that accompanies this debilitating disease, however, she always had that quiet, gentle spirit and the determination to overcome. Her faith in God would not move. She touched so many lives with her positive outlook, humility, and unwavering faith. We all learned what inner strength, patience, and determination not to quit in the midst of suffering looks like. It is easy for us to have a positive outlook when everything is going great and we feel fine, but the test comes when we hurt and we can't get past it. I saw my mother in so much pain that her face was drained to a chalky white. There were times when she would finally get to her feet after sitting too long and almost lose her breath, breaking out into a cold sweat from pain. Her theme was "One day at a time, sweet Jesus." Treatment for rheumatoid arthritis has come a long way since Mother's agony. She also developed osteoarthritis that caused her to be bedridden for the last two years of her life. Even in that state, she was a blessing to all who knew her.

We can count on God in times of suffering just as we can in the times when all is well. Just as He assured Paul and my mother with the words "My grace is sufficient for you," He is our all-sufficient Savior as well, as we meet with trials and suffering. There are many hurts in our world today—physical, mental, emotional, and spiritual. Jesus is the answer to them all! If we can keep our eyes on Jesus and build our hope on Him, we can overcome these obstacles one day at a time!

And He said to me, "My grace is sufficient for you, for power is perfected in weakness." (2 Cor. 12:9)

January 15
Blessed are those who are pleasant to live with.

I cross-stitched this little saying several years ago, had it framed, and hung it on the stair landing in our home so that all my family and I could see it regularly. We need little reminders to keep us focused on what is important in this life. Life offers so many distractions that throw us off course if we don't remind ourselves often who we really want to be in control of our lives and that it is He we want to please with our actions. Day-by-day living in such close communion with family is not always easy. We have to have a place and a time when we can let off steam. There is no better place than at home with people we love and those who love us in spite of our moments of ill will. However, we must always remember not to get so wrapped up in our own sensitivity that we aren't aware of the feelings of those close to us. Moodiness seems to be contagious at times; one bad mood can trigger another. But one good mood can trigger another as well. It's important that we try to be conscious enough of those around us that we see when there is a need for an encouraging word, a kind deed, or maybe just a hug. By God's grace, our marriage has lasted more than fifty years. We have decided at this point that we are going to take an aspirin and go on and make it last. Long marriages are getting to be a rarity these days. It is certainly not an easy road, blending two people with different upbringings, different beliefs, different habits, and opposite personalities. (I am going to ask God when I get to heaven why opposites are attracted to each other. I think God's answer to my question will be, "Because I want you to learn to depend on Me.") Truthfully, I don't see how any marriage lasts without God at its center. When we don't make Him the honored guest in our homes, we are bound to fail.

The Bible tells us that children are a gift of the Lord (Ps. 127:3). Yes, indeed they are! And so are grandchildren. Our three grown children and their spouses make life a joy, and our ten grandchildren are a sweet blessing in our old age. Our desire is to be a blessing to them and not a burden.

Bear one another's burdens, and thus fulfill
the law of Christ. (Gal. 6:2)

January 16
Three early risings make an extra day.

How are you fixed for time this week? Rushed? Pushed? Is your calendar already packed with chores and activities? Wow! Will it ever end? No, and we don't want it to! It's good to stay busy, to be active and occupied with worthwhile things. It's also good to have those quiet moments to yourself when you can stop, take stock, and reflect on what you have accomplished or get your priorities in order and your ducks in a row for your time ahead.

For many years my husband and I enjoyed rising about an hour before the children did and having that time to have a cup of coffee and a quiet conversation at the beginning of the day. I always cherished that time. When our nest became empty with no more children at home, my husband retired, and we had no reason to have to get up, we tended to sleep in a little longer. It was not long before we decided that we missed those special early morning times. We are now back to enjoying our quiet time, devotionals, and watching the sun come up. There is something about seeking God first, before the clamor of the world sets in, that anchors your day, helping you to arrange your thoughts and fix your plans. After my time alone with God and my husband, my early rising gives me time to take a walk and enjoy God's outdoors and the company of three walking buddies.

Jesus often felt it was necessary for Him to find a quiet place in the early morning hours to have time with His Father. In the book of Mark we see Jesus rising early to pray. The day before and even after the sun had set, He had preached, healed the sick, and cast out demons. He must have been weary and very tired, but that did not keep Him from rising early. "And in the early morning, while it was still dark, He arose and went out and departed to a lonely place, and was praying there" (v.35). Jesus knew from where His strength and guidance came.

May we always follow Jesus's example by seeking God first. Before your day begins, call on Him to be your strength and your guide for the new day. He will be there and will be much, much more. Have a happy day!

O God, thou *art* my God; early will I seek thee. (Ps. 63:1 KJV)

January 17
It's one thing to be active in our work for the Lord— quite another thing to be effective. —T. J. Bach

Our world today is moving so fast that I sometimes feel we are just busy being busy. Oftentimes we are at the church every time the doors open, yet we seem to be accomplishing so little in reaching out to those around us. I am reminded of the story of the little old woman who sat in her modest cottage at the top of the mountain and prayed each day for all the people in the valley below. She had grown too feeble to travel down the mountainside to show her love and to minister to them. Her ministry, nevertheless, was just as great because she did what she could. Corrie ten Boom is a beautiful example of effectiveness in a Christian life. She and her family suffered such heartache and persecution during her time in the Jewish concentration camps, yet never did she waver or get downtrodden in her Christian faith. She prayed for her enemies and those who persecuted her. It is said that in her last days after she suffered a stroke, she would sit at her window at the edge of the street and pray for each person who passed by. She did the best she could considering the shape she was in, and she did it for the right reasons. We become effective when we do whatever we do in Jesus's name and for His glory.

Being a quiet servant is not always easy. We seem to hunger for a pat on the back or desire recognition or compliments for our little servitude. Our old sinful nature tells us that we "deserve" praise for what we do. That is not God's way, even though it is often our way. In order to be effective in God's kingdom, He asks that we seek Him first, die to ourselves, and let Him lead.

There are many lessons in God's Word about how to live godly lives in order to be fruit-bearing Christians. Our good works are not what save us, so why do we think they must be recognized? "He saved us, not on the basis of deeds which we have done in righteousness, but according to His mercy, by the washing of regeneration and renewing by the Holy Spirit, whom He poured out upon us richly through Jesus Christ our Savior" (Titus 3:5–6). Jesus paid the price for our righteousness when we did not deserve it. We can be effective servants when we glorify Him in all we do.

But prove yourselves doers of the word, and not merely hearers who delude themselves. (James 1:22)

January 18
The man who removes a mountain begins by carrying away small stones.

Are you facing a situation today that seems overpowering? You can't see above, under, or around it? I know the feeling. However, there is a way. Remove one obstacle at a time. Face the little ones first, then the next ones won't seem so large. As Mary Kay Ash use to say, "Inch by inch, it's a cinch. Yard by yard, it's hard!" Just as we must take one day at a time, so we must take one obstacle at a time.

I am reminded of a man who looked on the dark side of everything. Everything that came up was an insurmountable obstacle. One day he found himself trapped in a cave after an explosion. His very life depended on whether someone found him. No one came. Life became real important to him. He had time to reflect and think about how he viewed life. He realized that the small things that had plagued him in the past were things he could have done something about, but the situation he was in now depended on someone else's help. Or did it? Gradually he began to remove one stone at a time until finally he could see the light of day and take in the fresh air. He came to realize after it was all over that, if he had sat down and said, "There are too many obstacles between me and the entrance to the cave," he would never have seen the light.

Life will never be free from obstacles, hindrances, and stumbling blocks. We live in a fallen world. It is important that we know who is in control and who is the enemy. God is in control, and the enemy (Satan) was defeated at the cross. Billy Graham once said, "I've read the last page of the Bible. It's all going to turn out all right." Sure, there are battles to be fought, rivers to be crossed, and mountains to be climbed, but our God is able to help us remove one enemy at a time, calm the rough waters, and cross over the steepest mountain.

Who are you counting on today to come to your aide? Your heavenly Father is always just a prayer away. Jesus said, "My sheep hear My voice, and I know them, and they follow Me; and I give eternal life to them, and they shall never perish; and no one shall snatch them out of My hand" (John10:27–28). He will do His part; we just have to do ours.

My help comes from the Lord, Who made heaven and earth. He will not allow your foot to slip; He who keeps you will not slumber. (Ps. 121:1–2)

January 19
You can measure a man by the opposition it takes to discourage him.

Is it going to be a good day? I hope so. It is up to you, you know. Life is unpredictable at its best. That is one thing that makes each day exciting and challenging. As Jesus walked on this earth, He never knew who was going to throw stones at Him. He never knew what criticism He would encounter from one day to the next. He was walking so close to His Father, as they were One, yet people questioned everything He did. Once, He opened the eyes of a blind man, and His own people did not believe it. One of his own disciples betrayed him and one denied Him. Did Jesus ever get discouraged? Possibly, but never to the point of losing sight of His purpose. "For I have come down from heaven, not to do my own will, but the will of Him who sent me" (John 6:38). No opposition was going to keep Him from His mission.

Just like Jesus, we too will often get knocked back, ridiculed, criticized, and even persecuted. Jesus said, "If they persecuted me, they will also persecute you" (John 15:20). Christians, those who name the name of Jesus, will receive opposition from the world. Who is the world? The world is those who have chosen to live outside of the will of the true and living God. They have rejected Jesus, and the cross is foolishness to them. Sadly, they are perishing (1 Cor. 1:18). Why are they so blind? Who is pulling the strings of deception and deceitfulness? It is the prince of darkness, Satan. He is crafty and seeks those whom he will devour. James 4:4 tells us that friendship with the world is hostility toward God. When Christians fall into the world's way, we lose our effectiveness as Christ followers. It is necessary for us to face opposition, even persecution, head on. Jesus never backed down and neither should we. How do you measure up?

Draw near to the Father that He might draw near to you. Satan makes sure that the negative is always there. That is why we must accentuate the positive! Discouragement is a tool of the evil one, and too often we allow him this stronghold in our lives. Let your focus today be on the power that comes with serving the living God.

**I came that they might have life, and might
have it abundantly. (John 10:10 NAS)**

January 20
Some of your best thinking is done when you are bored.

Have your children ever come in saying, "I am bored"? You just stand there amazed that, with all the television, toys, video games, good books, and so on, they could dare to make such a statement. Our quote for today came to me one day when my youngest was sitting around the house with a sad face. He had called every friend he knew to call to come and play, but they all had other plans. Out he came with this "bored" statement. That is when this revelation came to me. I had heard this from my two older children on other occasions, and I would always say, "Well, I can remedy that!" and I would find them a job to do. They soon learned that if they were bored, they didn't tell Mama! However, it occurred to me when my youngest made the statement just how much I cherish those moments when I have nothing to do. We think of bored as being a negative word, but from that time on, I have seen it to be a positive word and have tried to help my children to see it that way. When things are quiet and there is no specific thing to do, your brain has an opportunity to relate to creative ideas, to sort out things, to think of others, to pray, to reflect on all your blessings, to reminisce, to read God's Word, and even to spend one-on-one time with your mama!

Jesus often would steal away to a quiet place to rest or to pray. We find this many times in scripture. When Jesus was only twelve years old, He left the crowd that was traveling with His parents and He went back to Jerusalem. The caravan was a day's journey away from that city when Jesus went missing. Mary and Joseph returned to Jerusalem and "found Him in the temple, sitting in the midst of the teachers, both listening to them, and asking them questions" (Luke 2:46). The text tells us that they "were amazed at His understanding and His answers" (v.47). Maybe the young Messiah was bored with playing childish games and chasing rabbits. The time had come for Him to put away childish things and do the will of His heavenly Father. Don't let boredom rob you of something greater.

Be still and know that I am God. (Ps. 46:10a)

January 21
Avoid following the crowd. Be an engine, not a caboose.

People face peer pressure today more than ever before. We see it not only with the younger generation but with adults as well. Television, Facebook, and social media in general have made it possible to see how the other half lives, and our lives have been exposed to good and evil through these means. We are definitely influenced by others, so it is very important to know whose you are and where you stand.

One of the most deceptive lies in our world today, which is being swallowed by the young and old alike, is that fornication and cohabitation are okay. Sex of any kind outside the bounds of marriage is an abomination to God and is forbidden. Just because "everybody is doing it" does not make it right. When we condone what God has already condemned, our hearts are not right and we are living in sin and disobedience. God's Word is very clear about this; Paul includes the sexually immoral and adulterers in the list of those who will not enter the kingdom of God (1 Cor. 6:9–10). Fornication is the act of consummating a relationship that the two people have not committed to, making the act a lie and a sin. Marriage is a covenant, a promise, between a man, a woman, and God. God does not excuse sex outside of marriage or sexual perversion. Many older people are living together without marrying for convenience sake, setting the wrong example while practicing situational ethics. Their morals are determined by their situations, usually concerning monetary means that will be cut off if they marry. God frowns on such behavior. His way is to do the right thing and trust Him to meet your needs. In order to escape God's judgment, we must abide in His truth.

Daily meditation with God and searching His word to know the right direction is so important. He is the same yesterday, today, and forever (Heb. 13:8). All the answers for godly living today are in His Word. The Bible is our manual from God that could be entitled, "Instructions for the Human Being to Live By." When we follow His instructions, everything falls into place. After all, He did make us, and He knows best how we work. Yes, judgment is His, but His mercy is sure.

Step back and take a good look at yourself today. If you are leading, are you going in the right direction? Is your life on the right track? There is always someone looking at you. If you are following, are you following a leader who is going in the right direction? Someone once said that if you don't stand for something, you will fall for anything. Whether leading or following, make sure you are going God's way. If not, you will eventually derail.

Oh that my ways may be established to keep Thy statutes!
Then I shall not be ashamed. (Ps. 119:4–5)

January 22
Those who are willing to face the music
may someday lead the band.

When I taught younger tweens and teens in Sunday school, I found it to be a challenge to inspire our youth of today to be leaders rather than followers, particularly when it comes to their walk with the Lord in the marketplace. When I stand back and take a long look, I realize that they are faced with greater temptations, pressures, struggles, and adversity than we were faced with thirty years ago. It is more imperative than ever before that they be saturated in the truths of God's Word and that they are shown the hope and righteousness that comes from knowing Jesus as Lord and Savior. Youth are born leaders. They love to be in the middle of things and on the cutting edge. Giving them the proper direction is the responsibility of parents, grandparents, teachers, coaches, relatives, pastors, and all who love them and are concerned about their future and the future of this world.

Manasseh was twelve years old when he became the king of Judah (2 Kings 21:1). He was the son of Hezekiah, a good king. Sadly, Manasseh did not follow in his father's footsteps and proceeded to restore idol worship and practice witchcraft, divination, and other abominations to the Lord. Josiah was only eight years old when he was made the king of Judah following his father's death. Even though his father, Amon, was an evil king, Josiah "did right in the sight of the Lord" (2 Kings 22:2). Josiah destroyed idols and worshipped the true and living God. We see two scenarios here—an evil son who had a good father and a good son who had an evil father. What made the difference? Maybe it was the mothers; the scripture does not say. One thing we know for sure is that Josiah sought the Lord's direction even at an early age and Manasseh did not.

Our youth must see examples of God-fearing, Christ-loving adults. Seek out young people today and let them see Christ in you! Point them to the Way by the examples you set and the words you speak. Help them to face the challenges of the times head on with the assurance that if they seek Christ first and His righteousness, all things will line up as they should. He never changes and His way leads to life. They can then lead the way for a better tomorrow.

The fruit of the righteous is a tree of life, and he
who is wise wins souls. (Prov. 11:30)

January 23
A pint of example is worth a gallon of advice.

Jesus walked this earth for only thirty-three short years, but, oh, the impact He made and is still making in lives today. No other person in the history of this world has embodied the righteousness of our Savior, the perfect example of holiness, humility, and hope for all humankind. As He ascended back to the Father, He left us the most precious of gifts, the Holy Spirit, so that all who accept and believe in Him will have eternal life. We would do well to follow in the footsteps of Jesus. His example was as true as His words.

In His Sermon on the Mount in the book of Matthew, Jesus challenged us with these words:

Blessed are the poor in spirit, for theirs is the kingdom of heaven. Blessed are those who morn, for they shall be comforted. Blessed are the gentle, for they shall inherit the earth. Blessed are those who hunger and thirst for righteousness, for they shall be satisfied. Blessed are the merciful, for they shall receive mercy. Blessed are the pure in heart, for they shall see God. Blessed are the peacemakers, for they shall be call sons of God. Blessed are those who have been persecuted for the sake of righteousness, for theirs is the kingdom of heaven. Blessed are you when people insult you and persecute you and falsely say all kinds of evil against you because of Me. (Matt. 5:3–11)

Imagine being blessed for enduring all these things.

Jesus never asks us to do anything that He didn't do. We will never be asked to suffer the way He suffered. When we surrender to Him, He gives us the power to live out the above Beatitudes. Surrender is simply giving God permission to mold you into His likeness.

There is nothing that will come your way today that you and Christ cannot handle. With the Holy Spirit as our helper, we have the power to be like Jesus, to walk in His footsteps, and to follow His ways.

Do you feel that you can be the example that Jesus was? Do you want to be? You can, and you will be blessed!

I can do all things through Him who strengthens me. (Phil. 4:13)

January 24
The important thing is not who is right but what is right.

Have you been called on to take a stand lately? Have you found yourself in a situation where you had to make a choice whether to stand up for what's right or to go along with the crowd? It seems we find ourselves in this situation quite often in today's world. Oftentimes we wonder how we can make a difference in our little corner of this world. There is one way: stand up for what is right. God's laws never change. His word for us is always the same. Christians are to be light and salt in this world. Light dispels darkness, and salt adds flavor and preserves life. The psalmist declares the word to be a lamp unto his feet and a light unto his path (Ps. 119:105). In order to see our way clear in these days, we must go to the source of light. Jesus said, "I am the light of the world; he who follows Me shall not walk in the darkness, but shall have the light of life" (John 8:12).

There are many things we can do to take a stand for what is right. First of all we must be sure that what we project is in line with what God says. Somebody once said that opinion is no substitute for the truth of God's Word. Our words should bring glory to God; our opinions draw attention to ourselves. Just because the world around us is changing does not mean that we have to go along with changes that are contrary to God's standards. Christians are to be different, set apart, separate from the world and its ways. What might be right in the world's eyes might be totally wrong in God's eyes. Satan is the prince of the world, but God is the ruler of the universe. The person who has taken a stand for Christ must purposefully and intentionally stand for what Christ and the Bible say is right.

Today, make a difference! Today, let your light shine! Today, be the salt that adds flavor to someone's day and gives them life and hope.

Let your light shine before men in such a way that they may see your good works, and glorify your Father who is in heaven. (Matt. 5:16)

January 25
Truth is what God says.

When our daughter went off to college, she went from being a big fish in a little pond to being a little fish in a big pond. She met many challenges that she had not had to face before. One night she called home in tears over one of her classes. It seems the teacher had brought up the subject of abortion in the class that day, and it disturbed our daughter terribly. In the course of our conversation, I realized that she was as disturbed about what she couldn't or didn't say as she was about the issue. She knew in her heart how wrong it was, but she found herself in a position where she felt she was compromising with an opinion that she disagreed with just by not speaking up. It is hard for Christians to sit and listen to people impose their views on an entire class when those views go against what God's Word says and what they know in their hearts to be wrong. It turned out, however, that she was assigned to write a paper on the subject and would have an opportunity to pose her side of the argument.

As a Christian and a mother, I was grieved for the many students who sit in classrooms every day and listen to many teachers who don't know God's truth and who lead many a child down the wrong path by forcing the world's views on them. I am so thankful that my daughter recognized a wrong opinion and was genuinely concerned.

The movie *God Is Not Dead* displays in reality what goes on in many of our colleges and universities. Is it any wonder that many of our young people question life and live in a state of hopelessness? God is very much alive, and He wants all to know the truth, the way, and the life. When truth is compromised, those who do not know the God of truth listen to the distorted views of those who themselves do not know what the Bible says. Like in the movie, sometimes just one voice can speak through the darkness and be heard. Our prayer was that our daughter's paper would make a difference in the heart of her teacher.

God has no tongue but our tongue. He has no feet but our feet. He desires that we walk with Him and speak truth to a world that cannot hear unless we tell them.

And do not be conformed to this world, but be transformed by the renewing of your mind, that you may prove what the will of God is, that which is good and acceptable and perfect. (Rom. 12:2)

January 26
Tell the truth and tell it ever, costeth what it will, for he who hides the wrong he did does the wrong thing still.

Today's society is faced with a dangerous wave of situational ethics. We are seeing more and more humanistic approaches to moral and ethical choices. Right and wrong are not treated as moral absolutes; instead, they are considered relative to the person and the situation. God's laws never change, however, and such views of morality and integrity leave us lacking the values that God wants for His people.

Situational ethics says that you can lie if it saves someone some pain or gets you out of a bind. God says speak the truth (Eph. 4:25) and He will take care of the pain and the circumstances. Situational ethics says play the lottery so that our children will have money for schools and scholarships. God says seek me and do the right thing and I will meet your needs (Matt. 6:33). Situational ethics says abort an unwanted baby because you can't afford another child or it would be inconvenient. God says it is wrong to kill (Exo. 20:13). Situational ethics says live with someone outside of marriage to be sure before you tie the knot. God says that He will judge fornicators and adulteries (Heb. 13:4).

Daily we find ourselves in situations that call us to compromise our beliefs and our integrity. There is only one way, and that is God's way. His Word is clear as to how we are to walk and live our lives. Our ethics are not to be controlled by the situation we are in. Our situations should be controlled by our ethics, our moral principles based on God's laws. God's Word is absolute truth and our guidebook to follow. We must never compromise God's principles to be what the world wants us to be. Wrong is wrong, no matter who calls it okay.

Integrity is what we do and how we behave when no one is looking. Integrity is fairness, fidelity, honesty, honor, purity, trustworthiness, righteousness, virtue, and sincerity. A person of integrity can be trusted.

Stop and think before you act. Even better, pray.

There is a way that seems right to a man, but its end is the way of death. (Prov. 14:12)

January 27
Set the rules, then set the example.

Our lives have meaning when we live in ways that are upright and pleasing to the Lord. The proper solution to any problem and the correct plan of action must come from God. What are the benefits of living one's life to please God? True wisdom lets God lead. Only God can judge us accurately. Only God can establish our plans. God is our sovereign Lord, and He expects us to be obedient to Him. Obedience brings blessings. True success in life comes only through a lifestyle of trust in the Lord. The wise person humbly lets God guide his or her life, while the foolish person proudly rejects God's standards for life.

In the book of Daniel we see, from the first chapter and all the way through the book, a young man whose desire was to please God. From his birth, Daniel was taught the Jewish rules for living a life that honored God, and they were embedded in his heart. In his youth he was among the brightest and best looking of the Jewish young men taken to Babylon after the siege of Jerusalem. King Nebuchadnezzar sought to brainwash them to the ways of the Chaldeans. They were required to eat the rich food from the king's table and drink his wine. Daniel and three of his friends asked for permission to refrain from eating that diet and chose instead to eat vegetables and water. Their request was granted, and because they made a better choice, God blessed them with great knowledge, intelligence, and wisdom. He gave Daniel the ability to understand dreams and visions. Because they were the most outstanding, they were given places in the king's service.

God expects His children to set the right example. He has given us His rules to live by. Will you walk this day in a manner worthy of your calling? Like Daniel, we can take a stand and set the example for those around us. Daniel was a man of prayer with strong convictions, and God used him mightily. He will use you, and you too will be blessed!

Do all things without grumbling or disputing; that you may prove yourselves to be blameless and innocent, children of God above reproach in the midst of a crooked and perverse generation, among whom you appear as lights in the world. (Phil. 2:14–15 NAS)

January 28
Your children more attention pay to what you do than what you say. —Zig Ziglar

I do believe my mother's favorite saying—along with the Golden Rule to treat others as you would have them treat you—was "Actions speak louder than words." I've since heard others state it this way: "I can't hear what you say for seeing what you do."

We can't expect our children or anyone else's children to live as they should if we do not set the right examples before them. The great evangelist Billy Sunday said, "To train a boy in the way he should go you must go that way yourself." Their hearts are so tender and their faith is so strong to believe even what they cannot see. That is why Jesus used the analogy of a little child's faith when He taught how we must come into the kingdom of God (Matt. 18). We must come as a little child, open and receptive to His will for our lives. Jesus also had a strong word for all who cause these little ones to stumble in Luke 17:2: "It would be better for him if a millstone were hung around his neck and he were thrown into the sea, than that he should cause one of these little ones to stumble."

Oh, how important it is for us to be genuine Christians with no hypocrisy. Jesus is our role model. His actions spoke as loud as His words.

How can I look like my Father when all the world moves in?

How can I walk so straight and tall when the line I must walk is so thin?

How can I be all He wants me to be and show a hurting world His light,

When darkness creeps over like a curtain of black and covers my heart like the night?

I do not always take on His likeness tho I desire in my heart to do so;

But He loves me no matter how wretched and selfish, this one thing I know.

The cross made it real and offered the seal that settled that perfect redemption.

Lord, come dwell inside, forever abide to make me a new creation.

How can I look like my Father? There's only one way that I see.

Ask Him to come in and make His abode in this heart with so desperate a need.

Then I will take on His likeness, then the world will be able to see,

A light glowing out of the darkness, His glory shining through me! (Author)

Lord, let our words be seasoned with the salt of your wisdom and the honey of your sweet love. Let our children and grandchildren be blessed because we have been with you.

**And whoever receives one such child in My
name receives Me. (Matt. 18:5)**

January 29
Use it or lose it.

Jesus uses a parable to illustrate His point that we are to use to the fullest the gifts and talents that He has given us. The story in Matthew 25:14–30 illustrates His lesson to us. One man was given one talent (unit of currency) by his master, another two talents, and a third man was given five talents. The master went away for a while, and when he returned he inquired of the three men what they had done with their talents. The man with five talents had doubled his and now had ten talents. The master said, "Well done, thou good and faithful servant, because you have been faithful in using that which you have, then I will give you more talents." The one with two talents had likewise multiplied his. Then the master went to the man with the one talent to see how he had done. The man replied, "Master, you only gave me one talent, while you gave the others many talents. Besides, I knew you were a hard and cruel master, that you reaped where you had not sown, and so I took the one talent and buried it." The master replied, "Thou wicked and slothful servant." He then took the one talent and gave it to the one with ten talents. In this case, the talents were the possessions of their master, but the principle is the same concerning the capabilities that some have that others do not possess like teaching, serving, preaching, singing, playing musical instruments, and such. God is the master, He entrusts certain gifts and talents to all humans, and He delights in seeing us use our talents and expanding them. "To whom much is given, much will be required" (Luke 12:48).

Many talents go to the grave without ever being exercised, enjoyed, or shared—buried and never used. God blesses us all with different gifts of service. He expects each person to use his or her gifts, whether we have one or many, to the glory of God and for the good of His kingdom on the earth. God gifts His children, and our talents can speak to the world like nothing else, drawing humankind to Him if we use them in the right way. Are your talents buried? Go dig them up and share your blessings!

For to everyone who has shall more be given, and he shall have an abundance. (Matt. 25:29)

January 30
When you fail–and fail you might–
go again and hold on tight.

If at first you don't succeed, try, try again. I cut my teeth on this saying—again, one of Mother's favorites.

How far can you go without failing or falling? Life is filled with stumbling blocks that keep us tripped up. Things get in our path and cause us to stumble. Sometimes we hit the ground hard. Sometimes it is just a bump in the road of life, and sometimes we have to detour to avoid a hard fall or problems ahead. Where are you today? Has life thrown you into a curve and you feel as if you are losing control? Don't moan and groan. Don't roll over and die. Don't blame it on someone else or take your frustrations out on them. Go to the source of your strength and let Him deliver you from the pits of despair and set your feet on the straight and narrow path.

Many great people before you have failed and gone on to great things. Thomas Edison failed many times before he invented the light bulb. The Wright brothers crashed many a plane before they got it right. God used a simple staff to test Moses's faith and build his confidence when he questioned his own ability. First, God instructed Moses to throw it down, and it turned into a snake. Then He told Moses to lift it up, and when he did the Red Sea parted and the Israelites walked through on dry land. The main thing is to give it to God before you ever set out. Failure has never killed anyone yet. It might slow things down, but hold on tight and trust the One whose timing is perfect and can lead you through. If we don't get up when we fall, we will never know how far we can run.

Our lives are like an artist's canvas. What we paint on that canvas is up to each one of us. There will be times when we will drop the brush or smear the paint. Step back and look at the whole picture. Call on the source for your inspiration. Now make your corrections. Failing should only make you more determined to go again.

**My flesh and my heart may fail, but God is the strength
of my heart and my portion forever. (Ps. 73:26)**

January 31
When your cookies crumble, make a pie crust!

Probably one of the hardest things to do is to stay optimistic when everything around you is falling to pieces. How do we live in a shaky world that seems to be crumbling all around us? We can't, with victory, apart from Jesus Christ. With Jesus as the Lord and Savior of your life, you can stand firm and walk steadfast with the assurance of His unshakeable kingdom.

When hopelessness abounds, you would think a nation of people founded on the principles of the one true and living God would turn to that God for help and direction. Even though He has made it clear in His Word, the Bible, Americans seem to be second-guessing all the absolutes that He has laid down for us. We can't honor God and straddle the fence with indifference to the laws, morals, and teachings that He has laid out for us to follow. What must we do? God says to humble ourselves, to pray, to seek His face, and to turn from our wicked ways; then He will hear from heaven, then He will forgive our sins, and then He will heal our land (2 Chron. 7:14). America has been so blessed that we don't want to believe that God would show any wrath toward us. But just as God promised Israel that He would "uproot them" if they "turn away and forsake my statutes and commandments which I have set before you and shall go and serve other gods and worship them" (2 Chron. 7:19), so He will do to us.

It is time for us to wake up and rise to the task that is before us. We must return to the Christian principles on which we were founded. Repentance means that we do a complete about-face. When we repent and turn back to Him, *then* we will hear from heaven and *then* He will show us what our part is in changing our nation.

God's kingdom is not of this world, but He came that we might have an abundant life while we are on our earthly journey. The storm clouds will gather and the ups and downs will come, but there is hope. The sovereign God of the universe is in control, and all is well.

Look in the bag. Are your cookies in crumbs? What kind of pie will you make today?

**God is faithful, through whom you were called into fellowship
with His Son, Jesus Christ our Lord. (1 Cor. 1:9)**

February

How precious also are Thy thoughts to me, O God! How vast is the sum of them! If I should count them, they would outnumber the sand. When I awake, I am still with Thee. (Ps. 139:17–18)

February 1
When life gives you lemons, make lemonade!

Dwelling on the negative is what some folks do best. What a waste of time. Life is too good to mope and fret. Look out the window today and see the birds in the treetops. Did the sun come up today at your house? Did you awaken to a new day? Is your heart beating? Someone is in control who is far wiser than we are, and He told us in His Word not to worry or be anxious, "For this reason I say to you, do not be anxious for your life, as to what you eat, or what you drink; nor for your body, as to what you shall put on. Is not life more than food, and the body than clothing? Look at the birds of the air, that they do not sow, neither do they reap, nor gather into barns, and yet your heavenly Father feeds them. Are you not worth much more than they?" (Matt. 6:25–26). God is also watching that little bird and knows when it falls. He knows the number of hairs on every person's head. Should we ever doubt that He will take care of our needs or that He is watching over His children?

What is the eternal prize we all want? Heaven, right? Are you placing your faith in people? In things? In relationships? In achievements? In Hebrews 11 we see what is known as the roll call of the faithful because it lists Old Testament personalities who set examples by doing what God called them to do. Were all of these people perfect? No, they all had character flaws. Moses killed a man. Samson broke his vow to God. Rahab was a prostitute, and David committed adultery and murder. God hates sin, but he uses all of us, flaws and all, to do His kingdom work. We can learn from the victories and from the failures of those who have gone before us. Do you want to be used of God? Make yourself available to Him. He forgives, He saves, and He restores.

As one another's brothers and sisters in Christ, we must cheer one another on. It is not easy to be a Christian, to repel the lemons of this world (Satan being the most bitter), but we "press on toward the goal for the prize of the upward call of God in Christ Jesus" (Phil. 3:14).

Life, like lemons, can get bitter and sour at times, but we don't have to be overcome by its circumstances. Enjoy your lemonade today, knowing that heaven is your prize.

**And He has said to me, "My grace is sufficient for you,
for power is perfected in weakness." (2 Cor. 12:9)**

February 2
The man who rows the boat generally doesn't have time to rock it.

My mother used to tell us, "Sweep around your own door." I didn't know what that meant for a long time. However, age and experience are good teachers, and I soon learned to "tend to my own business." Jesus put it another way. He warned us to remove the beams from our own eyes before we try to get the splinter out of our brother's eye (Matt. 7:4).

So many times we get in an uproar about the overt sins of those around us when, in fact, our own hidden sins are possibly more harmful and hurtful than the sins of the person we are focusing on. God knows the heart, meaning that no sin is hidden from Him.

Like most children growing up, my siblings and I tattled on one another. I remember one time in particular tattling on my brother and causing him to get a whipping. After I saw the punishment that I had brought on him, I wanted so badly to take it back. I wanted him to suffer for aggravating me, but I cried along with him when his punishment came.

Do you weep over your own sin? Do you weep over your own doubt and disobedience? Do you cry out to God at times to create in you a clean heart and renew a right spirit within you? God knows our weaknesses and appreciates our honesty before Him. He rejoices when we are able to see our own sin and acknowledge it before Him. I believe that is why He loved David so and called him a man after His own heart. In all his sinful acts, David realized that his heart was wicked and only God could restore it to where it needed to be. Only the God of his fathers, only the Great Shepherd, only the righteous One could give him peace in his suffering over an evil and contrite heart. The psalms are filled with the laments and agonizing cries of this man who was so broken by the crushing burden of his sin.

We can know forgiveness after sin if there is repentance. We can know restoration and rejoice in a new day. The God of David is the Jesus who came to earth in human form to die for the sins of the world and to give each of us hope for eternity with Him. He alone can renew a right spirit in you and in me. Don't rock the boat unless you are sure that you have a good grip and are above reproach.

Therefore, however you want people to treat you, so treat them, for this is the Law and the Prophets. (Matt. 7:12)

February 3
A despairing world needs caring Christians.

Are there times when you just need someone to sympathize with you? Someone just to acknowledge that your sadness is okay or your suffering will not be forever? That someone is Jesus. He knows and He cares. "We do not have a High Priest who cannot sympathize with our weaknesses" (Heb. 4:15). How can we know that and rest in His truth? By coming "boldly to the throne of grace that we may obtain mercy and find grace to help in time of need" (v.16). Jesus knows our hurts. He knows all that is troubling us. He himself bore the same struggles and more, and He will not leave us comfortless. Do those around us know that?

When Jesus came to earth over two thousand years ago, His message to this despairing world was, "I love you, and I want you to know Me." He was God in human form, the Word made flesh, sent to redeem humankind to Himself, and He called those who would surrender their lives to Him to go and spread this "good news."

Our churches are filled with wonderful, caring people who have gotten comfortable in the pews. Jesus calls us to step out of our comfort zones. Jesus taught in the synagogues, but His primary ministry was done outside of the walls and in the fields that were white unto harvest. He calls us to go and tell, bring the lost in from the highways and byways so that they will not perish. The world's darkness and spiritual blindness can be extinguished only by His glorious light. Being too contented and not stepping out can often lead our churches to become stagnant and ineffective. We are commissioned by Jesus to go, teach, and baptize. His greatest promise and our greatest comfort can be that He promises to be with us. As He empowered the prophets, disciples, and apostles before us, He will also bless every effort we make to carry the gospel to the lost world.

As one of my favorite songs says, "People need the Lord," and caring Christians are the ones who can point them to the hope that is found only in Jesus. Resurrection Day will be much more rewarding if we are joined in the air by those we have helped to make that eternal flight.

Go therefore, and make disciples of all the nations, baptizing them in the name of the Father and the Son and the Holy Spirit, teaching them to observe all that I commanded you; and lo, I am with you always, even to the end of the age. (Matt. 28:19–20)

February 4
When I start to find fault with all that I see, it is time to start looking for what's wrong with me.

Sometimes I have days when nothing seems to go right. Everything that I attempt goes wrong, and everything I touch is disastrous. I feel like I need to get back in bed and roll out on the other side. On those days, normal circumstances often make me lash out or find fault when, otherwise, I would not notice.

I think a lot about ol' Paul, the apostle. All through his letters in the New Testament, he was encouraging believers. Many times he had to correct and reprimand them, but always before his instruction in righteousness he would encourage them in their faith, challenging them to live worthy of their calling. Certainly Paul had many days when much went wrong. After all, he had a "thorn in the flesh" that was ever with him, and he received much criticism just for his Christian walk. But even on Paul's worst days, whether in prison for preaching the gospel or being beaten or persecuted for his faith, he wrote words like, "My heart's desire and my prayer to God for them is for their salvation" (Rom. 10:1). His one goal in encouraging was to point those around him to Christ.

God calls us to be encouragers like Paul and to not be grumblers or complainers. A critical spirit discourages people and retards spiritual growth. It is so refreshing to be with those who are uplifting and the same every time you see them. The only way we can control our attitude and moods is with God's help. It is easy to get caught up in our circumstances and come to a standstill. I hope you will roll over and get out on the other side of the bed too and see the joy in a new day and a new opportunity. Paul was unstoppable. He knew what his goal was, and he ran the race with all the vigor he had. Let our intentions be to honor our Savior by pointing others to Him, the One who loves us best.

But encourage one another day after day, as long as it is still called today, lest anyone of you be hardened by the deceitfulness of sin. (Heb. 3:13)

February 5
A good way to avoid heart trouble: Don't run upstairs, and don't run down people.

Jesus did a lot of serious talking to His disciples in the Sermon on the Mount (Matt. 5–7). As He directed His teachings to them and all the people who came to hear Him, He was speaking to us today. His message was timely. Only the omniscient God could know that for two thousand years, His people would be confronted with and be battling the same obstacles, struggling with the same sins, and searching for the same answers as those weary pilgrims of His day.

In this same sermon, Jesus talked to us about seeking Him first and His righteousness (Matt. 6:33) in order that we would know how we should live, make our decisions, and enjoy the blessing of the abundant life. When we seek Him and His righteousness first, then all the things that we require in this life will be added to us. Philippians 4:19 declares, "And my God shall supply all your needs according to His riches in glory in Christ Jesus."

In chapter seven of His sermon, Jesus comes to us with His words about judging our fellow humans. We are instructed to neither judge nor condemn our brothers and sisters in Christ but to instruct them in love in what God declares in His word to be truth. The Holy Spirit is the One who convicts the heart of the believer of sin and disobedience. We don't need to condemn people for their sin; that is the Holy Spirit's responsibility. A fallen bridge is useful to no one, and a crippled heart cries out for encouragement and approval—not approval of their sin but a yearning to be corrected. Like a spoiled child or a wayward adolescent, the sinful person will go as far as they can until someone calls them down or they heed the voice of the Holy Spirit. Our Christian response should always be patience and love, never running them down with an arrogant spirit.

We must never compromise good for evil or truth for error but always look to Jesus, the author and finisher of our faith, for direction and instruction in righteousness. We are all sinners and accountable to God alone.

And if your brother sins, go and reprove him in private; if he listens to you, you have won your brother. (Matt. 18:15)

February 6
If you must publish someone's faults, then why not publish your own?

Today's tabloids are a booming business. They are in the grocery stores, on newsstands, bookstores, and anywhere else the publishers can get permission to place them. It seems that our society thrives on the news of the sins of others. Sin is newsworthy to the lost world. Others' sins seem to camouflage, disguise, or even justify, in the worldly mind, people's own shortcomings and failures to live up to God's standards. Christians fall into this trap of the evil one. Satan loves to entice the minds of those who strive to follow God's way. God has His own standard for the Christian's life. Romans 3:23 tells us that we "all have sinned and fall short of the glory of God." Christians are sinners saved by grace. So what makes the difference? *The cross made the difference.* Jesus took all of our sins and placed them on Himself. He paid a debt He did not owe because we owed a debt we could not pay. When we come to Christ, we are no longer slaves to sin. It's called walking in the Spirit and not walking in the flesh. Jesus paid the penalty for our sins on that cross, and through humility and repentance on our part, we can go to Him, confess our wrong, and turn away from it. Then He will forgive us and remember it no more. Forgiveness because of His grace is then ours.

Gossip can be just as destructive as a tabloid. Assassination of one's character is deadly and cruel. Spreading lies or even truthful things that should be held in confidence strikes a devastating blow and causes unnecessary pain. We would never want our sins broadcast; hence, broadcast not your brother's sins. We would never want someone to say things behind our backs, so why should we ever choose to do it ourselves? Bitter words can be poisonous and hurtful.

The next time you are standing in the grocery store checkout line, pray for those faces that you see plastered all over the tabloids. And the next time you taste a bitter word, swallow it so it won't go past your lips.

He who goes about as a slanderer reveals secrets. Therefore do not associate with a gossip. (Prov. 20:19)

February 7
Who but the Spirit gives power to our witness?

There are no gray areas in the Christian life. The color is either black or white. Jesus says in Revelation 3:16 that it makes Him sick for us to be neither hot nor cold. He would rather that we be cold than to be lukewarm. A lukewarm Christian makes Him nauseated and want to spew us out of His mouth. Jesus was adamant about this. Why? To border on the truth or to live a middle-of-the-ground life causes others to stumble and waters down the gospel message. He wants us to be wise, be discerning, and impart to the world around us a true picture of a risen Savior. We can't be His angels of light in a dark world if we are tarnished with a mediocre lifestyle. The Christian's life is to point others to the abundant life that only comes from a steadfast walk in the right direction. Jesus is the Light of the World, and we are to shine for Him. To compromise with the world is to say that we are no different from the world. Somebody once said, "If you don't stand for something, you'll fall for anything." How true that is.

Christians should know the absolute truth and walk in it. The Holy Spirit in us is our guide, our advocate. God's Word is our handbook to study, and we should follow its instructions. It's not always easy to stand firm and to put on the robes of righteousness. We can't in ourselves. However, with His armor we can withstand all the forces of evil that come our way, and then we can be victorious in our walk through this world, not conforming to lukewarm living. To please and glorify God needs to be our main goal in this life.

Are you satisfied with your Christian walk? Although we are justified, sanctified, purified, and indwelt by the Holy Spirit, Christians will not be glorified until we stand in His presence. "For I am confident of this very thing, that He who began a good work in you will perfect it until the day of Christ Jesus" (Phil. 1:6). Thank God today that He continues His good work in us until He takes us to heaven.

Therefore, take up the full armor of God, that you may be able to resist in the evil days, and having done everything, to stand firm. (Eph. 6:13)

February 8
If we could forget our troubles as easily as we forget our blessings, how different things would be.

Are you hanging onto something today—something that would be better if you let go and let God have it?

For some reason we want to hold onto and dwell on things that pull us down. Satan loves this kind of stinkin' thinkin'. If he can get us discouraged and downtrodden, that's where he will keep us. We complain, "Woe is me!" "I have been so mistreated," "Why does everything happen to me?" or "That's just my luck." Whine, whine!

How we must sound like the children of Israel to God. From the time He led them out of Egypt and the bondage of slavery that they were in for four hundred years, they continued to whine and complain if things were not just as they thought they should be. Even though God's blessings were evident and His faithfulness never failed, they constantly cried out to God for more and were impatient when it was not delivered in their timing. Even as God was writing the Ten Commandments and before Moses could get back down off the mountain with them, they had resorted back to idols, forming a golden calf for their worship rather than worshipping the true and living God who had been so patient with them. For generations to come, God would continue to send prophets, priests, and kings to help them keep their focus on Him, but invariably they would revert back to the worship of false gods and idols. He loves them still and continues His faithfulness, His blessings, and His striving.

Ask God today to help you get rid of stinkin' thinkin' and to be more intentional on praise and thanksgiving for His many blessings. Our blessings are so numerous. Go to the window and look outside. Wow, what a blessing! Write down at least one answered prayer. Wow, what a blessing! Look into the face of someone you love. Wow, what a blessing! Need we go on? Remember, God's faithfulness is to all generations. As it was and still is to the children of Israel, so it is to you.

Be anxious for nothing, but in everything by prayer and supplication with thanksgiving let your requests be made known to God. (Phil. 4:6)

February 9
If you go against the grain of God's laws, you get splinters!

Guilt is a terrible thing to live with. Psychologists say that some people have a guilt complex, and medical doctors say that guilt can make a person physically ill. Guilt leads many into alcoholism, drug abuse, and suicide. Perhaps we all have done things that we regretted later and felt guilty for doing, but do not despair. God has the answer.

God places in each of us a conscience, and aren't we glad that He does. A relationship with Him makes our conscience more sensitive. The indwelling Holy Spirit convicts the saved person of sin and helps one to stay on the right track. But even the lost person has a conscience and knows right from wrong. We have all heard of criminals who turned themselves in because the burden of the guilt of their crime was worse than the prison bars they would ultimately face. Many Christians are in their own prisons of guilt because they cannot forgive themselves and accept the forgiveness offered to them from Jesus's provision at the cross. By not accepting Christ's forgiveness, we remain in bondage and are, in essence, saying that Jesus's work on the cross was not enough.

God is gracious and good. He has made provision for our sins so that we do not have to live with guilt. Through the cross and spilled blood of Jesus, we have forgiveness. Do you know Him? Splinters of guilt from unconfessed sin fester, cause pain, and infect even the strongest person. God's laws are for our greater good and for abundant living. His shed blood and finished work on the cross rid us of infection and heal us. Because of the cleansing blood of Jesus, He forgives our sins and makes us white as snow. Call on Him for cleansing so that your life will be guilt free and ready for kingdom living and service. Confess, repent, and go God's way. Splinters are very painful!

**... how much more will the blood of Christ, who through the eternal
Spirit offered Himself without blemish to God, cleanse your conscience
from dead works to serve the living God?
(Heb. 9:14)**

February 10
Let us not rebel against delay. We must not steal tomorrow out of God's hands. God is never too late. He is always right on time.

Have you prayed for something only to have God tell you to wait? When God says yes to our requests, we are thrilled. If God says no, we are reluctant to accept it, but we move on. But what about "wait"? That is hard. "How long, Lord?" we want to say. "How long are you going to keep me waiting? Are you going to answer at all? Do you hear me, Lord? What do I need to do to get an answer from you? Give me a sign."

The Israelites were impatient and lacking in faith. We, like the Israelite people, grumble and complain. God's answer might be right at our fingertips, right after the next prayer. It could be that we are faithless rather than faithful. What is the reason God keeps us waiting?

Sometimes it is to teach us. Sometimes it is to grow our faith and trust Him through the process. Other times it might be a test from God to see if we will wait on Him or jump out in our own strength.

There were those who traveled to the promised land who took things into their own hands. Moses warned the Israelites who spurned God not to invade the land of the Canaanites and Amalekites because God was not with them. God had told them to wait, yet they took it upon themselves to step out on their own. "But they went up heedlessly to the ridge of the hill country, neither the ark of the covenant of the Lord nor Moses left the camp. Then the Amalekites and the Canaanites, who lived in that hill country came down, and struck them and beat them down as far as Hormah" (Num. 14:44–45). Not waiting on God can have serious consequences. There is a reason that God wants us to wait on Him. He knows the big picture. He has our best interests in mind. God gives His best to those who wait on Him!

For our citizenship is in heaven, from which also we eagerly wait for a Savior, the Lord Jesus Christ. (Phil. 3:20)

February 11
When you are down in the mouth, remember Jonah. He came out all right.

God cares for His own. He tells us that He will never leave us—salvation is forever—nor forsake us (Heb. 13:5). Nothing can separate us from the love of God. Nothing! Once we realize our own sinfulness, repent, turn from it, and accept the forgiveness and provision that God made for each person when He went to the cross for us, our salvation is sealed. By asking Jesus to come into our hearts, from that time on nothing can control our lives again unless we go against God's plan and will for our lives and choose to disobey Him. Even then, our God will work diligently to bring us back to Him. Like the shepherd of a lost sheep that has left all the others to stray, He will bring us back lovingly and patiently.

Jonah chose to be rebellious. He didn't want to go to Nineveh as God had instructed him to do. However, in a timely way, God got Jonah's attention. It's a fishy story, but it's not a tale. It's true (Jonah 1 and 2)! Jonah cried out to God from the stomach of a great fish, and God heard him. After three days the fish spit him up onto the shore, and Jonah got his direction right.

Are you in rebellion against the God who loves you more than His own life? Are you fleeing to Tarshish when God wants you in Nineveh? Jonah was trying to flee from the presence of the Lord. You see, when we are not being obedient, we don't want to listen to God. Like children who hide from their parents when they don't want to do their chores or go to the dentist, they often find themselves in deeper trouble. Disobedience causes suffering and consequences. What do we see Jonah do in the second chapter? "Then Jonah *prayed* (my emphasis) to the Lord His God from the stomach of the fish" (v. X). Call out of your distress to the Lord. He will hear you and help you get your direction right. God hears the prayers of his children.

The salvation of the righteous comes from the Lord;
He is their stronghold in time of trouble. The Lord
helps them and delivers them. (Ps. 37:39–40a)

February 12
Don't despair because you have occasional sinking spells. Just remember the sun has a sinking spell every night but comes back up every morning. –Dolly Parton

The Christian life is a journey of growth from start to finish. If we seek to know our Creator more each day and desire the things of the Spirit, then our journey will be a fruitful one. It is encouraging to know that God keeps working with us and on us until the day He takes us to our heavenly home. We do not come into the Christian life fully grown. Although we have everything at the point of salvation, we are like babes in Christ, growing and maturing at our own rate.

When you feel down and out and wonder why God continues to put up with you, just remember that you are His child and He loves you. Just as we love our own children even when they are bad, our God loves us and sees the potential in us. He is a patient God and will never give up on us. Our aim as Christians should always be to please Him and to walk worthy of His love.

Recently, I was alerted to the needs of a young woman whom I had known all her life. Some bad choices in her life had caused her to sink into a desperate situation. She had recently been diagnosed with a debilitating disease, she was unable to work, and she was without financial aid. She needed help. Her father had been her main go-to in times of need, but now he had moved away and was dying of cancer. As I ministered to her, I found myself questioning what I would do if I were in such a situation. She seemed to take everything as it was and dealt with it the best way she could. She was not bitter or whiny but very appreciative of the help that was being given to her. I felt my call was to help where I could, along with other friends, and encourage her.

Sinking spells come to the best of us. We have no idea what tomorrow holds. But one thing we can be sure of: like the sun rises and sets each day by the hand of our Creator, He will be our sustainer if we call on Him.

**For we do not have a high priest who cannot sympathize
with our weakness, but one who has been tempted in
all things as we are, yet without sin. (Heb. 4:15)**

February 13
If you find a path with no obstacles, it is probably a path that doesn't lead anywhere.

Have you ever seen an obstacle course? Many athletes train on courses that present challenges and require endurance. In the military, soldiers are expected to conquer an obstacle course before they can complete the training. The exercise is not an easy one. It involves mental and physical stamina.

Most everything in life has obstacles or barriers that we must get around or over in order to accomplish our goals. There is something about us that says it's more valuable if we accomplish it ourselves. Even though the easy way seems to be the way that we go for most often, it is the challenging things along the way that make the greatest impressions on us and teach us those lasting lessons.

Joseph, the next-to-the-youngest son of the patriarch, Jacob, is a good example of a life patterned by pitfalls and obstacles that came to him, but not necessarily by his own doings. Thrown into a pit by his older, jealous brothers, he was sold to a caravan of Midianite traders who took him off to Egypt, where he was bought by Potiphar, an Egyptian officer of Pharaoh. Soon after arriving at Potiphar's house, Potiphar's wife tried to seduce Joseph, causing him to be thrown into prison. Through a lengthy turn of events, Joseph was called in from his prison cell to interpret the Pharaoh's dream. Pharaoh recognized a "divine spirit" in Joseph and "set [him] over all the land of Egypt" (Gen. 41:41). The dream of Pharaoh came true just as Joseph had interpreted, and because there was a famine in their land, his brothers came to Egypt to buy food. Joseph recognized them, but they did not recognize him at first. When they finally did, Joseph assured them that even though they meant their actions for evil, God meant them for good and to preserve many lives (Gen. 45:5). Like Joseph's case, the obstacles we face are often for a greater good. Many times hardships come with rewards.

Try to avoid the pitfalls, but run the obstacle course of life with strength, determination, and endurance, knowing at all times and with all assurance that the One who made us has shown us in His Word where the obstacles are. Go to that infallible handbook and see for yourself. He would never have created us without showing us how we best can live. All the answers are in there—the Bible.

We also exult in our tribulations, knowing that tribulation brings about perseverance; and perseverance, proven character; and proven character, hope; and hope does not disappoint because the love of God has been poured out within our hearts through the Holy Spirit who was given to us. (Rom. 5:3–5)

February 14
The greatest pleasure of life is love. —Sir W. Temple

When we look at 1 Corinthians 13, considered the love chapter, we can see love spelled out clearly and plainly. Love is not infatuation or a sexual experience. Love is not passion, nor is it just saying the words "I love you." God's Word tells us what love is. Love is patience and kindness. True love does not envy, nor is it jealous, boastful, or proud and never haughty, selfish, or rude. Perfect love does not demand its own way and is not irritable or touchy. It does not hold grudges and will hardly even notice when others do wrong. It is never glad about injustice but rejoices whenever truth wins out. Love is loyal at any cost, always believing in the other person and expecting the best of him or her even to the point of standing up for another. (Paraphrased from The Living Bible). What a clear and vivid description of love from God's Holy Word. We are totally inadequate to love like that except through Christ. Lest we forget, God is love. Because He first loved us, we too have the ability to love as we should and as He has called us to do.

Today, February 14, has been set aside by the world as Valentine's Day. We see red hearts and Cupids everywhere. We buy flowers and candy for that significant other and plan dinner out with that special someone—all to express feelings and "love." Is this bad? Not at all. However, true love should be shown every day of the year. God's definition of this most precious emotion as we see in his Word is totally different from what the world has perceived it to be.

The story of Mary and Joseph comes to mind when I think of unselfishness, loyalty, kindness, and belief in the other person. When Mary became pregnant by the Holy Spirit, Joseph, who was betrothed to her, had only Mary and her welfare in mind. His first thought was not to disgrace her. After the angel of the Lord appeared to him, he took her as his wife and kept her a virgin until she gave birth. We see no jealousy or selfishness. We can see why God called Joseph to be Jesus's earthly father.

**But now abide faith, hope, love, these three; but
the greatest of these is love. (1 Cor. 13:13)**

February 15
Of all sad words of tongue or pen, the saddest are, "It might have been."

Have you ever realized that each decision you make each day alters your life in one way or another? Rarely do we ponder or agonize over the simple choices in life. That would be a pain. We move from one routine thing to another as if we know exactly where we are going and what we should do next.

Think about it! If you had chosen another job or career over the one you are in now, where would you be? Or if you had decided to live in a large city rather than the small town you are in now or vice versa, would your life be the same? Or, perhaps, if you had married a different person than the one who shares your life now, where would that decision have taken you? Maybe it's the seemingly insignificant choices, the practical things like eating this food over another, saving for a rainy day rather than living from paycheck to paycheck, or starting to study God's Word early in life rather than later that would cause your life to be different.

Life is made up of choices that only we can make for ourselves. We are products of our choices. There are blessings associated with choices, and there are consequences associated with choices. When we are younger children, our parents make many of our decisions for us, such as where we live, when we go to sleep, basically what we eat, and so on.

Our heavenly Father wants to be involved in the decisions we make. Whatever choices we make in life, whether large or small, enormous or insignificant, they can be made without regret if we seek Him first, abide in Him, and rely on Him always. Nothing is too great or small. He is interested in it all!

Don't let regrets cloud your life. Seek Him first!

O Thou who dost hear prayer, to Thee all men come. (Ps. 65:2)

February 16
If your efficiency doesn't have Christ sufficiency, it will result in deficiency.

I found out a long time ago that what I do on my own and in my own strength is in vain. Christ wants us to lean on Him. He tells us, "My yoke is easy and my load is light" (Matt. 11:30) and that if we are weary and heavy laden, we can go to Him and He is our strength. The promise that His grace is sufficient for all our needs (2 Cor. 12:9) is an enduring one and forever a truth we can claim and rely on. Jesus tells us that His power is perfected in our weakness, that when we are at our weakest, His strength abounds even more. Hallelujah!

We see much symbolism in the Bible referring to Jesus. We see Jesus as the cornerstone, the rock, the living water, the Way, the Truth, the Life, and many others. Today as I studied my Sunday school lesson before teaching, I focused on Jesus as the Bread of Life. Interestingly, Jesus was born in the city of Bethlehem, which means "house of bread." Bread is sustenance, necessary for life and health. It satisfies hunger and gives strength to the body. As we can't live without physical bread, we also cannot live without the Bread of Life. Many go through life missing the nourishment they need both physically and spiritually. When humans push away the Bread of Life, they miss the very substance that gives them strength and hope to live this life. Don't miss out on the Bread of Life. Your life will suffer a drastic deficiency.

Do you serve this all-sufficient Savior? Or do you find your labors void and in vain, futile? He wants to be your sufficiency each day and in every way.

Jesus said to them, "I am the bread of life; he who comes to Me shall not hunger, and he who believes in Me shall never thirst." (John 6:35)

February 17
When two egotists meet, it's a case of an "I" for an "I."

Jesus said in Matthew 16:24, "If anyone wishes to come after Me, let him deny himself, and take up his cross, and follow Me" (NAS). Deny himself? The world today is saying something quite different. It is telling us, "Look out for number one," "You deserve it," and "Don't let anyone or anything stand in the way of achieving your goals."

When we look at the word *sin* and see that the middle letter is "I," it becomes real clear. Focusing on me, myself, and I is definitely sinful. In order to know Jesus and experience an abundant life, we must first die to self and ask Jesus to come into our hearts. His indwelling Holy Spirit enables us to live a life that is selfless rather than selfish. Then and only then can we know and understand what it means to love Jesus first and then others.

Jesus says that we have to give ourselves away expecting nothing in return. On this principle, He will build His kingdom, and on the rock of those who believe and trust Him will He build His church. Thinking more highly of ourselves than we ought to is contrary to what God calls us to do (Rom. 12:3).

In the Sermon on the Mount from Matthew 5, Jesus teaches us:

Blessed are the poor in spirit, for theirs is the kingdom of heaven.

Blessed are those who mourn, for they shall be comforted.

Blessed are the gentle, for they shall inherit the earth.

Blessed are those who hunger and thirst for righteousness, for they shall be satisfied.

Blessed are the merciful, for they shall receive mercy.

Blessed are the pure in heart, for they shall see God.

Blessed are those who have been persecuted for the sake of righteousness, for theirs is the kingdom of heaven.

Blessed are you when men cast insults at you, and persecute you and say all kinds of evil against you falsely, on account of Me.

The world's way or God's way—that is our choice.

**For if anyone thinks he is something when he is
nothing, he deceives himself. (Gal. 6:3)**

February 18
He who provides for this life but makes no provision for eternity is wise for a moment but a fool forever.

Have you ever gone to a funeral and come away almost envious that you were not headed for glory with the deceased? I experienced that recently.

She was just twenty-nine years old, a young mother of two small children—one three years and one eight months old. Her husband was a baseball player and a devoted husband and father. Cancer had taken over her beautiful, young body and consumed her within eight months of her diagnosis. I had known her only about a year, having met her through my daughter.

Her life was so short. Her funeral was such a testimony of a life well lived, a life that had touched so many. She faced death with victory and confidence of eternal life. The service reflected that and challenged all in attendance to know the One she had served in life and with whom she would spend eternity.

Be wise. Eternity is forever. As the old song says, "This is not my home, I'm just a'passing through." We will spend eternity somewhere. It will be either heaven or hell. This is the time we have to make our choice. This is the opportunity you have to choose who you will serve.

Let it be Jesus. He is the Way to heaven!

Do not lay up for yourselves treasures upon earth, where moth and rust destroy and where thieves break in and steal. But lay up for yourselves treasures in heaven, where neither moth not rust destroys, and where thieves do not break through and steal; for where your treasure is there will your heart be also. (Matt. 6:19–21)

February 19
He who climbs the highest is he who helps another ascend.

Mountain climbing is risky business, with many dangers along the way. Many loose rocks, pitfalls, and obstacles could slow down or discourage the most experienced climber. Just concentrating on one's steps is a challenge.

I travel with my husband sometimes up into the mountains of Tennessee to buy horses. The beauty of the mountains, valleys, and landscapes is awesome. However, sometimes it is hard to concentrate on the beauty all around for seeing the danger on the curvy mountain roads. The canyons look bottomless. The climb up, while pulling a huge horse trailer, is strained and slow. The trip down the slopes is even more frightening. Just looking at the runaway ramps with their deep tire tracks and the highway skid marks gives me an eerie feeling. The trip down with a heavy load of horses requires good brakes to maintain a slow descent and avoid a runaway truck and disaster.

Life has its own mountain experiences. Each day there are obstacles in our paths, and each day there is beauty that surrounds us. Each day there are uphill climbs and downhill times. One thing is certain that we can always remember: we have a God who cares, protects, guides, and leads if we will listen and heed his direction. Many times we encounter detours on our paths that lead us away from harm and to a safer route. We would be foolish to ignore such warnings. When God has made it clear in His Word which way is best for us to live, then you can believe that it is the right way. Walk in it and be blessed. In following His ways, you can bless others as well.

Therefore let us not judge one another anymore, but rather determine this—not to put an obstacle or a stumbling block in a brother's way. (Rom. 14:13)

February 20
The best thing to do behind a person's back is pat it!

Let's resolve this year to "each one, encourage one." Have you ever been down for no apparent reason and then someone calls you with an encouraging word? Or maybe a complete stranger stops you on the street or in the mall and compliments you on something you are wearing or your hair. It could be a smile from an approaching motorist that lifts your spirits. Maybe it was a hug when you needed it most or a timely letter, card, e-mail, or text that gave you encouragement.

We never know whose life we might change with just a smile or a kind word. There is not one person who at one time or another does not need a pat on the back or a kind gesture from another human being.

Sometimes the smallest undertakings can be the greatest blessings. You may never know what a gift you were to someone, but your heavenly Father knows and will bless you for it.

We are called to be a lighthouse of His love and grace. The only true gift is a portion of yourself. Take time today to seek out someone who you think might need a "warm fuzzy." In 1 Peter 4:8, we are admonished to "keep fervent in your love for one another." In showing love we glorify our Father in heaven who is love and wants to teach us to love as He loves.

Don't forget the challenge! Each one, encourage one. Make this a goal and remember that the more we do things, the more they become a habit.

Good habits reap good benefits; bad habits reap bad consequences.

If therefore there is any encouragement in Christ, if there is any consolation of love, if there is any fellowship of the Spirit, if any affection and compassion, make my joy complete by being of the same mind, maintaining the same love, united in spirit, intent on one purpose. (Phil. 2:1–2)

February 21
A hundred mistakes are an education if you learn something from each one.

To pass through this life without making mistakes would be an impossible task. We all make them, and we inevitably suffer for them, learn from them, or both. Unfortunately, our old sinful nature that we derived from God's first son, Adam, causes us to make unwise choices at times, and we get sidetracked into thinking, like Adam, that we don't need to listen to our heavenly Father. Bad mistake!

I am reminded of Lot in Old Testament history. Being the nephew of Abraham was definitely a blessing. However, when the time came for them to part company and go in opposite directions, Lot made a bad mistake. Abraham offered Lot the first choice of all the land that was before them. Lot chose the rich, fertile land of the Jordan Valley, leaving Abraham to settle in the land of Canaan (Gen. 13:12). Lot moved his family and his tents to Sodom, which was a wicked city, not a good place to live and raise a family. Even though God got Lot and his family out of Sodom before He destroyed it, they were all influenced by the evil there, and ultimately his story got worse (Gen. 19:30–38). Abraham, on the other hand, was faithful. He never failed to build an altar to God and thank Him. God continued to bless Abraham and his descendants.

Mistakes can be valuable lessons if we realize them and learn and grow from them. Sin can wreak havoc on our lives and cause much heartache and grief. All mistakes are not sin; they are just bad choices, but many bad choices *are* sin. Remember that everything that glitters is not gold. Choose to do the will of the One who created you so that you will not mess up like Adam did, and Lot did, and on and on!

Behold, I have found only this, that God made men upright,
but they have sought out many devices. (Eccles. 7:29)

February 22
Birthdays are nice to have, but too many of them will kill a person!

Today is my special day, and I am happy to see one more! I look forward to eternity when my time comes, but until then I thank God for each one.

My siblings and I used to get so amused at my grandmother. She was a wonderful Christian lady and a blessing to all who knew her. We felt secure and warm just being in her presence. She was full of wisdom and a gifted storyteller. I loved to sit at her feet and listen to her stories.

Grandmother Griffin lived to be ninety-nine years of age, and in those later years her pat answer to "How are you doing?" was "I'm fine, darling. Just too many birthdays!" She was from a large family and outlived her parents and most of her siblings. She would laugh and say, "I've lived so long, Mama and Papa are going to think that I went the other way."

Jesus was only thirty-three years old when He died. He did not have many birthdays but, oh, what an impact He made in this world in the few years that He walked on this earth. His birth was a humble birth and His death a lowly death. He lived like a pauper, yet He was a king. He loved humankind, yet His own people rejected Him. He was sinless, yet He took on Himself all the sins of the world. The number of our days is not the important thing, but how we live them is.

We may be surrounded by gifts on our birthdays, yet how often do we stop to think about the greatest gift that has ever been given to this world, Jesus, our Savior and King? He came from heaven to be the perfect sacrifice for our sin, to redeem us by His blood and rise again that we might have eternal life if we repent of our sins, believe on Him, and invite Him into our hearts. Thank you, Jesus, for your redeeming love! You are my greatest gift on all my birthdays!

I know that there is nothing better for them than to rejoice and to do good in one's lifetime. (Eccles. 3:12)

February 23
The man who has a right to boast doesn't have to.

Humility is one thing that Jesus called on His followers to possess. A proud spirit is hard to deal with and projects a haughty nature. James 4:6 states that "God is opposed to the proud, but gives grace to the humble." James tells us that if we humble ourselves in the presence of the Lord, He will exalt us (James 4:10).

It is only in Christ Jesus and His death on the cross that we can boast. Our high position as believers is only because He humbled Himself by becoming obedient to the point of death, even death on a cross (Phil. 2:8). When we therefore humble ourselves before Him in abandonment, dying to self and living for Christ, our old selves are crucified and we live to walk in the newness of life. Salvation is eternal. It is once and for all, and born again, to be a new creation in the likeness of Christ.

A song I love to sing is called "I Will Glory in the Cross." The words are powerful.

I boast not of works, nor tell of good deeds
For naught have I done to merit His grace.
All glory and praise shall rest upon Him
So willing to die in my place.
I will glory in the cross, in the cross.

There is nothing that we can do to earn or deserve such grace. It is a free gift given to us through Jesus Christ and His righteousness. He died a shameful death, shedding his precious blood for us while we were yet sinners. If you do not know the Savior, cry out to Him today. He knows your name and will hear you. Repent and give your life to Him. Rejoice!

Have this attitude in yourselves which was also in Christ Jesus, who, although He existed in the form of God, did not regard equality with God a thing to be grasped, but emptied Himself, taking the form of a bond-servant, and being made in the likeness of men. (Phil. 2:5–7)

February 24
Many people, when they run into a telephone pole, blame the pole!

Calculate in your mind the times you have chosen to go against God's will in your life. Maybe you can't remember a time, or perhaps there are too many times to remember. Sometimes we jump out without thinking and certainly without taking time to ask God for His direction.

Adam and Eve had it so good in the Garden of Eden. The beauty of God's creation was everywhere, unmarred by human or beast at this point and everything for their pleasure. Even cool walks with their Creator were theirs to enjoy, as were lush fruit and perfect weather each day. No sin, no sadness. No gossip and no death. Only love, joy, peace, patience, kindness, goodness, faithfulness, gentleness, and self-control. They lived and walked by the Spirit. God had breathed into man the breath of life, and he was made in God's image. What happened? Why would humans choose to go against God and forfeit all, causing sin to enter the world?

Adam and Eve listened to the wrong voice. They had heard God when He told them to enjoy the fruit from all the trees in the garden except one, the one in the middle of the garden. It was the tree of the knowledge of good and evil. But as Satan tempted them to doubt God, they fell for it. They went against their Creator and fell for the deceiver's lies. The scriptures tell us that "the eyes of both of them were opened, and they knew that they were naked." Sin had come to this paradise. When they heard God walking in the garden, they hid from Him. God called to them. He knew what they had done. They then began to blame each other and then the serpent who had deceived them.

What a sad fate for God's first children and for generations to come. Sin entered the world that day, and humankind still plays the blame game. We are each responsible for our own sins, and with sin comes consequences.

Therefore, just as through one man sin entered into the world, and death through sin, and so death spread to all men, because all sinned. (Rom. 5:12)

February 25
Don't feed on the world's crumbs; get some delicious meals from the Bread of Life.

For several months I have been making friendship cakes. In case you are not familiar with it, it is a cake that you make by adding fruit and sugar to a starter that you have gotten from a friend. You must stir it every day for about thirty days, and then you are ready to bake your cakes, having enough starter to share with at least three friends and enough to start over again. It's a fun thing, and the cakes are delicious. However, you can't make this delicious cake unless you first have the starter. The starter is the life of the mixture because it ferments and gives flavor and life to the other ingredients.

Jesus is the Bread of Life. The richness of our lives depends on the One who was sent to this earth to be broken for us. God loved us so much that He came from heaven in the form of a man, Jesus, and laid down His life for the sins of this world. As the Bread of Life was broken for us, we were offered His Spirit to dwell in us. As yeast adds life to bread and the starter adds life to my friendship cake, Jesus gives life to each of us when we invite Him into our hearts. A life without Jesus is a life without flavor, a life without the nourishment we need to grow spiritually and enjoy the abundant life that He desires for all humankind. He alone gives the power to rise above our circumstances. Without Him we perish, not only from hopelessness in this life but from the eternal separation we evoke in the life to come.

Do you know a friend who needs a starter? Do you need a starter to introduce you to the Bread of Life? As our bodies crave physical food, we need to crave spiritual food. Jesus said, "I am the bread of life; he who comes to Me shall not hunger, and he who believes in Me shall never thirst" (John 6:35).

For the bread of God is that which comes down out of heaven, and gives life to the world. (John 6:33)

February 26
The Bible promises no loaves to the loafer.

The idea of work being a curse goes all the way back to the beginning of time. In the book of Genesis, Adam and Eve sinned and God put them under a curse. Because of the fall of humankind, God told Adam, "Cursed is the ground because of you; in toil you shall eat of it all the days of your life. Both thorns and thistles it shall grow for you; and you shall eat the plants of the fields; by the sweat of your face you shall eat bread, till you return to the ground, because from it you were taken; for you are dust, and to dust you shall return" (3:17b–19). As with all sin, there are consequences. Sin requires punishment, and God punishes in order to teach us and help us grow. Like a loving parent, our God disciplines us.

Before there was sin in the world, there was pleasure and provision. God made our world to be a paradise, free from hard labor and stress. Adam and Eve must have enjoyed their days together. There was no enmity between them, no arguing or ill will. They took pleasure in each other and their time with God. There were no nine-to-five workdays or deadlines to meet and no clothes to wash for they wore none. All was peaceful and pleasant.

We have never known the world as it was before sin entered paradise. We have had to learn from the onset of adulthood that if we want to eat and exist on this earth, we must work in order to sustain nourishment for these hungry appetites. Paul tells the church of the Thessalonians, "If anyone will not work, neither let him eat" (2 Thess. 3:10). When God put this curse on humankind, He was serious about it. There is a lesson to be learned, and God has a purpose in all things. The idle mind is the devil's workshop. Staying busy and accomplishing something is good for the mind and the body!

Laziness casts into a deep sleep, and an idle man will suffer hunger. (Prov. 19:14)

February 27
A Bible in the hand is worth two on the shelf.

God's Word: Part 1

Have you set aside a quiet time for yourself? That special time when it is just you and God alone? You probably have if you are reading this. Don't you agree that it is the best part of your day?

Spending time alone with the Father in order for Him to speak to you is a precious gift to yourself. How can we ever hear from God if we don't make ourselves available to Him? His Word is a lamp unto our feet and a light unto our path (Ps. 119:105). The psalmist cannot say enough about how he treasures the precepts of the Lord and meditates on them day and night. He says that they make him wiser than his enemies and give him more insight than his teachers. (vs. 98, 99). He says the words of God are "sweeter than honey to my mouth" (v. 103). I agree with the psalmist. There is no book like God's book, and it was inspired by Him and written for us.

Prayer should be a major part of this time as you voice your prayers and petitions to Him for your own personal needs as well as interceding for others. Always make praise a part of this time as you open the windows of heaven in thanksgiving to the one and only Holy God.

Don't let your Bible gather dust. It is so easy to get caught up in everyday life and let your time in the Word slip right by. He knows your name, and He will speak to you personally. Let us stand in awe that the God of the universe would even have time to have a quiet meeting with little old you and me! Like the psalmist, may we cry out to the Father, "I rise before dawn and cry for help: I wait for Thy words" (v. 147).

The sum of Thy word is truth, and every one of Thy righteous ordinances is everlasting. (Ps. 119:160)

February 28
A man has deprived himself of the best there is in all the world, who has deprived himself of this—a knowledge of the Bible. —Woodrow Wilson

God's Word: Part 2

"Study to show thyself approved unto God—a workman that needeth not to be ashamed, rightly dividing the word of truth" (2 Tim. 2:15 KJV).

Paul diligently taught Timothy as a son, mentoring him in the faith as they labored together. Studying God's word and knowing His truths is necessary if we are to mentor, teach, or witness to others. With God's help we can search His precepts, rightly dividing the word of truth until we know what God has to say to us. God called out His writers to communicate His very soul to us through the pages of His Word. It has no errors as He inspired every word, every concept, every precept, every parable, and every illustration. His Word is holy and precious to all humankind; however, if we never read it and let it speak to our hearts, it is just another book that we put on the shelf and dust off occasionally.

We will never be able to share Christ with the lost world if we do not learn His truths. The apostle Peter tells us that we are always to be "ready to give a defense to everyone who asks you to give an account for the hope that is in you" (1 Peter 3:15). What is the Christian's hope? Jesus and Him crucified. "For He was foreknown before the foundation of the world, but has appeared in these last times for the sake of you who through Him are believers in God who raised Him from the dead and gave Him glory, so that your faith and hope are in God" (1 Peter 1:20–21).

Know God. Know His Word. "And the Word became flesh and dwelt among us" (John 1:14). Jesus is the Word of God, and everything that proceeds out of His mouth is truth!

But the Word of the Lord abides forever. (1 Peter 1:25)

February 29
Other books have been written for our information; the Bible was given for our transformation.

God's Word: Part 3

Have you ever walked through a public library and felt the vastness of the knowledge surrounding you? It is amazing to realize that generations of intelligent men and women have been successful in passing on their wisdom and their thoughts through the pages of the many books that fill the shelves. The inventories of public libraries include books on every subject. Many are helpful, and many not so helpful. Many we read for entertainment. There's nothing like curling up with a good book. Many books are filled with teaching material and how-to instructions for do-it-yourself projects. There are history books and children's books. The list goes on and on. How long do you think these books sit on a library shelf before they are weeded out and replaced? Possibly several years, maybe longer, and then in order to make room for newer books by newer authors, they are sold at a book sale or destroyed.

There is much information encompassed in a library, but no book has the transforming power of the Bible. God's precious Word to His people has been around for hundreds of years. Because it is inspired by God, He has protected and preserved it for all generations. When we read God's Word, our minds are renewed and we are transformed. "And do not be conformed to this world, but be transformed by the renewing of your mind, that you may prove what the will of God is, that what is good and acceptable and perfect" (Rom. 12:2). God wants us to walk in His way, not the world's way. We have the promise from the Author that when we share his Word, it will not return void. Who do you know that needs some transforming power?

All scripture is inspired by God and profitable for teaching, for reproof, for correction, for training in righteousness. (2 Tim. 3:16)

March

**From the rising of the sun to its setting the name
of the Lord is to be praised. (Ps. 113:3)**

March 1
Give your life to God; He can do more with it than you can!

Why do human beings fight against God, the Creator of all humankind and the universe? His way has been tried and proven for generations upon generations. His way brings abundant life on this earth and eternal life after death. Rejection of His way brings destruction to life on this earth and an eternal separation from God in hell after death. Why would anyone choose not to follow Christ's way—the better way?

Well, humans have always thought that they knew more than God. Adam and Eve listened to Satan and came under the impression that they could be like God. Their disobedience brought sin into the world. The people of Sodom and Gomorrah were sure that their sinful pleasure was more important than following God's way. Those two cities were wiped off the map. Noah's audience that gathered as he labored on the ark for years in obedience to God was sure that they had everything under control as they laughed at Noah. They did not laugh as the waters came. The crowd that yelled, "Crucify Him! Crucify Him!" rejected Jesus to the end. When He rose again, death was conquered and victory for all humankind was won. Many rejoice even today, but still many do not.

These are just a few of the biblical accounts of disobedient behavior. We see many others as we read through the pages of God's Word. I'm sure you can look around you and see the same scenarios in our world today. Sin is sin whether it occurred six thousand years ago or today.

Jesus's death on the cross and resurrection from the grave made it possible for every person on earth to have forgiveness of sin and a new life in Him. We don't have to live outside the will of our Creator God. He made a way for us to enjoy the abundant life by accepting Him, repenting of our sins, and walking in His ways.

Therefore, if any man is in Christ, he is a new creature; the old things passed away; behold, new things have come. (2 Cor. 5:17)

March 2
People need loving the most when they deserve it the least. –Mary Crowley

Do any of us deserve to be loved? Do we earn love or the ability to love? Can we manufacture or generate love within ourselves just because the moment calls for it?

Love is a simple thing, yet it is so complex. It can appear as a surface emotion, yet it is so deep. The scriptures tell us that love "bears all things, believes all things, hopes all things, endures all things" (1 Cor. 13:7). The scriptures also say that love abides forever and never fails. What a powerful emotion, and God gives us control over it—like His love for us. He draws us to Himself but never forces Himself on us. He tells us to love our fellow human, then gives us His Spirit to help us to do it. He offers us love for a lifetime through the marriage relationship, then He strengthens the union in time with a deep and abiding love. He blesses us with children and grandchildren as an extension of that love, and we reap joy to overflowing.

The greatest love of all came when "God so loved the world that He gave His only begotten Son that whosoever believeth in Him shall not perish but have everlasting life" (John 3:16). Imagine leaving heaven and coming to earth to die for sinful people so that they can have forgiveness of sin and eternal life. We certainly did not deserve that kind of love, but the Father thought we did. He thought we were worth it. Imagine that!

Ask God to show you someone today with whom you can share that wonderful love story. Ask God to help you love as He loves.

You have heard that it was said, "You shall love your neighbor, and hate your enemy." But I say to you, love your enemies, and pray for those who persecute you. (Matt. 5:43–44)

March 3
Worry is a misuse of the imagination. —Mary Crowley

Do you know the antidote for anxiety? The antidote or cure for anxiety is to trust the God who made you, giving Him every problem that you are anxious about.

When Jesus was talking to his disciples in Matthew 6:25–34 and giving them the cure for anxiety, He was talking to us as well. It is a timely subject for us to address today as many struggle with anxiety and depression. Many today look for security in a good job, family, education, a savings account, and possessions. When we become slaves to our wants and desires, we are making idols of these things, which dishonors God and creates anxiety for Christians. God wants to bless us, and He knows the needs of His children. When we are anxious over material possessions, even the food we eat or the clothes we wear, He says that we are behaving like pagans (Matt. 6:32).

Worrying doesn't solve a single problem. In fact, it has been medically proven that worry and stress erode a person's health. The psalmist spoke of this long before any doctor or scientist came to that conclusion.

Commit your way to the Lord,
Trust also in Him and He will do it.
And He will bring forth your righteousness
As the light,
And your judgement as the noonday.
Rest in the Lord and wait patiently for Him;
Do not fret because of him who prospers in his way,
Because of the man who carries out evil schemes.
Cease from anger, and forsake wrath;
Do not fret, it leads only to evildoing.

For evildoers will be cut off, But those who wait on the Lord, they will inherit the land. (Psalm 37:5-9)

March 4
God will mend even a broken heart if we give Him all the pieces. –Mary Crowley

Trust is a word that is key to faith. God cannot work in us or through us unless we will Him or trust Him to do so. The more we trust Him with the pieces of our lives, the more He can work in us and our circumstances, thereby building our faith as we see Him at work.

In the year 1999, my family experienced grief in a way that we had never known before. My mother-in-law, who had been in our care for the previous twelve years, passed away in August of that year. We soon were faced with more grief as my mother died in October after being bedridden for two years. My younger brother had gone with us to pick out Mother's casket, and in December, we were picking out his. He had suffered a stroke and died in a matter of days. He had just seen his first grandchild come into the world, and now he was gone to heaven. Our hearts were broken and we were weary from grief.

When we are hurting it's hard sometimes to get past the grieving period. Our heavenly Father knows our every hurt. He knows our every need and is waiting for us to relinquish them to Him. He tells us to place our burdens on Him and He will bear them (Ps. 55:22).

Trust the God of all sufficiency to mend your hurts today. Give Him the pieces one by one, and watch the master healer as He gently restores and compassionately walks beside you.

**Come to Me, all who are weary and heavy-laden,
and I will give you rest. (Matt. 11:28)**

March 5
I love God's mathematics. Joy adds and multiplies as you divide it with others. —Mary Crowley

Have you ever watched a people-person in a crowd? They just seem to radiate with joy and attract others like a magnet. People are drawn to them, and they are most comfortable in the midst of it all. You can see the whole affair liven up as the joy is passed on from one to another.

What a gift! However, it's a gift we all can have. With Christ in us, we should all shine out like beacons. The assurance of being the child of a king should put us on shouting ground. "The Lord is my light and my salvation; whom shall I fear?" (Ps. 27:1).

When my precious grandchildren come in the summer for "Granny Camp," there is a lot of joy around! We have such fun, and they just play off of one another. Just to be together for a week is something that they look forward to—especially to be together at Granny and Papa's house. We have a big old farmhouse at the edge of town with plenty of room for them to romp and play. I try to keep somewhat of a schedule so that we can get it all in. They have to make their beds in the morning after breakfast, and then we go out on the front porch for our Bible time.

We do crafts out in my old bakery and try to get in a nature walk. The afternoons sometimes include a field trip off somewhere that I have planned ahead or board games, swimming, or free time. You have never heard so much giggling, chatter, squealing, and talking in your life. It is music to my ears. I do love to hear them enjoying one another and their time at our house, but my primary goal is to continue to shine Jesus into their lives as their parents have started a good work in them.

As God's children, we are to walk in a manner worthy of our calling (Eph. 4:1). As God calls us out of darkness and into His glorious light, may our joy overflow and merge into the lives of those around us who might need a spark to ignite a fire in their heart.

Thy wilt make known to me the path of life; In Thy presence is fullness of joy; In Thy right hand there are pleasures forever. (Ps. 16:11)

March 6
Don't say "if I can" but "How can I?"

Setting out on the journey of life and accomplishment, you need a positive attitude and faith in the One who will always walk beside you if you call on Him. You need to believe that you can achieve your goals. If you don't believe you can, certainly no one else will.

Noah is a good example of one who people could observe and mimic. He was surely a man of faith. The scriptures say that Noah "was a righteous man, blameless in his time." They also say of Noah that he "walked with God." He never backed down when God gave him the huge task of building the ark. Noah could easily have questioned God and His purpose in this, but he trusted his maker and believed in what he could not see. That is faith. Noah had to have a positive attitude as all those around him must have laughed and criticized what he had set out to do. "Thus Noah did; according to all that God had commanded him, so he did" (Gen. 6:22).

Putting your plans into action means revving up your engine and saying, "All aboard!" Before you start to move your "I know I can" train, put a banner on the engine that says, "Praying about this." The coal car reads, "Setting my goals" and is followed by a passenger car labeled, "Working my plan." At the end of the train, the side of the caboose reads, "Moving forward." As we see your train climbing the hill, we read the banner across the back: "With God I can do all things!"

Do you have a seemingly impossible task before you today? Ask God, "How can I accomplish this with your help?" He is waiting to walk with you through any- and everything that is facing you today. Ask Him!

Yet those who wait for the Lord will gain new strength; they will mount up with wings like eagles, they will run and not get tired, they will walk and not become weary. (Isa. 40:31)

March 7
You may give out, but never give up. –Mary Crowley

Paul was a good example of one who endured. His missionary journeys took him from Jerusalem to Rome and everywhere in between. He established churches and preached the gospel of Jesus Christ everywhere he went. He was diligent to encourage new Christians, and he wrote letters of encouragement and instruction to the churches. He met with much opposition from believers as well as unbelievers. He was abused and rejected, insulted and persecuted. He was thrown into prison and attacked from all sides. He never gave up or gave in. Paul never laid his armor down. Even though he lived with a "thorn in the flesh" (2 Cor. 12:7), he was faithful to the end. Paul had his eye on the goal of sharing the good news. He had his eye on the prize of heaven and wanted to take everyone with him. His faith was anchored in Christ, and he was devoted to His mission and call. Empowered by the Holy Spirit, he stayed the course.

We, like Paul, are called to that same mission. And we too are empowered by the same Holy Spirit if we have trusted Christ as Savior and Lord. We are weak, but He is strong.

Today, choose for yourself whom you will serve. Joshua said, "As for me and my house, we will serve the Lord" (Joshua 24:15). Is that your choice today? What is your answer to God's call? As we serve, we might give out, but we must never give up. God will make a way for us to reach the lost around us if we seek His face and call on His name. The fields are white unto harvest, and the laborers are few. We must each do our part.

My grace is sufficient for you, for power is perfected in weakness.
(2 Cor. 12:9)

March 8
Develop a swelled heart, not a swelled head. –Mary Crowley

Have you ever met people and known when you saw them or got into a conversation with them that they had a heart for God? Christian people have—or should have—a different persona. Jesus said in Matthew 7:16, "You will know them by their fruits." He likens a saved person to a tree that bears good fruit. He says in the verses that follow, "Even so, every good tree bears good fruit; but the bad tree bears bad fruit. A good tree cannot produce bad fruit, nor can a bad tree produce good fruit." Jesus is warning us about false prophets "who come to you in sheep's clothing, but inwardly are ravenous wolves" (v.15). The scribes and Pharisees of Jesus's day had swelled heads. They were "religious" yet unsaved. Jesus called them hypocrites and vipers for demanding one thing from the people and yet living by their own rules for themselves. They knew the law, the Ten Commandments, backward and forward, but they did not know the writer of the law. They refused to acknowledge Jesus and therefore missed salvation. Jesus told them in this same sermon that He had not come to abolish the law or the prophets but to fulfill it (Matt. 5:17). The Ten Commandments still stand; they are our plumb line. They are God's rules for us to follow. But Jesus came to write them on the hearts of believers, not on stone. We strive to keep the commandments because we love our Savior and want to live for Him, serve Him, and be obedient to His rules.

Does the world look at you and see a heart for God? Does the person who does not know Jesus see you and say, "I want what he or she has?" Is your heart enlarged, swollen, bursting with love for the One who saved you so that it overflows with love for those around you? Heavenly Father, let our hearts be filled with your righteousness, exceeding that of the scribes and Pharisees, so that we will point others to you. Amen.

Let your light shine before men in such a way that they may see your good works, and glorify your Father which is in heaven. (Matt. 5:16)

March 9
Be somebody. God doesn't take time to make a nobody.
—Mary Crowley

Ethel Waters said it this way at a Billy Graham revival in London: "Honey, God don't sponsor no flops."

Are you on the winning team? Have you chosen your side? It's time. We only have this short lifetime to get it right. I saw a bumper sticker recently that set me back. It read, "When all else fails, try God." Imagine that! Don't fall into that trap. God wants to be our first responder. Don't suffer through all the things the world offers before you see the light and call on Him. You don't have to. Go directly to God now. He takes you right where you are. He takes our junk and makes all things new as He leads us down the path of righteousness for His name sake. Our "nobodyness" becomes "somebodyness."

A transformed life is a beautiful life. Saul was a persecutor of Christians in New Testament history. He acknowledges himself that he was the "chief of sinners." He stood and watched as Stephen was stoned for his faith. In fact, he held the coats of those throwing the stones. Then, one day on the road to Damascus, Saul was blinded by a great light. Sometimes we have to become blind in order to see. God got his attention, and he was never the same. Even his name changed from Saul to Paul. We can thank Paul today for taking the gospel to the Gentiles. Aren't we glad today that God took a somebody in the *world* like Paul and made him a somebody in the *kingdom of God?* That is the power of salvation that can only come from knowing Jesus.

Call on Him today! He is on call twenty-four hours a day! He loves you and is patiently waiting for all who will come to surrender.

For God so loved the world that He gave His only begotten Son that whosoever believeth on Him should not perish but have eternal life. (John 3:16)

March 10
Attitude is a universal language. –Zig Ziglar

Do you ever feel like you need an attitude adjustment? What about the people with whom you live, work, and even go to church? Yes, we all need a little kick in the pants at one time or another.

The Bible is filled with many examples of God's conforming, molding, convicting, and scolding to get His people where He wanted them to be. In order to be useful vessels, we need to be selfless, obedient, loving, and faithful.

The children of Israel could not get it right. Over and over again God blessed them, and over and over again they were unappreciative and disobedient. They suffered in bondage for over four hundred years in Egypt before God freed them. They wandered in the wilderness for forty years on their way to the promised land because they failed to observe God's commandments and His statutes. After finally reaching the promised land, they were in captivity in Babylon for seventy years for idolatry and not worshipping the true and living God. There are consequences to sin and disobedience. God is patient, but He is also just, and His discipline can be swift.

Jonah did not want to go to Nineveh as God had directed Him to. However, after a little altering of his priorities by the influence of a huge fish, his direction changed rapidly. Joseph, Jesus's earthly father was a righteous man and didn't want to disgrace Mary when he found out she was pregnant. He "desired to put her away secretly." His state of mind changed considerably the moment the angel settled the question in his mind. Many times the apostle Paul had to adjust the thinking of the early church through reprimands done in love.

Listen. Hear what God is saying to you today concerning your attitude. Is it an attitude of selflessness, obedience, love, and faithfulness? Ask Him to adjust your attitude that you might be more like Him.

**Create in me a clean heart, Oh God, and renew a
steadfast spirit within me. (Ps. 51:10 NAS)**

March 11
You get the best out of others when you give the best of yourself. –Harvey Firestone

Try this today: when you see someone without a smile, give them one of yours. Goodwill is contagious. It is hard for even the worst of grouches to shun a smile or a kind word. It might not work the first time, but don't give up. God doesn't give up on us when we are down and out or have a bad day. You might be the only Bible someone ever reads. One of the sweetest examples of kindness and gentleness is described in the book of Mark as the little children were brought to Jesus to be touched by Him. Their parents knew that they would receive a blessing just by being in His presence. The disciples rebuked them, but Jesus quickly said to them, "'Permit the children to come to Me; do not hinder them; for the kingdom of God belongs to such as these. Truly I say to you, whoever does not receive the kingdom of God like a child shall not enter it at all.' And He took them in His arms and began blessing them, laying His hands upon them" (Mark 10:14–16).

Jesus always gives His best to His children. He is love, and if you are His you know it. How can we share the victory with others if we don't project it through our actions? We must exalt the Savior today before a world that is dying to know Him. What is your best? Is your heart in tune to the cries of the world? Sometimes it's the simplest act of kindness that touches the toughest heart. Jesus told the children, "Come to me." He speaks those words still today. Give of your best to the Master.

And just as you want people to treat you, treat them in the same way. (Luke 6:31 NAS)

March 12
Help others along life's way. It will come back to you one day.
—Author

How can we help someone today? How can we brighten the corner where we are? Try a smile in passing to some disgruntled or downtrodden person. What about a pat on the back or a hug for no reason at all? Offer up a prayer for someone that you know is lonely, hurting, or facing a big decision today. Maybe you need to make a phone call or two to offer encouragement. Is there a financial need somewhere that you can help with? A little goes a long way, and God blesses our every effort if we do it as unto the Lord. Amazingly we always are the benefactors because the blessings are ours in return.

One day a man was traveling on the road to Jericho. Some thieves attacked him, robbed him, and left him for dead. One man, a priest, passed him by as he lay on the road in need of a helping hand. A second man, a Levite, also passed by on the other side of the road, ignoring him. The third man to come along was a Samaritan. Jesus tells us that this man felt compassion. He stopped, bound the man's wounds, and loaded him on his donkey. He took him to the nearest town. There, the Good Samaritan took care of the hurt man. The next day as he had to be on his way, he left money for the innkeeper to take care of the injured man. Jesus asked this question as he finished the story: "Which of these three do you think proved to be a neighbor to the man who fell into the robbers' hands?" (Luke 10:25–37). I think we know the answer, don't we. It is the same today as it was then. Jesus replied, "Go and do the same."

We are commissioned to love God with all our hearts and our neighbors as ourselves. Who will you meet on your Jericho road today? Don't pass up a blessing!

Do unto others as you would have them to do unto you. (Matt. 7:12)

March 13
You don't have any guarantees for tomorrow, you can't do anything about yesterday, but you have today!

Life is eternal. We will spend eternity somewhere. For Christians, it will be in heaven, that glorious place where we will be forever with the King of Kings, our heavenly Father, God. For people who do not choose Jesus as Savior and ask Him into their hearts, they will spend eternity forever separated from their maker and will suffer for eternity in a place called hell. Oh, the horror of such a thought! God gives us all the same opportunity to get it right. In our allotted time on earth, we need to make the very best of it. As Joshua reminded the Israelites to "choose for yourselves today whom you will serve" (Joshua 24:15), we too must be reminded that we may not have tomorrow, so now is the appointed time to make our choice.

We must never be misled to think that we can serve God and the world. The world loves darkness; God's people love the light. God hates sin and does not tolerate it in any of us. His Son went to the cross and died a horrible death for our sins, so why would He tolerate it? "For God so loved the world, that He gave His only begotten Son that whosoever believeth in Him shall not perish but have everlasting life. For God sent His Son into the world not to condemn the world, but that the world through Him might be saved" (John 3:16–17). What a glorious promise! What a marvelous Savior! And it was all done for sinners like you and me.

Life is short at best. We must not be lukewarm. If the Holy Spirit is drawing you today and convicting you of your sinful state, of being lost, cry out to Him for forgiveness and ask Him to dwell in you with power from on high. Our God is mighty to save!

The Lord is not slow about His promise, as some count slowness, but is patient toward you, not wishing for any to perish, but for all to come to repentance. (2 Peter 3:9)

March 14
How you do what you do gives dignity to any honest labor.
–Zig Ziglar

I remember a time when I was a teenager visiting at a friend's house. I sat talking with her as she did the dishes. I became amused as she washed more and more dishes that it became a challenge for her to stack them just so in the drain rack so that they would not all come tumbling down. Each time she washed another dish, pot, or pan, she would work for several minutes to rearrange the draining, clean dishes so as not to cause an avalanche when placing another dish on the stack. I have thought about that so many times. Why didn't she stop and dry some of them? By the time she stopped to arrange and rearrange, she could easily have been finished with her chore with no danger of broken dishes. It's funny how little things like that stick in your mind. In hindsight I've also wondered why I didn't suggest that to her or, better still, take up a dry cloth and jump in to help her. Oh, well.

Isn't that the way we do, though? We often go around our elbows to get to our thumbs, missing the obvious. We wrestle with things in our lives, then just before the avalanche, we give them to God. Just before things come crashing down and our world falls apart, we call out to God.

The children of Israel are a good example of God's mercy as they struggled to do things their way. God delivered them from their enemies, He sent prophets to show them the way to go, He provided leaders, and He even gave them a king when they cried out for a king. They had been slaves in Egypt, laboring under the hand of an evil pharaoh until God delivered them in a miraculous way when they got between a rock and a hard place. And just before the avalanche caused by their disobedience, whom did they call on? That's right, God. Through Moses, God, the mighty deliverer, parted the Red Sea and saved the Israelites one more time. God is never late. We need not wrestle with life or dishes! Our God is able.

Commit your way to the Lord, trust also in
Him, and He will do it. (Ps. 37:5)

March 15
Christians are just ordinary people doing extraordinary things through the power of the Holy Spirit.

When you think of a sovereign God, what do you think of? A ruler sitting on a throne? A heavenly terrestrial being, greater than all the rest? Do you see a glowing face and long white robes?

In whatever way you picture God, He is all powerful and all knowing. He is omnipotent, omniscient, and omnipresent. He is more and greater than we can ever imagine with our earthly minds. Some things are certain—He does not make mistakes, He is never late, He is just, and He is faithful. God is merciful, and God is wise. These are just a few of God's attributes.

God's Word tells us that there are some things that God hates. We know that God hates sin. He sacrificed His Son to rid the world of the power of sin. Through Jesus, our perfect sacrifice, we have forgiveness of sin if we are His children and have surrendered our lives to Him. Rejecting Jesus and blasphemy against the Holy Spirit are the only unpardonable sins.

Proverbs 6:16–19 gives us a vivid picture of some of the sins that God hates. "There are six things which the Lord hates, yes, seven which are an abomination to Him: haughty eyes, a lying tongue, and hands that shed innocent blood, a heart that devises wicked plans, feet that run rapidly to evil, a false witness who utters lies, and one who spreads strife among brothers." Sin grieves God. If we are not led by the Spirit of God, then we will practice the deeds of the flesh which are "immorality, impurity, sensuality, idolatry, sorcery, enmities, strife, jealousy, outburst of anger, disputes, dissensions, factions, envying, drunkenness, carousing, and things like these" (Galatians 5:19–21). Paul goes on to say that "those who practice such things shall not inherit the kingdom of God."

He who is not with Me is against Me; and he who does not gather with Me scatters. (Matt. 12:30)

March 16
Act enthusiastic and you will be enthusiastic. —Dale Carnegie

Jesus calls all Christians to be light and salt in this world. But are we? Do you "shine out like a beacon light" as Jesus calls us to do? What about adding flavor and good taste to our environment and to those around us who need the living salt that only one who has been with Jesus can give? As we are called to be salt as well as light by the One who gives light to the world, let us not forget that as Jesus ascended back to heaven, he left us with a "great commission" to go out among the world and be His witnesses, spread the gospel, baptize in His name, and teach all those who will listen to observe all His teachings, His Holy Word. That is something to be enthusiastic about! Imagine being entrusted with such a command. But the comfort and assurance in that is that He said that He would be with us as we pursue such a task (Matt. 28:19–20).

Jesus wants us to get excited about doing His work in this world as we do His will and live the abundant life that He has made possible for us. We are to excite and inspire the crowds and the players in this huge arena. "You are the salt of the earth; but if the salt has become tasteless, how will it be made salty again? It is good for nothing anymore, except to be thrown out and trampled underfoot by men. You are the light of the world. A city set on a hill cannot be hidden.… Let your light shine before men in such that they may see your good works and glorify your Father who is in heaven" (Matt. 5:13–14,16).

As we seek to live an abundant life and to inspire those around us with our enthusiasm for knowing the risen Savior, may our goal be to glorify Him and point the lost world to the Way, the Truth and the Life, Jesus.

For God has not given us a spirit of timidity, but of power and love and discipline. (2 Tim. 1:7)

March 17
Talking is sharing, but listening is caring.

To be a good listener is one of God's greatest gifts, and not everyone has it. However, anyone can develop or improve this trait. To learn to be a good listener is to get the self out of the way and hear the person who is seeking to communicate with you. It is important to invest time and attention when other people are talking and to let them know that you care about what they are saying.

Listening is an area that I have recently put on my prayer list. If we are not careful, we will be so busy concentrating on what we want to say next that we fail to give full attention or show interest in what the person with whom we are engaged in conversation has to say. I have asked God to help me to be a good listener. I feel that in learning to listen to others better, I will learn to listen to Him better.

I love the story in 1 Samuel 3 of God's prophetic call to the boy Samuel. Samuel's mother, Hannah, had been barren before God answered her prayers and blessed her with a baby boy, whom she named Samuel. Hannah had made a vow to the Lord that, if He would give her a son, she would give him back to Lord. She was true to her vow, and at an early age, Samuel went to live with Eli, the priest and minister there. One night as Samuel slept, a voice called to him and woke him. Each time, he went to Eli thinking that it was Eli who had called to him. But each time, Eli sent him back. The third time, Eli realized that it must be the Lord calling to Samuel, so he told him to say to the Lord, "Speak, Lord, for thy servant is listening." Samuel did as Eli said, and he heard an important message from the Lord. The scripture goes on to say in verse 19 that "Samuel grew and the Lord was with him and let none of his words fail." How important it is for us to be good listeners. God always has a word for us if we will listen to Him, and people you encounter might need you to listen to them.

Like an earring of gold and an ornament of fine gold is a wise reprover to a listening ear. (Prov. 25:12)

March 18
Duty makes us do things well, but love makes us do them beautifully. –Zig Ziglar

Have you ever had a job to do that you weren't too excited about doing? But then some inspiration came into the picture and it changed your whole outlook? I've often made the comment that I need to have guests at least once a month so that I get some cleaning done in my house. I'm afraid I put off many chores until the next day unless I think I might be exposed as being a bad housekeeper. Let someone call and say that they are coming by, and I go into action. I am inspired! I have decided that procrastination is a disease, and I have it! I tell myself that I work better under pressure.

God calls us to many things. Spreading the good news is of highest priority and not something that Christians should put off. Many are dying each minute of every day without the saving knowledge of Jesus Christ. We are to tell them of how He came to earth so that He could take our sin debt upon Himself, how His crucifixion was for all of humankind, and how He rose again to live in the hearts of all who would trust in Him. We do not need to put off sharing such good news. It is a beautiful truth that needs to be revealed to all who will listen. Do you love those around you enough to reach out to them? Are you putting off what God has called you to do? What more inspiration do we need than the truth that God sent His only Son to die for us so that we could live the abundant life on earth and live throughout all eternity in heaven with our heavenly Father?

May we all not procrastinate on this very important mission but in love seek out the lost and share the greatest message of love that has ever been demonstrated—such a sacrifice, and we were so undeserving.

For He hath made Him to be sin for us, who knew no sin; that we might be made the righteousness of God in Him. (2 Cor. 5:21)

March 19
Make no small plans for they have no capacity to stir men's souls.

How do you see life today? Have you set any goals? Just as an athlete runs for the prize, we should set our goals in order to accomplish the most in life.

God entrusts each of us with talents and abilities. He expects us to use and develop these as we move along through life. Not to do this would mean that we are bad stewards of what God has entrusted to us. The ultimate reality is that when we plan and accomplish, we reap rewards. Surely if God makes plans, He expects us to as well. In Jeremiah 29:11, God sends a message through Jeremiah the prophet to those exiled by Nebuchadnezzar from Jerusalem to Babylon, saying, "For I know the plans that I have for you, declares the Lord, plans for welfare and not for calamity to give you a future and a hope." What blessed hope is ours when we have the assurance that mighty God has plans for His people. We can rest assured that His plans will be carried out and will never fail. His desire for His people is that we too establish plans—plans for tomorrow, plans for the future, plans for eternity.

Decide today to go for the gold. Map your course and run the race with endurance and determination. Know the rules and abide by them. Strengthen yourself through the power of the Lord, and in all you do seek to glorify Him. He never sends us on a mission for which He doesn't equip us. First of all, plan today whom you will serve, plan to stay the course, and plan to finish the race well! How can we stir people's souls toward salvation if we don't follow the plan that He has set forth for us? Know His plans first, then walk in them.

Then you will call upon Me and come and pray to me, and I will listen to you. And you will seek Me and find Me when you search for Me with all your heart. (Jer. 29:12–13)

March 20
You measure the size of accomplishment by the obstacles you have to overcome to reach your goals. –Booker T. Washington

There is nothing that compares to the mission that Jesus came to this earth to accomplish. Before the foundation of the world, He knew what He would have to do and when He would have to do it. His goal was to do the will of the Father. In obedience He became the perfect sacrifice that was necessary to free us from the bondage of our sin. God in human form paid our sin debt. The new covenant meant that the shedding of His precious blood and His death, burial, and glorious resurrection would make available salvation for all humankind. He became the perfect, sacrificial lamb of the old covenant so that we might no longer have to go through a high priest for forgiveness of sin but have direct access to our heavenly Father. As we cry out to Him in prayer, He hears and answers as we take our petitions before His throne.

A humble birth through a young virgin girl who "was found to be with child by the Holy Spirit" served as the divine entrance of the Savior into the world. At twelve He was teaching in the temple, making an impression on the elders of His day. His greatest mission began at thirty years old, when He called His disciples and began to evangelize the world. Despite many obstacles, He proceeded to do His Father's will, never drawing back from hardship or rejection. His work was accomplished at only thirty-three years of age when the very ones whom He came to save became an angry mob and called for Him to be crucified. Willingly He came and willingly He died on that cruel cross. With the words "It is finished," He sealed His commitment and accomplished His goal. As He took the sins of the whole world on Himself, all things were made new. The grave could not hold Him. He arose and ascended back to heaven. We serve a risen Savior today who is alive and accessible. If you don't know Him, you can. Just call out to Him today.

He is your praise and He is your God, who has done these great and awesome things for you which your eyes have seen. (Deut. 10:21)

March 21
Nothing is more frequently opened by mistake than the mouth.

Open mouth, insert foot! How many times have you heard this statement when you have spoken out of turn or spoken without thinking? Many, many times we put our tongues into motion before our brains. As a result, we immediately get hoof-in-mouth disease. This can be a painful disorder and often calls for extreme treatment. After removing the foot, we might have to put a bandage on the hurt we have caused and medicate with an apology and kind words.

One of Jesus's disciples, Peter, suffered from this disease big time. He was impulsive and forthright. Once, when Peter and some of the other disciples were out on the sea fishing, a storm came up. They were frightened. Then they saw Jesus walking toward them on the water. Only Peter jumped out of the boat and walked on the water to Jesus. Another time, in the upper room, Jesus began to wash the feet of the disciples, and Peter said to Jesus, "Never shall you wash my feet!" Jesus had to convince Peter by telling him that if He did not wash his feet, then he would "have no part with Him." Peter then settled down and said, "Not my feet only, but also my hands and my head." As you remember, he was the one who lunged forth and cut off the ear of the high priest's slave as the mob came to arrest Jesus before He was crucified. Soon after, he denied Jesus three times, a strange reaction after boldly coming to Jesus's defense. However, Peter was the one whom Jesus told three times to "feed my sheep." As Peter preached a powerful sermon on the day of Pentecost, three thousand were converted and later tens of thousands in Jerusalem.

Aren't we glad that hoof-in-mouth disease is not fatal? When we are truly repentant, God restores. He can take our harshest words and our most impulsive reactions, and with our repentant hearts He offers healing to those we have offended as we go to them in love.

This you know, my beloved brethren. But let everyone be quick to hear, slow to speak and slow to anger. (James 1:19)

March 22
Lord, fill my mouth with worthwhile stuff and nudge me when I've said enough.

I cross-stitched this little prayer and hung it in my kitchen right by my sink, reminding me daily to weigh my words and petitioning the Lord to give me a little nudge when I need to say no more. The truth is, I fall short many times, allowing the tongue to cut loose before giving enough prayerful attention to my words.

The tongue can be both a blessing and a curse. Like many other things, it is how we use it that makes the difference. God's instruction to us in the book of James is to "bridle the tongue." Like a horse that needs to be restrained, the tongue needs to be controlled. Proverbs 21:23 says, "He who guards his mouth and his tongue, guards his soul from troubles." In other words, we can cause ourselves a lot of unnecessary trouble by not watching what we say.

Blessings come from speaking kind words. When our hearts are in tune to the loving spirit of our heavenly Father, our words will flow as a sweet offering of His love. We are instructed to control our tongues with the reins of love, compassion, kindness, discipline, responsibility, and patience. We are to use sound judgment in what we say. In other words, we are to think before we speak. James spoke a lot about the tongue and how it can be a blessing or a curse. He said, "Does a fountain send out from the same opening both fresh and bitter water?" (James 3:11).

As Christians, we can destroy our witness in a moment when we speak gossip, obscenities, criticism, or the like. We are His ambassadors.

Let our speech always be seasoned with love. Turn a criticism into a compliment today!

Set a guard, O Lord, over my mouth; keep watch over the door of my lips. (Ps. 141:3)

March 23
Much more important than adding years to your life is to add life to your years.

We are seeing active senior adult groups in most of our churches today. They are such an inspiration and a blessing to us because they are filling their later years with creative activity. They fill the choir loft on designated Sundays and go to various places like nursing homes, other churches, and civic organizations to share their music. They have their own Bible studies in which they seek to continue to learn and know God's Word. They visit and seek out lonely seniors to help them to see that caring is sharing. They are involved in projects that help their churches minister to those in the community with special needs, and they reach out to one another, dining out together, seeing one another home, calling and checking on one another, and just being there for one another.

Our senior years can be our most beautiful if we bloom where we are planted. They can also be lonely years because many people lose their spouses of many years. That is why it is even more important to be involved and to reach out to others who need to know that someone cares. God has a place of usefulness for each of us no matter our age. It's not our ability that He desires but our availability. We should have more time than we have ever had to get involved in worthwhile mission projects and minister in areas that fit our physical capabilities. A phone call to a shut-in requires only a little time and very little effort, but it can be the highlight of someone's day.

Make a list of those in your church and community who might need a touch from you. Send a card, call them, or drop in with cookies or just for a visit. We are the hands and feet of Jesus while we are passing through this life. Let's shine for Him and brighten someone's day!

Therefore, we do not lose heart, but though our outer man is decaying, yet our inner man is being renewed day by day. (2 Cor. 4:16)

March 24
Go as far as you can see and when you get there you will always be able to see farther. —Zig Ziglar

We have to make many decisions in life. Some are important, and some are not so important. Some make no real difference at all, and some are life changing. Some decisions affect only ourselves, while others affect the lives of many.

Recently, I was talking with a senior friend. She and her husband had just made the decision to sell their home and move to a retirement village. They felt that making this decision now would eliminate heartrending decisions for their children to make later on. It was not an easy decision to make. However, after much prayer they felt that this was the right move for their golden years.

Even though we see God making the decision for Abraham and Sarah, they were obedient as God told them in their old age—Abraham was seventy-five—to pull up stakes and "go forth from your country, and from your relatives and from your father's house to the land which I will show you" (Gen. 12:1). When we walk by faith, God blesses us. Abraham was obedient, and God loves it when we listen to Him and obey. We are blessed today because of Abraham's right decision to follow God's way. God promised Abraham that he would be blessed and "all the families of the earth shall be blessed" (v. 3).

Consult the God of all wisdom today with any decisions that you need to make. None is too large or too small for Him. Seek Him first!

**In all your ways acknowledge Him and He will
make your paths straight. (Prov. 3:6)**

March 25
As you head toward your goals, be prepared to make some adjustments in your course. –Zig Ziglar

Life is very unpredictable. That is one thing that makes it so interesting and such an exciting adventure. Each day holds its own course. Some days are obstacle courses, and some days are smooth sailing. Each course produces joy or calamity, happiness or anguish, rejoicing or distress.

No one likes to experience the hurdles that we sometimes find in our path, but they will come. James says it like this: "Consider it all joy, my brethren, when you encounter various trials, knowing that the testing of your faith produces endurance" (1:2–3). A good athlete must train and endure to the end. Endurance brings results. We can overcome the hurdles in life in different ways. We can jump over them, go through them, or go around them. But as life goes on we see that it is those hurdles, the hard times, that make us stronger runners in life's race. As a sprinter masters the hurdles on the track, we too must run with endurance toward the goal, trusting the One who helps us soar over the hurdles in our path.

Have you already had to make some adjustments on your course? Have things not gone exactly as you thought they would? Do there seem to be more hurdles, and do they seem to get higher and wider and more numerous? Maybe you are praising God today for an uneventful race. Wherever you are on the journey of life, just know that there is One who knows your every need. Just as Moses instructed Joshua, "And the Lord is the one who goes ahead of you; He will be with you. He will not fail you or forsake you. Do not fear, or be dismayed" (Deut. 31:8). We too have that assurance, that promise. And heaven is the prize!

Let us run with endurance the race that is set before us, fixing our eyes on Jesus, the author and perfecter of faith. (Heb. 12:1b–2a)

March 26
Most locked doors are in your mind.

America is a nation of opportunity. We have the freedom to be what we want to be, go where we want to go, do what we want to do, and even worship how we want to worship. We are limited in what we set out to do only by our own selves. God has given to each of us talents, gifts, and opportunities. How we take advantage of them is up to us.

This story is told about Houdini, the master magician and locksmith. He boasted that he could open any jail cell in the world. The officials of a small town that had built a new jail offered to Houdini a challenge to see if he could open it. Publicity and excitement surrounded the event. Houdini was confident and began his task, but after two hours, he had not yet opened the cell door. Exhausted he fell against the door—and it opened. It was not even locked except in his mind, which meant it was as locked as if with a dead bolt.

Houdini had been told that the door was locked, so in his mind it was. How many opportunities do we miss because of fear of failure or because we listened to someone else? Maybe there have been times when you overanalyzed a challenge or questioned your own ability. Moses almost made that mistake. When God called him to lead the children of Israel out of Egypt, he asked God to let his brother Aaron do it instead. He said that Aaron was more capable than he was. But God believed in Moses and assured him that He would be with him, and Moses took on the task.

There are challenges in anything that we undertake, but with God at our side we do not have to put locks on our mind. Always pray about all decisions before you make them. He will direct you and be with you all the way. Push open your doors of opportunity today.

**But He said, "The things impossible with men
are possible with God." (Luke 18:27)**

March 27
It's easy enough to be pleasant when everything goes like a song; but the man worthwhile is the man who can smile when everything goes dead wrong.

I'm not so sure Job smiled when his whole world was falling apart around him, but one thing is certain: he knew where his strength came from and in whom he trusted.

Few people will experience the extreme tragedy that Job did. He was a wealthy man, with land and herds and many sons and daughters. Job loved God, and his faith was immovable. Then the test came. Everything was taken from him. He was in so much despair that he called out to God to kill him. His wife begged him to "curse God and die." Job's suffering took him low; however, he blessed God through it all. Job's response throughout was, "The Lord gave and the Lord has taken away. Blessed be the name of the Lord" (Job 1:21).

Where are you today in your suffering? Maybe you are saying, "Well, I have not seen any suffering. All is well." It will come. Jesus Himself said, "These things I have spoken to you, that in Me you may have peace. In the world you have tribulation, but take courage: I have overcome the world" (John 16:33). Where will your peace lie when trouble does come, when sorrow or suffering knocks at your door? Do you know the Prince of Peace, the great I Am, the sustainer of all comfort? Paul says that our God is the Father of mercies and God of all comfort (2 Cor.1:3). What blessed assurance we have to know that we are in the arms of the One who suffered so much for us. He promises that He "will Himself perfect, confirm, strengthen and establish you" (1 Peter 5:10). Let us all, like Job, when those times do come "come forth as gold."

**Shall we indeed accept good from God and
not accept adversity? (Job 2:10)**

March 28
When life knocks you down on your knees, you are in a perfect position to pray.

Have you ever been a part of an intercessory prayer ministry? The church that we are a part of has a wonderful prayer ministry. When people in a church start to pray, you see things happen.

God is so eager for His people to communicate with Him, call on Him, and fellowship with Him through prayer. Christians have a direct line to the Father. When Jesus said "It is finished" as He hung on the cross, the veil in the temple was ripped in two, giving us direct access to the Father. We no longer had to go through a priest, but we have the privilege of openly and directly praying to the Father. Jesus sits at the right hand of the Father, making intercession for us, and we have the privilege of interceding on behalf of someone else. That is so exciting to me!

You might know people who have given themselves over to sin or, perhaps, who have a sickness or disease. What a blessing to be able to cry out to the Father for them. Praying for our children, grandchildren, family, and friends helps us to have a part in their lives and welfare. You can pray to the Father, interceding on behalf of these people, and ask God to help them when they may not be able to see their own need or are unable to pray for themselves.

It is said that Corrie ten Boom, in her last days after she had suffered a stroke and could no longer speak, would sit by her window and pray for each person who passed by. I would love to have been prayed for by Corrie ten Boom. What a blessing to know someone is interceding for you and to be an intercessor. Jesus is your intercessor and is pleading to the Father on your behalf.

Hence, also, He is able to save forever those who
draw near to God through Him, since He always lives
to make intercession for them. (Heb. 7:25)

March 29
Don't be afraid of opposition: a kite rises against the wind, not with it.

Like a frail little bird or a flimsy paper kite that is tossed about by the wind yet soars upward, we too gain greater heights and stronger wings from the obstacles we encounter as we move forward and upward. If we allow ourselves to rest in our disappointments or remain discouraged in our failures, then we will forever be grounded and never accomplish the feats we desire or set out to accomplish.

There is a little song that I love to sing called "Little Flowers." It serves to remind me of this very thing. It goes like this:

Little flowers never worry, when the winds begin to blow
And they never, never cry when the rain begins to fall;
Tho' it's wet, and oh, so cold, soon the sun will shine again;
Then they'll smile unto the world, for their beauty to behold.
When the clouds begin to gather, and the storm begins to grow;
Little flowers don't complain, tho' they're tossing to and fro;
Oh, I guess they've learned the secret, they don't fret because they know
If it never, never rained, then they'd never, never grow.
So let it rain, let it rain, let it pour,
Let old trouble keep a knockin' at my door;
If we learn the right from wrong, it will help to make us strong.
Lord, please help us learn the secret even little flowers know;
If it never, never rains, then we'll never, never grow.
(Words and music by Danny Lee)

Our God is faithful to love and keep us in good times and hard times. His mercies are new every morning, and as we tread against opposition, just remember that God is greater.

**The Lord is my strength and my shield: My heart
trusts in Him and I am helped. (Ps. 28:7a)**

March 30
Most of us would get along well if we used the advice we give others.

A teacher is one who passes on knowledge to others. I have never taught a Sunday school class or spoken to a group with a lesson that I was not speaking to myself first. Each time I study or each time I hear myself impart a revelation from the Bible, I can hear it speaking to me.

It is amazing how inadequate we can feel in ourselves. I thank God that He promised us His Holy Spirit to be our teacher. A few years ago I was asked to speak at a spiritual growth conference in our town. I was humbled. What could I possibly say to a gathering of Christian ladies who, I was sure, were more capable than I? The Lord made it clear to me that He had called me for this time and this hour and I needed to step out of my comfort zone. *Sure, they are capable and they are able, but I am calling you this time,* I felt He was saying to me.

When we come to Jesus for salvation, we each have a calling on our life. Our sins are forgiven, and we can accept His finished work on the cross. We are no longer slaves but joint heirs with Jesus. Being in the family of God is a great position to be in. By His stripes we are healed. By His grace we are set free to speak His truth. No longer are we in bondage, but we can enjoy the freedom that comes with a right relationship with the only One who knows how to impart the truth to us. Keeping His truths to ourselves is being disobedient and selfish.

Let His love motivate you today to reach out beyond your comfort zone to share the pure truth of His glorious gift of salvation. In studying we learn and in learning we gain knowledge to share and to grow.

Be diligent to present yourself approved to God as a workman who does not need to be ashamed, accurately handling the word of truth. (2 Tim. 2:15)

March 31
To profit from good advice requires more wisdom than to give it. –Churton Collins

Listening is sometimes the hardest thing we do. However, we learn more when we listen, and many times we are more helpful that way. Many people out there need someone to just listen and let it go no further. A good listener holds in confidence what is shared with him or her.

Wars bring on much posttraumatic stress disorder (PTSD). Many of our soldiers are deployed out of a safe and comfortable environment into hostile, stressful, and excruciatingly painful settings that bring on what one soldier called a "shift of the mind" ("From Suicide to Seminary," *Missions Mosaic,* April 2016). Suicidal thoughts often drift into the mind from the sufferings that the conditions and circumstances of combat and surroundings bring. When and if soldiers do return home, many suffer endless days of withdrawal from society because of fear of losing control or just the fear of being in a crowd.

Healing can come for many through a person who cares enough to listen to their struggles. Caring for a person's needs involves much more than physical healing. The world is filled with those who need a listening ear or a shoulder to cry on. A caring spirit is a gift from God. Empty and lonely people seek out those who are sensitive to the needs of others and those who care that they are hurting. Oftentimes, however, those hurting people withdraw into themselves, and we need to be intentional about recognizing the signs.

God's love becomes evident in people's life without their ever saying a word when we caringly listen to the heart of a hurting friend or a stranger who, perhaps, God sends our way. Always point them to the One who gives peace and restores. The One who knows our every need and struggle and hears our cries for help.

In my distress I called to the Lord, and He answered me. From deep in the realm of the dead I called for help, and you listened to my cry. (Jonah 2:2)

April

It is good to give thanks to the Lord, and to sing praises to Thy name, O Most High; to declare Thy lovingkindness in the morning, and Thy faithfulness by night. (Ps. 92:1–2)

April 1
Men and pins are useless when they lose their heads.

Have you ever sat at a sports event and watched a parent or an angry fan completely lose control over a silly ballgame? I sometimes wonder, if a video were made of their actions, would they believe it was them? I have seen sweet, sensible people turn into monsters. Once, I saw a mother jump the fence to get to the official calling the game in which her son was playing. You can see big, strong, burly men practically foaming at the mouth in anger over a call. Do they really think anyone is listening to them except to shake their heads in embarrassment for them and for their children, who are surely not happy with their behavior?

People cease to be effective when they lose their heads. Our actions influence other people. As Christians mature, they learn that they are responsible for the effect of their actions on others. There is, however, justifiable anger. Jesus exercised this when He went to the temple and found people defiling the house of prayer, the place of worship, by buying and selling there. He took up a whip and drove out those who were dishonoring God's house. Such sacrilegious actions would have continued had He not taken charge and handled the situation. Those in charge had allowed it to go on.

In our world today, there are many opportunities for justifiable anger—innocent babies being killed in the womb; the innocence of our children being taken away by vicious men and women who engage them in child pornography and sex trafficking; the recruiting of our young people into homosexuality, brainwashing them to believe that they were born into that lifestyle. All of this and so much more causes anger to build up in all of us, especially Christians. We must be wise to know when to speak out and when to express our anger at the evil that we see taking place around us. Call on Him for discernment.

**A hot-tempered man stirs up strife, but the slow to
anger pacifies contention. (Prov. 15:18)**

April 2
People are funny! Everyone wants to live a long time, but no one wants to get old!

My dear, precious grandmother lived to be ninety-nine years old, and she was such a delight to be with. Her mind was clearer than mine, and she had that wonderful, sweet, Christian spirit that I have always admired. When you would ask her how she was feeling, she, with a twinkle in her eye, usually gave her pat answer: "Oh, I'm fine, honey. Just too many birthdays," or "I'm fine for the shape I'm in."

Abraham in the book of Genesis lived to be 175 years old. God promised Abraham that his descendants would be as many as the stars in the sky. Genesis 15:6 says, "Then he believed in the Lord; and He reckoned it to him as righteousness." God gives His best to those who believe and trust in Him. Isaac was born to Abraham and Sarah when Abraham was 100 years old. As God is always faithful and His promises never fail, He made Abraham's descendants a mighty nation, Israel, and from that line came our Savior, Jesus Christ.

Old age is not to be feared or dreaded. The promise of eternal life is far greater and gives us the hope of a greater future. As the apostle Paul said, "For to me, to live is Christ and to die is gain" (Phil. 1:21).

I hope if I live to a ripe old age that I will grow old gracefully with a sweet spirit and a sense of humor. I think Grandmother would say to love the Lord, stay in the Word, and do for others. Her life has been a testimony to me. Growing old is a blessing just like being born is a blessing. Genesis 25:8 says, "And Abraham breathed his last and died in a ripe old age, an old man and satisfied with life." God, let us all live our lives to the fullest and be satisfied with life and the legacy we will leave.

A gray head is a crown of glory. (Prov. 16:31)

April 3
Never answer an angry word with an angry word. It's the second one that produces a quarrel. –A. A. Nance

My mother's words ring in my ears: "It takes two to fuss." I have a sister and two brothers, and I know that there must have been times that my parents wanted to cover their ears and run. However, having three children of my own now, I see, as I am sure my wise parents saw, that those times of arguing and bickering with brothers and sisters are times of airing out differences and releasing frustrations. If we can't do that at home, then where can we do it? The important thing is not to let your disagreements give opportunity for the devil to crouch and stir up anger to the point where hatred and evil creep in to destroy relationships. I had a wise mother who always made sure that we worked out our differences in a loving way. We were encouraged to apologize to each other when we needed to, and we received punishment by my parents' authority when necessary. I hope that my children will say that was their parents' approach as well.

Cain and Abel were the first children of Adam and Eve. By this time, sin had entered the world. Cain became angry because God honored Abel's offering but did not honor his. The scripture in Genesis 4 states that "Cain became very angry and his countenance fell." The Lord asked Cain why he was angry and why his countenance had fallen. He went on to warn Cain that sin was crouching at his door and that he must master it. Cain did not listen to the Lord, allowed sin to overtake his heart and mind, and killed his own brother, Abel. When we do not first listen to the instruction from the Lord, disregarding His warnings, we will slip easily into the dangerous territory of sin and disobedience. One angry word unchecked leads to another and another.

The home is the best training ground to teach children to learn to control anger and learn that being a peacemaker shows maturity. Learning this early on enables a child to answer with a kind word, thereby squelching a quarrel and heading off unbridled anger.

A gentle answer turns away wrath, but a harsh
word stirs up anger. (Prov. 15:1)

April 4
We do not stop working and playing because we grow old; we grow old because we stop working and playing.

As I approach the later years, I can identify more with the inclination to slow down. A good night's rest seems more important, a simple task is not as simple as it used to be, and my idea of playtime is time spent with the grandchildren.

People view the retirement years in many different ways. Some see freedom of work and stress and an eternal holiday. Some see an opportunity to pursue another avenue of interest, a hobby, a sport, or perhaps a different job. Some join every senior-adult activity in sight and have a ball. Still others come to a halt and start planning their funerals!

Jesus said, "I came that they might have life and might have it abundantly" (John 10:10). What does He mean by *life*? More years? More fun? Better health? Jesus said this as he told the parable of the Good Shepherd. When He speaks of life, He means only the life that comes with knowing Him, the Good Shepherd. The sheep hear the voice of the shepherd . They know that voice and follow him. So it is with all those who hear the voice of the Holy Spirit when He calls—they answer the call and follow Jesus. Jesus is the Good Shepherd. Just like today, so many of that day did not understand what He was saying to them. Apart from knowing Jesus, there is no abundant life. You can live out your years, even have fairly good health the whole time and some fun along the way, but if you want the life that God desires for you, the peace and joy of the abundant life and eternal life, you must know the Good Shepherd. Jesus said, "I am the good shepherd; the good shepherd lays down His life for the sheep" (v. 11). He freely laid down His life for us on the cross so that we could have the abundant life.

Trust the Good Shepherd with your remaining years if you have not already. Say to yourself or out loud, "Life begins at (your age)," and live it to the fullest. Work and play will be much more rewarding!

It is the Spirit who gives life; the flesh profits nothing; the words that I have spoken to you are spirit and life. (John 6:63)

April 5
Today you are you, that is truer than true. There is no one alive who is youer than you. —Dr. Seuss

This is such a lovely time of the year. Winter seems to be melting away, and spring begins to bud out. Birds start their singing early in the morning, and all the new growth seems to sing and shout for the new season. God is so good; His miraculous creation is ever before us, inviting us to enjoy each new day and praise the Creator with singing and thanksgiving.

Before the world was ever formed, God was thinking of you! As God spoke creation into being with all its beauty and majesty, He was thinking of you. His Word tells us that after He completed each day's work, after all was in place according to His design, He looked at it and saw that it was good. On the sixth day, our God "created man in His own image, in the image of God He created him; male and female He created them. And God blessed them" (Gen. 1:27–28a). "And God saw all that He had made, and behold, it was *very* good" (v. 31, emphasis added). God then rested and sanctified the seventh day. How blessed we are to be blessed by God. He blessed us from the beginning, and now let us bless Him with our lives. Imagine a holy, loving, and mighty God knowing you before the foundation of the world. We could never comprehend it!

Praise God from Whom all blessings flow.

Praise Him all creatures here below.

Praise Him above ye heavenly host.

Praise Father, Son and Holy Ghost. (Doxology)

Look at the little things around you and be thankful. Shout songs of joy. Compete with creation in praise to the Holy Trinity.

This is the day that the Lord hath made. I will rejoice and be glad in it. (Ps. 118:24)

April 6
How you act speaks so loudly, I can't hear what you say.

During this season of Easter, we focus on the cross and all that it means to us. Would I have been one of those in the crowd that day calling for Jesus to be crucified? Would I have turned my back on the Chosen One as He hung there that day shedding His precious blood for the remission of my sins? Would I have cast lots for his garments or taken my turn to drive the nails into His hands and His feet? Someone had to pierce His side. Would I have been the one?

My Jesus hung alone that day.
My sins were His burden;
My debt He would pay.
Why couldn't I step forward and say,
"I'll suffer here, release Him I pray!"
But just like the rest, I stood and I watched,
Counting the blows to each spike head and notch.
Shouting and clamoring for the perfect space
To see this man, Jesus, tortured and erased.
You are thinking, I know, "Oh, you were not there.
That was many years ago, how could you share
In a scene such as this in days long gone by?
That would be impossible, even if you try."
But my face is sad, for I know I'm in that mob
Each time I reject Him, each time I choose to rob
This crucified Savior of all mankind
Of freedom to live in my heart and my mind. (Author)

Easter is a time of reflecting on the cross, but the celebration comes as we rejoice in a risen Savior. Jesus is no longer on the cross and He is no longer in the grave. He is risen! In spite of us all, He lives!

**He said, " It is finished." And He bowed His head
and gave up His Spirit. (John 19:30)**

April 7
Make hay while the sun shines!

The Bible has a lot to say about those who shun work. God intended for us to be productive on our journey through this life and not to sit back on our fingers and lean back on our thumb.

There are blessings in working, and the fruit of the harvest is so rewarding. It is hard to tolerate a lazy person. The New Testament has a lot to say about working, whether it is manual labor or laboring in the Lord's work. In 2 Thessalonians 3:10, Paul issued this statement as an order to the church at Thessalonica: "If anyone will not work, neither let him eat." My mother always told me that an idle mind is the devil's workshop, and I believed her. How sad it is to see someone spend a whole lifetime trying to avoid what actually is a blessing.

Laziness is a bad habit that turns into a disease that, untreated, grows rapidly and destroys. When we sit idle, it gives the devil open season to prey. He loves to fill a life with boredom, depression, anxiety, irresponsibility, failure, gossip, worry, and so on. Such are the things that laziness brings. There is so much pleasure in rest after the labor. The feeling of accomplishment brings encouragement, and productivity brings profit and success. Adam and Eve chose to listen to the devil as they walked in the garden. They had plenty to do in that perfect place, but they chose to disobey.

Don't be idle. Don't give the devil a foothold. Seek to be a productive human being, and life will be so much more rewarding. Don't put off until tomorrow what you can do today. Ask God to direct you to a good work ethic, to take you to a higher level of acceptance of work, and to give you the strength to complete the task.

He who gathers in summer is a son who acts wisely, but he who sleeps in harvest is a son who acts shamefully. (Prov. 10:5)

April 8
If at first you don't succeed, try, try again.

Some of the most successful and renowned people in days present and past have failed over and over again to reach their goals, but they kept striving, kept pulling themselves up by their bootstraps and surging ahead. You have probably heard the story about Walt Disney. He was fired from his job and told that he "lacked imagination and had no good ideas." And yet, millions have enjoyed his amazing theme parks. Thomas Edison's teachers told him he was "too stupid to learn anything," but he went on to hold more than a thousand patents and invented some world-changing devices, like the phonograph, practical electrical lamp, and a movie camera. Vincent Van Gogh painted hundreds of paintings but sold only one in his lifetime. If he had given up on his artistic ability, the art world would be missing hundreds of paintings from a true master *(Business Insider)*. Success is not determined by how many times you tried but by how you reach your destination.

I have heard it said that faith is never surprised at success; it expects it. Believe in yourself and your abilities, but more than that, believe that God is a rewarder of those who seek Him. God never said life would be easy. He did say, however, that He would be with you. Remember, David slew the giant with a single stone and a mighty God. That same God is your refuge and your strength. Call on Him. His desire is that you succeed at what you do. Success is not found in wealth and things but in a right relationship with Him. Seek Him first, and these other things shall be added unto you as He sees fit. Trust Him and don't give up!

**Do not fear or be dismayed; tomorrow go out to face
them, for the Lord is with you. (2 Chron. 20:17b)**

April 9
Today is the first day of the rest of your life—make the most of it!

The cross of Calvary is the heart of Christianity and the single most important event in human history. Where would humankind be today had it not been for the cross? It is obvious as we look around and see the sin in the world that we need a Savior. We would be enslaved by our sin and separated from Holy God. Jesus came to earth for the purpose of redeeming humankind to God. Sin brings death. The cross and what was accomplished there bring life. Jesus brought hope to a sinful world as He willingly gave up His life for all humankind. We can become sons and daughters of God by willingly and openly accepting His perfect Son. Because God recognized the lost nature of His greatest creation, humankind, He came to earth in human form, Jesus, to be the propitiation for our sins. Jesus was God's all-sufficient sacrifice. The death, burial, and resurrection of this perfect Lamb made it possible for everyone who accepts Him to come into the kingdom. Rejecting the cross and the One who died there means being lost, separation, and spiritual death. Accepting the cross means salvation, becoming a new creation, and not being enslaved by sin but forgiven by the blood of Jesus. God defeated sin and death at the cross, and praise God we can rejoice in that victory!

Will you start anew today? The sacrifice was for you. You can serve a risen Savior, a God who is alive and loved you enough to sacrifice Himself for you. "For God so loved the world that He gave His only begotten Son. That whosoever believeth in Him should not perish but have everlasting life. For God sent His Son into the world, not to condemn the world, but that the world through Him might be saved" (John 3:16–17).

And He Himself is the propitiation for our sins; and not for ours only, but also for those of the whole world. (1 John 2:2)

April 10
Give to the world the best that you have and the best will come back to you.

God gave His best to us when He sent Jesus to this world. Our best back to God is surrender—surrender to the One who came to give us abundant life on earth and eternal life in heaven. Jesus came for the purpose of dying for sinful humankind. Even though we were in our sin, Christ died for us. No sin has ever been committed that Jesus's blood does not cover, and He will forgive all sin no matter its depth if we repent and cry out to Him.

The burden of our sin was what Jesus suffered on the cross. The weight was tremendous. It was not the spikes, the spear, or the crown of thorns. The sin debt of the world was what He suffered. When His Father turned His back on Him—because God cannot look on sin—Jesus cried out in anguish, "Father, why hast Thou forsaken me?" At that moment He was completely alone and separated from His Father and from the Holy Spirit. He was bearing my sin, your sin, and the sin of generations past and generations to come. All the sin of all the world, past and present and future, was placed on Him at that moment.

When we reject what Jesus did for us, when we do not accept Him as Savior and Lord, He grieves. He again feels the pain and suffering of Calvary. He desires that no one perish but that all come to repentance and be saved. God gave us His best. Give Him your best—you!

As I walk this path day by day,
I meet many along my way.
Will I share Jesus or will I delay
Holding back and too shy to say,
"Do you know my Jesus? Let us pray,
That today's the day that you will say,
'Jesus come in, I ask you to stay.'"
How can I give my best today?
By giving my own life away! (Author)

Beloved let us love one another, for love is of God. (1 John 4:7)

April 11
Anytime you condone what God has already condemned, you are in a mess. –John Sullivan

Look into God's Holy Word and see what He has condemned as sin. Then take a look at our world today and note what we condone. God's Word tells us that "the fear of God is the beginning of wisdom" (Prov. 9:10). It is an unwise people who go their own way, ignoring what God, their Creator, is against. America has fallen into the trap of disobedience. We are not only disobedient to God's laws, the Ten Commandments, but also to humans' laws and the ones that our nation was founded on.

The children of Israel strayed over and over again from the truth, and they had to suffer for their disobedience. Someone once said that when you choose to sin, you choose to suffer. Christians do not need to tolerate what God has already said is wrong, much less participate in it. If God tells us in His Word that it is wrong and we choose to do it anyway, then we are already judged. "For the Lord gives wisdom; from His mouth come knowledge and understanding. (Prov. 2:6).

Look today at Exodus 20 and go one by one through the Ten Commandments. Observe how our world and its people have distanced themselves from the laws of God. We have listened to the wrong voices, walked the wrong paths, heard the wrong drumbeats. Commit yourself to make any changes necessary in your world and your walk. Hear the voice of the One who knows and loves you and wants the best for you. One voice can change the course of history, and one spark can set a nation ablaze with fire from on high. God plus one is a majority. Let's do our part today!

For God has not given us a spirit of timidity, but of power and love and discipline. Therefore do not be ashamed of the testimony of our Lord. (2 Tim. 2:7–8a)

April 12
Our faith is unmerited because it is by grace. It is unlimited because it is by Christ Jesus.

Do we deserve all that Christ has done for us? Certainly not, but that is the beauty of it all. His love is unconditional. His love has no end. It always has been and always will be! His love is all sufficient. It is all that we need! His love has no limits. Even when we are at our worst and unlovable, He loves us! *Wow*! Do you know another love like that?

In our world today, we struggle to find deep and lasting love that is abiding. I have been married to my husband for many years. To be truthful, there have been difficult times. However, because we love each other and made a covenant with God and each other, we have worked through the hard times. I always tell young couples that each time they work through those difficult times, they are tying that knot tighter. Sometimes it is easier to run from conflict than to work through it. But what have you gained when you run? Nothing but more conflict and greater hurt, extending far beyond your relationship.

Oswald Chambers said, "If human love does not carry a man beyond himself, it is not love." Many rely on affection and feelings to determine love. Our world today is caught up in the physical appearance of the opposite sex rather than character, integrity, and spiritual depth. Going beyond oneself means to put others before your own selfish desires. Whether it be a husband, wife, children, friend, or acquaintance, love of any kind must be unselfish.

Love is what Calvary was all about. Jesus loved us so much that He was willing to take the sins of the whole world on Himself. When that blood was shed, it provided hope for all humankind and showed us what true sacrificial love is. Generation after generation can know the power of forgiveness and no longer be in bondage for their sin. If there is true repentance, His forgiveness is yours. His precious blood redeemed us. It is a mystery how God could love us so!

For God so loved the world that He gave His
only begotten Son. (John 3:16)

April 13
Friendship is priceless; it cannot be bought or sold, for it is a gift of the heart.

One of God's greatest blessings in this life is the friendship of another human being. God puts people in our lives who enrich and bless us by their very existence.

When I was probably between ten and twelve years old, I would go to G.A. Camp at Norman Park, Georgia, in the summer for a week. It was a time I always looked forward to. I met many friends from other churches in the area. It was always a special time because, even at that young age and even though I didn't realize it then, I was developing friendships that would carry on through the years. We would write letters for weeks. Some relationships lasted the space of time and miles, and some fizzled. One particular friendship that I still cherish today was sparked at that camp so long ago. Janie and I lost touch for a while. As life got busy with high school and college, our correspondence ceased. Coincidentally, after six years of marriage, my husband and I ended up in Janie's hometown. She and her husband, Mike, were living in Texas at the time. When they came home to visit their families, they would visit the church she had grown up in, which happened to be my current church. You can imagine our excitement when, after all those years, we reunited and caught up on our lives. A few years ago Mike retired, and they have moved back closer to home. We often have lunch or just enjoy short visits at church when they are in town. The warmth of her friendship is always present. She is such an encourager and a blessing to me. The friendships that are inspired by our loving God are the best and most lasting!

Reach out to someone today. You never know how deep, how wide, how long, or how strong those ties that bind will be. Friends are one of God's greatest blessings.

A friend loves at all times. (Prov. 17:17)

April 14
A worker's appetite works for him, for his hunger urges him on. –Prov. 16:26 NAS

Have you ever been so hungry that your stomach pinched? Hunger creates a gnawing pain that does not go away until it is satisfied. So it is with the appetite for anything that you desire. The hunger for that thing spurs you on. It may be food, it may be success, or it may be a hunger for the Word of God. Whatever the basis for your hunger is, it can be the driving force toward accomplishing what it takes to satisfy that hunger.

Bad habits, too, can create an appetite. That is one reason that we should never give in to the temptation of evil and sin. People who get taken in by bad habits like drugs, alcohol, illicit sex, pornography, and so on never set out to let it be a controlling force in their lives, but our bodies and minds can crave bad as well as good and we can become addicted to sinful lust that takes over our lives. Colossians 3:2 says, "Set your mind on the things above, not on the things that are on earth." Things above are things of God, things that He desires for us to have an abundant life, a future and a hope. Things of this earth are worldly things that do not satisfy. The prince of this world, Satan, longs to "steal, and kill, and destroy" (John 10:10).

Hunger pangs make a lazy person work for bread. Setbacks are not easy but can be rungs on the ladder of success to spur us on. Disappointments and heartaches can develop maturity in our spiritual growth and make us hunger for a word from God. Seek after the Bread of Life, Jesus, who satisfies the greatest hunger and is the great healer for those who desire to be free from the appetites that lead to destruction.

**But grow in the grace and knowledge of our Lord
and Savior Jesus Christ. (2 Peter 3:18 NAS)**

April 15
The fear of the Lord is the beginning of wisdom, and the knowledge of the Holy One is understanding. —Prov. 9:10 NAS

We can know God in His fullness. He tells us that. It is a matter of submitting to Him and having a teachable spirit. Christians should have a hunger and thirst for the knowledge of God. To fear Him is not necessarily to be afraid of Him but to have a healthy desire to know Him more and to desire the things of a Holy God, knowing and believing that He is our Creator and He knows best. Reverential fear means that we hold in reverence the One who holds all wisdom and knowledge, the One whose judgment is sure and fair. We can't be wise unless we know who supplies all wisdom. Knowledge and intelligence can come from books and earthly scholars, but wisdom comes from the One who created our minds, our hearts, and our souls. That should put us in awe and fearful anticipation.

Hanging over the bed in my guest room is an antique piece of needlepoint that reads, "Do right, Fear not." I love the look of the old piece and the frame it is in. It hangs perfectly over my grandmother's antique sleigh bed. But most of all, the message is invaluable. I am seriously thinking of stitching a needlepoint similar to it to pass down to my grandchildren that reads, "Fear God, Be Wise," a message to them as they walk this journey through life.

When we tell God that we no longer want Him in our schools, in our government, on our money, or in our everyday lives, we must know that we have lost the reverential fear that we must have to be blessed by Him. "How blessed is the man who finds wisdom, and the man who gains understanding" (Prov. 3:13).

Take My yoke upon you, and learn from me, for I am gentle and humble in heart; and you shall find rest for your soul. (Matt. 11:29)

April 16
The Lord is far from the wicked, but He hears the prayer of the righteous. –Prov. 15:29

We distance ourselves from God on our own. He never moves. He is the same yesterday, today, and forever (Heb. 13:8). Sin separates us from our Holy Father. He can't bear to look on sin. He knows what it does to His children—it pulls us away from His presence. As we draw away from Him in sin, our wickedness grieves Him. However, He continues to call out to us as He beckons us back to Himself, waiting always to hear our prayer of repentance. As we realize our sin and confess it, we become righteous, in right standing, before Him.

David in the Bible is a good example of a repentant sinner. A man after God's own heart, David did some wretched things to satisfy his own selfish desires. One sin always leads to another unless it is taken to the foot of the cross. Lust breeds sin, and then comes spiritual death. As David committed adultery with Bathsheba, that sin led to the death of her husband, Uriah, whom David sent to the front line of battle to be killed so that he could marry Bathsheba. Murder followed adultery. God sent the prophet Nathan to rebuke David, and David repented. God's grace is amazing. He will not let His children stray far before He draws them back into the fold through discipline or coaxing. Our loving Shepherd loves us so.

I grieve today as I think of those who do not know of God's provision for us through Jesus Christ. The lost must cry out to God, repent of sin, and ask to be saved. The saved must cry out to God, repent of sin, and plead for God's amazing grace to wash away their sins. We are all wicked, but through Jesus we can be made righteous. Pray for a lost person by name today!

**Even so consider yourselves to be dead to sin, but
alive to God in Christ Jesus. (Rom. 6:11 NAS)**

April 17
He is on the path of life who heeds instruction, but he who forsakes reproof goes astray. –Prov. 10:17

Jesus tells us that the gate that leads to destruction is wide and broad and there will be many to pass through it. He calls us, however, to enter through the narrow gate that leads to life. He says that this gate is small and that there will be few to find it (Matt. 7:13).

If you have raised children, you can see this picture clearly. When they are small you do everything in your power to get them on the right track. You practically walk them through those young years, holding their hands and pointing them in the right direction. As they get older—say, ten or twelve—they are pulled from your grip by friends and peers, thus veering off the path and then back again by your nudging. As they approach the teenage years, their peers and acquaintances have a greater influence on them. The wide gate becomes more inviting because more are going that way. Then they are on their own in college, the workforce, and marriage. Which gate will they choose? Have they listened to instruction or forsaken reproof? Have they made that all-important decision to follow Christ down the narrow road, or will their decision be to take the wide road of the world that leads to destruction?

John Bunyan's *Pilgrim's Progress* illustrates brilliantly that the narrow road is not easy. "Christian" encounters many dreadful pitfalls along the way. Satan is constantly trying to lure him into sin and frightening him into turning back from the narrow road that Christian knows leads to the lights of the Holy City. He has chosen the narrow way, but it is not easy.

God gives us a promise in Proverbs 22:6 that if we train our children up in the way that they should go, when they are old they will not depart from it. We need always to pray for them and instruct them in righteousness, pointing them to that narrow gate.

I will instruct you and teach you in the way which you should go; I will counsel you with My eye upon you. (Ps. 32:8)

April 18
It's not how you start but how you finish that counts.

A good name can go before you, and it will also follow you. This is also true about a bad name. My mother always told me that it takes a whole lifetime to build a good reputation and one destructive act to tear it down. How true.

One thing that we can leave our children that is greater than any monetary inheritance is a good name. Parents should strive for a reputation that is exemplary of one whose eyes are fixed on Jesus. Such a legacy goes far ahead and lingers far behind. Good people can leave a good reputation according to worldly standards by living a life of honesty, integrity, and even generosity. However, if the Creator of all things that are good and righteous is left out of their lives, then it is a superficial and short-lived legacy. It's time to get it right.

Paul is a good example of one who started out on the wrong track. He was a strong persecutor of Christians. By the world's standards, he was doing what he should do to rid the world of The Way, a doctrine being preached by Jesus and His followers. His reputation changed drastically, however, when his life was radically changed by the One, Jesus, who called him to repentance and salvation. Paul was literally blinded so that he could see the light. After his conversion he became a dynamic missionary to the Jews and Gentiles. Through Paul's preaching, God opened the way for the Gentiles to be drafted into the promise and for many to come to believe.

Maybe you started out on the wrong road. Maybe you made mistakes that you think could never be forgiven by a Holy God. Don't sell the heavenly Father short. He waits earnestly for sinners to come with a repentant heart. It is never too late to get it right. As they say, "It's not how you start out but how you finish."

A good name is to be more desired that great riches. (Prov. 22:1a)

April 19
If you don't stand for something, you will fall for anything.

Jesus spoke out strongly about being wishy-washy. A lukewarm Christian was sickening to Him. He said that it would be better for us to be either hot or cold than to be lukewarm.

Why do you think Jesus would say such a thing? Milk-toast Christians have no influence. They come across as wimpy and ineffective. Shouldn't it show if Christ has done a work in our lives? Christian people are called to stand firm. This not only pleases God, but it wins the respect of unbelievers. God called us to live holy lives. We are His representatives here on earth. Salvation sets us apart, and we are to be different. If we go with the flow of the world's way, where will the difference be seen?

God called Joshua to lead the people of Israel into the promised land after God's servant Moses died. Why did God call Joshua? Because he was different from all the rest. He was faithful, honest, and a proven leader. He knew the scriptures and was led by them. Over and over, God told Joshua, "Be strong and courageous, for the Lord your God is with you wherever you go." And Joshua believed God. Joshua had seen Moses's obedience and faithfulness played out before him for many years. Joshua's own name means "The Lord is salvation." God knew that he would not fall for anything but would remain faithful to do what He called him to do. "And Israel served the Lord all the days of Joshua and all the days of the elders who survived Joshua, and had known all the deeds of the Lord which he had done for Israel" (Joshua 24:31).

Jesus did not call us to be faithful so He could then abandon us. Like Joshua, He promises to be with us "to the end of the age" (Matt. 28:20). When Jesus went to heaven, He promised us a helper, the Holy Spirit, who enables us to stand firm when all around us is as shifting sand beneath our feet.

**Be on the alert, stand firm in the faith, act
like men, be strong. (1 Cor. 16:13)**

April 20
When you are down and all seems in vain, lift your head high and sing a refrain. –Author

Make a joyful noise unto the Lord
All ye lands.
Serve the Lord with gladness;
Come before His presence with singing.
Know ye that the Lord He is God;
It is He that hath made us
And not we ourselves;
We are His people and the sheep of His pasture.
Enter into His gates with thanksgiving,
And into His courts with praise.
Be thankful unto Him and bless His Name.
For the Lord is good; His mercy is everlasting,
And His truth endureth for all generations. (Ps. 100)
Music and singing revive the soul and rejuvenate the spirit. The psalmist expressed his feelings and emotions through the words of his songs. Each poetic psalm came from the heart and projected the mood and emotion of the writer. From happiness to utter despair, singing can express the very depths of the soul. David wrote many of his psalms when he was in agony over his sin. Also, he rejoiced in many at the faithfulness and deliverance that God brought to him.

Sing a new song today. God's mercies are new every morning. That is something to sing about. Sing a song to revive your own spirits or to someone else to revive theirs. The best singing is in praising our glorious king. It can be a cleansing and a blessing!

Shout joyfully to the Lord, all the earth; Break forth and sing for joy and sing praises. (Ps. 98:4)

April 21
When folks are distant, they might need you to move in closer. –Author

Some people feel threatened if they find themselves getting too close to others. This could be a result of insecurity. There is usually a reason for such behavior. Perhaps they lost someone close to them or were rejected at one time by someone. Maybe closeness makes them feel uncomfortable or obligated. Whatever the reason, it is important to recognize the signs and respect their space.

How satisfied are you in your own skin? Insecurity can come across as confidence. Sometimes insecure people are narcissists, always talking about me, myself, and I. Their accomplishments are above everybody else's—in their eyes, anyway. Insecurity is sad in that, because they appear to be very self-confident, they are probably desperately lacking confidence in reality and need to constantly be reassured.

In a loving and caring way, we need to reach out to those around us. We need to offer them trustworthiness and loyalty. Rather than despairing because people turn their backs on us, perhaps we need to recognize the symptoms of their deeper problems and offer a caring heart and an understanding spirit with reassurance and compassion.

Look around you today. First make sure you are not wearing a chip on your own shoulder, then reach out gently and touch a life that obviously is hurting. When we are born again, we should have a new nature. Perhaps the insecure person you know has not had that life-changing, Spirit-indwelling encounter with the Holy One. Share the ABCs that can make the difference in that life: A—admit that you are a sinner, B—believe in your heart that Jesus is God and that He came to earth and died and rose again for forgiveness of sin, and C—confess with your mouth to others that He is the Lord of your life. Salvation gives freedom, peace, and confidence. Salvation can bridge the gap!

Little children, let us not love with word or with tongue, but in deed and truth. (1 John 3:18)

April 22
Inch by inch it's a cinch. Yard by yard
it's hard. –Mary Kay Ash

Things can be overwhelming at first glance. Maybe you are facing a new job, a difficult task, a large debt, or a challenging relationship. God never promised us that life would be a bowl of cherries or a rose garden. He gave us clouds as well as sunshine and bodies that suffer as well as rejoice.

When God created the world that we live in, He did not create it in a day. He certainly could have. He is God! But He took a full six days, and then He rested on the seventh. Our wise and all-knowing God even told us on which day He made what. He didn't have to, but He did. When Jesus walked on earth, He never rushed into the things that He set out to do. First of all, it was with much prayer that He went before His heavenly Father, waiting to hear from Him for direction and timing.

When things seem bigger than you are, break them down and take one step at a time to accomplish the goal or solve the problem. If you have Jesus, you have everything anyway, and there is nothing too great that the two of you together can't achieve. Petition the Father in prayer to help you and wait for His answer.

If you do not know the Savior, then that needs to be the first step you take. Go to Him, repent of your sins, and ask Him to save you. He is faithful and just to forgive your sins and to cleanse you from all unrighteousness (1 John 1:9). Go to church and publicly profess Him as Lord of your life. He takes you where you are, and everything after that is a move in the right direction. All your problems will not go away, but you will be a child of the One who will walk with you through any and all situations as you seek Him in all you do, inch by inch.

Watch the path of your feet, and all your ways
will be established. (Prov. 4:36)

April 23
You can't move forward going backward.

I love to feel like I am accomplishing something every day. If we aren't moving forward, we are standing still, going backward, or getting stagnant. No progress is being made, and certainly being at a standstill lays hold to laziness.

As we read and study God's Word, we see that He had a plan from the beginning, even before the foundation of the world. He moved forward with His plan, and still today His ways are made known to us. As we read and study the Bible, we are amazed at how our great God orchestrates things to implement His plan. He has always called out prophets, priests, and kings for His purpose. He uses ordinary people—men, women, and children empowered by the Holy Spirit—to fulfill His great and mighty work for His people.

I have found that daily planning is helpful. Unlike Holy God, we are not sovereign, omniscient, omnipotent, or eternal. However, God has granted to all who will accept Him the gift of the Holy Spirit, our helper.

Calling on Him to help us in whatever we set out to do ensures much better results than relying on our own abilities alone.

List on paper today the ten most important things you need to accomplish. Or maybe you choose to mentally go over what needs to be done, according to their priority. Whatever your strategy, plan to accomplish something. Accomplishment brings satisfaction and fulfillment. Pray about it, asking the Holy Spirit for guidance and discernment. Some projects may carry over to the next day. Some may even be long term, but always have a plan and work that plan. The right helper can make the difference. Don't we all love it when a plan comes together!

I will never cease to be amazed at how God works in different situations and through different people to accomplish His purpose and bring about all the promises that He has made known to us. God did not create us as ornaments for His great green earth. He intended that we move forward, that we bloom and prosper. Don't get stagnant and stinky!

The mind of man plans his way, but the Lord
directs his steps. (Prov. 16:9)

April 24
Paul encouraged, Abraham obeyed, Moses listened, and they all prayed. —Author

God's people are to be people of prayer. It is no different today than it was in days of old. God wants to hear from His children just as we want to hear from ours. Talking and having fellowship with our heavenly Father is of the highest order and reaps the greatest blessings. David Jeremiah says that prayer is the key to unlocking God's prevailing power in our lives.

Imagine praying to the same God that Paul, Abraham, and Moses prayed to. Try to grasp the reality of a God so personal that He knows us each by name. He knows the number of hairs on each and every person's head. He is a mighty God, powerful and omnipotent, yet approachable, faithful, loving, and just. He desires more than anything to have a relationship with His people. A relationship is dead and ineffective without conversation. How can we know God if we don't spend time with Him? I married my husband many years ago. I cannot imagine what kind of marriage we would have had if in all that time I never spent time with him, never talked to him, and never confided in him. Do you think I would know him very well? We certainly would not have much of a relationship. God knows us even if we never spend time with Him, but He wants us to know Him. In order to know our Lord and Master, we must seek Him and trust Him. When we hurt, we need to cry out to Him. When we rejoice, we need to praise Him. When He blesses us, we need to thank Him. He wants to impart to us His righteousness and peace.

Prayer is the key that unlocks the doors of heaven. You are carrying a key to a wealth of power and grace if you are His child. Don't misplace it!

Pray without ceasing. (1 Thess. 5:17)

April 25
Love, live, laugh, and listen.

These four L's stretch long and say much. In a nutshell, they express much knowledge for living.

God is love, and His love never fails. If both of these are true, what does God expect from us? He calls on us to love Him first and then we can love others as we should. In Matthew 22:37 and 39, Jesus said to "love the Lord your God with all your heart, your mind and your soul and love your neighbor as yourself." He goes on to say that unless we keep these two commandments, we cannot keep the rest. He reminds us that "everyone who loves is born of God and knows God" (1 John 4:7).We love because He first loved us (1 John 4:19).

We should live with the same zest for living that any child of a king does. Our inheritance of eternal life is worth more than the wealth that any earthly king can give. No earthly fortune can compare with the riches of the glory in Christ Jesus that is ours if we trust in Him. Life is fleeting, and our heavenly Father desires for us the abundant life, here and in heaven. Each day is precious.

Laugh often. Laughter cleanses the soul and makes a merry heart. It is contagious and spreads joy and goodwill. Have you ever found yourself in a state of uncontrollable laughter? It seems to happen to me when I get extremely tired. I call it getting giddy. But it is so freeing and cleansing. Laughter can break down barriers and promote healing.

Learn to be a good listener. We can learn more with our mouths closed and our ears open. The psalmist says, "Even a fool, when he keeps silent, is considered wise" (Prov. 17:28). Everybody needs a friend who will listen to them. Jesus is the best of all friends and the best of all listeners. Apply the four L's today. You will be the benefactor.

When a man's ways are pleasing to the Lord, he makes even his enemies to be at peace with him. (Prov. 16:7)

April 26
If you want children to turn out well, give them twice the time and half the money.

Children are God's most precious gift to us. Over the span of time that I have been writing these devotionals, my children have been growing up. Today just happens to be my youngest child's birthday, and I look back today wondering where the time has gone. That precious little boy, whom it seems we just brought home from the hospital, has grown into a fine young man with dreams and aspirations of his own.

Our three children are five years apart in age. It has been interesting to observe the changes in our society over the years and to be careful as parents to remain faithful to God's ways and not man's ways in permissiveness. God's laws never change, and it is so encouraging to know that we have a place to go to get absolute truth. When the sand beneath our feet is shifting, we can be confident in this very thing—that our God never changes. He says, "I am the same yesterday, today and, yes, forever" (Heb. 13:8). His Word is as relevant for us today as it was for Abraham, Isaac, Jacob, David, Paul, and John. These men, as well as other men and women in the Bible who sought God and listened to Him, are examples of faithfulness. They sought God in the good times and also in the hard times. We can learn from them.

Young children and teens want their parents' time and attention more than anything else. Too many children are put in front of the television or given electronic games and devices to entertain them rather than being offered time with a parent or a loved one. If we allow the world to influence our children, we should not wonder when they crave the things of the world.

Play a board game with your child today. Get your daughter interested in a sewing project or bake a cake together. Read together or just engage your children in a conversation. Love them by listening to them.

These commandments that I give you today are to be upon your heart. Impress them on your children. Talk about them when you sit at home and when you walk along the road, when you lie down and when you get up. (Deut. 6:6–7 NIV)

April 27
Eat to live, don't live to eat.

Our appetites can get us in trouble sometimes. It is like anything that we go to the extreme with either way. Paul told the church at Corinth that "food is for the stomach, and the stomach is for food; but God will do away with both of them" (1 Cor. 6:13). He made it clear to them that their bodies were for the Lord. Paul was trying to help the Corinthian church, and us, to see that just because there is not a law against something like eating, we still need to be aware of God's restrictions on things that keep us from being what He calls us to be as ambassadors for Him. "Or do you not know that your body is a temple of the Holy Spirit who is in you, whom you have from God, and that you are not your own?" (v. 19). When we let anything take over our bodies, our thinking, or our lives, they become as harlots to Holy God. They become masters of our will and pull us away from Him.

God gave to each of us a good mind and the capability to make right choices. Unlike animals, we can discern right and wrong, good and evil. If we make the wrong choices, we must suffer the consequences. If we make the right choices, then the blessings are ours and He is glorified.

Whether it is our hunger appetites or our moral appetites, God gives us the power and a sound mind to control both. Eve let her appetite for the forbidden fruit lead her to sin by being disobedient to God. As she offered the fruit to Adam, sin multiplied and we all have had to suffer for their disobedience. Thanks be to our loving God who made a way for us to be delivered from the bondage of sin through the blood of His Son, Jesus Christ.

Because our bodies are the temple of the Holy Spirit, He wants us to be intentional about how we care for them. Make wise and healthy choices for your own good, for the ones who love you and for the One who indwells you.

**For you have been bought with a price: therefore,
glorify God in your body. (1 Cor. 6:20)**

April 28
God treats all men justly. O, that all men would treat Him justly.

What does it mean to be just? The dictionary says, "righteous and fair in action or judgment; impartial." How refreshing it is to know that we can rest in the Lord knowing that He is fair in all His ways and that we can find shelter under the wings of an Almighty God. God is faithful. Even when we aren't, He is. God is just, and His justice is fair. He loved us enough to come to earth to die for us, but He doesn't put up with ugly always. He is a patient God and desires that no one should perish, but neither will He strive with humankind forever (Gen. 6:3).

The prophet Micah delivered a message from God to the Israelites telling them what the Lord required of them. The message is for us as well, that we might know the heart of God. He calls on us to be just as he is just, to love mercy as He is merciful, and to walk humbly with Him, not proudly or arrogantly but in humility, as we serve Him (Gen. 6:8).

God holds us accountable for our actions. If a person is lost, then his or her actions are accountable to the Son of Darkness, Satan. The Holy Spirit will continue to strive with the lost person, but there is a point in time when He pulls away if He is continually rejected. If we are children of God, Christians, and Sons of Light, then we are accountable to Holy God and He expects us to walk by the power of His Spirit. If we do not, He decides what is necessary to set our feet back on the narrow path.

God's justice is sure, and His wrath is swift. When those who are called by His name stray, He gently leads us back to the fold. However, if we persist in our defiance, His discipline can get harder. Let us thank our Father today for His holy wrath that keeps us walking with Him.

For Christ also died for sins once for all, the just for the unjust, in order that He might bring us to God, having been put to death in the flesh, but made alive in the spirit. (1 Peter 3:18)

April 29
Leisure is a beautiful garment, but it will not do for constant wear.

After five years in business, I sold my gift shop. The business had grown rapidly and steadily. It had gotten to be more than one person could handle, so I was going to have to make a decision about hiring a full-time employee. At just the right time, a man came looking for an established business to buy. A friend of mine in the real estate business approached me about selling, and I was ready. I had worked myself silly. I loved what I was doing, especially seeing people and interacting with them on a daily basis. I loved being creative and innovative. I had always stayed at home with my children, so stepping out on this little venture after our youngest was almost sixteen was exciting. Being a stay-at-home mom had always been my first dream, and thanks to my hard-working husband, I had been blessed to be able to do that. My little shop was just a short distance from our home, which was good because we were caring for my mother-in-law at the time. To have my own little gift shop had been a secret dream of mine for a while. It was a wonderful experience and I enjoyed it very much; however, I decided to sell and go back home.

I'm back home now, and retirement is wonderful. I am writing, reading, and loving grandchildren. I even take my daddy fishing every once in a while. I could get used to this. Life is a wonderful blessing, and opportunity is all around us. Leisure soon ended as my mother became bedridden and needed me. God's timing is amazing. He knew I would be needed to help with her as a caregiver, and what a blessing that was.

Try your wings today or enjoy the shelter of His wings as you rest from your labor.

**Come to Me, all who are weary and heavy-laden,
and I will give you rest. (Matt. 11:28)**

April 30
That man lives twice who lives the first life well. –Robert Herrick

Age is something that we rarely think about when we are children. Only when we reach about fourteen do we long to be older. Usually, we long for sixteen in order to get a driver's license, then eighteen to graduate high school and go to college. Then comes career, marriage, home, and family, and aging just happens.

My aunt who is approaching ninety knows that I am writing a devotional book, and she asked me one day if I had written anything on aging. As I began contemplating, I couldn't think of one day that I had covered that subject. So I began thinking of the life that we live if, in fact, we live long enough to be considered old. The life span is so much longer today than it was even in the1930s. I received an email a few years ago with information about how much longer people are living today than in years past. In the 1930s, according to this information, the average life span was only thirty-four years of age. We consider life to be just beginning at that age now.

One gem of wisdom that I have acquired in my lifetime is that it is not the number of years that we live but how we live the year that God grants to us. Eternity is forever. As the old song says, "This world is not my home, I'm just a-passin' through." Would you want to live in this old body for eternity? Even if we are relatively healthy, we know that it is just a matter of time before these old bodies wear out. Jesus refers to them as our "earthly tent." A person who suffers a long time in this life welcomes death and the open arms of the Father, the all-sufficient One. As He calls them to their eternal home, there is no more pain and suffering, sadness and grief, or worry and anguish. There is only peace, joy, love, and kindness.

We have only one opportunity to make the choice as to where we will spend eternity. God does not make that choice for us. We are the only ones who can make it. It has to be decided between the cradle and the grave. Where will you spend eternity?

**It is appointed unto man once to die and
then the judgment. (Heb. 9:27)**

May

The night is almost gone, and the day is at hand. Let us therefore lay aside the deeds of darkness and put on the armor of light. (Rom. 13:12)

May 1
A winner never quits, and a quitter never wins.

Winning at life is something that we all want to do. To some, winning in this life is the accumulation of material wealth and things. To others, it is power or prestige. Still others desire degrees and titles that label them as having attained education and knowledge. Many battle for achievement and recognition. There is nothing wrong with any of these things. However, there is everything wrong with all of these things if we make them our gods. Jesus said in Matthew 16:26, "For what will a man be profited, if he gains the whole world, and forfeits his soul?"

Our most important priority is our relationship with Christ Jesus. As we seek him first, moving in the direction that He leads us, all the things we attain in life will fall into their proper place. Then and only then are we truly winners.

Paul, who had a rough start, finished well. God saw something in this man, Saul, a radical Pharisee, that we would never have seen. He saw his heart. After a heart change by the living Savior, Saul got a new name, Paul, and set out to run the race for the Master with new zeal and a purpose. Jacob, one of our Old Testament patriarchs, also did not start out well. Having stolen his brother Esau's birthright and becoming a fugitive early in his life, God had to get his attention in a dream, in which Jacob saw a ladder ascending from earth to heaven. The Lord stood above it and spoke a word to Jacob: "I am with you, and will keep you wherever you go.... I will not leave you until I have done what I have promised you" (Gen. 28:15). God knew Jacob's heart better than he did. God honored Jacob with a new name, Israel; the Lord became his God; and God kept His promise. Jacob had twelve sons—hence the twelve tribes of Israel. From this line came our Savior, Jesus.

Do you want to be a true winner who never quits? Run to the finish line with the One who knows your heart. He is your guarantee for the abundant life here and for all eternity.

Whatever you do, do your work heartily, as for the Lord rather than for men; knowing that from the Lord you will receive the reward of the inheritance. (Col. 3:23–24a)

May 2
The trouble with opportunity is that it usually comes disguised as hard work.

Our oldest son is a hard worker. He made the statement when he got out on his own that he wanted a job for which he would get compensated more for the amount of effort he put forth. With an outlook like that and a desire to work hard, we knew that he would always be able to make a good living. Many people today work harder at getting out of work than they would have to if they got a job and stuck with it. Recently, I was taken in by a scam artist who hacked into my computer. He literally talked me into buying a protection service for my computer that was totally unneeded. My son-in-law is my computer go-to person, but it was only after the fact that I could talk to him and get his input. He told me that I did not need the service and I certainly did not need to pay what I had for it, *giving the scammer all my information and credit card number*! Thankfully, my credit card company was able to stop the transaction. I felt so stupid and gullible. (Sometimes it doesn't pay to be so trusting.) I learned a hard lesson real fast.

Why wouldn't a person with so much knowledge and persuasive ability take that gift and use it for good rather than in a dishonest way? We will never know what makes evil triumph in some when good would be better. I think we know, but we don't want to believe anyone could be so controlled by the evil one.

God gave us all different talents and abilities, and He expects us to use these in constructive and productive ways. Not only can we gain monetary benefits from hard work, but we develop a sense of security and well-being from accomplishment. Whether brain or brawn, your hard work will be rewarding.

> **Here is what I have seen to be good and fitting: to eat, to drink and enjoy oneself in all one's labor in which he toils under the sun during the few years of his life which God has given him; for this is his reward. (Eccles. 5:18)**

May 3
Age may wrinkle the skin, but lack of enthusiasm wrinkles the soul.

I am a beauty consultant with Mary Kay Cosmetics and have been for a number of years. I started when my youngest child started going to school. I guess you could say that I know the importance of a good skin care program, and I know what the years and the elements can do to the skin. As sad as it may be for some to see their youth slipping away with the years, it is even sadder to observe the lack of excitement and enthusiasm for life that we sometimes see with the aging process. Our zeal for living should not be based on whether we have smooth or wrinkled skin or whether we are in the spring or the winter of our lives. God has provided for us abundant living at every level, in every stage, and in every season of life.

I don't know who said this saying, but I think it speaks volumes regarding the sadness of a wasted life: "When I came to die, I discovered I had not yet lived." Will you leave a legacy of hopelessness and despair? If we aren't living, aren't we already dead? Did not Jesus say that He came that we might have life and have it more abundantly (John 10:10)? Apart from a relationship with the living Savior, there is no life! Jesus is the Way, the Truth, and the Life (John 14:6). He said that we can go our own way and gain the whole world, but what does it profit us if, in doing this, we lose our souls (Matt. 16:26)? As Jesus taught his disciples, he is teaching us today when He said, "Do not be anxious for your life, as to what you shall eat: nor for your body, as to what you shall put on. For life is more than food, and the body than clothing." He went on to talk about the birds and the lilies and how He looks after them, and He says that we are much more valuable to God than they are (Luke 12:22–27). Don't stop buying your Mary Kay, but is living a godly life not more important than worrying about years and wrinkles?

**But seek for His kingdom, and these things
shall be added to you. (Luke 12:31)**

May 4
Happiness is doing work you like to do.

I love to bake, and it has turned into a profitable little home business. Some people, I am sure, would think, *What a drudgery*, and would shudder to think of spending their time in such a way. However, each thing I bake is a challenge and a created work of art to me. It is a service for those who do not like to do such things, and there is satisfaction in the supply and demand of it.

Perhaps you are trying to accomplish something that someone else is good at instead of fulfilling your own need for accomplishment. You wonder why you are not happy in your work, in your committee role, or even in the sport you are trying to play. One of our grandsons would have made a great left-handed pitcher, but he never went out for baseball. All of his friends were playing football, so that is where he wanted to be. But he was not built for football. He is tall and slim, had a great arm, and was born with all the ability to be a good baseball player. He spent lots of time on the sidelines at football games. We could have been wrong, but we will never know.

God gave to each of us different talents, gifts, skills, and abilities to build on. As large or small as it might seem to you, God can make it a source of great joy, fulfillment, and profit if you surrender all to Him and let Him direct you in the way that you should go. Moses thought his brother, Aaron, was more capable to lead Israel than him, but God made it known to Moses that He did not call Aaron but him. We must not shy away from our own talents, gifts, skills, and abilities because we might miss God's greatest blessings for our lives.

I went on to open a small country store with gifts, antiques, homemade candies, and cakes. What a blessing it was to me and, I hope, to my customers. Wesley, just out of college, is pursuing what he loves, computer technology. He is in the right field!

**Commit your works to the Lord and your plans
will be established. (Prov. 16:3)**

May 5
Wisdom is knowing what to do next, skill is knowing how to do it, and success is doing it.

Are you pointed in the right direction? Is your compass God-controlled? Are you self-oriented or Spirit-oriented? Have you consulted your manual, your handbook, your Bible? Do you have the victory of the cross?

To be wise is to follow your Creator's leading, moving in the direction He has for your life. As you place your footsteps in His, He equips you with the skill you need to do what He calls you to do. You become God's anointed, and through Him success is imminent. God knows what to do, He knows how to do it, and He will do it through you if you allow it.

God only has my hands to do His work,

He only has my feet to go,

My eyes are His to see the need,

My ears to hear those that hurt. (Author)

Joshua was old when he called all the elders, their heads, their judges, and their officers of Israel together to remind them of all that God had done for them. He instructed them not to turn to the right hand or to the left from the book of the law of Moses but to keep those laws and to cling to and love the Lord their God. He also reminded them that "not one word of all the good words which the Lord your God spoke concerning you has failed" (Joshua 23:14b). He also reminded them of what would happen if they transgressed the covenant of the Lord: God's anger would burn against them.

God is a jealous God. He is jealous for His people because He loves us. He calls us to be wise. In being wise, we make the right choices. We succeed when we do all things God's way.

But the wisdom from above is first pure, then peaceable, gentle, reasonable, full of mercy and good fruit, unwavering, without hypocrisy. (James 3:17)

May 6
All you send into the lives of others comes back into your own.

Giving is a part of life that we all need to lend more attention to. Giving of oneself is the best of all gifts. Ask a lonely child if he would rather spend time with a television set or with a parent or friend. As much as many children embrace television, computers, music players, and computer games, they would certainly prefer the fun, companionship, and time with a parent or a playmate. Ask an old person, a widow, a single parent, or anyone, for that matter, how much a visit, a card, or a telephone call means to them.

When we give others our time, attention, love, and devotion, we are giving them a lasting treasure with which nothing can compare. Have you ever stood at the edge of a pond or lake and tossed a pebble into the water? Imagine that the pebble is what you give. As you toss it in, it makes ripples on the water. The small waves go on and on, each one forming another. No matter where you are standing, those waves come back to you, as well as reaching distances all around the circle. The ripple effect goes on and on.

Jesus instructed us, "Give, and it will be given to you; good measure, pressed down, shaken together, running over, they will pour into your lap. For by your standard of measure it will be measured to you in return" (Luke 6:38). We will never do anything for someone else and not get the blessing for it.

Investing in the life of another human being takes us to another realm. The world is full of people who are desperate for love and attention—people who just want to know that someone cares about them enough to spend a little time with them. Go the distance today and toss a pebble or two. You will be the blessed one!

Blessed are the pure in heart, for they shall see God. (Matt. 5:8)

May 7
You are just as happy as you make up your mind to be.

The human race seeks happiness in many different ways. Our desire to be entertained has caused us to believe that we can press a button and be stimulated to happiness. Many seek happiness in worldly pleasures and alcohol or drugs. For others, travel and adventure is what they depend on. Happiness for many is found in family and friends. Material things and possessions serve as a substitute for happiness in a materialistic world.

A rich, young ruler wanted so much what Jesus had to offer but would not part with his worldly possessions in order to have it. His desire was to hold onto the world with one hand and God with the other, but Jesus wants us to sell out to Him. We cannot have two masters. We cannot love the things of this world and love God as we should. It causes a split personality. What causes us to be so earthly minded that we miss out on the heavenly benefits? Satan takes pleasure in distracting us and causing us to believe that we need to "eat, drink, and be merry for tomorrow we may die." He got one thing right! One day we will die, and this old life will be over. But eternity is forever and ever. We need to live with heaven on our minds. Surrendering all to Jesus in this life brings dual happiness—happiness now and happiness later. Jesus said, "I am the resurrection and the life: he who believes in Me shall live even if he dies, and everyone who lives and believes in Me shall never die. Do you believe this?" (John 11:25–26).

We all at times have looked to some of the temporal things for temporary gratification. Happiness is knowing Him in His fullness. The Christian's joy is not dependent upon circumstances, things, or stimulants but has its source in the Holy Spirit. Through Him we can know true happiness.

**The disciples were filled with joy, and with
the Holy Ghost. (Acts 13:52)**

May 8
He who dares for nothing need hope for nothing.

I suppose no one sets out in this thing called life knowing exactly where to go and how he or she will get there. However, there is one thing that most people soon realize: It is up to me as to what I do with my life. If you sit down, life will pass you by. If you lay down, life will run you over, but if you stand up and run a good race, you will come out a winner.

Somehow, we always go back to Paul in the Bible when we want a good example of one who ran the race of life well. So many times, Paul used the metaphor of running a race to describe life. Like many people, Paul did not have it all together. He certainly did not start out well. A devout Jew, Paul was a staunch advocate for Christian persecution. It took him a while, but he eventually found the Way. Once he became a Christ follower, his life took on a whole new dimension. His conversion put him on the other side of the spectrum, and he was the victim of much persecution himself.

The Christian life is not an easy, trouble-free life. God never promised that. He did, however, promise that He would always be with us and would never forsake us (Matt. 28:20, Heb.13:5). How can this be? Can God be with every one of His children all the time? Yes, He can! He is sovereign; He is omnipresent. He is everywhere at all times. Amazing, huh? That is the God that you, too, can know if you will call on Him with a repentant heart and trust Jesus as your Savior.

Even when is seems that wickedness and evil prevail all around us, our God will always sustain us.

Don't be satisfied with the world's way. Little becomes much when God is in it. Hope is found in Jesus Christ.

God rewrote the text of my life when I opened the book of my heart to his eyes. (2 Sam. 22:25)

May 9
Life's road is dotted with many tempting parking spaces.

As we travel down life's highway, it's tempting to pull over and park along the way. That's fine. Resting is good because it gives us time to think, learn, plan, and regroup. But don't ever stop and stay. Life offers to the human race an abundance of opportunity. When we pull in and park too long, we risk a stalled engine, a dead battery, fuel leaks, and flat tires. It takes a lot of motivation, effort, and repair to get going again if, in fact, in these old worldly bodies, we even want to move on.

In Noah's day, lots of people were in parking spaces. They were satisfied with life as usual. They looked around and saw "everybody else is doing it" and decided that was the way to go. Noah was the exception. He was listening to God and was obedient to do what God called him to do. "But Noah found favor in the eyes of the Lord" (Gen. 6:8). God honors obedience. Out of all the people in parking spaces, satisfied with the present life, Noah had found the reason to move forward, and his obedience to hear God and to move forward at His command saved him, his wife, his three sons, and their wives for all eternity. "Noah walked with God" (Gen. 6:9). He did not pull into a safe place to park and stay there. His goal was to please God and to trust Him, even if that meant building a huge boat on dry land with no signs of rain.

Have you been parking on a side street too long? Has your engine corroded? Do your tires need to be pumped up so that you can move on? Are you in someone else's parking space? Take a good look today. Think about what you need to do to get those spark plugs fired up again. Pull out of that parking place and move on along with Jesus onto His fantastic interstate. His road is narrow, but it is the right road. Abundant life and a glorious eternity are ahead when we trust Him.

"For I know the plans that I have for you," declares the Lord, "plans for welfare and not for calamity to give you a future and a hope." (Jer. 29:11)

May 10
The three C's of life: choices, chances, changes. You must make a choice to take a chance or your life will never change.

Choices belong to the ones making them. Both blessings and consequences come with individual choices. We are each responsible for our own choices, whether good or bad. I have heard it said, make good choices today so you don't have regrets tomorrow.

A career choice can be a lifelong decision. The career you choose can lead you down paths you never would have gone had you not chosen that career. Look at your choice of husband or wife. Have you ever thought about how different it would be had you married someone else? Maybe you have had to make a choice about moving or not moving. Had your choice been different, your job and friends would be different.

Sometimes it is necessary to take a chance, to step out into the unknown. However, chances and choices should always be made after first going to the One who can see the big picture and can lead us to make the right decision. Always we must seek God and ask Him to direct us. He knows us, loves us, and wants the best for us. I always find peace in knowing that I can go to Him and He will direct my path. "The mind of man plans his way, but the Lord directs his steps" (Prov. 16:9). Chances are not chances when the Lord is in charge. They might be unknown waters to us, but not to Him.

With choices and chances, we often find ourselves in the midst of change. God told Abraham at age seventy-five, "Go forth from your country, and from your relatives and from your father's house, to the land which I will show you" (Gen. 12:1). God promised to make a great nation from Abraham's seed, to bless him and make his name great. Abraham obeyed, but he would encounter many changes. He and his nephew, Lot, would go separate ways and he would step out of God's will and have a son by his maid, but God would bless him with a son, Isaac, by his wife Sarah when he was a hundred years old. "Is anything too difficult for the Lord?" (Gen. 18:14). Change is good when God is in it!

And your ears will hear a word behind you, "This is the way, walk in it," whenever you turn to the right or to the left. (Isa. 30:21)

May 11
When people are at their worst in cruel hatred, God is at His best in gracious love.

There is no other expression that will ever demonstrate His love for us more than the cross. It is hard for us as human beings to fathom that kind of love. It would be unbearable enough to think of sacrificing your own sinful son for a good or sinless people, but what love for us that God gave His perfect, sinless Son for a perverted and sinful world. "But God demonstrated His own love toward us in that while we were yet sinners, Christ died for us" (Rom. 5:8).

The cross expressed so much to a helpless world. We are enemies of God if we are not followers. Why would anyone resist such love? Jesus could have called ten thousand angels to take Him from that cross, but instead His love for us made Him willing to go through anything that we might know that kind of love.

I love my children so much, as I am sure you do. I have heard it said that a mother's love is next to God's love. That is a wonderful analogy, but I don't believe any of us can know the extent of our heavenly Father's love for His children. He knows how many days are appointed to each of us. He knows the number of hairs on our heads. Our God catches our tears in a bottle and keeps us in perfect peace when we trust in Him. I love my children, but I am not capable of any of those things.

Many are the hurts in this old world. Most are a result of our sinfulness. God showed us how to love through Jesus. Jesus's earthly ministry exemplified God's love. In John 15:12 He said, "Love one another as I have loved you." How did and how does He love us? Unconditionally and with an everlasting love. Can you love like that? Can I love like that? It's a challenge, but let's try!

In Him we have redemption through His blood, the forgiveness of our trespasses, according to the riches of His grace, which He lavished upon us. (Eph. 1:7)

May 12
The church is the adhesive that holds this world together.

"Behold I lay in Zion a choice stone, a precious cornerstone, and he who believes in Him shall not be disappointed" (1 Peter 2:6). The church's foundation is built on Jesus Christ. Jesus came into the world to redeem lost humankind and to establish His church. As people came to know and trust in Him, they began to worship together as a body of believers who followed the Way. Jesus said in John 14:6, "I am the way, and the truth, and the life; no one comes to the Father, but through Me." Before his conversion on the road to Damascus, Paul was a persecutor of the Way. Jesus blinded him so that he could see the true light. His name changed from Saul to Paul when he was saved and the Holy Spirit filled him (Acts 9). Paul was certainly not disappointed. He was baptized "and immediately he began to proclaim Jesus in the synagogues, saying, 'He is the Son of God'" (v. 20). Paul became the greatest of missionaries, establishing churches and pointing people everywhere to the Way.

Many forces come up against the church, forces from within as well as from without. However, Jesus says that the "gates of hell shall not prevail against it"(Matt. 16:18). The church is a body of baptized believers who have chosen to follow His way. Like Paul, they have responded to the call and been filled with the Holy Spirit. A born-again Christian is a new creation who repents and turns from his or her old, sinful way of life and follows God's way.

The world is searching everywhere for what can be found on every other street in America, the church. The love and fellowship, the security and fulfillment, the peace and joy, and the support of the saints should always be a drawing force to a world that is longing for each of these things. God's people are the church. We have a responsibility to reach out in love and draw them in so that when Christ returns one day for His bride, the church, they will be included.

**Grace be with all those who love our Lord Jesus
Christ with a love incorruptible. (Eph. 6:24)**

May 13
A rock is organized sand.

It seems that about every few months I am involved with a bunch of women to plan a tea or a shower for a bride. We always have a large group of ladies who want to help, and someone has to head it up so that we can get organized. A meeting is called, and each person is assigned some kind of refreshment to bring. A time is set to begin and end the affair, and we each have various responsibilities so that the party will come together without a hitch.

Organization is important in whatever you do. School teachers must have a lesson plan. Doctors must look over a patient's chart before they operate. Firefighters and emergency medical technicians know exactly what they must do to get to the call as soon as possible. Garbage workers and paper deliverers have planned routes. Organization is crucial for things to be accomplished as they should be.

Jesus was a great organizer. His first priority was prayer as He looked to His Father for guidance in everything. He knew that His purpose for coming to earth was to do the will of His Father, and He prepared for His ministry until He was thirty years old. He was baptized by John the Baptist, as God said He would be, and then He began to proclaim the gospel whereby people could be saved. He called and trained twelve men to minister with Him. The cross was His mission and His main purpose, and He accomplished His mission as He arose from the grave and ascended back to heaven. In just three short years, Jesus brought forgiveness for sin and salvation to lost humankind through His sacrifice as the perfect Lamb. With no more need for the blood of bulls and goats, His own blood became our redeeming sacrifice—hence, the new covenant.

As our Savior went back into heaven to sit at the right hand of the Father, He left the Holy Spirit for all who would ask Him into their heart. Have you organized your life to include this Jesus?

**The ants are not a strong folk, but they prepare
their food in the summer. (Prov. 30:25)**

May 14
Hate sin, but love the sinner.

In our world today we see many things being substituted for genuine love. The word is used so loosely that it is no wonder we cannot identify what true love is: "I love pizza!" "I love your dress!" "I love my cat so much!" and on and on it goes. Lust is substituted for love, and a selfish sexual relationship is mistaken for genuine love. Many marriages dissolve because they were founded on physical attraction rather than love, which goes beyond that.

In 1 John 4:8, we read that God is love. Not only that, but while we were yet sinners, He loved us and sent His Son to die for us so that we could have forgiveness for sin and everlasting life (John 3:16). If God is love, should we so desecrate His name by using a substitute for what love truly is?

We can look in 1 Corinthians 13 to find the excellence of love, the kind of love that God is calling us to:

Love is patient, love is kind, and is not jealous; love does not brag and is not arrogant, does not act unbecomingly; it does not seek its own, is not provoked, does not take into account a wrong suffered, does not rejoice in unrighteousness, but rejoices with the truth; bears all things, believes all things, hopes all things, endures all things. Love never fails.

God's love can overshadow the worldly substitutes for love. Many today, even Christians, are being deceived by what the world has perceived as love. "All have sinned and fall short of the glory of God, being justified as a gift by His grace through the redemption which is in Christ Jesus" (Rom. 3:23–24). We can be grateful that our God of love has taken upon Himself our sin and we can be forgiven by His grace.

Just as God hates sin because it separates us from Him, so we should as well. But just as He loved us enough to die for us, we too must love those who do not know Him so that they will know Him by our love.

Let love be without hypocrisy. Abhor what is evil; cling to what is good. Be devoted to one another in brotherly love. (Rom. 12:9–10)

May 15
Bitterness is like drinking poison and hoping the other person will die.

Bitterness eats at you from the inside out. It can absolutely cause you to become physically ill. To harbor bitterness, anger, and resentment in your heart only serves to cause despair, erode your health, and damage relationships with those around you.

I am reminded of Joseph, son of Jacob, in the book of Genesis. His brothers resented him terribly because he was a favorite of his father. Their bitterness toward Joseph drove them to drastic measures as they devised a plan to get rid of him. After throwing him in a pit they sold him to an Ishmaelite caravan. Joseph was spared his life only because one of his brothers, Judah, intervened for him. Joseph went on to do great things as he practiced purity and devotion to God. If Joseph had nursed bitterness and hatred toward his brothers for what they had done to him, his life would have come to a different end. Instead, years later when his brothers traveled to Egypt and appealed to Joseph, who was now in a position of power, for help, he said to them, "Don't be afraid, for am I in God's place? And as for you, you meant evil against me, but God meant it for good in order to bring about this present result, to preserve many people alive" (Gen. 50:19–20).

God takes bitter and makes it sweet. "God causes all things to work together for good to those who love God, to those who are called according to His purpose" (Rom. 8:28). Are you carrying around a bitter spirit today? Do you love God? Then ask Him to free you from the bitterness that is consuming your spirit and literally keeping you from having the blessings that He desires for His children. God gave Joseph the upper hand. He could have held back from giving his brothers the very food they needed to sustain them, but Joseph had long ago forgiven his brothers and God blessed him. Bitterness hurts you more than anyone else.

For if you forgive men for their transgressions, your heavenly Father will also forgive you. (Matt. 6:14)

May 16
Love is active and costly.

Paul was possibly in Ephesus when he wrote his first epistle to the Corinthians. The Corinthians' morals were at a low level. Being in an affluent commercial city, the people of Corinth failed miserably at living holy lives, loving one another, and knowing the gospel of Christ. They were worldly, wealthy, and prosperous and felt that they needed no one, especially God. As Paul helped the people there to learn about love, he helps us even today to learn what God expects of us. The chapter of 1 Corinthians 13 is often called the love chapter as it instructs us in what God-ordained love looks like.

Godly love can be explosive; it grows, develops, strengthens, and multiplies. It spreads as we learn to be genuine and sincere in our love relationships with others. Whether in our homes, churches, marriages, friendships, or our love for our Lord, true, genuine, sincere love is contagious. The more love we give away, the more it multiplies. It is like ripples on the water when a pebble is thrown in—it continues to form a circle of ripples and waves that go on and on.

With love comes responsibility. True love is sacrificial. We might have to give up something to meet the needs of another person. Love does not seek its own way, nor does it seek vengeance. Love promised and not demonstrated is hypocritical. Love must be sincere if it is to be effective. Only Christ in us can help us to love like that.

Paul's message is as relevant today as it was to the Corinthians. Paul's message is God's message given over and over again. As God handed down the commandment to "love the Lord your God with all your heart and with all your soul and with all your might" (Deut. 6:5), He showed His love for us when He sent His only Son to the cross for us. And as God continues to love and bless us with all spiritual blessings, we can know how important it is for us to love actively at any cost!

... but the greatest of these is love. (1 Cor. 13:13)

May 17
The mind of man plans his way, but the Lord directs his steps. –Prov. 16:9

Whatever you set out to do, it is important to plan your course of action. If you want to landscape your yard, it is important to at least have a mental plan if not a diagram on paper of how you want your beds laid out. This avoids moving and shifting plants later or living with a mistake. You would not think of building a house without first having plans drawn up, designing and displaying the floor plan that suits the needs of your family.

One thing I have enjoyed on my computer is Mapquest. I can type in where I am and where I want to go, and it will give me a map as well as directions that I can print out in just seconds. I can plan out my trip with ease before I ever leave home.

The biggest plans we make are for our lives and futures. The Bible tells us that our heavenly Father has a plan for each of our lives. Just as God spoke through the prophet Jeremiah to the people that Nebuchadnezzar exiled from Jerusalem to Babylon, God speaks to us and through us today. Through His infinite wisdom, He knows the hearts of all people. He knows the wickedness of people's hearts, and He knows the hearts that are truly His. Aren't we glad that He directs our paths if we trust him with them? Seek Him first today and see where He takes you. He loves you and desires only the best for your life and your future. God's message through Jeremiah is our message today. His plans promise us a future and a hope.

How do we know God's plan for our lives? The directions are found in His handbook that He left just for you, the Bible. There is not one thing that you will face in this life that He has not covered in His Word to us. Go there today. It is your "mapquest" for life. "Study to show yourselves approved unto God, a workman who needeth not to be ashamed, rightly dividing the word of truth" (2 Tim. 2:15).

For I know the plans that I have for you, declares the Lord, plans for welfare and not for calamity to give you a future and a hope. (Jer. 29:11)

May 18
Plan the work and work the plan.

As God continued to speak to the people in Jeremiah's day, He continues to strive with us today through this very book in the Bible. God laid out for them and for us what we need to do. He had just told them in the previous verse that He had a good plan for their lives to give them a future and a hope. Now He directs them in what they need to do in order to receive this blessing and His promises. "Then you will call upon Me and come and pray to Me, and I will listen to you. And you will seek Me and find Me, when you search for Me with all your heart" (Jer. 29:12–13).

God gives us specifics in His plan. He petitions us to do certain things, then He will do certain things. Isn't that the way a wise planner implements a plan? You can't move to the second phase of a plan until the first is accomplished. I get amazed at God's ways, and He wants to teach us those ways if we will call to Him through prayer and search for Him with all our hearts. It does no good to call upon God, to pray and seek Him, if we are not going to follow His directions when He gives them to us as He says He will.

Jeremiah was a prophet appointed to the nations by God to warn them of God's judgment if they did not turn back to Him. They would not listen. America, too, stands in danger of God's judgment. As a nation founded on the principles of an all-sufficient God, we have fallen far from Him. America and the world have had the benefit of many wonderful, God-fearing, Bible-teaching evangelists and preachers only to turn from God's ways to doing what is right in our own eyes as the Israelites did. How sad it is to watch a nation like America, so blessed with all the good things of the Creator—life; liberty; the pursuit of happiness; freedom of worship, speech, and government—turn its back on God and follow its own way. If we do not learn from the past, we have to suffer the consequences. God is calling us back!

**Blessed is the man who trusts in the Lord and
whose trust is the Lord. (Jer. 17:7)**

May 19
Trials can make us bitter or better.

God comforts us in our affliction so that we can comfort others. Trials often come as a result of circumstances or disobedience. God sometimes allows trials and tribulations in order to strengthen and grow us spiritually. Trials are hard. If you have had none, get ready! They will come. Through it all we are never without access to the Father. He is there for us, and when we call on Him, He hears us and works all things out for our good, if we are His children (Rom. 8:28).

You might say, *Why do people who are trying to follow Christ and trying to walk in His ways have to suffer?* Why not? Christ, the only perfect person who ever lived, suffered persecution, hate, temptation, rejection, verbal abuse, blasphemy, and pain. Hebrews 5:8 tells us that Jesus learned obedience from the things He suffered.

Do you desire to be more like Jesus? Do you desire obedience? Do you desire spiritual maturity? Trials grow us. Adversity can teach us things we never would learn any other way. Hardships can cause us to call out to the only One who can help us. Trials challenge our deepest needs and cause us to face adversity head on. Don't pass through a trial without asking God to show you what He is trying to teach you through it. Don't miss it or you might have to go around again. If we don't listen to that still, small voice any other way, it might take a trial to stop us in our tracks. Spiritual maturity is important if we want to follow Jesus. His footprints lead us to heaven. We are smart to walk in them.

I am reminded of Joni Eareckson Tada and her beautiful life. After a diving accident, she was left paralyzed from the neck down. As she trusted God with her infirmities and what was left of her shattered body, He has blessed her with a wonderful ministry. She has impacted many lives and inspired all of us through her courage and beautiful testimony.

Adversity and trials will either harden us or soften us. God always remains faithful. How we respond to the difficulties in life is up to us. People in whose lives God has proved faithful can comfort others.

Consider it all joy, my brethren, when you encounter various trials, knowing that the testing of your faith produces endurance. (James 1:2)

May 20
The Christian life is not the hundred-yard dash; it's cross-country.

When the Olympic Games came to Atlanta, we were all excited and challenged. Many athletes participated in the games after training long and hard hours to develop their athletic skills. They trained not only physically but mentally and emotionally. They made every effort to learn the rules and to abide by them in order that they might qualify. Their anticipation of winning the highest award, the coveted gold medal, is always the goal of those who compete in the Olympics.

God wants us to walk in victory. We are defeated only by our own choosing. Jesus said, "I have come that you might have life and have it more abundantly." The provision was made for us when, at the cross, Christ said, "It is finished." With those three little words, He sealed the victory. He tore open the curtain of separation between humans and God whereby we can now have direct access to the one and only God who can offer a victorious life to His children. God made a great sacrifice for humankind. He came to earth as Jesus to give us victory over sin and death. If you are His child and have chosen Him over the world and Satan, then you have received the highest award you will ever need.

Are you offering to your children the victorious life? Are you teaching and training your children in the ways of God? Are you as a family going to church, reading the Bible, and praying together? Do they know that you love God with all your heart and your neighbor as yourself? Do your children see you putting God first, before worldly pleasures and material things? Children are little athletes who need to be taught discipline in how to win the prize of the higher calling of Christ Jesus. We are all born with an old sin nature that takes us in the wrong direction if it is not channeled in the right direction. Just as Olympians need direction in their training from their coaches, so our children need it from us. Run the race with them. They need your influence!

... let us also lay aside every encumbrance, and the sin which so easily entangles us, and let us run with endurance the race that is set before us, fixing our eyes on Jesus. (Heb. 12:1b–2a)

May 21
No one can make a fool of you without your permission. –Eleanor Roosevelt

Human beings can obviously do some very foolish things. We move through life trying to be so cautious, yet in our most guarded moments we still falter and fail. Many people are quick to pick up on the weak moments of others. They jump onto embarrassing moments to amplify them and call attention to what might be overlooked or unnoticed if not exposed so openly by the insensitivity of others.

Jesus was put in this position many times as He walked this earth. I am reminded of the time His authority was questioned in Luke 20:1–8. The chief priest and scribes approached Him to confront Him about His credentials to preach, heal, and so on and who gave Him the authority. They were seeking to put Jesus on the spot and discredit Him. Jesus, in His wisdom, rerouted the question, and it fell right back into their laps as He said to them, "I shall also ask you a question, and you tell Me: was the baptism of John from heaven or from men?" They knew that any way they answered it, they would be trapped by their own teachings. They took the low road, saying that they did not know where it came from. "And Jesus said to them, 'Neither will I tell you by what authority I do these things.'"

I marvel at how Jesus always had the right answers. And He still does today. Many foolish people turn their backs on the truths of God's Word to us. Many choose to believe anything but what God says. Scientists, philosophers, naysayers, and skeptics all cling to their own worldly views rather than trusting their Creator God, who knows all.

We must never trust in the foolishness of this world and humans' ways over God's ways. "Words from the mouth of a wise man are gracious, while the lips of a fool consume him" (Eccles. 10:12).

**Let no man deceive himself. If any man among you
thinks that he is wise in this age, let him become
foolish that he may become wise. (1 Cor. 3:18)**

May 22
Life is short. Walk uprightly.

As far as age goes, many people in the Old Testament lived extremely long lives. Adam lived 930 years. He had sons, who are named in Genesis 5, and they lived long lives, as well. Methuselah goes on record as the oldest man to ever have lived, as he reached the age of 969 years. Noah was 950 years old when he died. It is hard for us to imagine such longevity. Even today there are those who live to be 100 years or older, and yet many die as babies or children.

Life at its very best is so short and fleeting. The older we get, the more we realize the swiftness of a lifetime. My grandmother lived for ninety-nine years and we still didn't have her long enough. Life, however, is not measured in years, if you think about it.

Some people live more in one day than others do in a lifetime. We are to love life, to walk uprightly, and to seek our Maker for the abundant life. He has promised us that if we seek Him first in this life, all the other things that He has promised us will be ours, "added unto you" (Matt. 6:33). Knowing Him makes for a richer, fuller, and more meaningful life. He promises us this, and who would know better than He? God has always been, even before the beginning of the world and the creation of it. God, Jesus, and the Holy Spirit have always been. God came to earth to redeem humankind through Jesus, and He lived on earth only thirty-three years, yet the impact of His life was profound.

Christians are called to walk tall, uprightly, and to be bold in our witness. We are to be on a mission as we travel through this time that God has allotted us. We are to abound in all the pleasures of the abundant life in Jesus Christ, but our primary purpose is to be about the Great Commission of telling others how they can be saved (Matt. 28:19–20). Share *real* life today!

**I know that there is nothing better for them than to rejoice
and to do good in one's lifetime. (Eccles. 3:12)**

May 23
Our inadequacies are irrelevant if the Lord chooses to add His blessing. –James Dobson

We are nothing in ourselves, but in Him we are all things. We are made in God's image, so we are like Him. However, we are unlike Him in that we have a sinful nature, while He is a perfect, sinless, holy God. But God knows our inadequacies and loves us anyway. He tells us to call on Him and He will show us great and mighty things.

David was a shepherd boy, but God saw him as a king. Paul was a tent maker, but God saw him as the greatest of missionaries. Moses was open with his confessions of inadequacy, begging God to use his brother instead, but God saw him as the one to lead His chosen people out of Egyptian bondage. Christian people are just ordinary people doing extraordinary things through the power of Jesus Christ. He enables us and equips us as long as we are willing to be faithful to doing His will. With God's blessings added to our willingness, we are a dream team. God always gives His best to those who leave the choices with Him.

Where are you today when it comes to giving it all to God? Are you willing to place it all in the Master's hands? Do you feel inadequate today, not knowing why you were even called to be His child? Does life seem to be slipping on by and you can't see one thing that you have accomplished for the kingdom? Get in line! I know the feeling! I ask God often to show me my usefulness in His kingdom, and I always seem to get a little God wink in my spirit that says, *Little becomes much when you place it in My hands.* Then He blesses me with a heart to touch or a mission project. Maybe it's a card or a phone call to someone whom He has laid on my heart. It seems little to us, but to Him, we are His hands and feet. We are His love, His comfort, His tenderness, and His voice. We are so many things that say "Jesus loves you" to someone.

For I was hungry, and you gave Me something to eat; I was thirsty, and you gave Me drink; I was a stranger, and you invited Me in; naked and you clothed Me; I was in prison, and you came to Me. (Matt. 25:35–36)

May 24
Money and things do not satisfy. They only create more hunger.

One can never acquire enough things to satisfy his or her cravings. There is always a hunger for more. It seems to be in our nature to seek after the things of this world, knowing all along that material things, in themselves, cannot satisfy. More than once, I have seen the realization of this in my own life. Recently, I had a yard sale to thin out my closets and get rid of things that I had not worn or used in quite some time. I am a pack rat of sorts, and things seem to accumulate over the years. I needed some space. Guess what! It was no time before I was shopping again, replacing the old (but not worn out) with the new (much like the discarded) and filling up the same space. Aren't we strange creatures? Always wanting more and better. There is a certain euphoria about buying and accumulating money and things.

Solomon was amazingly wealthy. He was David's son by Bathsheba and was chosen by God to build the temple. He asked God for wisdom, and God blessed Solomon with great wisdom. "And all the earth was seeking the presence of Solomon, to hear his wisdom which God had put in his heart" (1 Kings 10:24). Sadly, Solomon grew to love luxury and fell into idolatry and polygamy. "And Solomon did what was evil in the sight of the Lord, and did not follow the Lord fully, as David his father had done" (1 Kings 11:6). It is believed that Solomon wrote the book of Ecclesiastes, in which he pours out his heart in confession that all his pleasures and possessions were futile in light of knowing God and fearing Him. He realized that God has also set eternity in the heart of humankind (Eccles.3:11). We should not desire the things of this world; they do not satisfy. He tried it and "all was vanity and striving after wind and there was no profit under the sun" (Eccles. 2:11).

One thing that I have learned to do that helps me with any material cravings is to fast. Yes, we can fast from materialistic spending as well as fasting from food. God honors our efforts to set aside any obstacle that hinders our walk and witness.

**He who loves money will not be satisfied with money,
nor he who loves abundance. (Eccles. 5:10)**

May 25
Know God early before foolishness and folly come. –Author

Have you ever observed the innocence of a small child—the trust, the confidence, the security of his or her world? Ask a small child to jump to you from a kitchen cabinet or the side of the swimming pool into deep water, and he or she will likely eagerly jump into your arms.

Such trust is what our heavenly Father expects from us. His desire is for us to fall into His outstretched arms and know the security of His strength and the warmth of His love for us. We can't know these things until we first trust Him enough to let go of where we are standing and plunge from our own lofty perch. It is by faith that we must let go and by faith that we must trust the One who will never disappoint.

It seems that age and maturity cause us to lose a bit of that innocence and make us doubt the ones in our lives who are trying to direct our paths. As children grow, we see their nature go from innocence to independence. They choose to trust in their own judgment, choose their own way, and have less confidence in the ones who truly love them. Humankind's hearts are inclined that way. The old sin nature that we are born with, the one that came down to us from Adam, has a way of making us doubt the innocence of a pure heart and move away to make our own selfish choices. Like Adam, we stop trusting the Creator and His Word to us, often believing a lie instead. If we are not careful, we will follow the way that seems right to man, by the world's standards, but in the end there is destruction (see Prov. 14:12). We see this turning most in the teenage years or early adulthood after a person leaves home. Unless curtailed, it becomes a way of life.

God calls on us to trust Him and to follow His Way. It is the way that leads to the abundant life. He is sovereign and knows our every weakness. He is patient and waits for our whole heart. We must come with trust in Him like the little child, willing to step out without fear and hold fast to the One whose arms are outstretched to us.

**Remember also your Creator in the days of your youth,
before the evil days come and the years draw near when you
will say, "I have no delight in them." (Eccles. 12:1)**

May 26
Wisdom is better than strength. —Eccles. 9:16

How do we acquire wisdom? The world offers a counterfeit wisdom through books and knowledge. We can know what is in every book in the library and still not be wise. Intelligence is not wisdom. We can learn about all things and know nothing about spiritual things. True wisdom comes from God because wisdom is knowing truth and God is truth. He says in John 14:6, "I am the way, and the truth and the life." Knowing God empowers us with a heart to hear God, enables us to make wise choices, and provides us with a tutor, the Holy Spirit, who teaches and disciples us to know God and the ways of God.

Proverbs 9:10 tells us, "The fear of the Lord is the beginning of wisdom, and the knowledge of the Holy One is understanding." Does this mean that we are to be afraid of God and be fearful of His presence? To a certain degree, yes. But don't we always fear someone whom we love and respect? It is not a frightening thing but an awe of that person and a desire to please him or her. Fear for Holy God is a reverential awe. It is honor, respect, and adoration for who we know He is.

As Solomon, the son of David, gave instructions to his son, he advised him to listen to him and to his mother so that he would be open to the things of God. God gives us an enormous blessing if we have godly parents. I was so blessed, and I never fail to thank God for that wonderful gift. We are also called to be parents and mentors and lead those in our charge to know God and walk with Him. My parents have gone on to be with the Lord, but I still reap the benefits of their godly wisdom and instruction.

A wise man or woman chooses God. A foolish man or woman rejects God. They may have knowledge of all things yet lack true wisdom because they reject the One who truly knows all things. "For the Lord gives wisdom; From His mouth come knowledge and understanding" (Ps. 2:6).

If any of you lack wisdom, let him ask of God …
and it shall be given him. (James 1:5)

May 27
A joyful heart makes a cheerful face. —Prov. 15:13

What countenance are you carrying around with you every day? What do others see as they walk past you on the street or drive past you in your car? What does your family see? Is it a happy face or a frozen frown?

Our faces project our innermost feelings. What we feel inside is reflected through our faces, and we can give off either radiance or gloom. I have cross-stitched several pieces for friends as well as for our home of the little saying that encourages me every time I see it: "If you see someone without a smile, give them one of yours." Did you know that something as simple as a smile can make a person's day? Try it sometime. Walk through the mall and smile at an approaching shopper. You will see him or her light up. You will also feel a sense of encouragement and brightness yourself. It seems to give you a connection with your fellow man. When we smile, our eyes sparkle, and the eyes are the window of the soul.

Oh, that we could remember to do this each time we walk down the street; through a crowd; or into the office, a dining hall, or a ballgame. Christians are to shine out like beacons. As Jesus instructed his disciples in Matthew 5, He instructs us:

You are the light of the world. A city set on a hill cannot be hidden. Nor do men light a lamp, and put it under the peck-measure, but on the lamp-stand; and it gives light to all who are in the house. Let your light shine before men in such a way that they will see your good works and glorify your Father who is in heaven. (vv.14–16)

Even the psalmist cried out to God, "Lift up the light of Thy countenance upon us, O Lord!" (4:6). A joyful heart and a cheerful face should be our banner to the world.

I will be glad and exult in Thee. (Ps. 9:2)

May 28
If you wish to reach the highest, begin at the lowest.

The best way to accomplish anything is to take it one step at a time. Mary Kay Ash, of cosmetic fame, always said, "Inch by inch it's a cinch; yard by yard it's hard." There are those who are able to start at the top, bypassing the hard part, but they miss some valuable lessons and training that would be to their advantage had they started low and worked up.

Step-by-step progress is very important no matter where we are in life. Young children never start out running. They first crawl and then balance by supporting themselves to stand. They then progress one step at a time, unsure at first, but eventually gaining confidence to rapidly move across the floor. Athletes train, learn basic skills, then move forward at their own pace to gain confidence and momentum to accomplish their goals. Businesses and corporations train their people first, then encourage them to move up the corporate ladder through hard work and determination. A ladder would not be a ladder if it only had top rungs. Each step takes us to a new level of learning and accomplishment, experience and maturity.

God has the ultimate plan for starting low and finishing high. People who choose to follow Jesus must be born again (John 3). We start over, in a sense, to a new life that is in Christ by dying to ourselves and giving our lives over to the One who can make all things new. In our relationship with Christ, we start out as babes, feeding on the milk of the Word, the basics of His teaching. The more we study His Word and walk in His ways, the stronger we become in our Christian walk. We are then ready for the meat of the Word, deeper truths that grow us to be more mature Christians. When Jesus ascended back to heaven, He said that He was leaving to those who would accept Him, the Holy Spirit, as our teacher, comforter, and helper. He indwells us to empower and convict us in order that we might walk steadfastly in this world.

**Set your mind on the things above, not on the
things that are on earth. (Col. 3:2)**

May 29
Houses are made of wood and stone, but homes are made from love alone.

My daughter and I recently went to the beautiful Biltmore Estate for a day. Unfortunately, we had allowed only a day when what we really needed was a week to explore this tremendous and magnificent estate of the Vanderbilt family in Asheville, North Carolina. The French Renaissance chateau has two hundred and fifty rooms surrounded by eight thousand acres of forest, farmland, and pleasure gardens. George Vanderbilt opened the doors of the Biltmore House to family and friends for the first time on Christmas Eve 1895. The house features many luxuries that were unheard of in the 1800s, like central heat, mechanical refrigeration, electric lights and appliances, and indoor plumbing. Priceless works of art and furnishings are displayed throughout the massive rooms. It was hard to take it all in but a beautiful sight to behold. We were so glad that we made the trip.

When I think about Jesus's words to his disciples as He prepared to leave this world, I get homesick. The Biltmore mansion does not compare to the mansions our Father has planned for those who love Him. "In my Father's house are many mansions; if it were not so I would have told you. I go to prepare a place for you" (John 14:2 KJV). In 1 Corinthians 2:9 we see, "But just and it is written, 'Things which eye has not seen and ear has not heard, and which have not entered the heart of a man, all that God has prepared for those who love him.'" Revelation 21 describes the Holy City, the new Jerusalem that is "made ready as a bride adorned for her husband" (v. 2). In these verses, God gives to John a glimpse of the city. "Her brilliance was like a very costly stone, as a stone of crystal-clear jasper" (Rev. 21:11). He goes on to describe its beauty, with gold and precious stones. There will be no need for sun or moon there for God's glory will be there. Read it in its entirety to see all that is prepared for those who love Him. Now that is love!

**Unless the Lord builds the house, they labor
in vain who build it. (Ps. 127:1a)**

May 30
Sin is missing the mark of God's moral standard.

When we think about sin, we immediately think of Adam and Eve and that first act of sin and disobedience in the Garden of Eden. God had made everything so beautiful and had placed the first man and woman right in the center of a wonderful paradise. Everything was theirs to enjoy. All creation, perfect and without blemish, was before them and in submission to them. It was a perfect world. We see in Genesis 2:16–17 that God spoke to the man and instructed him that he was free to eat from any tree in the garden except one, the tree of the knowledge of good and evil. He even told him that if he ate from it, he would surely die. God then created a woman for Adam so that he would not be alone but have a helpmate. You know the story. We see it acted out every day now. Satan came to Eve and convinced her to doubt God and to listen to him. She ate the forbidden fruit and then gave it to her husband, and he ate (3:6). Satan tempted them, they succumbed, and sin entered the world.

Why did Adam and Eve sin? Why do we sin? God takes disobedience very seriously. Disobedience is sin, and sin brings about separation from God. When we listen to Satan or anyone else rather than God, we risk deadly consequences. God loves us and wants the best for us. Why do we doubt that? Adam and Eve hid from God after they sinned. We, too, hide and want no part of God, His church, or His people when we are involved in sin. Sin separates us from the sweet fellowship of a loving God.

God created a perfect universe that was free of death, disease, pain, suffering, and sin. Humans chose disobedience over righteousness. "For the mind set on the flesh is death, but the mind set on the Spirit is life and peace" (Rom. 8:6). To be right with God brings abundant life!

Jesus said, "Keep watching and praying, that you may not come into temptation; the spirit is willing, but the flesh is weak." (Mark 14:38)

May 31
The more you work, the more you want to accomplish. The less you work, the lazier you get. –Author

Work is a blessing and a responsibility that all Christians should take seriously. A good work ethic is important and reflects the character and attitude of a dependable person.

Jesus grew up working with his earthly father as a carpenter. You can be sure that Jesus was a very good carpenter, a skilled worker, and diligent in whatever He undertook. Mark 6 tells us that later, when Jesus began ministry and was teaching, healing, and performing miracles in Nazareth, the people recognized him as "the carpenter" and questioned His wisdom and ability to do all the miraculous things He was doing. They saw Him as a skilled worker, not a scholar. Like any good father, Joseph saw to it that Jesus was trained in a skill that would occupy his young mind until time for His earthly ministry to begin.

Jesus's good work ethic served Him well as He set out at age thirty to do His heavenly Father's business. Even at twelve years of age, He told His parents that He was about His Father's business when they found Him after three days in the temple in Jerusalem "in the midst of the teachers, both listening to them, and asking them questions" (Luke 2:46). The scriptures say that "they were amazed at His understanding and His answers" (v. 47). We don't know much about Jesus's life from this time until He was thirty years old. Perhaps, as He worked in His father's carpentry shop making furniture for those in His village, He would spend His spare time in the synagogue, studying the scriptures and learning from the priest and elders. It is unsure. But we do know that Jesus is amazing and different from the average person. He was fully God and fully man. He is our example, and we can look to Him concerning all standards for living, including work.

Whatever you undertake, do it as unto the Lord and to the best of your ability. Always give 100 percent to your chore or job and be faithful, prompt, and dependable.

Poor is he who works with a negligent hand, but the hand of the diligent makes rich. (Prov. 10:4)

June

The Lord's lovingkindnesses indeed never cease, for His compassions never fail. *They* are new every morning; great is Thy faithfulness. "The Lord is my portion," says my soul, "therefore I have hope in Him." The Lord is good to those who wait for Him, to the person who seeks Him. (Lam. 3:22–25)

June 1
Believe that you can even when your heart says you can't. —Author

Faith That Works: Part 1

In Christ all things are possible. How do we put our faith to work? Paul challenged Christians in Rome to become a "living sacrifice" and to strive for excellence in their faith. We know that it is impossible to please God without faith. So how do we know that we have faith? And if we do, how do we put it to work?

Faith is trusting God even when you can't see where He is taking you. "Faith is the assurance of things hoped for, the conviction of things not seen" (Heb. 11:1). Faith is believing that God will do what He said He would do. Faith is Abraham as God told him to sacrifice his son, Isaac. Faith is Noah as God commissioned him to build an ark. Faith is David as he faced the giant Goliath with only a slingshot and a few stones. Faith is Mary as she believed God when He told her that she would be the mother of the Messiah, Jesus, and how they each responded, showed that they believed God, and were obedient to do what He asked. God gives His best to those who trust Him to do what He says He will do. We must never underestimate the power of a living Lord, a mighty God, a faithful Savior. As we trust all that we are to Him and "believe that He is, and that He is a rewarder of those who seek Him" (Heb. 11:6), He will honor our faith and bless us for it. God spared Isaac, God spared Noah and his family, God protected David as he defeated the giant, and God rewarded Mary as she was favored by God to be the mother of the Son of the Most High and became blessed among women.

Has God asked you to do something in your life that required faith? Have you believed God and trusted Him with the outcome? I don't know that I would ever be listed among the saints in the Hall of Fame of the Faithful, but my desire is to please Him and to diligently seek Him.

Together today let us ask God to bless our "mustard seed" faith, and I know that He will.

God is greater than our heart, and knows all things. (1 John 3:20b)

June 2
Know Him. Listen. Step out.

Faith That Works: Part 2

We know that we have faith when we see ourselves trusting God. As we trust Him more, He imparts to us more faith; that is, our faith grows and we in turn trust Him more, and on and on. Ann Graham Lotz once said, "I'd rather step out and risk failing than not listen to God and stay in my comfort zone."

God doesn't just say, "Okay, you have faith and you have faith and you have faith." No. He allows us to grow our own faith through trusting Him and believing that He will do what He promises in His Word He will do. It is only when we step out and trust Him when circumstances look impossible that He can show us and grow us in faith. Do you see the teaching method? He teaches us, but it is up to us to teach ourselves. We are both the teacher and the pupil because it has to be by our own will. We determine our own faith growth. What a wise God we serve!

Moses was called by God to lead the Israelite people out of the Egyptian bondage that they were suffering under and into the promised land. This was not an easy task. The Israelites were many and were made to carry the workload in Egypt. The Egyptians did not want to lose their labor force, so it would be a hard task to convince them to let the people go. The sons of Israel had lived in Egypt for 430 years. God used Moses and many plagues to convince Pharaoh to let them go. The exodus of the thousands finally came. As they approached the Red Sea, Moses stretched out his hand over the sea, and God caused a strong wind to make a way through the sea for all the Israelites to walk across on dry land. God then told Moses, "Stretch out your hand over the sea so that the waves may come back over the Egyptians; over their chariots and their horsemen" (Exo. 14:26). What if Moses had refused to step out and do what God called Him to do? God did it all but used Moses. Moses knew God—he listened and he stepped out!

**Faith comes by hearing and hearing by the
word of God. (Rom. 10:17 KJV)**

June 3
The difference between servitude and servanthood is the difference between have to and get to. –Jane Fryar, Thank You for Serving with a Heart like Jesus

We are living in a society that is not geared toward serving others more than the self. God has made it so clear to us that we are to love Him with all our heart and love our neighbor as we love ourselves (Lev. 19:18). Those we love we want to serve. Do you love your neighbors? Do you know your neighbors? How can we love someone that we do not even know? Our neighbors are not necessarily the people who live next door. I believe God expects us to love our fellow humans as we would someone who is dear to us. He even says to love them as we love ourselves. *Wow*! We are good at looking after number one, aren't we?

I am reminded in this of the story of Moses and how his precious mother bravely made a wicker basket and covered it with tar and pitch so that it would float in the Nile River. She then placed Moses in it in order to save her son from the Egyptian king, who was having all the Hebrew baby boys killed. When Pharaoh's daughter went to the Nile to bathe, she found the baby Moses. Moses's sister had been watching the small basket from a distance and immediately went to Pharaoh's daughter to offer to find a Hebrew woman to nurse the baby. Who do you think she brought to her? Moses's own mother. We see a clear picture here of servanthood, "get to." Moses's mother would become a servant to the princess in order to get to care for her own son. She was not forced to do it, nor was she required to do it; she did it out of love. God calls on us to love like that, even as a parent for a child, as a wife with a servant's heart to serve her husband, or a friend who "loveth at all times" (Prov. 7:7). Selflessness leads us to give of ourselves because we have a heart to. Servitude is forced service. One who is forced to be a slave or a servant as punishment resents it.

Where is your heart today? Is servanthood on your radar?

But now we have been released from the Law, having died to that by which we were bound, so that we serve in newness of the Spirit and not in oldness of the letter. (Rom. 7:6)

June 4
Sometimes we can't see the forest for the trees.

God expects Christian people to have vision. What is vision? When we open our eyes, we are able to see. When we close our eyes, all is darkness and we are unable to see even our own hands before our eyes. This is your physical vision.

Spiritual vision is the ability to see ahead. God's vision for us as His people is that we see things that others don't see. As we step out in faith, trusting Him for each step that we take, He opens our eyes to new frontiers for ministry, witnessing, sharing, and caring. He empowers us to hold on, to stand firm, and to keep the faith. Vision helps us to rid our perspective of apathy and keep our sights on progress. He inspires us to move ahead, to have hope in all things, and to pursue the seemingly impossible task.

When we receive spiritual vision that comes to us as we trust in the One who knows all things past, present, and future, we receive the guidance and direction we need to follow Him in blind faith. We hear His warning and heed the impending judgment that comes as a result of disobedience. He lights our way, showing us the potholes and cliffs of sin to avoid.

When a nation's leaders lack spiritual vision, all under them suffer. A nation groans in hopeless pursuit as its people sense and feel the pain of hopelessness and despair. Many do not know or recognize what is missing, nor do they understand the ramifications of sinful behavior and willful disobedience to God's laws. It is often obvious to Christians who are grounded in truth and those with any knowledge of the Bible at all, but to those who cannot see, whose vision is cloudy, who experience total spiritual blindness, or who can't see the forest for the trees, it is life as usual.

Let us be wise to keep our focus on our heavenly Father. He opens our spiritual eyes and illuminates our path. He keeps us moving with vision and purpose in the right direction.

Where there is no vision the people perish. (Prov. 29:18)

June 5
It is only when men begin to worship that they begin to grow. –Calvin Coolidge

God's faithfulness is beyond our widest and broadest sense of comprehension. When we are faithless, He is faithful. When we are weak, His strength is made perfect. When we cease to listen, He continues to speak.

When my mother called me one night to tell me that my youngest brother would have to have surgery, I was shocked. The doctor had told him that he had a tumor and that there was a fifty-fifty chance that it was malignant. He was a picture of health—this could not be! This kind of news makes you numb. You can't feel a thing for a while, and your mind goes into a spin. Before hanging up the phone, Mother and I agreed that there was nothing that we could do but that we knew someone who could do something; we would join our hearts in prayer and watch God work. Peace came and so did God's healing. He underwent surgery, but there was no malignancy. God is in control, and He is faithful. Even if the outcome had been different, we knew we could trust God with this battle.

Worship comes to each of us when we choose to trust God with our circumstances. Worship is to give honor and respect to the faithful One. He sees the big picture and blesses His children by "causing all things to work together for good" when we place them in His hands. The wonderful Christian singer Babbie Mason wrote and sings a song that expresses it well. She sings it this way: "When you can't see His hand, trust His heart."

Will you worship today? God desires our worship in good times and hard times. We know not when the battles will come, but they will come. Our reverence of Holy God is an act of love and obedience, trust and praise to the One who loves us and wants to bless us. "Worship the Lord with reverence" (Ps. 2:11), and grow in grace and truth.

**My grace is sufficient for you, for power is
perfected in weakness. (2 Cor. 12:9)**

June 6
The blood of the cross makes me safe. The Word of God makes me sure. —Jess Hendley

Jesus's atonement for our sins at the cross paved a road of security for the believer. When we trust Him as Lord and Savior, accepting His act of love as our own, then we can rest in Him and know that we are in right standing with Almighty God. The cross pardoned a sinful world and saved it from the penalty of incarceration. We no longer have to be bound up by our sin. In Christ Jesus, His grace has made us free indeed! When He puts that confidence in our hearts, we don't want to do the things that displease or hurt Him. Our joy comes through serving Him and sharing the good news with those who have not heard.

A few years ago, I had the privilege of joining with two others ladies to minister to a young lady whom we had seen grow up in our church. She had made some bad choices concerning drugs and had strayed away from the Lord. She spent time in jail, lost custody of her child, and let her marriage fall into shambles, and things did not look so good for her. My friends and I approached her about getting together for a time of Bible study and encouragement to seek to bring her back to her walk with the Lord and to help her see the dead-end street that she was headed down. She was open to it, but it was hit and miss on the commitment. That was fine! We were grateful to see her whenever she could meet with us. Amazingly, over time we saw a complete turnaround as she realized her sinful state, gave it to the Lord, and chose to walk His path. Her marriage failed, but she got her child back and is holding down a responsible job.

Jesus rejoices when one sinner is brought to repentance. His word is so powerful, and we should never fail to use it to convict those who are struggling with sin. God's Word is clear and sure!

But before faith came, we were kept in custody under the law, being shut up to the faith which was later to be revealed. (Gal. 3:23)

June 7
A righteous relationship with Jesus will heal any situation.

God guides His servants through tragedy and suffering. He never promised us that just because we are His we would be exempt from the hard things. Even God's own Son suffered, and from that suffering He learned obedience (Heb. 5:8).

Suffering is not an easy road. It hurts, and we feel desperate and all alone. We cry out to God and can't feel Him there. We pray and don't see anything happening. *Why can't I feel spiritual?* we may think. *Where is my trust and confidence?* But we continue to persevere. We move ahead blindly. Then, faith takes over. "Faith is the assurance of things hoped for, the conviction of things not seen" (Heb. 11:1). God knows our hurts and disappointments. He never leaves us comfortless. His peace comes, and we look back and see that He was there all the time.

God expects those who love Him to leave the choices and decisions to Him. We are just to "believe that He is, and that He is a rewarder of those who seek Him" (Heb. 11:6). Our response to Him should always be faithfulness and believing that He can, even when we see hopelessness and feel helpless. We should believe that He will even when there is no evidence and believe that He is there even when we feel abandoned. He honors this. The psalmist put it this way. "It is good for me that I have been afflicted; that I might learn thy statutes" (Ps. 119:71)

When we trust God blindly, that is faith. When we move ahead in our darkest hours and see nothing ahead to encourage us, that is faith.

When pain is unbearable and there is suffering on every side and yet we persevere, that is faith. In all adversity, God can teach us if we are willing to pay attention. Many times I have said, "God, don't let me miss what you are trying to teach me in this." And I have always been able to see it when I look back. You will, too! His grace is sufficient.

Let us therefore draw near with confidence to the throne of grace, that we may receive mercy and may find grace to help in the time of need. (Heb. 4:16)

June 8
Faith is the pencil of the soul that pictures heavenly things. –T. Burbridge, A Dictionary of Thoughts, p. 200

Hillary was our first grandchild. One of her favorite things to do was to draw and color pictures for the refrigerator art gallery. Since then we have had seven more grandchildren, and they all have loved art and crafts. They love to create things, to draw and display their masterpieces. I remember that when Hillary was about four years old, a little tiny thing, she would grasp that pencil just right with those precious little hands, then with a serious expression, she would contemplate what great work of art would go onto that clean sheet of paper. It wouldn't take long before she would jump right into her project with all the enthusiasm and zeal of a four-year-old. The years have yielded more perfected masterpieces from Hillary and all the rest, but none is any more precious than another and each one is a treasure.

Faith is like a child's artwork and our lives like a clean sheet of paper before us. We do not know what the finished picture will look like. We can only imagine what we would like to see on the pages of our life. By faith we must trust our lives to the One who gives life. Fixing our eyes on Jesus, the author and perfecter of faith (Heb. 12:2a), we can contemplate our next move with confidence and assurance that His plan for our masterpiece will far exceed any Rembrandt. Jesus said, I have come that you might have life and have it more abundantly. When we trust God by faith to go before us and light the way, we can be assured that the picture of our lives will reflect Him.

Do you want to see heavenly things, blessings that only God who loves you can give? Then trust Him by faith to walk through life with you. Let today be the day that you ask Him to hand you a clean sheet of paper and by faith walk with Him.

Now faith is the assurance of things hoped for, the conviction of things not seen. (Heb. 11:1)

June 9
He surely is most in need of another's patience, who has none of his own. –Lavater, A Dictionary of Thoughts, p. 470

Have you noticed lately how few patient people there are in the world? Go to the grocery store and stand in line at the checkout counter. Listen, if you dare, to the grunts and grumbles as the line slowly moves along. What about the line at a restaurant? The hungry bears are growling with enthusiastic pessimism. Try the doctor's office or the dentist's office. In that nice, clean, comfortable atmosphere with music playing, you hear impatient patients. We have all been guilty at one time or another, but if we aren't careful, it can become a bad habit.

You have heard the saying "the patience of Job." Now Job, if anybody, had an excuse not to be patient. He was stripped of all his possessions, his children, livestock—everything. He was covered with boils and suffered greatly. His friends didn't see how he could be patient with all the adversity that God had allowed Satan to put on him. Even his wife told him to curse God and die. Job, even in all of his sorrow and suffering, held fast to the promises of God. Job's words were, "And as for me, I know that my Redeemer lives, and at the last He will take His stand on the earth. Even after my skin is destroyed, yet from my flesh I shall see God" (Job 19:25–26). We see in Job extreme patience in extreme circumstances. Cannot we have simple patience in meager circumstances?

Patience is a virtue and something we all must work on. A man named George Horne once said, "Patience strengthens the spirit, sweetens the temper, stifles anger, extinguishes envy, subdues pride, bridles the tongue, restrains the hand, and tramples upon temptations."

Like Job, we need to live with eternity in mind, shaking off the small stuff and focusing our minds, attitudes, and optimism on the good that lies ahead if we are children of God.

When your patience is finally in full bloom, then you will be ready for anything, strong in character, full and complete. (James 1:4 TLB)

June 10
Sorrow for having done amiss is fruitless if it issue not in doing so no more. –George Horne, A Dictionary of Thoughts, p. 565

True repentance comes hard and slow sometimes. Many are sorry for what they do, but few admit it. The reason God wants us to be sorry for our sin is so that we can repent and turn away from that sin. We can't turn and walk in His direction if we are still walking headlong and headstrong in our own direction. Sin separates us from God and hinders the working out of His plan for our lives. Somebody once said there is greater depravity in not repenting of sin when it has been committed than in committing it at first.

Why would David ever be considered a man after God's own heart? What did God see in David that He loved and that grabbed His heart? Could it be that David was broken over his sin? Could it be that when he sinned, he was totally sorrowful and repentant to the point of despair? David knew one thing that many so often miss: he knew where to go to find peace. He knew the One who forgives, the One who could restore the joy of his salvation. In Psalm 32 we see David's cry to the Lord:

How blessed is he whose transgression is forgiven, whose sin is covered! How blessed is the man to whom the Lord does not impute iniquity, and in whose spirit there is no deceit! When I kept silent about my sin, my body wasted away through my groaning all day long. For day and night Thy hand was heavy upon me; my vitality was drained away as with the fever heat of summer. I acknowledged my sin to Thee, and my iniquity I did not hide; I said, 'I will confess my transgressions to the Lord,', and Thou didst forgive the guilt of my sin.

God holds each of us accountable for our own sins—not someone else's sin, only our own. He also expects us to take responsibility for those bad choices and make them right. He paid a great price for us to have forgiveness of our sin, the sacrifice of His precious Son, Jesus.

For the sorrow that is according to the will of God produces a repentance without regret, leading to salvation; but the sorrow of the world produces death. (2 Cor. 7:10)

June 11
Solitude shows us what we should be; society shows us what we are. –Cecil, A Dictionary of Thoughts, p. 629

In your quietest moments, those moments of solitude you have to yourself, you are able to look inwardly and reach upwardly. God loves those times in our lives when we surrender our intimate feelings to Him and share peaceful moments of tranquility in His presence. Those are the times He can speak to our hearts and we listen best and hear Him.

Life gets so cluttered and complicated at times that we lose our perspective and it gets hard to focus on what is real and lasting. We get caught up with the superficial and obvious and lose the depth we need to deal with life's simplest struggles or lose sight of some of life's most divine blessings.

Jesus lived a solitary life while he was on earth. He was born in a solitary setting, a stable. He often withdrew from the disciples to pray and from the crowds to rest. He was not flamboyant, nor was He obscure. He always made Himself available to those around Him who wanted to hear His words or to be healed or ministered to. Jesus's main focus was His mission, to do the will of His Father. Jesus brought hope to the world and to those who trust in Him; He gives peace and the assurance of eternal life with Him. You see, there is no peace without knowing Jesus.

Are you caught up in the rat race of the world? Have you been deceived into thinking that to be still and peaceful is a waste of time? Do cell phones, television, radios, or other distractions keep you from hearing what you need to hear from the One who wants to have time with you? We will never hear from God if we drown out His voice as he tries to speak to us. Draw near to Him today, and He will draw near to you. Comfort yourself in knowing that He is always there.

Be still and know that I am God. (Ps. 46:10 KJV)

June 12
With God all things are possible.

The vastness of this universe is but a reminder of the greatness of Almighty God. In just six days our Creator God created the entire universe, as well as man and woman. It's amazing when you think about it. And how did God do all of this? He spoke it into being. After He had spoken the world into existence, He acknowledged the Trinity as He said in Genesis 1:26, "Let Us make man in Our image, according to Our likeness." From the beginning, we see God, Jesus, and the Holy Spirit. As you walk through the scriptures of God's Word, you see God, Jesus, and the Holy Spirit throughout the pages. For so long I did not grasp the truth of the Trinity in the Old Testament. For some reason the Genesis 1:26 scripture was not one that jumped out at me. Since God has given me the revelation of that truth, I have been able to see the three in one all throughout the Word of God. To see the foreshadowing of Jesus in the Old Testament, before He ever came to earth in the form of man, has been exciting and mind-boggling. The Holy Spirit working in the hearts of Old Testament prophets and kings and God speaking so that they knew and understood without a doubt His full instructions puts me in a state of awe for the God of the universe and my Savior.

I rejoice today, as I am sure you do, that I know the King of Kings and Lord of Lords and that He knows me. I rejoice that Jesus is Lord of my life and that the power of the Holy Spirit indwells my heart, soul, and mind and humbles me to the point of tears. God is still creating man and woman in His image. If you respond to the calling of the Holy Spirit today and ask Jesus Christ to come into your heart, you will be born again. You will become a new creation in Christ and will live for eternity with God. Call on Him today. To be created anew sounds impossible, but all things are possible with God, Jesus, and the Holy Spirit—the Holy Trinity!

Come near to Me, listen to this: From the first I have not spoken in secret, from the time it took place, I was there. And now the Lord God has sent Me, and His Spirit. (Isa. 48:16)

June 13
A person on the wrong path of life is not without hope, just on the wrong foundation. –Lex Bowen

My faith is built on nothing less
Than Jesus' blood and righteousness.
I dare not trust the sweetest frame,
But wholly lean on Jesus' name.
On Christ the solid rock I stand
All other ground is sinking sand
All other ground is sinking sand.

This great old hymn by Edward Mote is a testimony of a life committed to walk by faith. Our foundation will not hold for this life if it is not built on Jesus. He is the solid rock. Many people walk through life, arm in arm with the things of this world, with never a thought of the shifting sand beneath their feet. It is often subtle, easing in as the waves on the beach. The clouds gather, the storms come, and the sand begins to move beneath their feet. Suddenly, the fall is great and the cries are piercing. In their pit of despair and hopelessness, they cry out to the only One who can rescue them from the distress and sinfulness of this world. God hears only the cries of repentance of the lost people. He is willing to save and to rescue the perishing if they repent and turn from the things of the world, putting their feet on solid ground and following His ways. Only then will He pull them from the pitfalls of the world and set them on solid ground. The Lord knows those who are His and calls on those who are saved to abstain from wickedness (2 Tim. 2:19). It is by faith that the saved build their lives on a foundation that is found only in Jesus, the lasting foundation that is solid and firm. When the storms of life come, He is the One we can turn to and be assured that we will not be moved.

And everyone who hears these words of Mine, and does not act upon them, will be like a foolish man, who built his house upon the sand. (Matt. 7:26)

June 14
Pray as if it's all up to God and work as if it's all up to you.

God expects us to pray believing that He will work all things out for our good (Rom. 8:28). However, He also wants us to diligently work to bring about results because faith, if it has no works, is dead being by itself (James 2:17).

Abraham was a man of God and he believed God, and it was reckoned to him as righteousness (Gal. 3:6). It was because of Abraham's faith that God imputed a right-standing relationship between Himself and Abraham. God called him friend. We never see Abraham resting on his laurels or saying that because God was his friend, he would do nothing but wait for Him to do something. No, he was about God's prophetic plan. He was not without sin or error, but his work was to honor God through obedience and to glorify God's kingdom on earth.

When do we enter God's kingdom? When Jesus enters us. His kingdom is eternal, and we live eternally because of His indwelling presence in us. When we are born again, His kingdom comes. Somebody once said that to glorify God means to extol Him, agree with what He says about Himself, worship Him in the splendor of holiness and submit to Him in humble obedience to all He says do. We must never refrain from praying. God made a clear path for us to Himself at the cross. The curtain in the temple was ripped in half, making it possible for every believer to have direct access to the Father. We had no more need for a priest to deliver our prayers or to plead for forgiveness on our behalf. We can go directly to the throne of grace with our prayers and petitions and present them to God. He hears the prayers of repentance of the lost, and his mercies are new every morning.

Always be faithful to pray and diligent to work to accomplish His purpose for you on earth. It is not by works that we are saved, but because we are saved we want to work to glorify Him.

**For just as the body without the spirit is dead, so also
faith without works is dead. (James 2:26)**

June 15
Don't quit. Remember, winners never quit and quitters never win.

This little quote reminds me of the story in Luke 11. One of Jesus's disciples came to Him as He was finishing His prayer time and asked Him if He would teach him to pray. After quoting the Lord's Prayer to him, Jesus proceeded to tell him a story about the persistence of a man who went to his friend at midnight to ask for bread. The man inside the house said that he and his family had gone to bed and he could not get up to give him anything. The man outside continued his plea for bread until his friend came and gave him all that he needed. Jesus said because of his persistence, his needs were met.

How persistent are you in prayer when you go to the Father? Do you continue to pray, or do you stop praying when you do not get an answer right away? Jesus goes on to say in verses 9–10, "And I say to you, ask, and it shall be given to you; seek, and you shall find, knock, and it shall be opened to you. For everyone who asks, receives, and he who seeks, finds; and to him who knocks, it shall be opened." How sad it is for many of us when we stop just short of getting an answer from God, or maybe someone who is praying for us sees no results so they stop praying. We are to pray without ceasing, even when the answer is nowhere in sight.

We can't be winners in anything we do unless we are diligent in our efforts, unless we are fervent and unrestrained in our endeavor to move forward. Our commitment and dedication must go beyond the average in order to advance to winning status.

How do we accomplish this? How can we, whether it be in prayer, the race of life, our Christian walk, or any earnest attempt worth time and energy, prepare ourselves for the persistent walk by faith? We must first sell out in total abandonment to the Lord Jesus Christ. Then through Him and Him alone we can proceed with persistent determination.

**And all things you ask in prayer, believing,
you shall receive. (Matt. 21:22)**

June 16
You can make giving a way of living. –Mary Kay Ash

Remember the old saying "practice makes perfect"? Well, I think it could apply here. If we make it a practice to help those around us, listen to them, and reach out to them, then such giving becomes a way of living.

I think often about my grandmother, whom I called Grandmother Griffin, and the way she lived her life. She did not have fine things, nor did she seem to desire them. When I went to her house, it was rare that I ever left without some little something she had made or wanted to share with me. It could be anything from a jar of her homemade mayhaw or blackberry jelly, a crocheted pair of bedroom shoes or a doily, a freshly made apple tart, or maybe a book that had meant a great deal to her. Whatever she had, she generously gave away.

When Jesus called His disciples, He gave them instructions for service. He told them to go to the lost sheep and to preach to them. He told them to "heal the sick, raise the dead, cleanse the lepers, cast out demons; freely you received, freely give" (Matt. 10:8). Jesus Himself said that it is more blessed to give than to receive (Acts 20:35). What do you have to give away today? Maybe it is a little time that you can share with a lonely person or with your child or grandchild. It could be a few dollars or a meal for a homeless person. Give a listening ear to a neighbor who is hurting or a card to encourage a friend. A smile is a great thing to give, and it costs nothing. I love to make bread and cinnamon rolls to give away. There are so many things we can give that say love in a special way. But the best gift that we could ever give to anyone is to share the plan of salvation. As Anne Graham Lotz says, "Just give me Jesus!" Jesus said, "Give and it will be given to you; good measure, pressed down, shaken together, running over, they will pour into your lap. For by your standard of measure it will be measured to you in return" (Luke 6:38).

Now this I say, he who sows sparingly shall also reap sparingly; and he who sows bountifully shall also reap bountifully. (2 Cor. 9:6)

June 17
The only true gift is a portion of yourself. –Emerson

The things we send into the lives of others like sympathy, joy, love, kindness, understanding, and forgiveness are the gifts that come from the heart and are lasting. To care about someone enough to give them words of encouragement, inspiration, and guidance indicates a heart of compassion and the true spirit of giving.

Nothing is more reassuring than to know that you have someone to go to when you hurt, when you need advice, or when you need a listening ear or a shoulder to cry on. Perhaps it is your husband or wife, a close friend, a parent, or your child. A caring and compassionate person is truly a blessing from a loving heavenly Father and a treasure worth more than gold. My mother was that kind of person. She listened, sympathized, comforted, and pondered it all in her heart like Jesus's mother, Mary. Whatever I shared with my mother, I knew that it was safe, and her advice was never biased or condemning.

Even more precious than a godly mother or anyone else close to you is the One who always hears us. God promises that He will never leave us or forsake us. He hears our deepest cries and catches our tears in a bottle. He holds us in the palm of His hand, and under His strong wings he shelters us. He knows how many hairs are on your head. He knew you before you were formed in your mother's womb. My God, the one and only true God, promises me that He loves me with an everlasting love and will guard my every step. How comforting it is to know that the One who created me knows my name and tells me that because I am His, there is therefore now no condemnation. I long to please Him. I love Him because He first loved me. All He requires of me is to accept His Son, His greatest gift to us, to love Him with all my heart, and to be obedient to follow the things that He teaches me in His Word. Let us together seek Him first, then we can be that true gift to someone.

And God is able to make all grace abound to you, that always having all sufficiency in everything, you may have an abundance for every good deed. (2 Cor. 9:8)

June 18
Absence makes the heart grow fonder. —Thomas Haynes Bayly, A Dictionary of Thoughts

When Jesus ascended back into heaven, I can just imagine how His disciples must have longed for Him. For three years, during His earthly ministry, they had been with Him constantly. Even though He left a comforter, the Holy Spirit, to console and teach them, they still missed His presence among them. The void of His warmth, His compassion, His fellowship, and His teaching would grieve them until they would one day see Him again. Jesus left them instructions as He departed from the mountain to heaven, back to the presence of His Father. In His absence they were to "go therefore and make disciples of all the nations, baptizing them in the name of the Father and the Son and the Holy Spirit, teaching them to observe all that I commanded you; and lo, I am with you always, even to the end of the age" (Matt. 28:19–20). The disciples immediately did as Jesus said. They went out fishing for lost souls. God knew that they would have plenty to keep them busy.

Have you ever for some reason had to miss church for a Sunday or two? Didn't you miss your brothers and sisters in Christ? When we come to Christ, we seem to form a bond with other Christians. We have a longing to be with those who are like-minded, loving, and supportive. Iron sharpens iron, so one man sharpens another (Prov. 27:17). That is why God commands us to forsake not the assembling of ourselves together. By coming together, we can encourage one another to grow spiritually, to witness, and to be faithful. It is the same when people you love go away or you are separated for a while—you long for their return. God said that He put eternity in our hearts. So, like the disciples, we long to see our God and spend eternity with Him. Until that time, let us love those in the body of Christ, His church. Oh, Jesus, how we long for your return!

And lifting His hands to heaven, He blessed them, and then began rising into the sky, and went on to heaven. (Luke 24:50 TLB)

June 19
Always rise from the table with an appetite, and you will never sit down without one. – Penn, A Dictionary of Thoughts, p. 2.

Bulimia is a sad sickness that has shown its ugly head in our society in the last thirty years. Its victims are held in the grasp of an insatiable desire to eat uncontrollably and then purge or vomit to get rid of all the food in which they have indulged. It becomes a psychological disorder, a battle of mind and body, ultimately leading to serious consequences, even death if not gotten under control.

Like all of our emotions and desires, God wants to be in control of them. He created us and knows best how we function. The greatest part is that He loves us and cares when something is out of whack or dysfunctional. Appetite for food is one of those natural or habitual desires that we seldom think about giving God control over. However, overindulging in anything is sinful and can create problems if we allow it to get out of hand. God wants control of our minds and bodies, not to manipulate or dominate them but to manifest Himself in us and through us. He wants us to live in peace and happiness, surrendering every area of our lives to Him. Let us learn to eat to live and not live to eat.

Jesus said, "I am the bread of life; he who comes to Me shall not hunger, and he who believes in Me shall never thirst" (John 6:35). Of course, our Savior is talking about spiritual food, the true bread, that which gives life. "For the bread of God is that which comes down out of heaven, and gives life to the world" (v. 33). If you suffer today from a physical eating disorder, take it to the One who gives us the true bread that sustains us. Jesus is waiting to aid you in any battle that entangles you in order to enable you to get back on the right track. His provision is mighty to sustain you as you fight any battle in this life.

I can do anything I want to if Christ has not said no, but some of these things aren't good for me. Even if I am allowed to do them, I'll refuse to if I think they might get such a grip on me that I can't easily stop when I want to. For instance, take the matter of eating. God has given us an appetite for food and stomachs to digest. But that doesn't mean we should eat more than we need. (1 Cor. 6:12–13 TLB)

June 20
The actions of men are the best interpreters of their thoughts. –Locke, A Dictionary of Thoughts, p. 4

I guess this could be another way of saying that actions speak louder than words. It amazes me that if you put three people in a room and ask them the same question, you would most likely get three different answers or opinions. How can two Christians look at the same incident and draw different conclusions if we each say we are seeking God's will? If you have ever been to a church business meeting, you know exactly what I am referring to. We, hopefully, are all seeking God's will and direction, yet so many times differences of opinion on how to handle the affairs of His church flare up, leaving questions as to which way to go. In such cases, it is best to just stop and pray, asking God for direction and guidance.

I love the scripture where God speaks through the prophet Isaiah to the people of Zion, the inhabitants in Jerusalem, declaring to them that "the Lord is a God of justice" (Isa. 30:18). He told them that "He (God) will surely be gracious to you at the sound of your cry; when He hears it, He will answer you" (v. 19). Verse 21 follows through with assurance that we might not hear the answer right away, but if we wait for God's timing, He is faithful to give us the answer. "And your ears will hear a word behind you, 'This is the way, walk in it,' whenever you turn to the right or to the left."

Only the wisdom of God is the answer. People's minds only function on a human level; God in His wisdom knows best. He sees the big picture. He can see beyond what our limited eyes can see. After prayer and as we seek to do and say what God lays on our hearts to do and say, we can look back to see how He handled it and it will bring glory to Him. Then our actions will truly speak louder than our words or thoughts as in obedience we follow His leading.

For the mouth speaks out of that which fills the heart.
(Matt. 12:34 NAS)

June 21
As the flower is before the fruit, so is faith before good works. —Whately, A Dictionary of Thoughts, p. 199

We are surrounded by peach trees in our area. Out of the wintertime of late February and early March come signs of the future harvest. The peach farmers watch anxiously as the long, bare branches suddenly begin to bloom with little flowers. Each flower represents a potential peach and is guarded and protected as best possible from the elements of the remaining bitter cold days until spring. When spring comes with the sunshine and showers, the flowers will turn to young fruit, and by summer will be mature, ripe peaches.

In all the signs of the harvest, whether peaches or the Christian life, evidence should be visible of new life and growth. Before any of us can produce good fruit, we must first come to the only One who can give life. Jesus said, "I am the vine, you are the branches; he who abides in Me, and I in him, he bears much fruit; for apart from Me you can do nothing" (John 15:5). We must come to Christ in simple childlike faith, trusting Him to work in and through us. As we bloom, His protective hand guards and guides us. We are nurtured by our heavenly Father, and we grow as we seek Him through prayer and His Holy Word.

Faith in Jesus must come before we can do the work that produces quality fruit. Then and only then will others "see your good works and glorify your Father who is in Heaven" (Matt. 5:16).

Many blooms fall off the peach trees before harvesttime, never to become edible fruit. So it is with His humankind. Again Jesus said, "Abide in Me, and I in you. As the branch cannot bear fruit of itself, unless it abides in the vine, so neither can you, unless you abide in Me" (John 15:4). A person who never comes to the vine in order to get life is dead already, as are his or her works. The true source of life is not there. Come to know the true source of life, and by harvesttime, you should be mature and ready for the kingdom of heaven.

Walk in a manner worthy of the Lord, to please Him in all respects, bearing fruit in every good work. (Col. 1:10)

June 22
Faith is to believe on the word of God, what we do see, and its reward is to see and enjoy what we believe.
–Augustine, A Dictionary of Thoughts, p. 199

Stepping out in faith is not an easy task. However, God makes it clear that it is impossible to please Him without faith (Heb. 11:6). We must believe that He is the rewarder of those who trust Him and believe that He will do what He says that He will do. Then and only then will He bless us. Like all the saints who are listed in the Hebrews Hall of Faith (Hebrews 11), we must learn to hear from God and act on what we hear.

How do we learn to hear from God? How do we discern the voice of God? Jesus said, "My sheep hear my voice, and I know them, and they follow Me" (John 10:27). Each person in the Hall of Faith heard and obeyed. Noah heeded the warning and built the ark; Abraham heard the call to move to another place, not knowing the place he would be going; Sarah considered God faithful to give her a child because He had promised He would; Moses chose God's people and the greater reward over the riches of Egypt; and Rahab, the harlot, repented and was obedient to hide the spies sent by Joshua. What do we see here? Ask, believe, trust, obey. Then how do we hear from God? We ask Him to show us, we believe that He will, we trust when we can't see anything happening, and we live in obedience to His Word. As His Word says, He is a rewarder of those who seek Him.

Are you hearing His voice today? Do you read your Bible to hear a word from God? It is God-breathed, you know. Do you pray? If you are His child, you have a straight line to your heavenly Father through prayer. We must always remember that sometimes His answer to us is "no" or "wait." It is not always "Yes, I will do it your way." He wants the best for His children, just like we want the best for ours. Trust Him and know that He will never let you down.

Blessed are they who did not see, and yet believed. —John 20:29

June 23
Give yourself away with love.

Have you ever taken someone flowers or a box of candy and signed the card, "With love" and then your name? It's a nice thing to do, and it is always received with much thanks and appreciation. The best gifts, however, are those that we give in service to those we love and our fellow humans.

I am reminded of the story of Anne Frank. She and her Jewish family and some family friends were in hiding for two years as they fled persecution of Jews from the German Nazi soldiers. Those two years were spent in a small space at the back of her father's business. At the time of Hanukkah, one of the Jewish holidays, she yearned to give a gift to each one of those who were in this desolate hiding place. She put much thought into this seemingly impossible effort. When the time for their subdued Hanukkah celebration came, she presented each one with a special gift. For some it was a sacrifice of her rations and for others the promise of a chore, her time and energy to do something for someone else. Anne Frank kept a diary of their time in that small space, detailing the loneliness and desperation that she felt. For a young teenager, the days were endless, but she managed to survive by writing down their daily activities and her thoughts in her diary. It was found later and given to her father, who was the only one of her family to survive the horrors of the Holocaust. You can read all accounts in the book from her diary, *The Diary of Anne Frank*.

I am sure that Anne Frank never dreamed that the kind and small deeds of giving herself away would ever be known, much less published, but when we give of ourselves, it doesn't matter. It is from the heart and a gift worth giving. Her only intention was to bless others. God blesses the small things that we do as well as the greater things.

He Himself said, "It is more blessed to give
than to receive." (Acts 20:35)

June 24
Nothing but a good life here can fit men for a better one hereafter.

You have heard the old saying, "Make hay while the sun shines." Well, that applies to life and eternal life as well. Whoever you choose now, Jesus or Satan, is who you get to live with when you die. Eternity is forever and ever, and we will spend it somewhere. When Jesus left earth and ascended back to heaven, He said that He was going back to prepare a place for us so that where He is we may be also (John 14:2–3).

Heaven is a glorious place, and we all want to go there. However, Hell is just as real but is a place of torment. Many people deceive themselves by thinking that such a loving God would not allow people to go to hell. He doesn't. We make that choice ourselves. Not choosing for Him is choosing against Him. Therefore, we have made the choice to be separated from Him in this life and throughout eternity. It is a bad choice and not His desire at all.

We have a food ministry in our church. On the third Thursday of each month, we open our doors to the needy and give them food for the body and food for the soul. I serve as one of the counselors who offers the plan of salvation to all first comers. We first find out where they are spiritually, whether they have a church that they attend, and if they would like to hear more about Jesus. We never have anyone to refuse the gospel, which makes this a very successful ministry because that is our purpose. After going over some questions with them, I have an illustration that I like to use. I draw a horizontal line across the page. I put a "B" for *birth* at the left end of the line and a "D" for *death* at the right end of the line. Beside the "D" I draw a vertical line. I then write a capital "H" at the top and another "H" at the bottom of the vertical line. I tell them that the top one represents heaven and the bottom one hell. I then ask them where they want to go when they die. Of course the answer is always heaven. Then I ask them if they have asked Christ to be their Savior. If they say that they have, then we place a cross at their point of salvation. If they have not, then I share the plan of salvation with them, telling them that the distance between "B" and "D" is the only time that we have to make that decision about where we will spend eternity. They listen and understand, then we pray!

**It is appointed for men to die once and after
this comes judgment. (Heb. 9:27)**

June 25
The Bible is a perfect treasure of divine instructions.

God's Word keeps us grounded. Because what He says is truth, it keeps us on solid ground. When we read it, we gain knowledge of who He is, how He thinks, and what He expects of us. When a person has no knowledge of God's truths, he or she flounders around looking for purpose and meaning to life. A wise person always wants to know more of God. "Fools hate knowledge" (Prov. 1:22). To them the things of God are foolishness (1 Cor. 2:14).

"Every word of God is tested; He is a shield to those who take refuge in Him" (Prov. 30:5). But the "god of this world (Satan) has blinded the minds of the unbelieving, that they might not see the light of the gospel of the glory of Christ, who is the image of God" (2 Cor. 4:4). Satan longs to distract, discourage, and disable humankind. That is why our faith should not rest on the wisdom of men but on the power of God (1 Cor. 2:5). The Holy Spirit holds the key to the wisdom that humankind must possess in order to have the true wisdom of God. That is a mystery to those who will not believe (1 Cor. 2:7–8). Other people do not know our thoughts; they are a mystery to them. Only the Holy Spirit knows. Likewise, no one knows the thoughts of God except the Spirit of God (1 Cor. 2:11). "Now we have received, not the spirit of the world, but the Spirit who is from God, that we might know the things freely given to us by God" (1 Cor. 2:12).

God's Word gives us light into the very heart and mind of God. As we come to Him by faith, He reveals to us words taught to us by the Spirit, freely given in His inerrant Word. We must not neglect the reading of His Word if we want to hear from our Creator God.

Jesus is God's last word to humankind. "He is the radiance of His glory and the exact representation of His nature, and upholds all things by the word of His power" (Heb. 1:3). Jesus is the Word made flesh. He is full of grace and truth (John 1:14). He is God come to earth, to redeem humankind. But as many as receive Him, to them He gave the right to become children of God, even to those who believe in His name (John 1:12). He was rejected and abused, just as His Word is rejected, abused, and neglected today.

Do you desire the abundant life? Do you want to live victorious? Do you seek solid ground? Absolutes? You have to want it. Go to the source of all knowledge and truth today. Seek Him and let Him lead you through His instruction manual, the Bible, to know truth.

In the beginning was the Word, and Word was with God, and Word was God. (John 1:1)

June 26
A smile is the shortest distance between people.

A simple smile can bridge a gap that even words can't express. That little facial expression can offer approval and show acceptance. A smile breaks down barriers and invites goodwill. A smile generates love and opens the way to new friendships. It melts the heart of a lonely soul and comforts the spirit of a dying man. A smile reveals the heart and mirrors the soul.

Jesus went about doing good, and I can just imagine that He drew people to Himself by the warmth of His smile. People followed after Him as He walked down the streets of the villages or along the countryside. I cannot imagine that the men He called to be His disciples would have wanted to follow Him if He had approached them with a frown or a scowling expression. As Jesus went about, He drew all people to Himself. You can be sure that He was pleasant and openly displayed a pleasing countenance. Humankind recognized that He had been with God, even though they didn't realize that He was God.

Do those around you know that you have been with the Almighty God? Is the expression on your face an indicator of your heart condition? The joy in your heart should show on your face. We used to sing a little song entitled "If You're Happy, Notify Your Face." If you have joy in your heart, let it show. If you love others, let it show. If you delight in the things of your heavenly Father and are thankful, let it show. Even if your day is not good, sometimes a smile lifts your own spirits and gives you a new perspective on your situation. In Psalm 4:6, David cried out to the Lord, "Lift up the light of Thy countenance upon us, O Lord." We all want to know that our heavenly Father is smiling on us and that his heart is not grieved toward us as we try to live for Him. Walk in His ways so that you will have something to smile about and so will He!

Happy is he ... whose hope is in the Lord his God. (Ps. 146:5)

June 27
God is fair. God is just. God sent Jesus just for us. —Author

Many options are offered to us, many doors that we can enter as we walk along the corridor of life. However, only one is "the Way." Only one leads to the life that God wants for His children. Even before God created the first man, His plan was for perfection. The world and everything in it was perfect as God spoke it into being. God's first children, Adam and his helpmate, Eve, were perfect. "God saw all that He had made, and behold, it was very good" (Gen. 1:31). There was no sin and no death. It was perfect, very good! What happened? With Adam's disobedience came the curse of sin, and God, being a just God, had to deal with it. Sin does not go unpunished; there are consequences.

Just as God's first children had to learn that valuable lesson, so we must learn that as well. God does not tolerate sin and disobedience. He would not be a just and loving God if He did. Just as we discipline our children, God disciplines His children. It is because He loves us.

If you have raised any children or are in the process of getting them raised, you can identify with how our heavenly Father must feel about each of His children. We want the best for our children and try our hardest to help them make the right choices. We point them to the right doors and make sure that they know the dangers that lurk behind the other doors. God warned Adam and Eve, but they did not listen. Oftentimes we do the same thing; just as our children do not always listen to us, as loving parents we try to help them avoid bad choices.

In his Twenty-Third Psalm, David said, "He guides me in the paths of righteousness, for His name's sake." Like David, we can be assured that when we call on Him, He will guide us. He makes His way plain in His Word and as He speaks to our hearts. His great sacrifice of His only Son should certainly point us to His Way. Are you a rebellious child or an obedient child? Was His sacrifice in vain, or have you claimed it as your own?

Truly, truly, I say to you, he who hears My word, and believes Him who sent Me, has eternal life, and does not come into judgment, but has passed out of death in life. (John 5:24)

June 28
A test is to see how far you have come
and how far you need to go.

I shudder to think about taking a test. I still have dreams sometimes, like many people, do that I am in school. I walk into the classroom, the teacher says to get ready for a test, and I realized that I have not studied. I am unprepared. It's a nightmare.

Sometimes, like Job in the Bible, we are tested. God allowed Satan to sift or test Job to see if his faith was real. God knew Job's heart, but Satan didn't. Sometimes we face very difficult tests, and other times they are just quizzes and not so hard. We are not tested for God's benefit, for He knew before we were formed just what choices we would make. We are tested for our own benefit, to see how far we need to go in the area of faith and trust. Sometimes it is God's way of showing us where we are in our Christian walk.

It is easy for us to say, "I have faith," "I believe," or "I trust God." But when trials come, how much faith do we have? Do you trust Him with your needs? Do you believe that He is sufficient? Noah is a good example of one who walked with God. Noah was a righteous man, a preacher (2 Peter 2:5). In all his days before the flood, Noah sought to tell those walking in wickedness to repent. None listened. God told Noah to build a huge boat, an ark, because He was sorry that He had made humans (Gen. 6:6) and was going to destroy the earth. Noah heard God. He passed the test of faithfulness as he listened to the Creator and heeded His instructions. It was indeed a test for Noah, for it took him seventy-five years and much ridicule and abuse from worldly people to complete the task. He could have easily thrown up his hands and said "This is too difficult," but He followed through. He passed the test. Like Job, whose faith was real, are you prepared for the tests? The quiz? They will come.

**Examine me, O Lord, and try me; Test my mind and
my heart. For Thy lovingkindness is before my eyes,
and I have walked in Thy truth. (Ps. 26:2–3)**

June 29
Love and a cough cannot be hidden. –Herbert,
A Dictionary of Thoughts, p. 372

Try to suppress a cough or a sneeze. It is virtually impossible. It is going to come no matter what. The dictionary describes love as intense affection, meaning that when this great emotion grabs you it is extreme in degree, an overwhelming feeling, and not likely to be held back.

This is the kind of love with which we are to love God, our Father and Creator. We are to love Him with all of our hearts, minds, and souls. If our love for Him is as it should be, we will not hide it. We *could* not hide it. Our very instincts would explode with evidence of Christ in us and our desire to know Him more and serve Him better. Love is a powerful feeling and must be given as well as received. God showed His love for us in a most dramatic way—the cross. While we were yet sinners, God came to earth to die for us. It is a love unsuppressed.

I met my husband while we were in college. He was a senior and I was a freshman. I loved college and everything about it. I was perfectly happy to go my four years and then hopefully settle down with a loving husband, a home with a picket fence, and a few precious children. That had been my dream. But he came along and changed all that—the timing, that is. We fell in love from the first time we met. When he surprised me with a ring after we had been dating only six months, I said yes. What was I thinking! What about all the richness of college life, new friends, sock hops, my home economics degree? I never looked back. Love never fails. Not following this man was never an option. My love for him could not be held back. After all these years, I look back and know that I would do it again. We have definitely had bumps in the road, times when giving up and giving in would have been the easy way, but like God's unending love for us, we will hold fast to the end.

How does your love for the One who never holds back anything for you measure up today? Jesus gave the ultimate sacrifice, His life. Is your love for Him a love that cannot be hidden?

Let the redeemed of the Lord say so. (Ps. 107:2)

June 30
It takes the lowering of the shield for only one moment for a soldier to be fatally wounded.

"Be of sober spirit, be on the alert. Your adversary, the devil, prowls about like a roaring lion, seeking someone to devour. But resist him, firm in your faith" (1Peter 5-8-9a).

A crack in our armor can be detrimental to our safety in our world as we know it today. What kind of armor is a Christian to put on? Spiritual warfare is real, and there is true and present danger if we are not equipped to handle the foe. Ephesians 6 tells us how to "be strong in the Lord, and in the strength of His might." It is not flesh and blood that we war against, but rulers and powers and world forces of this darkness. Our struggles are against the spiritual forces of wickedness in the heavenly places (v. 12). Christians' protection is the full armor of God. We are to gird our loins with truth and put on the breastplate of righteousness. We are to shod our feet with the preparation of the gospel of peace and take up the shield of faith. The helmet is our salvation, and the sword is the indwelling Spirit, which is the Word of God. We are to pray without ceasing, being on the alert at all times. We are called to intercede for other Christians and also for those who preach the gospel (vv. 13–19).

Today is our oldest son's birthday. He is a big guy and a mighty man of valor. He stands for truth and lives out his faith every day. His business is a ministry as he encounters renters in a low income area. He has faced those who were not so accepting and amiable, but the shield of faith always prevails.

Christians must stand firm, holding fast to the shield that protects us from the darts and spears of the enemy. When we let down our guard, we cease to be effective to a world that is searching for truth and steadfastness. Not only do we lose our effectiveness as witnesses, but we set ourselves up for moral and spiritual failure.

Polish your armor today. Repair any cracks. Strengthen the arm that holds the shield. Now step out in faith!

Go, and may the Lord be with you. (1 Sam. 17:37)

July

And My people who are called by My name humble
themselves and pray, and seek My face and turn from their
wicked ways, then I will hear from heaven, will forgive
their sin, and will heal their land. (2 Chron. 7:14)

July 1
A house divided against itself cannot stand. —Abraham Lincoln

Do you feel that your spirit is at war with your flesh? That there is internal warfare going on in your very being? You are right. It is. Satan struggles daily, moment by moment to control your mind and to pull you from sincere devotion to Christ. Even though you belong to Christ, you still do battle with Satan because of your old sin nature that was passed on to you through generations from Adam and his disobedience. Because of this old sin nature, we must constantly call on our heavenly Father for strength to resist the temptations that are ever before us. You see, God has already won. Satan just doesn't know it yet!

A few years ago I opened an email that was very disturbing. It contained a video of a busload of small Syrian boys going to a camp where jihadists would continue the brainwashing tactics forced on them. As one of their leaders interviewed them for the camera, they sang songs of hate and jihad. They expressed their love for Bin Laden, saying how they wanted to be like him and their desire to be a suicide bomber. When asked who sent them on this trip, they said that their parents did. It broke my heart—children being led by evil forces and encouraged in it by their parents. They were being deprived of knowing the love of their heavenly Father, the love that Christians try to instill in their children from birth. We are surely up against the forces of darkness in these times. Sadly, many have gone into eternity never knowing the One who came to die so that they could live with Him forever in peace. They justify their evil deeds as pleasing Allah.

Christ's death on the cross was the perfect sacrifice for forgiveness of sin, even for those with such a mind-set. Accepting Him as Lord and Savior makes us one with Him and gives us the power that we need to win the battle against Satan and to live the abundant life. Our world is divided. Satan is alive and well and seeking whom he might destroy. He knows his time is short, and he knows who wins. Will you ask God to show you where you can make a difference today?

For the weapons of our warfare are not of the flesh, but divinely powerful for the destruction of fortresses. (2 Cor. 10:4)

July 2
What you send into the lives of others comes back into your own. –Mary Kay Ash

There is no reward like the feeling you get from helping someone. To give expecting nothing in return has its own reward. Those who give joy to others can't keep it from themselves because it flows back to them. Think about Christmastime. Don't we always look to see the reaction of the person to whom we give a gift? The pleasure that we get from their liking what we gave them is usually much greater than any gift that we received. Jesus spoke that very truth when He said, "It is more blessed to give than to receive" (Acts 20:35).

Growing up, we always went to my grandmother and granddaddy Griffins' house for Christmas with the cousins. It was a fun time because we saw cousins whom we didn't see all through the year. We didn't exchange gifts with one another, but our grandparents always had something for everyone there, and there were a lot of us there! It was not much, usually something that they made or found on sale, but each of us would always make sure that they knew how much we appreciated it. Their joy was in seeing that each of us received a little part of them. They had put themselves into each gift and loved seeing us open them.

When the greatest gift that was ever given to this world came down from heaven to rescue humankind, the world did not receive Him well. God was pleased to come to earth in the form of man. He was pleased to be the propitiation for our sin. He prophesied His coming in the Old Testament. He announced His coming through the angel Gabriel in the New Testament. He prepared Mary's and Joseph's hearts that Mary might be the mother of the Messiah, Jesus, God in the flesh. The angels and the shepherds rejoiced. The wise men came. But John said that as Jesus ministered among those He came to save, "He came to my own, and those who were his own did not receive him" (John 1:11). He was referring to the Jews and all who reject Him. Open your heart today to the One who has given His life for you. The greatest gift is yours for the receiving.

The generous man will be prosperous, and he who waters will himself be watered. (Prov. 11:25)

July 3
Work will win when wishing won't.

I once heard a story of a little boy who sat on a stump and wished all day. At the end of the day, he had wished all his wishes away! You won't get much accomplished with wishing. Wishing is like spinning your wheels in one place. God expects us to put some wings to our wishing just like He wants us to put feet to our prayers.

There have been many times when my children were small that I would walk through the house and see dirty dishes, clothes piled up to be washed, floors that needed mopping, windows that longed for some scrubbing, and on and on. With a wish and a sigh, I would survey the obstacle course, but nothing changed. The temptation to put it off was great, but I knew that was just prolonging the tasks and they would get worse instead of better. There was nothing to do but to dig in. As I took it on, one chore at a time, it was all soon accomplished. Wishing and hoping are futile without actions. Wishing is like a mirage in the desert. In our mind we can see, picture, and even imagine what that cool drink of water would taste like or that clean house would look like. But in all reality, it is not there. We can never be satisfied with wishing or dreaming. It does not make it so.

The Lord gives us many opportunities of service. Paul made it clear to the church at Corinth that "each man's work will become evident…. If any man's work which he has built upon it remains, he shall receive a reward" (1 Cor. 3:13–14). We are not saved by our works, but we work because we are saved. God has no hands but our hands and no feet but our feet. He expects us to glorify Him by the things we do for his kingdom while we are on this earth. Just like the little boy on the stump wishing, we often *wish* we could do more, *wish* we could go visit the sick, *wish* we could go share Christ, *wish* we could give more, but we never seem to make it happen. "Commit your way to the Lord, trust also in Him, and He will do it" (Ps. 37:5). God plus one is a strong workforce!

**Commit your works to the Lord, and your
plans will be established. (Prov. 16:3)**

July 4
Be just and fear not; let all the ends thou aimest at, be thy country's, thy God's, and truth's. – Shakespeare, A Dictionary of Thoughts, p. 471

This day every year reminds us of the sacrifices of our forefathers as well as those of the veterans, men and women past and present, who served and those who still serve to preserve the freedoms that we enjoy today. Many were wounded and scared. Many have suffered the emotional trauma of wars and battles, and many died. As the quote that we know so well today says, "All gave some and some gave all." All suffering and sacrifice was done for life, liberty, and the pursuit of happiness. For a nation that was founded on the principles of God's Word, we must never stray from the truths that He has made known to us in His Word in order to be blessed by Him.

Why is Holy God so passionate about obedience to His Word? Because He loves us so much that He doesn't want us to have to experience the consequences that come with sin and disobedience. He paid a big price for us to have forgiveness for our sin when He gave His only Son as penalty for our sin. Jesus came to earth to suffer and die an agonizing death in order that we might have freedom from the bondage of sin. We as a nation cannot disregard the sacrifice God made for us for our eternal security any more than we can disregard the sacrifice of the lives of our servicemen and -women for our earthly safety and national security. Freedom is not free. Someone must pay. Jesus paid it all. God is a patient God, not desiring that any should perish but that all would come to Him and spend eternity with Him.

Pray for our servicemen and -women today as many are in harm's way and many have not accepted the Savior who came that they might have eternal life and live free indeed. Because of our forefathers, our veterans, and those who still serve to ensure the security of this great United States of America, our rights to free speech and worship have been preserved. We can still openly proclaim "in God we trust."

Blessed is the nation whose God is the Lord. (Ps. 33:12a)

July 5
Shattered dreams can become substantial foundations.

Many a lofty goal have been set after some plan or dream had fallen apart or dissipated before ever getting off the ground. If we fall down and then stay down, it gets harder and harder to get up again. Falling or failing is not a sin; neither is it a disgrace. It only becomes a failure when we stay down or roll over and play dead.

I am reminded of something that I saw on television. It was such a picture of courage and the instinct to survive. A baby elephant was born with something like club feet. Because of his large size, his front feet were bent over at the knee joint in the womb. It was impossible for him to stand tall enough to reach his mother's milk. His mother and sister were futile in their efforts to help him as they struggled with their trunks to lift him. Without his mother's milk he would die. The young elephant calf collapsed from exhaustion after the long struggle. Night was coming, and the rest of the herd was moving on. His mother and sister refused to leave him. It would be a long night. The next morning, he again worked to stand. Weak but determined, he rose to his bended front knees. Then with all that he had left in him, he straightened out those knees and leaned back as if to lock them in place. He reached up for the first taste of his mother's milk. All was well. He had overcome adversity.

Everyone has something that they have to overcome. If your shattered dream, struggle, trial, heartache, or pain has not come, then get ready because it will. How do I know this? Jesus tells us so. "These things I have spoken to you, that in Me you may have peace. In the world you have tribulation, but take courage, I have overcome the world" (John 16:33). Paul learned a great lesson about this and shares it with us in Romans: "And not only this, but we also exult in our tribulations, knowing that tribulation brings about perseverance; and perseverance, proven character; and proven character, hope and hope does not disappoint, because the love of God has been poured out within our hearts through the Holy Spirit who was given to us" (5:3–4).

O taste and see that the Lord is good. (Ps. 34:8)

July 6
If we have not peace within ourselves, it is in vain to seek it from outward sources. – Rochefoucauld, A Dictionary of Thoughts, p. 472

Jesus came that we might have spiritual peace—not peace as the world knows peace but a peace that only comes from knowing and trusting Him. It's a peace that surpasses understanding. Why do you think God tells us that He is our refuge and our strength, our very help in trouble? Why does He say to call on Him and He will show us great and mighty things? Why does He tell us that He has placed in us a desire to know Him and to have a relationship with Him?

Anxiety and depression can be physical or psychological problems. Not all mental illness results from a lack of spiritual commitment. God has called us to have a relationship with Him, not just know about Him, and until we do we cannot know peace. History tells us that there is a God, just like we know that there was a first president, George Washington. But just knowing about God is not personal. We can know what the entire Bible says after reading it through over and over, but until we know the God of the Bible, we cannot claim His promises and be blessed as we live by His words. To have a relationship with God, we must believe God and know that He is the author of our faith. We must accept Jesus, who is God in the flesh—God who came to earth to suffer and die on the cross in order for humankind to have a personal relationship with Him (salvation) and forgiveness for sin. Jesus said, "I am the way, the truth and the life. No man comes to the Father (God) except by Me" (John 14:6).

In order to have a relationship with someone, we purpose to spend time with them. Love and devotion grow between us. There is trust and intimacy. There is commitment and conviction. So it is at a point in our lives when we make the choice to follow the One who gave us life. We must realize our sinfulness and cry out to God to forgive us and save us, realizing that we cannot save ourselves. As God hears our cry, He cleanses us from all unrighteousness, and as we invite Him into our hearts, His Holy Spirit indwells us to give us the power to live the Christian life and enjoy a relationship with Holy God.

Nations are always crying for peaceful settlements. Nations go to war and fight. They struggle to arrange peace talks between leaders. They bargain and bribe for peace. People and nations will never know peace apart from knowing Jesus Christ. Are you in God's army or on the battlefield with the world's fight to win a winless war? God has already won. The victory is yours!

These things I have spoken unto you, that in
Me ye might have peace. (John 16:33)

July 7
Learn Him. Know Him. Share Him.

As Christians today, we sometimes feel like the Christians of old who were thrown into the arenas where they were made a mockery of or torn apart by wild beast for sport. When we do step out to take a stand, we risk embarrassment and humiliation. Our words are often taken and used against us or twisted to mean something entirely opposite of our intent. Should we pull back then? Should we retreat to our comfort zones? Should we clam up and not be heard? May it never be that we would reject truth and swallow the lies of godless people. God's truth is a mystery that we can rejoice in and embrace. It is the mystery of all truth that belongs to those who trust in the One who is truth. When the spirit of truth abides in the surrendered heart, then we can know the peace of making the right choices. He gives discernment, guidance, and boldness as we face hard decisions and doubt. When the choices are hard and life closes in, He is our confidence.

God has called us to boldness and promises to be our refuge and strength. The psalmist cries, "In God I have put my trust, I shall not be afraid. What can man do to me?" (Ps. 56:11). Conviction about living a godly life comes with knowing the One who gives life. May we never base our convictions on the things of this world. Outside of Christ, our convictions are worldly. We see things as the world sees them. Satan is the god of this world. May we never choose to walk in that way. Yet many do, not accepting the better way.

Lord, help my convictions to always line up with your will and your Word. Your Word is like a two-edged sword. It cuts deep, causing us to have convictions, yet it comforts and encourages. It gives life and hope and wisdom to your children as we read your words and apply them to our lives and receive your blessings. Help us always to stand for your truths so that we will not fall for Satan's lies. Lord, give us boldness to fight off the wild beast in the power of your might.

It is no shame to suffer for being a Christian. Praise God for the privilege of being in Christ's family and being called by His wonderful name. (1 Peter 4:16 TLB)

July 8
"Self" living is a lost cause.

Jesus said, "If anyone wishes to come after Me, let him deny himself, and take up his cross, and follow Me. For whoever wishes to save his life shall lose it; but whoever loses his life for My sake and the gospel's shall save it. For what does it profit a man to gain the whole world, and forfeit his soul?" (Mark 8:34–36 NAS).

When we come to Christ, He does not want what's left after we have done our own thing. He does not care for our crumbs. He doesn't even want our willingness without obedience or our brokenness without humility. God desires that we lay our entire being on the altar. He wants to be in charge. It is sinful to put ourselves on the throne and to assume that our choices, attitudes, and behavior can reflect Christ without His leading. That is to set ourselves up as God. God-control is better than self-control.

One of Jesus's most outspoken disciples was Peter. He thought that he had all the answers but, if in doubt, was always willing to ask. He was ready to follow Jesus, but being a typical Galilean, he was oftentimes quick-tempered and spoke out without thinking, trusting in his own impulsive nature. Peter was often the spokesman for the disciples, as his curious and inquisitive nature begged for answers from Jesus. Three times Jesus asked Peter if he loved Him, and three times Peter said that he did. After the third time, Jesus told him to feed His sheep, meaning to share the gospel with the lost. We well remember Peter's attempt to walk on water, sinking as he took his eyes off Jesus, and then his denying that he knew Jesus the night before the crucifixion. Like Peter, we each have much "self" to deal with. But also like Peter we have the same Savior who sees what we can be. After Pentecost Peter was a different man. The power of the Holy Spirit radically changed him. He went on to preach to multitudes and many were saved. He told the younger men to "clothe yourselves with humility toward one another, for God is opposed to the proud, but gives grace to the humble" (1Peter 5:5b). In the end Peter was crucified upside down because he said that he was not worthy to die as his Lord had died. Selflessness was his dying testimony.

It's amazing what God can do when we get "self" out of the way! Are you ready to die to self?

I am the vine, you are the branches; he who abides in Me, and I in him, he bears much fruit; for apart from Me you can do nothing. (John 15:5)

July 9
If psychiatry leaves God out, ultimately we shall see psychiatrists going to each other for treatment. – Billy Graham, Day by Day with Billy Graham, 1976

God is our sustainer. He is our very present help in trouble. He is our peace and the fortress that we lean upon. He never changes, and He is holy. He provides for our needs and exercises loving-kindness toward His children. He is our protector and is all-knowing and all-powerful. He is omnipresent. He is the great I Am. He is King of Kings, the Lord of Lords, and the Prince of Peace. God is God, and when we come to a time when we fail to realize this truth, then we will have reached finite mentality and fail to be what God has created us to be. We are to fear God in a holy and reverent way, acknowledging Him as the one true and living God.

If God is all these things, then why does much of humanity purpose to leave Him out, to ignore Him, to not acknowledge Him as the only Way to life on earth and life eternal? Did the Creator of all not put in each of us a desire to know Him? We see in Acts 1:18–19 that we are without excuse: "For the wrath of God is revealed from heaven against all ungodliness and unrighteousness of men, who suppress the truth in unrighteousness, because that which is known about God is evident within them; for God made it evident to them."

People are groping in darkness today because many parents, psychiatrists, and counselors fail to give godly advice to those who seek it from them. God's Word is filled with answers to all of our problems, but few read it. "Seek the Lord while He may be found; Call upon Him while He is near" (Isa. 55:6).

God created us for fellowship with Him. We are far above the animals and just a little lower than the angels. Bask in His love for you, knowing that He is God, your Creator, and that He has placed in you a desire to know Him!

Bless our God, O peoples, and sound His praises abroad, Who keeps us in life, and does not allow our feet to slip. (Ps. 66:8–9)

July 10
The fullest and best ears of corn hang lowest toward the ground. —Edward Reynolds, A Dictionary of Thoughts, p. 282

Jesus came down hard on the Scribes and the Pharisees. They were the religious leaders of that day, and Jesus called them exactly that, "religious." It is one thing to be a Christian and quite another to just play the part. Play-acting or hypocrisy infuriated Jesus as seen in Matthew 23, especially in those who were supposed to be righteous and lawful. Their proud and arrogant ways were contrary to the teachings of Jesus who, even though He was God, was humble in spirit. His attitude toward such things has not changed.

As Jesus washed the disciples' feet the night before He was crucified, He painted a picture for us of what true humility is. Jesus had walked with these men on the dusty roads around Jerusalem for three years. He was their Lord, their teacher, their rabbi. They loved Him and He them. He had taught them how to pray, and they had seen Him heal the sick and cause the blind to see. He was truly God. Humility was Jesus's character. Born in a stable and raised by a carpenter, He was a man of sorrow and acquainted with grief. Like a lamb He would be led to slaughter; like a sheep that is silent before his shearers, the disciples would see their Master slain in the days to come. His human side was that of a humble man, yet He was God. As outspoken Peter asked Jesus, "What then will there be for us?" (Matt. 19:27) concerning their reward for leaving everything to follow Jesus, He said to them, "Many who are first will be last; and the last, first" (v. 30).

Jesus calls us to be humble in spirit and holy as He is holy. We must die to ourselves and all our lust, and in humility we must take up our crosses daily and follow Him. We are to fear the Lord in such a way that we show Him all honor and glory. Only in our humility and gentleness of spirit can Christ have freedom in our hearts.

Take My yoke upon you and learn from Me, for I
am gentle and humble in heart; and you shall find
rest for your souls. (Matt. 11:29 NAS)

July 11
After crosses and losses men grow humbler and wiser. –Franklin, A Dictionary of Thoughts, p. 282

What does it take to get us to a place where we are humble in spirit, where we are gentle and merciful? Jesus, in His own words, called on us to commit to such an attitude of humility. He called His disciples aside to be sure that they heard Him as he spoke the Beatitudes. His words were truths to them of how they could be happy and blessed if they followed these instructions found in His teaching in His Sermon on the Mount recorded in Matthew 5.

Blessed are the poor in spirit ...

Blessed are those who morn ...

Blessed are the gentle ...

Blessed are those who hunger and thirst for righteousness ...

Blessed are the merciful ...

Blessed are the pure in heart ...

Blessed are the peacemakers ...

Blessed are those who have been persecuted for the sake of righteousness ...

Blessed are you when men cast insults at you and persecute you and say all kinds of evil against you falsely, on account of Me ...

Jesus is speaking these same words to us today as He spoke to the multitudes that day. The challenge is no greater now than it was then.

Do we have to become broken to become humble? Do we have to suffer or experience tragedy to know what humility is? I should hope not, but sometimes it comes to that. There will always be crosses to bear, and there will always be times when we must choose to lose in order to win the greater reward. Jesus said, "And he who does not take his cross and follow after Me is not worthy of Me" (Matt. 10:38). Jesus only asks us to die to ourselves and let Him fill us. We will then be blessed in His sight and know true humility, mercy, gentleness, purity, and righteousness.

And whoever exalts himself shall be humbled, and whoever humbles himself shall be exalted. (Matt. 23:12)

July 12
The truest end of life is to know the life that never ends. —Penn, A Dictionary of Thoughts, p. 362

To know God in His fullness should be our goal for this time we have on earth. Even though that is hardly possible, we should strive for that end. In striving and keeping our eyes on the "prize," we find the strength and faith to press on.

Recently, a newspaper reported on a young mother and her child who perished in a winter ice storm. It seems their car slid off the road and into a pond. The mother was able to get herself and her young child out of the sinking car only to walk wet and cold in freezing temperatures and collapse. Authorities found their frozen bodies less than six hundred feet from a farmhouse.

We never know what tomorrow holds. That young mother set out that day probably to run some errands or maybe to visit a friend. Maybe she had a church meeting or was about to drop the child off at day care. We don't know. But one thing we do know is that the lives of these two on this earth is over. We can only pray that the young mother had not put off the most important decision of this life—where she would spend eternity. There are no more chances once we breathe our last breaths. Now is the appointed time to make our choice. Heaven is for those who choose Jesus and hell for those who reject Him. We must never put off salvation, because we never know when our appointed time is.

Pray, read your Bible, go to church, seek God, and know'Him. Hold fast to the promises of our heavenly Father and know that even though the struggles are hard and the path is lonely at times, there is peace in knowing that heaven is our final destination. Paul said it like this to the church at Philippi: "For our citizenship is in heaven, from which also we eagerly wait for a Savior, the Lord Jesus Christ" (Phil. 3:20).

You know the right choice. Make it today if you have been putting it off.

And this is eternal life, that they may know Thee, the only true God, and Jesus Christ whom Thou has sent. (John 17:3)

July 13
It is easy to look down on others; to look down on ourselves is the difficulty. –Peterborough, A Dictionary of Thoughts, p. 281

Prejudice is a hard pill to swallow. It infringes on our very souls and pulls us toward bitterness, hatred, and malice. To despise another human being because of the color of his or her skin, religion, or background is a far cry from what Jesus taught. He said that we are to love our neighbor as ourselves. Imagine that!

People of this world will never know how to love like that until they know Christ. Billy Graham made the statement, "Only Christ can solve the complicated racial problem that is facing the world today. Until people of all races come to accept Christ as Savior, they do not have the ability to love each other."

Sadly, the scribes and Pharisees of Jesus's day had a very pious, self-righteous attitude. As they sought to live by the letter of the law, they missed the principles of the new covenant. Jesus said that He came to write the laws on our hearts as we come to Him for salvation (Matt. 5:17). A heart that is truly His has no room for prejudice and hate. In Galatians 6:2–3, Paul calls on us to "Bear one another's burdens, and thus fulfill the law of Christ. For if anyone thinks he is something when he is nothing, he deceives himself." The indwelling of Christ in us allows us to possess the supernatural power to love unconditionally. Prejudice is like poison that not only destroys another person but eats away at your own heart.

Thank you, Jesus, that you don't love me for who I am. Thank you that you don't prejudge me. Your mercy and grace to me make me ever grateful for your love and sacrifice when I was so unlovable. Help me to love all those around me with the same kind of love that you love me.

Do nothing from selfishness or empty conceit, but with humility of mind let each of you regard one another as more important than himself. (Phil. 2:3)

July 14
A bad man is worse when he pretends to be a saint. —Bacon

The dictionary describes a hypocrite as a person given to hypocrisy and defines *hypocrisy* as "the act or practice of pretending to be what one is not; esp., false assumption of an appearance of virtue or religion." The Lord frowns on such behavior especially from those who name the name of Jesus, Christians. He made it clear in His Word when he spoke His woes to the scribes and the Pharisees.

Many people are turned off by people in the church who talk Christianity but do not walk the walk. I have always been amused at those who would let someone else keep them from worshipping if they themselves are walking as they should. I am sure you have heard the saying, "If you ever find the perfect church, don't join it because you will ruin it." There are no perfect people, and there are no perfect churches. Christians are only sinners saved by grace.

It is true that if we name the name of Jesus and call Him our Lord, if He lives in us and we represent Him, then we are to walk upright and not cause anyone to stumble. Evangelism is the churches basic mission, and we cannot be effective if we are not striving to live a godly life and seeking to be obedient to the One who has called us out of darkness and into His glorious light. Jesus said that it would be better that a millstone be tied around our neck and we be thrown into the sea than to cause someone else to sin (Luke 17:2). Jesus follows this by saying, "If your brother sins, rebuke him and if he repents, forgive him." By *brother* He means another Christian. In the church, we are to love one another enough to go to people we believe are sinning and help them to get back on the right path. We are also to be grateful to those who make us aware of things in our life that repel those who are seeking. Jesus warns us in Matthew 7 to "beware of the false prophets, who come to you in sheep's clothing, but inwardly are ravenous wolves" (v. 14).

Woe to you, scribes and Pharisees, hypocrites! For you are like whitewashed tombs which on the outside appear beautiful, but inside they are full of dead man's bones and all uncleanness. (Matt. 23:27)

July 15
Integrity is how you act when no one is looking.

I recently read a book by Gary Aldrich entitled *Unlimited Access*. Aldrich retired after being an FBI special agent for twenty years. He was assigned to the White House during the George Bush Sr. administration and retired after two years into the Clinton administration. It is appalling and saddening to read the information that Aldrich reveals about the Clintons. The character flaws that were so evident from top to bottom made the people of his office at the FBI cringe. They found "an apparent total disregard for honesty, integrity, or even cooperating with me, with the FBI," Aldrich wrote. It is very disturbing when we hear such things about anyone, but when it is regarding someone who holds the top position in a nation that was founded on Christian principles, whose behavior should be exemplary, whose conduct should be above reproach, it is heartbreaking.

It is disheartening to observe a person who has allowed the world to slip in and rob him or her of the traits that God deems important to our very nature. God has established moral and ethical absolutes that set us apart from the heathens. When we totally disregard these, we place ourselves in the position of a lower standard of living, which ultimately leads to destruction. God's Word is clear as He spoke through Moses when he said, "And be sure your sins will find you out" (Num. 32:23). There are no secret sins. God sees all, hears all, and knows all. He knows what we are thinking before we think it, and He knows our hearts. He expects us to be people of integrity. Our example is Jesus. God showed us the way to behave when He became a man, Jesus, and walked among us.

Whether we are in the White House or in a little shack in the woods, God expects from each of us the character of a person of integrity. Know His Word and you will know how to live.

Finally, brethren, whatever is true, whatever is honorable, whatever is right, whatever is pure, whatever is lovely, whatever is of good repute, if there is any excellence and if anything worthy of praise, let your mind dwell on these things. (Phil. 4:8)

July 16
You can take my life, but you will never take my freedom. –William Wallace

I can't think of many things worse than being imprisoned. The idea of not being able to come and go as I please or to make my own decisions and choices is unnerving. We have all seen the scene in a movie where someone is put in a jail cell and the door is slammed shut behind him or her. The jailer puts the key in the lock, turns it, and the person inside is confined to a small, desolate space for the duration of his or her sentence.

Mankind was made to be free. Paul teaches in Galatians that we "were called to freedom" (5:13). Christ came that we might be free from the legalistic burdens of the law (the Ten Commandments) that are impossible to keep. They are to never be cast aside but are to serve as a plumb line, a measuring rod for us to know how God expects us to live. Jesus fulfilled the law. The perfect sacrifice of God's Son on the cross, His shed blood for the remission of sin, made it possible for all humankind to receive the indwelling Holy Spirit. When we receive Him into our hearts, God writes on our hearts His laws. We obey because we are His and want to please and glorify our Father. That is freedom!

Many are in bondage, more than they ever were during the slave era. The world is so enslaved by sin that it is failing fast under the load. When we allow sin to enslave us, we are slaves to the one who is our master, Satan. We are then in bondage, locked down. But there is hope. Jesus holds the key. He will set you free if you call on him, repent, and turn from your sin. The primary reason Jesus came to earth was to destroy the works of the devil. We either underestimate or overestimate the power of Satan. Jesus came to unravel and break the chains that bind us because of sin. We first must recognize the enemy, whether it be Satan or our own selfish desires. Know who you are at war with, put on the armor of Christ, and stand firm against the enemy. Paul warns us to never "turn your freedom into an opportunity for the flesh" (v.13).

**If therefore the Son shall make you free, you
shall be free indeed. (John 8:36)**

July 17
You can be as close to the Lord when you feel nothing as when you're in the grip of spiritual passion. –James Dobson, Life On the Edge, p. 182

Do you ever have dry spells—times when, spiritually, you are in the desert with no oasis in sight? Do you pray and feel that your prayers are going nowhere, that you are just going through the motions? Maybe you feel like the psalmist when he said, "Out of the depths I have cried to Thee, O Lord. Lord, hear my voice! Let Thine ears be attentive to the voice of my supplication" (Ps. 130:1–2).

Think of Job and how he must have felt as he watched everything that He treasured slip away. Job had seven sons and three daughter and many possessions. He had many servants and was well known and respected in the east. Job was "a blameless and upright man, fearing God and turning away from evil" (Job 1:8). Satan asked God for permission to test Job, to see if he would still be faithful if everything was taken from him. God allowed it, and everything was taken from Job—his children, his livestock, all his possessions, his servants, everything. Job was surely in the desert. "Where are you God?" he must have cried out. However, "Through all of this Job did not sin nor did he blame God" (v. 22). To his wife he said, "Shall we indeed accept good from God and not accept adversity?"(2:10). Even though God allowed these trials to come on Job, he never doubted that God was with him and that He loved him. Job grieved and questioned why he was ever born, but he remained steadfast in his love for God.

God never moves. He is always there for us. We might move, falter, and fail, but He remains always faithful, always steadfast. Are you in the desert today? Are you in a dry and thirsty land? Draw close to the One who can comfort and sustain you through good times and bad times. Drink of the cool, living water and feel the warmth of His Spirit as He ministers to your soul. As you struggle out of the pit, He is your refuge and your oasis.

**My flesh and my heart may fail, but God is the strength
of my heart and my portion forever. (Ps. 73:26)**

July 18
Life's a hard game. Aren't we glad we don't have to play it alone?

God's grace is sufficient for all our needs. He always sustains us and watches over us. How do we know this, and how can we be sure? We can know and be sure because He tells us and assures us all throughout His Word that He will "never desert you nor will I ever forsake you" (Heb. 13:5). We can rest on that promise. Paul goes on to say, "The Lord is my helper, I will not be afraid. What shall man do to me?" (v. 6). There will be times in this life that we will be persecuted or ridiculed for what we believe or perhaps for the stand we take, but we, like Paul, can have the assurance that although "we are afflicted in every way, but not crushed; perplexed, but not despairing; persecuted, but not forsaken; struck down, but not destroyed" (2 Cor. 4:8), we can stand firm with confidence. To have no convictions is to fall for anything. To be milk toast in a society where people do not know what they believe only saturates you in the status quo.

Have you come up against any giants lately? They are out there. I seem to find myself in more situations than ever that cause me to have to call on God for direction and discernment. To have convictions and to stand by them is often very hard. Sadly, we make enemies of those who do not see things from a Christian perspective. God tells us not to compromise with the world but to "consider it all joy, my brethren, when you encounter various trials, knowing that the testing of your faith produces endurances." (James 1:2–3). Christians are to be the light and salt of the world. By standing firm in love without compromise, we might be able to win over those who have no conviction about anything.

God promises that when we "walk through the fire" He will be with us. What more assurance do we need?

**Blessed is the man who trusteth in the Lord,
and whose hope the Lord is. (Jer. 17:7)**

July 19
Everything that glitters is not gold.

Have you ever felt a little resentment in your heart toward someone who is living totally contrary to the way that God calls us to live and yet seems to prosper and have everything go so well? It can be a struggle in a Christian's life because there is a conflict between right and wrong. We sometimes want to believe that, because we are obeying the rules and living at the foot of the cross, we deserve a reward. But our reward is that He is with us always.

The story of the prodigal son in Luke 15:11–32 gives us a clear picture of one who thought that the world and its glitter held more bang for his buck than sticking around and waiting for his father to die to get his inheritance. The younger of two sons said to his father, "Father, give me the share of the estate that falls to me." The father divided his wealth between the two sons. The younger son went his way and "squandered his estate with loose living" (v. 13). As time passed, his stomach began to pinch from hunger and he ended up in the pigpen eating what the pigs were eating. "When he came to his senses" (v. 17), he immediately thought of his father and what he had left for this worldly life. Returning home, his father ran to meet him, hugged him, and kissed him. He apologized to his father and repented. His father told his servants to bring out the fatted calf, a robe, a ring for his son's finger, and sandals for his feet. They celebrated. The older son, on the other hand, was jealous for he had been faithful to stay with his father even though he too had gotten his inheritance. "The father gently said to him, 'My child, you have always been with me, and all that is mine is yours. But we had to be merry and rejoice, for this brother of yours was dead and has begun to live, and was lost and has been found'" (v. 31–32).

God has a good plan for our lives. However, many go for the glitter of the world and miss out on the blessings that have always been there for them. Never be jealous or resentful of those who are chasing the things of the world. When things look good on the outside, often there is a hurting soul who needs you to reach out to them.

Jesus said, "There will be more joy in heaven over one sinner who repents, than over ninety-nine righteous persons who need no repentance." (Luke 15:7)

July 20
The most pathetic person in the world is someone who has sight but no vision. –Helen Keller

When Helen Keller was stricken with a devastating disease at the age of nineteen months, it left her both blind and deaf. It was 1880 in Tuscumbia, Alabama. In 1887, at the age of six, she came to know a wonderful lady and teacher, Anne Mansfield Sullivan. Helen was a quick study; a gifted child in spite of her handicap; and in 1904, she graduated cum laude from Radcliffe College. Many from all over the world have benefitted from her work with the blind and deaf. Her determination and courage were passed along as she became a writer, a lecturer, and an inspiration to all who knew her and her story. Helen Keller was a blind person but had more vision than many who can see.

When you look around you, what do you see? Is it a community, a nation, a world that is reaching out, or do you see desperate people, visionless and going in circles? Before Anne Sullivan came into Helen's life, she was a "half-wild" child, very disruptive and unruly. Having very little knowledge of her surroundings because of her handicap, she was desperate.

How can each of us generate foresight and a supernatural stimulation for purpose and well-being into the life of another? How can our desire for happiness and Christianity for others be projected into a callous society where vision for such things is dim? Let us begin today to make a list of those in need of the reforming power of Jesus Christ in their lives. We must commit to pray for them daily and, when possible, share with them what Christ has given us. His transforming, powerful grace can flow through each of us to give vision and hope to a world that without Him has no hope. Like Helen Keller—who lacked physical vision and hearing, leaving her desperate—we too are desperate and visionless without the knowledge of the Savior, Jesus.

Where there is no vision, the people are unrestrained. (Prov. 29:18a)

July 21
Don't marry the person you think you can live with. Marry the one you can't live without. — James Dobson, Life on the Edge, p. 102

Marriage is a big step. God ordained marriage to be a sacred and holy institution. It is not just a marriage license or a "piece of paper" like some would like to believe. Marriage is a covenant, a promise, between a man and a woman and God. God's idea for marriage is one man for one woman for all time—that is, it should last for eternity.

When people enter marriage lightly or without much thought for the future or for the ones they are marrying, they set themselves up for a fall. God hates divorce and has established all the ground rules for a happy marriage in His Word. Mutual love and respect are foremost in laying the foundation for a lasting marriage. Cohabitation is far from God's plan. Not only is it sin with all indications of fornication, but statistics show that 75 percent of the marriages of people who have lived together in a relationship before they get married end in divorce compared to an already astounding statistic of 50 percent of all marriages ending in divorce of those who didn't live together before marriage.

Christ should be at the center of all marriages. Perhaps there have been people who have a happy marriage who do not know Christ, but it is rare. Just imagine those marriages being Christ-centered. They would be heavenly.

If we start out by building our marriages on the foundation of Jesus Christ, holding each stone together with the mortar of love and respect, the walls will never come tumbling down. A Christ-centered marriage is described in 1 Corinthians 13, where Paul lays out the excellence of love.

Love is patient, love is kind, and is not jealous; love does not brag and is not arrogant, does not act unbecomingly; it does not seek its own, is not provoked, does not take into account a wrong suffered, does not rejoice in unrighteousness, but rejoices with the truth; bears all things, believes all things, hopes all things, endures all things.

This is the God-ordained equation.

Love never fails. (1 Cor. 13:8)

July 22
Where there is no hope there can be no endeavor.
–Johnson, A Dictionary of Thoughts, p. 279

Hope makes us try harder. It tells us there is reasonable assurance that something can be done, whatever the talk, whatever the challenge. Hope is that glimmer of expectation that spurs us on when all evidence is contrary to that hoped for.

God's Word tells us that when we inherited the promises by faith in Christ Jesus, this hope we have is as an anchor of the soul, a hope both sure and steadfast (Heb. 6:19). Hope is missing something desired if it is void of Christ. In the Old Testament the prophets foretold the promise of the coming Messiah. The people looked forward to the hope of the One who would come to redeem them. We, on the other hand, look back on the cross in the New Testament and rejoice in the assurance of the hope that is ours if we put our faith in the One who has accomplished a living hope through Christ Jesus and His shed blood for all humankind. There is an old hymn, "The Solid Rock," that we can sing with confidence: "My hope is built on nothing less than Jesus' blood and righteousness." Hope in Christ is assurance. Hope without Christ is uncertainty.

Hope is steadfast and sure, overwhelming certainty if its foundation is the rock, Jesus Christ. One thing we can count on is that hope founded in Jesus does not disappoint. Why? "Because the love of God has been poured out within our hearts through the Holy Spirit who was given us" (Rom. 5:5).

Webster's dictionary states that an *endeavor* is "an effort made to do or get something; attempt; try." Stop today and praise the One who has made hope a positive for you and not a negative, the One who has taken the "effort," "attempt," and "try" out of it for you! We can inherit the promises of the Old Testament and the reality of the New Testament. Our only action verb is to *accept* it by faith!

For by grace you have been saved through faith; and that
not of yourselves, it is a gift of God. (Eph. 2:8)

July 23
We are never beneath hope, while above hell; nor above hope, while beneath heaven. – Shakespeare, Dictionary of Quotations, p. 278

Since our hope is in Christ Jesus, what about those who do not know Him as their personal Savior? Oh, what a challenge for us there. As long as there is a heaven and an earth, and as long as we have breath to tell, we need to witness to the hope that we have in Him. Peter stresses that we are to always be "ready to make a defense to everyone who asks you to give an account for the hope that is in you" (1 Peter 3:15). When humans take their last breath or the trumpet sounds the coming of the King of Kings, our time for choice making is up.

Joshua told the Israelite people that they needed to "choose today whom they will serve" (Joshua 24:15). They could worship idols and the things of the world, or they could choose to serve the one true God. They could not have it both ways. The same is true with us today. God is jealous for those He loves. He wants our whole heart.

As we choose for Christ, we live with the hope of glory and eternity with Him. When we choose against Him, we choose for the world with its hopelessness and despair. Such a choice leads to eternal separation from Holy God and the inevitable choice to spend eternity in hell. Hell is a real place just like heaven is a real place. In fact, the Bible talks more about hell than heaven. Jesus told the story in Luke 16 of a beggar and a rich man. The beggar lay at the gate of the rich man's house just hoping for some crumbs that might fall from the rich man's table. It happened that they both died. The beggar was taken to paradise by the angels, and the rich man went to Hades and was tormented. He cried out for mercy and for the beggar to dip his finger in water and cool his tongue because he was in agony in the flames. Then he cried out for someone to go and warn his five brothers about this place of torment called hell so they would not come. Jesus continued his story by saying, "If they do not listen to Moses and the prophets, neither will they be persuaded if someone rises from the dead" (v. 31). Don't delay!

For God hath not destined us for wrath, but for obtaining salvation through our Lord Jesus Christ, who died for us. (1 Thess. 5:9)

July 24
Saul looked at Goliath and said he was too big to hit. David looked at Goliath and said he was too big to miss.

I love the story of David and Goliath. What a mountain of courage for such a young boy! He moved with boldness toward the challenge that was before him. He was not asked to take on this huge giant of a man who had been taunting Saul and the men of Israel for days, but when he arrived at the camp and saw the situation that they were in, he stepped up to the plate. His first order of business was to identify the enemy—a wise approach in any circumstance.

David was a youth—a handsome, young shepherd boy. He was a skillful musician and a mighty man of valor. He didn't know much about battle, armor, and swords. His weapon of choice was a slingshot and a stone to fight off fierce lions and bears as he tended his father's sheep. But there was one thing David did know: he knew personally the living God. David said to Saul, "The Lord who delivered me from the paw of the lion and from the paw of the bear, He will deliver me from the hand of this Philistine" (1 Sam. 17:37). He never doubted from where his help would come. From the moment he heard the challenge that Goliath had been giving to Saul and his army for days, he never hesitated. David shouted out to the Philistine giant, Goliath, "You come to me with a sword, a spear, and a javelin, but I come to you in the name of the Lord of hosts, the God of the armies of Israel, whom you have taunted"(v. 45). With the simple weapon he knew how to use, the slingshot and a stone, he stepped out and in boldness prevailed.

Do you know where your help comes from? Saul was a king, and David was only a shepherd boy. Goliath was huge in stature, and David was only a child. Goliath was dressed in all his armor, while David wore his shepherd tunic. Goliath had Goliath, but David had God!

The Lord is my strength and my shield. My heart trusts in Him, and I am helped. (Ps. 28:7a)

July 25
When our little bit is combined with His greatness, the team is unbeatable. —James Dobson, Life on the Edge

"But he who boasts, let him boast in the Lord. For not he who commends himself is approved, but whom the Lord commends" (2 Cor. 10:17–18). Can we even conceive of the magnitude of being teamed up with God? That He would allow us to be on His team is an awesome thought. People struggle on their own to accomplish the simplest goals that they set for themselves, not realizing that God stands ready to lead, direct, guide, and keep us in all we do if we just call on Him. Many a person drudgingly moves through life, hoping to attain some worthwhile legacy yet never even considering God. All the while God is crying out, "Try Me! Trust Me! We can be an unbeatable team."

You may have heard the saying, "Little becomes much when you place it in the Master's hands." The story of Jesus feeding the five thousand people who had gathered around Him to be taught and healed is only one example of the magnitude of the miracles of our Lord. From just five loaves and two fish, Jesus fed the multitude of people, who stayed well into the evening. The disciples had said to Jesus that He should send the people home because it was getting late, but Jesus said, "They do not need to go away; you give them something to eat!" (Matt. 14:16).

After ordering the multitudes to recline on the grass, He took the five loaves and the two fish and looking up toward heaven, He blessed the food, and breaking the loaves He gave them to the disciples, and the disciples gave to the multitudes, and they ate and were satisfied. And they picked up what was left over of the broken pieces, twelve full baskets. (vv. 19–20)

Why do we hesitate? Why did the disciple hesitate? Oh, we of little faith! Jesus said it Himself in John 15:5 when He said, "I am the vine, you are the branches; he who abides in Me, and I in him, he bears much fruit; for apart from me you can do nothing." Are you a team player?

**Commit your works to the Lord, and your
plans will be established. (Prov. 16:3)**

July 26
Caring is sharing.

When we become Christians, it is our responsibility to tell someone else what Christ has done in our life. Good news is hard to keep under wraps, and the fact that we have been redeemed or deemed not guilty should put us on shouting ground.

Some people have the mistaken idea that the spread of the gospel is the responsibility of only ministers and missionaries. When Christ does a work of grace in us, we are called to take that message of salvation and saving grace to another lost soul. If we care, shouldn't we share? A personal testimony is so powerful, and a changed life is an outward sign of an inward miracle of the heart that only Jesus can do. As we preach by example in our daily walk, we can witness through our obedience and faithfulness. Whether it is tithing and giving to missionaries who can go where we cannot go or giving our time and talents to be used where we are needed as we serve in our churches, commitment to the kingdom is our calling.

As we are joint heirs with Jesus to the kingdom of heaven, we can be partners with Him to help fulfill His mission here on earth. When salvation comes to us as we die to ourselves and invite Jesus into our hearts, we are immediately indwelt by the Holy Spirit, who helps and equips us to live a victorious Christian life as sheep among the wolves. It is not easy in this world, but nothing that is good and lasting comes easy.

Don't hold back today! If you care about those around you who are going to hell without knowing the One who can rescue them, then make it a point today to share what Christ has done in you. We never need to try to talk someone into accepting Christ because someone else can come behind us and talk them out of it. Only the Holy Spirit can convict and lead them to Jesus. We just need to care enough to plant the seed. God will send others along to water and grow the seed to salvation.

**Come and hear, all who fear God, and I will tell of
what He has done for my soul. (Ps. 66:16)**

July 27
You can't out give God!

Just as we like to give good gifts to our children, so our heavenly Father likes to give good gifts to us, His children. His abundance is far greater than ours, for what we have is His already, yet He entrusts it to us for our own good pleasure.

God likes to see His children be willfully generous. He calls on us to take our tithe back to the storehouse (our church) and give our gifts over and above our tithe. If you have ever put this to the test, giving sacrificially, you have seen what God will do. He tells us in Malachi 3:10 that He will open the windows of heaven and shower us with blessings unmeasurable.

The story of the rich, young ruler is a sad one. This young man went to Jesus one day and asked Him what good thing he would need to do to obtain eternal life (Matt.19:16). Jesus told him that he must keep the commandments and went over them with him. The young man assured Jesus that he had done that but asked, "What am I still lacking?"(v. 20).

Jesus told him to go and sell his possessions and give to the poor, "and you shall have treasures in heaven; and come, follow me" (v. 21). These verses go on to tell us that the young man went away sorrowfully because he had much and he did not want to give it up to follow Jesus. He chose the world's riches over God's immeasurable abundance.

It is not our little bit or our abundant riches that God wants. It all belongs to Him anyway, and He can take it from us if He desires to do so. But He wants our obedience. We put our little tokens in the offering plate thinking that we have done something amazing for God. He owns the cattle on a thousand hills and the wealth in every mine, as the little chorus says. We can't out give God! If you never have seen God at His most generous, then do your part and watch Him do His!

Now He who supplies seed to the sower and bread for food, will supply and multiply your seed for sowing and increase the harvest of your righteousness; You will be enriched in everything for all liberality, which through us is producing thanksgiving to God.
(2 Cor. 9:10–11)

July 28
You can't teach your children to like spinach if every time they see you eating yours, you gag. –Ruth Graham

Setting a good example is the only true teacher. Words come easy and often sparsely, but a person's actions seldom lie. Jesus said, "For the mouth speaks out of that which fills the heart" (Matt. 12:34).

Sometimes it's hard to be a parent. Loving parents want only the best for their children. Sometimes, however, we find ourselves in a position of no return—do or die. We are placed in situations where our true character and integrity are challenged. In other words, our true colors come through. These are moments when we really need to stop, step back, and evaluate our reactions. No one else on earth influences our children like we do as parents. If a parent does it, in the child's mind, it's all right.

Prejudice, slander, hate, and immorality are all negative influences that affect our offspring. If we want them to taste the good things of life, then we must feed them a diet of integrity, good parenting, discipline, and truth from God's Word.

I had a good example of godly parenting. My mother and daddy set out from the beginning to give us a loving home where Jesus was always welcome. We were taken to church every time the doors were opened, it seems, and they didn't drop us off either; they were very involved in the activities of the church. I can remember when we had revival meetings morning and night. We would all go before school and then back again at night. Church was our second home, and God's people were our extended family. We loved it! The preacher and his family were invited to our house for homemade ice cream and pound cake some Sunday afternoons in the spring and summer, and that was a fun time.

My siblings and I talk about this a lot. We are all so thankful for parents who taught us to love God and love others and lived out that lifestyle before us. Always practice what you preach!

Hear, my son, your father's instruction, and do not forsake your mother's teaching. (Prov. 1:8)

July 29
Eventually we all get across the finish line. Winners just think of a better way to get there.

God is loving and powerful, but He is also holy and despises sin. God is merciful and patient, but He is also wrathful and has a limit to how long He will tolerate sin and disobedience.

If God never called us to repent and turn away from our sinful ways, we might never choose to obey Him. His purpose is that we live our lives in light of Him and His ways. You see, His provision for us is for the abundant life. He paid a big price in order that we might have forgiveness for sin and win the prize of abundant life here and eternal life with Him. His only Son's broken body and shed blood for the remission for our sins made it possible for us to cross the finish line. Paul states in Phil. 3:14, "I press on toward the goal for the prize of the upward call of God in Christ Jesus." God issues to each of us the "upward call" to follow Him. Satan's way leads us to destruction. Paul goes on to make the point even clearer. "For many walk, of whom I often told you, and now tell you even weeping, that they are enemies of the cross of Christ, whose end is destruction, whose god is their appetite, and whose glory is in their shame, who set their minds on earthly things" (vv. 18–19). Yes, we will all finish the race, but without Christ, we lose the race and end up in eternal hell.

This life will be over either way one day, but when we finish, when we breathe our last breath, God wants us to come home to live with Him for eternity. If we choose to reject Him and live in disobedience, heaven will not be our eternal home. Say no to the world and yes to heaven. Think of a better way, a winner's way. Jesus said, "I am the way, and the truth and the life; no one comes to the Father, but through Me" (John 14:6).

Test yourselves to see if you are in the faith; examine yourselves! Or do you not recognize this about yourselves, that Jesus Christ is in you—unless indeed you fail the test? (2 Cor. 13:5)

July 30
Seek correction from God before you seek direction from God.

God hates sin. He could not even look at His own Son on the cross as Jesus took upon Himself the sins of the whole world. Sin is an ugly sight. It destroys lives, homes, families, and nations. It shows its ugly head in the most beautiful places and disguises itself in the most cunning of ways. Sin delights in boasting of its prey and entices in the most seductive ways. Proverbs 6:16–19 lists some sins that God hates.

There are six things which the Lord hates,
Yes, seven which are an abomination to Him:
Haughty eyes, a lying tongue,
And hands that shed innocent blood,
A heart that devises wicked plans,
Feet that run rapidly to evil,
A false witness who utters lies,
And one who spreads strife among brothers.

Because Jesus paid our sin debt at the cross, we have freedom not to sin. When we come to Him, acknowledging Him as Savior and Lord, we are given the privilege and amazing grace that we do not deserve through the power of the Holy Spirit. Because of His mercy, He forgives our sins and remembers them no more. When He forgives us, His words to us are the same as the ones He spoke to the woman who was caught in adultery when he forgave her: "From now on sin no more" (John 8:11). People who continue in the same sin after God's mercy has been shown to them are lacking repentant hearts and have chosen to go against God's grace with a rebellious spirit. Paul said in Romans 1:18 that "the wrath of God is revealed from heaven against all ungodliness and unrighteousness of men, who suppress the truth in unrighteousness." The truth is, God loves us so much that He is happy to forgive us. But He expects us to do our part by turning away from sin and living in obedience to the truth of His Word. His divine correction is to point us in the right direction.

**Or do you think lightly of the riches of His kindness
and forbearance and patience, not knowing that the
kindness of God leads you to repentance? (Rom. 2:4)**

July 31
Genuine love is an expression of the deepest appreciation for another human being. –James Dobson, Life on the Edge

When you love someone, you want to please them. You seek out things that will bring joy to those you love. It is a natural outpouring of a heart that loves and appreciates another.

With love comes responsibility, commitment, and loyalty. Whether it is a marriage relationship, a family relationship, or a friendship, love carries with it an awesome responsibility to reach out in genuineness to show that love.

I am a touching person. It is hard for me to greet someone without reaching out to them with a hug, a kiss, a handshake, or a pat on the back. It is part of my heritage on both sides of my family, and I don't apologize for it. We are a big family on all sides and love one another very much. God expects us to show affection for one another. He strokes us every day with His loving-kindness and tender mercy. He hugs us with little winks that tell us that He is near. God is love and we know it!

I can't help but believe that when young Mary, who was pregnant with our Savior, went to visit her relative Elizabeth in the hill country, she did not give her a hug as she greeted her. The scriptures only tell us, "When Elizabeth heard Mary's greeting, the baby leaped in her womb; and Elizabeth was filled with the Holy Spirit" (Luke 1:41). Elizabeth, who was thought to be barren, was pregnant with the forerunner of Jesus, John the Baptist. These family friends came together to love and encourage each other as they had received the blessings of these promised ones from a loving God. Elizabeth's expression of appreciation for Mary's faithfulness to believe God's promise is evident in verse 45. Genuine love comes from the One whom Mary carried in her womb—the God of love, Jesus.

And walk in love, just as Christ also loved you, and gave Himself up for us, an offering and a sacrifice to God as a fragrant aroma. (Eph. 5:2)

August

How blessed are those who observe His testimonies,
who seek Him with all *their* heart. (Ps. 119:2)

August 1
Patience is bitter, but its fruit is sweet. –Rousseau

It is not always easy to wait. Whether it is waiting to eat, waiting for a bus, waiting for a special holiday like Christmas or a birthday, or waiting on God for an answer or direction, waiting is hard and tests our endurance or lack of it.

The dictionary explains that to be patient is to endure "without anger or complaint." *Wow!* Not only do we have to wait, but we have to be nice about it. How can we accomplish such a task as learning to be patient? Paul says in the book of Galatians that patience is one of the fruits of the Spirit. So the more we become like Jesus, the more patience we will see in our own lives.

Have you ever bitten into an orange in order to break through the skin enough to start peeling it? It is very bitter, isn't it? But once you get to the delicious sections of the fruit—oh my, how sweet it is! Why is patience so hard? Why does it make us so irritable to have to wait, and why do we complain when things don't happen when we want them to or when we think they should? Why do we lose our composure with others? Could it be that we haven't broken through the hard shell around our hearts and gotten to the sweetness of the Spirit?

Our heavenly Father is our example. He is so patient with us that it should make us ashamed. He endures abuse each time we show our immaturity. He calls us to forbearance and tolerance. A child's rage shows that he wants his way now. Rome was not built in a day, as the saying goes, and God is most assuredly on His own timetable, steadily "working all things according to His purpose" (Rom. 8:28). Thank goodness He is patient with us and His patience calls us to repentance.

Is your orange peeled yet? Are you enjoying the sweet fruit of patience? "You too be patient; strengthen your hearts, for the coming of the Lord is at hand" (James 5:8).

The Lord is not slow about His promise, as some count slowness, but is patient toward you, not wishing for any to perish but for all to come to repentance. (2 Peter 3:9)

August 2
Go to church. Don't wait for the hearse to take you.

When you die, what will happen to you? Where will you go from there? Well, how well have you planned for the future? Do the thoughts for your future include eternal life, life after death? If so, in what direction are you planning to go?

It is a foolish man or woman who does not plan ahead. However, many a person goes through life day in and day out with never a thought for tomorrow. It is sad but true. I have taken notice of the obituaries lately (we do that the older we get, you know), and I have seen many long write-ups that mention all the dead person's earthly accomplishments but never mention a church affiliation or any indication of a spiritual life. Death is no respecter of persons. How can we forget our Creator when the earth is filled with His glory? His Creation screams His majesty. How do some see it and others ignore the clearly obvious?

It's been that way since humans made the wrong choice in the Garden of Eden. God did not have it planned that way. God gave precise instructions to the first man and woman, who had enjoyed full access to all that was beautiful in this paradise. There was only one stipulation: "From the tree of the knowledge good and evil you shall not eat, for in the day that you eat from it you shall surely die" (Gen. 2:17). God is serious about obedience, and He always keeps His promises. If He says to do it this way, then He does not mean for us to do it *that* way, which usually means our way. Adam and Eve did not listen, and as a result, death and disobedience, sin, entered the world. God could have left it at that, but because He loves us so much, He gave us a way to escape the sting of death, Jesus. His foreshadowing, the hope of His coming, is seen right there from the beginning (3:15). He came, and He conquered!

Going to church does not make you a Christian, and neither does riding to the church in the hearse when you have breathed your last, but in this life it is at church that you hear the message of salvation and grow spiritually so that after accepting what Jesus accomplished for you on the cross, you can spend eternity with Him.

God has given us eternal life, and this life is in His Son. (1 John 5:11)

August 3
Anything that the mind of man can conceive and believe, he can achieve.

Even though to some this might sound like a health, wealth, and prosperity saying, it really is not. Our direction in this life is determined in many ways by what we set our minds on. That is why it is so important at the onset of this life to know Christ. The scriptures tell us, "Set your mind on things above, not on the things that are on earth" (Col. 3:2). God knows the future and wants the best for everyone, and He gives the best to those who trust Him with it. There are many roads that one can travel. Some lead to opportunity and prosperity, while others are pathways to destruction and failure.

We are blessed to live in a land that is so filled with opportunity. America affords many advantages and is a safe harbor for those seeking solitude and hope. People can accomplish their goals if they work to do so. Diamonds are rocks until they are chiseled and polished and all the facets of the prisms are cut. We are born into this world with individual personalities, abilities, and gifts. God created each of us in His image and for His own good pleasure. Even though we are His creation, He gave each of us a mind and free volition. We are not people that He controls like puppets on a string. He gives us the freedom to make our own choices.

With freedom to choose comes great responsibility. Especially as Christians, we are obligated to make good and godly choices. As we call on God to direct us in whatever we endeavor to accomplish, He will direct our paths and will protect and keep us moving in the right direction. "And your ears will hear a word behind you, 'This is the way, walk in it,' whenever you turn to the right or to the left" (Isa. 30:21).

Determine yourself today to first seek God and His righteousness, to second focus on noble goals, and to third go for it!

Therefore, gird your minds for action, keep sober in spirit, fix your hope completely on the grace to be brought to you at the revelation of Jesus Christ. (1 Peter 1:13)

August 4
Sow seeds of kindness. Reap a crop of friends.

One of the fruits of the Spirit is kindness. Paul wrote that those fruits that are evident in a Christian's life are indicative of the indwelling Holy Spirit.

We are naturally drawn to a person who is kind. Kind and gentle people radiate this trait through their actions and their countenances. It is a natural outpouring of a heart that cares for others, and kindness generates a spirit of love toward others. Who can ever deny the warmth of such a person. A kind deed, a kind word, a gentle answer, and a loving smile are all part of love that shows itself through kindness.

Where do we see the best example of such a person? Yes, Jesus. The Bible tells us that He went about doing good. His kind and gentle manner caused the little children to want to come to Him, and He encouraged them. Multitudes followed Him for His teaching but also for His compassion for them and His gracious spirit. I doubt that the twelve who dropped everything to follow Jesus would have done so for a cruel or merciless person. No, you know yourself if you have asked Him to come into your heart that His presence in you gives you peace and a desire to reach out to others with love and kindness. Peter reminds us that when we come to Christ, we can put aside our old ways "if you have tasted the kindness of the Lord" (1 Peter 2:3). With His help, we can live out the fruit of the Spirit in our lives.

Are you scattering seeds of kindness that will reap an abundant harvest? Paul said, "If we live by the Spirit, let us also walk by the Spirit" (Gal. 5:25). If we see people as Jesus sees them, then being kind to our fellow humans should come naturally and we will reap an abundant crop of friends. They will be blessed, and we will be blessed!

Be ye kind one to another, tenderhearted, forgiving one another, even as God through Christ hath forgiven you. (Eph. 4:32 KJV)

August 5
Don't stay away from church because there are so many hypocrites. There's always room for one more. —A.R. Adams

It frightens me to see in my lifetime the invasion of sin and hypocrisy that exists in our churches. We can often look around our own congregations and see people who are blatantly living in sin yet occupying a pew on Sunday morning as if their walk is straight and upright. Thank goodness the churches are for sinners as well as saints.

God calls those who name the name of Jesus to be holy as He is holy. When the church begins to look and act like the world, then what difference is there? Christians are called to be different, and with Christ's Spirit living in us, that should not be a difficult task. Christianity should not be a chameleon-type existence in which we change our convictions like the chameleon changes its colors. Our walk should be such that we reflect Christ outside the church as well as inside. Then our churches will remain holy and without stain.

It is a known fact that all of us sin. The scriptures are clear about that. And if we know our own hearts, we know that apart from Jesus there is no good in us. Romans 3:23 tells us, "For all have sinned and fall short of the glory of God." But when we look over a few chapters, we can see that God made a way for us to repent and turn away from our sin and be forgiven. "But God demonstrates His own love toward us, in that while we were yet sinners, Christ died for us."(5:8). By God's grace, with His taking our sin debt, those who have named the name of Jesus, Christians, can go to Him and ask for forgiveness for their sins. True repentance for our sin does not mean that we continue in sin, acting like they don't exist. The Holy Spirit convicts us of sin if we belong to Christ. True repentance is being sorry for your sins, turning away from them, and going in the opposite direction.

When God's grace is abused, that is like spitting in the face of God. He paid a huge price for our sin by dying a horrific death on a cruel cross. A hypocrite is one who lives a lie with no peace in his or her life.

You are from God, little children, and have overcome them; because greater is He who is in you than he who is in the world. (1 John 4:4)

August 6
Waste of time is the most extravagant and costly of all expenses. –Theophrastus

The older a person gets, the more precious time becomes. Moments, days, months, and years fly by, and we begin to see the reality of life as being like the blink of the eye. Time wasted is eternity wasted. God's Word teaches us that if we trust Him in this life, we will fade into eternity when we take our last breath on the earth. What a wonderful promise! That is why it is important for us to use our time on the earth wisely and always make choices that glorify God and point others to Him. Dr. Seuss said, "Sometimes you will never know the value of a moment until it becomes a memory."

To waste time is foolishness because it can never be restored. When a moment is gone, it is gone forever and we are one step closer to eternity. Paul longed for the time that he would be "absent from the body and present with the Lord" (1 Cor. 5:8). I can see this myself the older I get. If we live long enough, we find that we have more loved ones living in heaven than on earth, and we long for that reunion. I saw a plaque that read, "Dear God, thank you for this beautiful life and forgive me if I don't love it enough." God wants us to love our lives, but He cautions us not to love it so much that we try to hang onto it and fail to plan for eternity. Eternity is a long time, and we will spend it somewhere. Jesus comforted his disciples with these words: "For I go to prepare a place for you. And if I go and prepare a place for you, I will come again, and receive you to Myself; that where I am, there you may be also" (John 14:2–3). Heaven is prepared for those who trust Jesus as Savior and Lord.

Use your time wisely today. Invest your time in what is real and lasting. Paul warns us in Ephesians not to be foolish, "but understand what the will of the Lord is" (5:17).

Therefore be careful how you walk, not as unwise men, but as wise, making the most of your time. (Eph. 5:15–16)

August 7
Every man's life is a plan of God. —Horace Bushnell

For I know the plans I have
for you, says the Lord.
They are plans for good and
not for evil, to give you a
future and a hope. (Jer. 29:11)

God desires no evil thing to come into our lives. However, because of the sin and disobedience of Adam and Eve in the beginning, when they chose to listen to Satan rather than God, God's perfect world became imperfect. With the evil one came tragedy, suffering, disease, hurt, and hardship. The fruit from the Tree of the Knowledge of Good and Evil, which God told them not to eat, opened the eyes of humankind to make their own choices, good or evil.

Because Adam and Eve chose to reject God's perfect plan, we as sons and daughters must endure despair and disappointment and the enemy known as death. But fear not! God has overcome the world. At the cross, Satan was defeated, and through faith in Jesus we can claim our new hope. Hope is Jesus, our strength and comfort in the midst of the storms of life. Hope is Jesus, redemption and salvation. Hope is Jesus, eternal life with our Creator.

You see, even back in the Old Testament book of Jeremiah, when God spoke these words to the prophet, God gave us a foreshadowing of the coming Savior who would give us a future and a hope. God's plans are perfect and always come to fruition. Our God is omnipotent, all powerful. Our God is omnipresent; He is everywhere. And our God is omniscient; He has infinite knowledge.

Do you doubt that He can carry out the plans that He has for your life, a plan for good and not for evil? Trust Him today to guide your steps and lead you in the direction that you need to go. "Is there any God besides Me, or is there any other Rock?" (Isa. 44:8).

**What we suffer now is nothing compared to the
glory he will give us later. (Rom. 8:18)**

August 8
God help the man who won't marry until he finds a perfect woman, and God help him still more if he finds her. —Ben Tillett

I suppose everyone who sets out to get married and walks down the aisle of matrimony feels that he or she has all the answers to a happy and fulfilling life. We have all had the thought—surely anyone in love "as much as we are" can make it through any obstacle that might be thrown in our path. Reality sets in real early. Much responsibility and accountability is required here. There must be give and take, and it all must be done in love and with patience. There is your way and there is my way, and again it must be resolved lovingly. Then one day when things settle a bit, the honeymoon is over, and one or maybe both say, "What have I gotten myself into?"

Marriage is not easy at its best. God never said it would be. But marriage is not just a piece of paper called a marriage license. Marriage is a covenant between a man and a woman and God. A covenant is a promise, an agreement, and is not to be entered into lightly. "What God has joined together, let no man put asunder" (Matt. 19:6). Those words are part of the traditional marriage vows, and God will do His part to protect and honor this agreement. It is up to the couple to hold up their end of the bargain. Anything worth having is worth working for. A good marriage and a loving home for your children are worth anything you have to do to make them good and godly.

God's heart must grieve when He sees the young people and many old people today who are living together outside of marriage. There seems to be no shame as they justify this lifestyle in their own minds. Divorce is rampant, and adultery seems to be a way of life for many.

No one comes into marriage perfect, nor will we die in our marriages perfect, but God expect us to keep our promise to Him and to the ones we have vowed to love till death do us part. After we tie that knot, we must work through those ups and downs, pulling that knot tighter and tighter.

Let marriage be held in honor among all. (Heb. 13:4)

August 9
The reward of a thing well done, is to have done it. –Emerson

I have always enjoyed little projects like sewing and painting and refinishing furniture because the satisfaction of a job well done is immediately evident and rewarding. Accomplishments are gratifying to most people, and they spur us on to bigger and better things. As we tackle the more significant projects, the payment is the same. It is the finished product, the completed task, that rewards us.

To successfully achieve a goal, whether great or small, we must first set out to do it. An airplane will never fly if its starter is never ignited. A computer must be turned on before it can ever give out one bit of information. We can't accomplish a thing until we get motivated to get started.

What motivates you? What gets you moving? What causes you to put your talents to work? We all have talents. God blessed some with more than others, but we all have areas that we excel in, and when we operate in those talents, we feel a sense of completeness.

Jesus tells a story in the book of Matthew 25 about talents. There was a man who was going on a trip, and he called his servants to him. They each had different abilities, so he gave them each talents according to their abilities. To one he gave five talents, to another two talents, and to the third he gave one talent. Immediately the one with five talents doubled his. The one with two talents gained two more. But the servant with one talent went out and buried his talent in the ground. When the master came home from his journey, he "settled accounts with them" (v. 19). He was so proud of the two who had doubled their talents and said, "Well done, good and faithful servants; you were faithful over a few things, I will put you in charge of many things" (v. 21). Sadly, the servant who had buried his talent ended up with nothing. He was called wicked and lazy. Then the master took his talent and gave it to the one with ten.

Jesus expects us to use the gifts that He gives us and be good stewards of them to not only bless our own lives but to bless others.

It is required of stewards that one be found trustworthy. (1 Cor. 4:2)

August 10
Turn your dreams into facts. It's up to you.

The games have begun! Yes, 'tis the season for the summer Olympics and for athletes from all over the world to come together to compete against one another for prizes. Will their hopes and dreams and years of hard work pay off in the days ahead as they give their all to accomplish that for which they have trained? There will be many victories, and there will be many heartaches from defeat.

When Atlanta hosted the Olympics several years ago, the theme of the games was "Go for the Gold," and it rang out all over the world. To play on that theme, the Southern Baptist Convention chose the theme "Go for the Goal" for Vacation Bible School and other outreach programs. Each statement expresses a positive challenge to give your best efforts to what you are striving to accomplish.

Just as an athlete works and trains for years for Olympic competition to win that coveted gold medal, so should the Christian work diligently to reach the lost world for Christ. Christians are to pray and prepare, plan and practice to witness to and win the lost. We must "run with endurance the race that is set before us, fixing our eyes on Jesus, the author and perfecter of faith, who for the joy set before Him endured the cross, despising the shame, and has sat down at the right hand of the throne of God" (Heb. 12:1b–2). What is so exciting is that we are in a win-win situation. We like Paul can boast that we "can do all things through Christ who strengthens me." Christians are not alone in our effort to win. If we have chosen for Christ, we have already won. God just calls us to live victorious because the victory is ours in Christ Jesus. He carries us across the finish line, and we can rejoice in what he has already done for us at the cross.

Dreams are just dreams until they become facts. Your dream of eternal life is a fact if you put your trust in the One who has made it possible. Trade your earthly medals for heavenly ones. It is up to you!

I press on toward the goal for the prize of the upward call of God in Christ Jesus. Philippians 3:14

August 11
I pray because the need flows out of me all the time, waking and sleeping. It doesn't change God, it changes me. –C. S. Lewis

Prayer—what does it mean to you? God loves His time with each of us. I have always loved it when I can spend one on one time with my children. It just seems like I can get to know their hearts a little better. Those heart-to-heart talks seem to be like glue that bonds us to one another. God desires that from His children as well. Even though He knows our hearts already, it is still His joy when we come to Him open and vulnerable, laying our needs as well as our praises before Him.

Paul's message to us in Colossians 4:2 is to "devote yourselves to prayer, keeping alert in it with an attitude of thanksgiving." Why does God want us to devote ourselves to prayer and to stay alert? Because He knows that we are weak and prone to sin. There is an adversary, the devil, who is prowling around seeking whom he can destroy. If we stay close to the One who gives us the power to combat the fiery darts of the evil one, then we can keep our guard up and our armor in check. Galatians 5:16 reminds us that if we walk by the Spirit, we will not carry out the desire of the flesh. Prayer keeps us in touch with our Creator, grounded and protected.

The cross of Jesus Christ made possible so many blessings for the one who chooses to believe. One of the greatest blessings is that as He "yielded up His spirit.… Behold the veil of the temple was torn in two from top to bottom" (Matt. 50b–51a). That one amazing act gave us direct access to the Father whereby we can pray to Him without a mediator. Imagine such a thing, that even in death, He was thinking of fellowship with us! As the disciples asked Him to teach them how to pray, He gave them the model prayer that we often pray along with our own petitions to Him. We know it as the Lord's Prayer (Matt. 6:9–13).

Don't neglect this wonderful privilege of prayer. God wants to hear from you today. God never changes. He is the same yesterday, today, and forever. But you will be changed if you spend time with Him!

Pray without ceasing. (1 Thess. 5:17)

August 12
God knows us completely and loves us anyway.

God's love for the Israelite people goes far beyond the imaginable. Their disobedience led to much discipline and punishment at the hand of God throughout the Old Testament. They are God's chosen people, and yet many of them still to this day choose not to acknowledge Jesus as the Messiah sent by God. Even though they know the Old Testament prophesy sent to them by God through the prophets—that Jesus would come as He did—they choose to ignore it. Thankfully, many Jews have seen the light and have come to Christ, but many refuse and reject salvation through Jesus, the new covenant (Jer. 31:31–34). Hopefully, they will come before it is too late.

The Jews are not the only ones who decline to accept the miracle of the new birth. We are born again to a new life in Christ when we die to ourselves and are raised to walk in the newness of life with Him. Baptism by immersion is a beautiful picture of that. You may say, *How do I die to myself?* You admit that you are a sinner (Rom. 3:23), "you confess with your mouth Jesus as Lord, and believe in your heart that God raised Him from the dead, you shall be saved" (Rom. 10:9). Salvation is by faith in the One who died for your sins. He was the perfect sacrifice that was needed in order for us to be redeemed. At salvation, our old lives are crucified so that Christ can live in us in the form of the Holy Spirit.

Through the new covenant, Jesus showed His amazing love for us. In the old covenant, God wrote the laws on stone, the Ten Commandments. In the new covenant, He writes the laws on our hearts when we come to Him for salvation. Our new hearts want to please Him. Praise God that He saved the apostle Paul to bring this beautiful promise to the Gentiles and we were grafted into the promise of redemption (Rom. 11).

Yes, He knows us very well. He is a loving God, but He is also a just God. He punishes and disciplines us in order to keep us on the straight and narrow path. Like a loving and wise parent, He provides direction and desires that we stay close to Him through prayer, Bible study, and church attendance. He knows your name. You are His chosen possession.

I am the good Shepherd; and I know My own,
and My own know Me. (John 10:14)

August 13

Little drops of water, little grains of sand, make the mighty ocean and the pleasant land; so the little minutes, humble though they be, make the mighty ages of eternity.
–Julia A. Fletcher Carney

"There is an appointed time for everything. And there is a time for every event under heaven.... He has made everything appropriate in its time. He has also set eternity in their heart, yet so that man will not find out the work which God has done from the beginning even to the end" (Eccles. 3:1, 11).

Time—where does it go? Wherever it is, we will never see it again once it has passed by. But that is okay. We need to move forward and not backward. Ecclesiastes also tells us that people do not know their time (9:12). The Bible instructs us that it is appointed unto humans once to die and then the judgment comes. Such facts make it even more imperative to guard our time wisely.

God has allotted to each of us a portion of life called time. Each second is precious. God expects us to be good stewards of our time on this earth and use each moment to our best advantage, always seeking to glorify Him and advance His kingdom on this earth. This life passes very quickly at its best. Is eternity secure for you? Does your vision for life and eternity include Christ?

God spoke through His prophet Hosea to the people of Israel, begging them not to waste time but to come back to Him. "Sow with a view to righteousness, reap in accordance with kindness; break up your fallow ground, for it is time to seek the Lord until He comes to rain righteousness on you. You have plowed wickedness, you have reaped injustice, you have eaten the fruit of lies, because you have trusted in your way" (Hosea 10:12–13). There is no time to waste. Are you trusting in your way or His way? Is eternity for you in sight, or is it in the far distance? You can't know. But one thing is clear: you need to spend your time wisely so that you can spend eternity with the One who loves you.

**I know that there is nothing better for them than to rejoice
and to do good in one's lifetime. (Eccles. 3:12)**

August 14
Little becomes much when placed in the Master's hand.

Our simplest efforts become great accomplishments when God is in them. It is that choice to let Him have control that makes the difference. How do we let go and let God? How do we trust when we cannot see? God assured Israel that He would always be there to help. "Thus says the Lord who made you and formed you from the womb, who will help you, do not fear" (Isa. 44:2). All through His Word He assures those who trust in Him that He will never leave them or forsake them. God never gives us a task to do for which He does not go before us to prepare the way.

In trusting we prove our faith. In believing that God will do what he says He will do, we trust and step out in faith. Abraham, Isaac, Jacob, Noah, and Mary, the mother of Jesus, all believed that God would do what He said He would. Many more throughout the Bible trusted what they could not see, just as many who have lived since the Bible was written have done. God takes our crumbs and makes loaves of bread. He takes our brokenness and causes good to come from it. He is glorified when we depend on Him, when we surrender our all to Him and let Him lead. Scripture tells us that it is impossible to please Him without faith (Heb. 11:6). Don't we want to please God? Yet how many times are we reluctant to trust Him? This same scripture tells us that "he who comes to God must believe that He is, and that He is a rewarder of those who seek Him." The psalmist states over and over, "How blessed is the man who trusts in Thee!"

The Lord of Hosts will never lead us down a path alone if we are His children. He walks beside us and many times carries us, continuously blessing and always growing us that we might be more like Him. Place your smallest and largest gifts, challenges, and efforts in His hands today and see what happens!

Many, O Lord my God, are the wonders which Thou hast done, and Thy thoughts toward us; There is none to compare with Thee; If I would declare and speak of them they would be too numerous to count. (Ps. 40:5)

August 15
People are lonely because they build walls
instead of bridges. –Joseph Fort Newton

I used to think loneliness came as a result of separation from those you love or from solitude—being alone or by yourself. However, loneliness can be felt in a room filled with people or during happy, fun-filled times. You don't have to be isolated to feel desperately alone.

Suicide among our young people is rampant. What can cause such a desperate act to take place in a society filled with so many people and so much going on around us? The desire to intentionally harm oneself defies all logic to those who seek to hang onto life as long as possible. If you have never suffered from depression and despair or a drug or alcohol addiction, it is harder to sympathize with those in this struggle. Many soldiers come home from war with the burden of posttraumatic stress syndrome, their memories haunted with visions of violence and death. For many other people, a chemical imbalance in the brain impairs their ability to cope. Whatever the cause, it is real to the people suffering through this horrible nightmare.

Loneliness among our older people is also a problem to be reckoned with. Many senior adults spend numerous lonely hours in their homes, in a nursing home, or even in a crowd, feeling isolated from the world around them. Many have lost their independence and ability to function as they once could.

Needless to say, we have a mission field all around us. Showing God's love to those around us is what God calls us to do. It has been said, "God loves us more in a moment than any one person could love us in a lifetime." Hurting people all need to know that love and be comforted by it. We can help them build bridges in order to free themselves from the walls that they so often erect in self-defense. Somebody once said that our weakness is a vessel for His power and our flaws a canvas for His grace. Let us today be on the alert as we seek out the lonely and the hurting.

**Come to me, all who are weary and heavy-laden
and I will give you rest. (Matt. 12:28)**

August 16
Beauty is only skin deep.

I can hear my mother say it right now. She would never let us get prideful or think more highly of ourselves than we ought to. What a gift to have a mother like that. We always knew that we were special to her and to Daddy, but we were not made to think that the world owed us something or that it revolved around us.

A prideful heart is a wretched condition. The Lord said, "The heart is deceitful above all things, and desperately wicked: who can know it?" (Jer. 17:9). We would like to believe that all humankind is good and noble and that our intentions are always honest and forthright. However, since the Garden of Eden, humans' choice has been to sin rather than stay perfect. Ugliness entered into the world in spite of a perfect environment just as God said it would if disobedience was the choice. And it was. The rebellion of humankind was with us long before the apostle Paul reminded us that "all have sinned, and fall short of the glory of God" (Rom. 3:23).

Beauty comes to each of us only when God's righteousness enters into our hearts. The outward appearance is but a facade. We can possess beauty beyond measure and yet be wretched, deceitful, and immoral. The indwelling Holy Spirit makes the difference—Christ in us, our hope of glory! As we look at Abraham and his nephew, Lot, in the book of Genesis, we see that they both had prospered and their herdsmen were squabbling among themselves. Abraham made the decision that it was time for them to separate and go in different directions. Abraham gave first choice of the land to Lot. Lot looked over toward the valley of the Jordan, and his eye saw only the beauty of the green grass as "it was well watered everywhere" (v. 10). Lot surely knew of the wickedness of the two cities there, Sodom and Gomorrah, but his eyes only saw the facade, the outward appearance. Only Lot and his two daughters survived as God eventually destroyed these two immoral cities and Lot's wife turned to a pillar of salt. God, let us always live in the beauty of your holiness.

Charm is deceitful and beauty is vain, but a woman who fears the Lord, she shall be praised. (Prov. 31:30)

August 17
Earth hath no sorrow that heaven cannot heal. —Moore

God's grace is sufficient for all our needs, and nothing touches humankind for which God has not made provision. God knows our every hurt and heartache. The same Christ who makes provision for all things that are good and abundant in our lives is also adequate in times of sorrow and suffering. In the book of 2 Kings, we see King Hezekiah gravely ill. The Lord sent His prophet Isaiah to tell him to "get his house in order, for you shall die and not live" (2 Kings 20:1). Distraught, he cried out to the Lord, weeping bitterly. God sent Isaiah back to Hezekiah with a message: "I have heard your prayer, I have seen your tears; behold I will heal you" (2 Kings 20:5). Nothing escapes God. Did you know that He catches your tears in a bottle? (Ps. 56:8). He hears your cries and comforts you in times of need.

My dear friend has just passed through a devastating period of suffering and heartache as she found her granddaughter after she had died from suicide. Such pain can be unbearable unless we walk through it in the arms of Jehovah-Shalom, our God of peace. "The Lord is near to the brokenhearted, and saves those who are crushed in spirit. Many are the afflictions of the righteous; but the Lord delivers him out of them all" (Ps. 34:19). What reassurance from Jehovah God who loves His own beyond measure and sustains us in times like this. That does not mean that the days ahead will not be filled with moments of tears and much sorrow for my friend, but the comfort of Holy God along with family and friends will help to make the days ahead bearable.

Someone once said, "Never doubt in the dark what God has shown you in the light." He has shown His faithfulness to all generations. So whatever you are suffering through and whatever the source of your suffering, our God can refresh your spirit and give you peace.

Thou hast turned for me my mourning into dancing; Thou hast loosed my sackcloth and girded me with gladness; that my soul may sing praise to Thee, and not be silent. O Lord my God, I will give thanks to Thee forever. (Ps. 30:11–12)

August 18
One makes a living by what he gets; he makes a life by what he gives.

Making a living is essential in a lifetime on this earth. Our bodies require food, and clothing is a desired and necessary commodity. The accumulation of earthly treasure is a priority for many people; however, Jesus said that it is the treasures that we build up in heaven that are lasting. What does He mean? He means the things we give away, the love and compassion we give to others, giving of our means to the poor, being humble and showing a servant's heart in our actions, living in peace with our fellow humans, and giving generously while expecting nothing in return.

Giving back to God through His church should be first on our list. To tithe is not a suggestion from God but a command if we truly want to be obedient to Him. By our obedience we are blessed and our churches are equipped to serve. There is no way that we can outgive God. He tells us to test Him in this and see "if I will not open for you the windows of heaven, and pour out for you a blessing until it overflows" (Mal. 3:10). Our heavenly Father wants to bless us, and this is just another way that He can do it. Because He commands us to tithe, we are robbing God when we don't (v. 8).

These are the things that are lasting. All the toys that we accumulate on this earth will rust away. Moths, insects, and rodents will eat away at all the rest eventually, or they will just waste away. But the things we give away in Jesus's name come back to us multiplied.

The greatest treasure we can give is the knowledge of Jesus Christ. I believe that this would be a good day for you to share your testimony with someone. You will never know what a blessing you can be to someone until you step out in faith. The blessing will be yours!

Give, and it will be given to you; good measure, pressed down shaken together, running over, they will pour into your lap. For by your standard of measure it will be measured to you in return. (Luke 6:38)

August 19
Late repentance is seldom true, but true repentance is never too late. –R. Venning

What we are seeing more and more of in our society today is sin without remorse. There seems to be no shame or regret accompanying much sin and, therefore, no repentance. The idea seems to be to convince oneself that sin is not sin, and then it will cease to be sin. Whoa! Can we do that? Of course not. Even people with the most hardened of hearts know when they sin. In the book of Romans, Paul talks to us about the two natures and the conflict that occurs as we try to live as we should on our own: "For the good that I wish, I do not do; but I practice the very evil that I do not wish" (v.19). When we try to live this life by the strength of our own flesh, we will fall short every time. Like Paul we must realize that "the law of the Spirit of life in Christ Jesus has set you free from the law of sin and death" (v.2).

Following a morning church service a while back, a young man who was visiting our service approached me. He put his arm around my shoulder, looked right into my face, called my name, and very warmly said, "How are you?" I was stunned and openly surprised. He was a young man, and years before, I had sung in his wedding. It was no secret in the community that, even though he was married, he was living at this time with a young woman who was not his wife. Would you not think that a person so openly living in sin would hide himself from anyone who knew him? Not so. He sought me out. He obviously had convinced himself that it was all right if that was what he wanted. Maybe he came to church that day to seek out someone who would confront him with truth, and I missed the opportunity. I will never know.

It jolts and jars us as Christians when those who profess to be Christians behave in such a manner. We know that "all have sinned and fall short of the glory of God" (Rom. 3:23), but if we are children of God, His Holy Spirit convicts us of sin immediately and calls us to repentance. Without repentance there is no remission of sin.

How blessed is he whose transgression is forgiven,
whose sin is covered! (Ps. 32:1)

August 20
He prayeth best who loveth best. —Coleridge

A heart filled with love is a heart true and transparent. One easily sees and knows the depth and genuineness of such a heart and such a love. When we come into His presence, God requires a clean heart, free of sin, repentant, and forgiven. For that kind of cleaning up, we have to go to Him, "for God is greater than our heart, and knows all things" (1 John 3:20). We need only to come to the throne of Christ with such a heart if we desire His faithful response to our prayers. "Beloved, if our heart does not condemn us, we have confidence before God; and whatever we ask we receive from Him, because we keep His commandments and do the things that are pleasing in His sight" (vv. 21–22). Christ loves a heart that is truly His. He loves a heart that beats with gratefulness for His provision and grace.

When Christ died for us, He didn't expect us to take it lightly. When the sins of the world were placed on Him, who was without sin, He didn't expect us to reject such a love as that. It grieves Him and renders invalid, for those who turn their backs on such a gift, the very sacrifice He made for the sins of all humankind. The repentant heart is the one God hears. We need to take with all seriousness and thankfulness His heart of love that made it possible for sinful people to have pure and sincere hearts of love. Then we can approach His throne of grace in prayer with thanksgiving and with our petitions.

Do you have a special place that you go to in order to meet God each day? We must take our prayer lives seriously. They are not only a privilege but a defense against the schemes of the devil. "Put on the full armor of God, that you may be able to stand firm against the schemes of the devil" (Eph. 6:11). When we love God, we want to spend time with Him. Loving God more helps us love others more.

Who may ascend into the hill of the Lord? And who may stand in His holy place? He who has clean hands and a pure heart. (Ps. 24:3–4)

August 21
Human life is a constant want, and ought to be a constant prayer. —S. Osgood

I have heard it said, "If you can't enjoy what you have, how can you be happier with more?" God must get really amused at us. Our hands are always outstretched as we say, "Gimme" instead of stretched upward as we say, "Use me."

It seems more and more that we hear of people church-hopping. They grumble and complain about a church not meeting their needs or not having this program or that program. Many find fault with the pastor, or with some it is the music. With others it might be a staff member or a person with whom they don't agree. Perhaps they disagree with a decision that was made. Whatever the reason or choice to leave their church, it could not be relevant enough to pull out and move on. Your church family should be your second family. We should love and sustain one another in times of need, always growing in grace and the knowledge of Jesus Christ. The church is the bride of Christ, and He is displeased and saddened when His bride is not functioning as it should. He has called us to work together in order to exalt His kingdom. Selfishness sometimes gets in the way, and we forget what the purpose of gathering as a body of believers is. If our own wants are our only focus, then we have missed Christ's purpose for His church.

Let us today commit to be what God has called us to be as we go forth into the world from our churches. Jesus has called us to be salt and light in the world. Salt adds flavor and also preserves. Light dispels darkness, and as light shines forth, His purpose can be seen more clearly.

As Christ's ambassadors, let us preserve the flavor of knowing the One who gives life and shine out like beacons in order that the hope of our risen Savior might light up this world.

Ask God today not what He can do for you but what you can do for Him!

Create in me a clean heart, Oh God and renew a right spirit within me. (Ps. 51:10 KJV)

August 22
Heaven is never deaf but when man's heart is dumb. —Quarles

God says that He will open the windows of heaven for us if we will but ask Him (Mal. 3:10) Not only will He open the windows, but He will pour out blessings like we have never seen. When we cry out to God with a pure heart, He never turns a deaf ear on our prayers. When we whisper a prayer, His ears are just as attuned to our weak and feeble prayers as they are to our most heartfelt and agonizing petitions.

There are, however, hindrances to our prayers. God does not hear the prayers of an unbeliever, except the prayer of repentance for salvation, nor does he hear the prayers of a believer who is practicing sin without repentance. John recalls what the blind man who was healed by Jesus said to the Pharisees as they reviled him for following Jesus. The man said to them, "We know that God does not hear sinners; but if anyone is God-fearing, and does His will, He hears him" (John 9:31).

Why would any of us not want to have open communication with the God of the universe? He has made it so simple and effortless on our part. When the curtain in the temple that allowed only the priest to go into the Holy of Holies was torn from top to bottom after the crucifixion, we were given complete access to the presence of Holy God. God paid a big price to give us that privilege. Jesus became the redemption for sin, past and present. That divide was abolished by Jesus's death and sacrifice. Hebrew 10:19–22 talks about "a new and living way."

Since therefore, brethren, we have confidence to enter the holy place by the blood of Jesus, by a new and living way which He inaugurated for us through the veil, that is, His flesh, and since we have a great priest over the house of God, let us draw near with a sincere heart in full assurance of faith, having our hearts sprinkled clean from an evil conscience and our bodies washed with pure water.

Don't be dumb when it comes to prayer! God wants to hear from those who have a surrendered heart.

And this is the confidence which we have before Him, that, if we ask anything according to His will, He hears us. (1 John 5:14)

August 23
An investment in knowledge always pays the best interest. —Benjamin Franklin

We invest in a lot of different things in our lifetimes. As young people, many of us leave home after finishing high school, with plans to invest in a college education. When the time is right and the right person comes along, we may invest in a life partner through marriage. Then the little ones might come along, and as parents we invest a lot of time and effort into the lives of our children. Many husbands and wives invest years into their careers in order to make a good living for their families. With that comes an investment in homes, cars, furniture, and things in general. This is a natural process and one that God ordained when He gave us life.

Many have knowledge of the Creator but have not invested their lives in knowing and serving Him. I can know about college, but until I go and become a part of the process, I have not invested in continuing my education. To know Christ, we must invest our lives in Him in order to have a relationship with Him and grow in the grace and knowledge of Him. The book of Proverbs has a lot to say about knowledge and wisdom. Knowledge can come from the Bible inspired by God or from books written by people, but true wisdom comes from God. "For the Lord gives wisdom; From His mouth come knowledge and understanding" (Prov. 2:6). A wise person always wants more of God. The scriptures tell us that "Jesus kept increasing in wisdom and stature, and in favor with God and men" (Luke 2:52). As we seek to know God more and more in our relationship with Him, it pleases Him and we grow in wisdom from Him. James tells us, "If anyone lacks wisdom, let him ask of God, who gives to all men generously and without reproach, and it will be given to him" (James 1:5). So many blessings come with the Christian life, and wisdom is one of the richest. Invest in a Spirit-filled life today and enjoy the riches in Christ Jesus.

. ... from childhood you have known the sacred writings which are able to give you the wisdom that leads to salvation through faith which is in Christ Jesus. (2 Tim. 3:15)

August 24
It is easier to leave angry words unspoken than to mend a heart those words have broken.

Hurtful words go deep and linger long in the hearts and minds of those attacked by them. Many a person has fallen victim to the abusive words of a parent, teacher, boss, or bully. Hateful words cut to the core, leaving their victims demeaned, degraded, and defeated. Verbal abuse can be as destructive as physical abuse. Harmful and bitter words attack the very souls of people and can destroy their emotional health and self-esteem as quickly as any weapon. The old saying "Sticks and stones may break my bones, but words may never hurt me" is totally untrue. Run that by someone who has been prey to the mean-spirited tongue of another and see if that holds true. Many can shrug it off, considering the source, but you can be sure that the echo is still there.

Many people use words to retaliate and kill others dead with a single statement. I once knew a teacher like that. It's hard to imagine that people could be so bitter that they would take out their frustrations on innocent children, but she did. The destruction she caused with her overpowering, abusive personality will never be known in full, but you can rest assured that there were damaged souls. In Psalms we see the tongue described as a sharp sword (57:4, 64:3) and as a serpent (140:3). In Isaiah it is a consuming fire (30:27). James 3:6 describes the tongue as a fire and "the very world of iniquity." The tongue can spread much gossip and destroy the character of another. James goes on to ask the question, "Does a fountain send out from the same opening both fresh and bitter water?" (James 3:11). If our tongues confess Jesus as Lord, may it never be that we would use them to tear down others.

Think before you speak. Weigh your words. They need to be sweet, not bitter. They need to encourage, not tear down.

Let your speech always be with grace, seasoned, as it were, with salt, so that you may know how you should respond to each person. (Col. 4:6)

August 25
Have you fifty friends? It is not enough. Have you one enemy? It is too much. —Italian Proverb

A genuine friend is truly a gift from God. I am reminded of a little song I sang in Sunday school as a child: "Make new friends, but keep the old. One is silver, and the other is gold." Blessings come to us in many different ways, and friendships rank way up there at the top. In Proverbs we read that "a friend loves at all times" (17:17). Friendship is not something that you pick up and put down. True friendship is a loving, genuine commitment to another person. It is a dedication to support and encourage that person in good times and in bad times.

An enemy, on the other hand, is one who works against another person. An enemy can cause much distress and hurt in the life of one he or she sets out to destroy. Did you know that when we are friends with the world we become an enemy of God? (James 4:4). Satan is our worst enemy, but he disguises himself as an angel of light. He is the prince of this world, and that is why "friendship with the world is hostility toward God" (v. 4). We never want to choose the things of this world over Holy God. James goes on to say, "Submit therefore to God. Resist the devil and he will flee from you" (v. 7).

David and Jonathan were devoted friends. The scriptures tell us, "The soul of Jonathan was knit to the soul of David, and Jonathan loved him as himself" (1Sam. 18:1). David had already been anointed by God to be the next king after King Saul, even though Jonathan was King Saul's son. However, Jonathan never showed any jealousy toward David. David went on to marry Jonathan's sister. When King Saul's heart was hardened against David and he sought to kill him, Jonathan warned David and intervened, speaking to his father and reminding him of all that David had done to deliver Israel. Saul listened to his son this time but later turned against David again. Jonathan made a covenant with David to warn him of his father's plans to kill him. Such friendship is God ordained. A true friend sticks closer than a brother (Prov. 18:24).

Greater love has no one than this, that one lay down his life for his friends. John 15:13.

August 26
None is so blind as he who will not see.

Stubbornness is a sad disease and comes forth like ignorance. If a person cannot see the hidden, that is one thing. But to refuse to see the obvious is sadly illogical.

I guess the saddest example of obvious blindness would be turning away from a loving and beckoning heavenly Father, who wants nothing but the best for His children. To refuse to follow the One who created you in exchange for following after Satan and the world with all of its lust and sinful pleasures is a bad choice, but it is sadly the one made in the lives of many. When people choose sinful living over godly living, they are obviously blinded. The Bible tells us that Satan's only weapon is to blind us to keep us from seeing Christ and the gospel that frees us from the bondage of sin. "And even if our gospel is veiled, it is veiled to those who are perishing in whose case the god of this world has blinded the minds of the unbelieving, that they might not see the light of the gospel of the glory of Christ, who is the image of God" (2 Cor. 4:3–4).

New Testament Saul of Tarsus was blinded twice—once by Satan and once by God. Saul was a persecutor of Christians and an enemy of the church. He stood by and watched as Stephen, "a man full of faith and of the Holy Spirit" (Acts 6:5), was stoned to death. Acts 8:1 says that "Saul was in hearty agreement with putting him to death." Satan had Saul blinded so that he would not see the truth of the gospel. But our God is greater, and He had a better plan for Saul. One day as Saul was journeying to Damascus, suddenly a light from heaven blinded him. He fell to the ground. Jesus spoke to him and asked him why he was persecuting Him. For three days Saul could not see. The Lord sent a certain disciple named Ananias to lay hands on Saul so that he might regain his sight and be filled with the Holy Spirit. Saul arose and was baptized, and his name became Paul because he his eyes were opened and "he began to proclaim Jesus" (9:20).

But whenever a man turns to the Lord, the veil
is taken away. 2 Corinthians 3:16

August 27
Encouragement after censure is as the sun after a shadow. —Goethe

I remember that when my children were little, if I ever had to scold or spank them, I relished those little arms around my neck as they retaliated with love and appreciation for deserved correction. This gave me an opportunity to respond with encouragement and to teach a life lesson in how to behave in a proper manner.

Our heavenly Father demands holiness from us. He knows, however, that we will fail and fall short of His righteousness, but He never, ever gives up on us. In loving-kindness and gentle persuasion, He nudges us on toward perfection. Sometimes we respond readily, while other times we are rebellious and distant. His correction is necessary if we are to be light in this dark world and reflect his goodness.

When your soul is downcast within you, you can remember and be encouraged by the fact that God has always helped you and met your needs. You can be reassured by the steadfastness of God's mercy and grace as you remember His faithfulness in the past. As the sun breaks through the clouds after the storm, so our heavenly Father's light dispels the darkness and restores spiritual truth and encouragement.

I write this in October as the harvest moon is so beautifully shining through my kitchen window each morning. Its beauty makes me want it to linger. However, from the shadows of the morning, a new day breaks, and I can again rejoice in the light of His creation. God is so good! We don't have to look far to know the comfort of His presence or to be inspired by the wonders of His hands.

God, help us to know that when you discipline us, it is for our own good and to keep us on the straight and narrow. You have told us that the way to destruction is wide and the way to You is narrow and few will find it. Thank you for your encouragement and guiding hand. Amen.

Send forth your light and your truth, let them guide me. (Ps. 43:3)

August 28
A man who hides behind the hypocrite is smaller than the hypocrite. —W. E. Biederwolf

To hold to a pious attitude of oneself is certainly not noble and definitely not Christian. Jesus frowned on the scribes and Pharisees because of their attitude of moral superiority. This group of religious leaders boasted of their ability to keep all the religious laws, yet they let fall through the cracks compassion, love, and concern for their fellow humans. Jesus came out strongly in His Sermon on the Mount when He told His listeners that "unless your righteousness surpasses that of the scribes and Pharisees, you shall not enter the kingdom of heaven" (Matt. 5:20). What did Jesus mean by this? For one thing, none of us is righteous except through Him, by Him, and because of Him. Righteousness gained any way except through Jesus is as filthy rags. Many people struggle to live right in their own power. They think that doing good things and going by all the rules makes them righteous and in right-standing with Jesus. It is not so. God's remedy for our sin and for us to become righteous is found in Jesus. Paul spells it out in 2 Corinthians 5:21: "He made Him who knew no sin to be sin on our behalf, that we might become the righteousness of God in Him." In our true repentance, He exchanges our sin for His righteousness! Praise God!

When our earthly children are born into our families, they immediately are in right standing with our families. They are given our names, our love, our protection, and our guidance. That is how it is with our heavenly Father. When we are born again into the family of God, we are saved by His amazing grace and covered by His righteousness. We are given his name, child of God, He loves us with an everlasting love, and He keeps us in perfect peace and guides us in His ways. May we never boast of our own deeds but rejoice in the righteousness of the One who saved us.

The wisdom that is from above is first pure, then peaceable, gentle and easy to be entreated, full of mercy and good fruits, without hypocrisy. (James 3:17)

August 29
Going to church doesn't make you a Christian any more than going to a garage makes you an automobile. —W. A. "Billy" Sunday

The Christian life is a miraculous experience. God has no limits when we open our hearts to Him to work His will and His way in our life. A changed life is like the transformation of the caterpillar that turns into a beautiful butterfly. It is the miracle of a changed attitude and a different focus as if scales were lifted from your eyes. The transformed, born-again person sees everything differently. Christians have a supernatural love for their fellow humans, more patience and tolerance, and are new creations with Christ at the center. Christians yearn to share their experiences with those around them and desire the same inner peace for all humankind. Christians have the same desires for the lost world that God has, and that is that none would perish, but all would come to repentance and salvation through Jesus Christ. Jesus said, "I have come that they might have life, and might have it abundantly" (John 10:10). The change that Jesus makes when He comes to dwell in the human heart is unmistakable, undeniable, and totally incomprehensible!

Jesus says that people will know His followers by the fruit that they produce. Those fruits are love, joy, peace, patience, kindness, goodness, faithfulness, gentleness, and self-control (Gal. 5:20–22).

Truly, we can never go to church enough to earn our salvation. We can never give enough to the church in order to be saved. We can't serve on enough committees or sing the loudest in the choir. We can't be good enough, patient enough, kind enough, or loving enough to earn a place in heaven. No, salvation comes by faith in the One who died on the cross over two thousand years ago for you and me in order that when we die to ourselves, He can come live in our hearts. The indwelling Holy Spirit gives us the ability to live as children of God.

Therefore, if any man is in Christ, he is a new creature; the old things passed away; behold new things have come. (2 Cor. 5:17)

August 30
Love gives itself; it is not bought. —Longfellow

Prostitution has gotten to be big business in our society. People long for fulfillment of their desire to be loved and seek after it even in sinful and perverse ways, hoping to satisfy that longing. They buy sex, not love. Love goes deep and has feelings of caring and giving. Love is kind and is not envious of the other person. True love is not self-centered, but God-centered. We can see a true picture of God-centered love in 1 Corinthians 13. Paul outlines love at its best, expressing that of all the spiritual gifts, love is the greatest, the "more excellent way" (12:31).

In a society where we have to look long and hard for a happy marriage, and we have to defend the virtues of love and courtship that we were taught and that are so clearly defined in God's Word, is it any wonder that generations are seeking after a counterfeit love known as lust and sex? Adultery, fornication, homosexuality, and pornography are rampant among the old and the young. These beasts poison the mind and put an indelible impression on the brains of any who choose to indulge. They are no longer called what they are, sin, but masked as freedom of expression. Our children are exposed to filth and debauchery on every hand, even as loving parents fight to protect them from it. James 1:14–15 warns us this way: "But each one is tempted when he is carried away and enticed by his own lust. Then when lust has conceived, it gives birth to sin; and when sin is accomplished, it brings forth death." *LSD* stands for "lust, sin, death," a deadly combination.

Christians are called to show what genuine, true love really is. We are to openly, unselfishly, and unapologetically reach out to those around us, offering to them the heartfelt love and example that comes only from knowing the Savior of Love. "The one who does not love does not know God, for God is love" (1John 4:8). We must speak out against the evils that seek to comprise the values and truths of the gospel. To be silent is to approve.

Let all that you do be done in love. (1 Cor. 16:14)

August 31
God might not be early, but He is never late.

Have you ever prayed about something, seeking God's guidance and direction, only to wait? That is hard, isn't it? Perhaps you made the decision that you would not move on a certain thing until you have clear instructions from God, maybe even putting out a fleece like Gideon did in Judges 6:36–40, desiring a sign from God, yet you hear nothing, so you wait. Then the day comes when you have to make a judgment on the issue. You have had no clear answer from God, but the choice has to be made. You move ahead, and your choice was the right one. Did that just happen? No way!

Many times I have relied on the scripture from the prophet Isaiah as he spoke God's words to the people of Zion: "And your ears will hear a word behind you, 'This is the way, walk in it,' whenever you turn to the right or to the left" (30:21). If you are a child of God and follow His ways, then that still, small voice in your spirit will lead you in the way that He has for you. His ways are not like our ways. He speaks to our hearts, our senses, and our innermost beings. The indwelling Holy Spirit enlightens children of God to the things of God. Paul reminds us in 1 Corinthians that "we have the mind of Christ" (2:16). We can know. If we go in the wrong direction, our Father will call us back or change our direction. Our decisions to move forward should be based on His Word to us either through prayer or as we study His scriptures. Many times I have looked back and seen how He worked things out in His own miraculous way and in His own time. His ways are always right, always fair, and always on time.

What decision do you have to make today? Are you trusting that the One who loves you most of all will come through for you? He will—guaranteed. "I will instruct you and teach you in the way which you should go; I will counsel you with My eye upon you" (Ps. 32:8).

His promises to us never fail!

But as for me, I trust in Thee, O Lord, I say, "Thou art my God." My times are in Thy hand. (Ps. 31:14–15a)

September

This is the generation of those who seek Him, who
seek Thy face—even Jacob. (Ps. 24:6)

September 1
Sorrows are our best educators. A man can see further through a tear than a telescope.
A Dictionary of Thoughts, p. 63

You have probably heard, as I have on occasion, someone say, "How could a loving God allow such a thing to happen?" It is not our prerogative to question God's plan. God is all-knowing, and He can allow or hinder things from happening. We don't always know or understand, but we aren't supposed to. God does not have to check in with us first. He is God. Sometimes God allows failures and defeats in our lives. Sometimes He allows death and disease. We are not to question His wisdom, but still He wants us to cry out to Him in our desperation. After all, we live in a fallen world. When sin entered God's perfect world through the disobedience of Adam and Eve, so entered the consequences of disobedience and death.

Many times we experience hardships out of our own need for discipline and alignment. Sadly, America is looking God's discipline right in the face. We have lost our reverential fear of Holy God. We have turned our back on the very principles of His Word that we were founded on. We have spit in the face of God and told Him that we don't want His covenant laws in our nation anymore. We have spurned His Word and told our schoolchildren that it cannot be read in their schools and that they cannot they pray to their Creator. We have created a holocaust by killing our young before they ever have a chance to live. We have embraced sin to do what is right in our own eyes. When there is no plumb line, when absolute truth that only comes from God's inspired Word is ignored, the foundations of a family, a nation, and a world will crumble.

If we let the waters of our lives flow from the main channel, then we get into troubled waters and gradually make our own streams and then rivers. And before we know it, we are drowning in oceans of our own making. God strives to keep us flowing on course. Sometimes it takes tears to see clearly and learn to fear and revere the One who loves us.

**Shall we indeed accept good from God and
not accept adversity? (Job 2:10)**

September 2
Show me the man who would go to heaven alone, and I will show you one who will never be admitted there. —Feltham

"The Lord is not slow about His promise, as some count slowness, but is patient toward you, not wishing for any to perish but for all to come to repentance" (2 Peter 3:9). Like our Lord, we are to have the same attitude toward our fellow humans. We are to work diligently to share the message of Christ's redemption in order that no one will perish. John in his gospel tells us that we know that we have passed from darkness (lost nature) into light (salvation) because we love other people. Saved people care about what happens to their fellow humans. They desire to reach out and rescue them from the desperate fate that is theirs without Christ. Jesus's last words to us as He ascended back to heaven are found in Matthew 28:19–20: "Go, therefore and make disciples of all the nations, baptizing them in the name of the Father and Son and the Holy Spirit, teaching them to observe all that I commanded you; and lo, I am with you always, even to the end of the age." These words are known as the Great Commission and are a command to all who name the name of Jesus.

When Jesus called two brothers, Simon who was called Peter and Andrew, to be His disciples, they were fishermen. Jesus told them to come and follow Him and He would make them fishers of men (Matt. 4:19). The scripture tells us that "they immediately left the nets, and followed Him" (v. 20). James and John, who were also fishermen, did the same. Jesus is calling us to follow suit. If we have chosen to follow Him, the Great Commission is our command. One day we will stand before the Father. Let us pray that we can rejoice with the souls that we have led to Christ.

Are you fishing today, or are you just out for a boat ride?

Then He said to His disciples, "The harvest is plentiful, but the workers are few. Therefore beseech the Lord of the harvest to send out workers into His harvest." (Matt. 9:37–38)

September 3
It is better to have loved and lost than never to have loved at all. –Tennyson

Blaise Pascal (1623–1662), a brilliant French mathematician, philosopher, and Christian believer, stated, "If the Christian claim is right, we have everything to gain and nothing to lose. If it is wrong, we have lost nothing." This statement has come to be known as Pascal's wager.

Jesus said it this way: "For what will a man be profited, if he gains the whole world, and forfeits his soul? Or what will a man give in exchange for his soul?" (Matt. 16:26).

There are certain things that we should not take a chance with, most especially if God has ordained it in His Word. Establishing a relationship with our Maker should be our priority since the desire for that bond was placed in us before we ever entered this world. Without knowing Him personally, we have a void in our hearts that cannot be filled any other way. Second, where we will spend eternity should be of greatest importance. Our time on earth is brief at its best, and eternity is forever after. There is no second chance once we breathe our last breath. Decision time is over.

Can the unbeliever afford the risk of unbelief? Is it not a greater risk to avoid Christ and His redemptive plan? Many people waltz through life with never a thought of commitment to their Maker. You can be "perfectly happy" and be spiritually wretched, pitiful, poor, blind, and naked (Rev. 3:17). The world offers a counterfeit plan. Satan, the Great Deceiver, tricks many into trusting his lies. Jesus said, "Come unto Me, all you who are weary and heavy-laden, and I will give you rest" (Matt. 11:28). Busyness is no substitute for salvation. He offers to us an eternal plan. Not only does He save us for abundant living on this earth, but His promise is for an eternal home with Him.

Seek Him first. Know and love Him your whole life. You will be blessed more than you can ever imagine and, oh, the eternal benefits!

I advise you to buy from Me gold refined by fire, that you may become rich, and white garments, that you may clothe yourself, and that the shame of your nakedness may not be revealed; and eyesalve to anoint your eyes, that you may see. (Rev. 3:18)

September 4
A cynic is a person who knows the price of everything yet knows the value of nothing.

The world is brand-name crazy. Even small children get caught up in the saga of labels and name dropping. When we stop and really think about it, we can see the foolishness of it all. One brand over another is so insignificant, and yet there are those who will do without rather than settle for the substitute.

Sadly, our society has seen murder over a certain brand of athletic shoes. Just recently a young man in a nearby town was killed for his sporty automobile. We are appalled at such actions, and yet how much do we individually get caught up in the seduction of advertisement, rushing out to buy things we see advertised in the paper or on television that are played up to be the "latest thing" or "new and improved"? If we lose our own focus regarding what is valuable and what is not, then we too will get pulled into this materialistic mind-set and lose sight of what is truly valuable in this life.

The book of Proverbs offers to each of us a wellspring of godly advice and wisdom. The world, which is a term for lost humankind, does not possess the wisdom to discern what is valuable and what is not. "How blessed is the man who finds wisdom, and the man who gains understanding. For its profit is better than the profit of silver, and its gain than fine gold" (Prov. 3:13-14). What we value in life speaks volumes about our integrity and honor. When things become more important to us than people, then we have lost our sense of loyalty to what is right and real in this life. "Do not let your heart envy sinners, but live in the fear of the Lord always"(Prov. 23:17).

What is valuable to you? I hope that it is your relationship with Jesus. He tells us in Matthew 10 how much He values us. He knows when a sparrow falls and how many hairs are on your head. His words to us are, "Therefore do not fear; you are of more value than many sparrows" (v. 31). Let us always value what God values.

> **God made men upright, but they have sought out many devices. (Eccles. 7:29)**

September 5
The greatest happiness of life is the conviction that we are loved, loved for ourselves, or rather loved in spite of ourselves. —Victor Hugo

Unconditional love is a true test of our character. We all want to be loved like that, but we often have problems when it comes to loving unconditionally. We want to put limitations on our love and place requirements on the objects of our affection. This is not to say that we don't have guidelines to live by and standards for righteous living, but rather to say, as God says, that we are to love with an everlasting love, a steadfast and true love.

God's chosen people, the Israelites, were often disobedient and ungrateful. They cried out for an earthly king when they had the King of Kings as their conqueror and deliverer. They worshipped idols when God was in their very midst. They whined and complained when God delivered them from Egyptian bondage, grumbling over and over again with ungrateful disregard for all that God had delivered them from. God's disgust turned to anger, and He spoke out, "How long shall I bear with this evil congregation who are grumbling against Me? I have heard the complaints of the sons of Israel, which they are making against Me" (Num. 14:27). The Israelites' rebellion caused God to have to act in a way that they had not expected. They would not see the promised land. Only their children would be allowed to enter, while the older generation would die in the wilderness.

God's love is unconditional, but it is just. His justice comes to those whom He loves in order to teach us obedience. It is so hurtful when those we love the most go against God's laws and seek their own selfish pleasure. Our sinful nature leads us to turn our backs on the commandments that He has written on our hearts. However, our godly nature, which only comes with knowing Christ as Savior, allows us to love them in spite of reservations and hurt. God continues even today to strive with the children of Israel, many of whom do not acknowledge Jesus as the Messiah. But He loves them still as He does all humankind and calls us to repentance that we may all become children of God.

I have loved you with an everlasting love. (Jer. 31:3)

September 6
If I take care of my character, my reputation will take care of itself. —D. L. Moody

Eleanor Roosevelt once said, "Character building begins in our infancy and continues until death." We never can stop striving to be the best we can be morally and spiritually. The character of humans is the conscience of society and holds society accountable. We must never grow weary of being good and moral people, even though all around us there is immorality and indifference to spiritual things. Paul expressed it like this to the Galatian Christians: "And let us not lose heart in doing good, for in due time we shall reap if we do not grow weary" (Gal. 6:9). What did Paul mean when he said that "we shall reap if we do not grow weary"? Just what Jesus meant when He said, "For I go to prepare a place for you ... that where I am, there you may be also" (John 14:2, 3). We will reap our eternal reward in the presence of Jesus forever. What greater reward for character building and godly living could there be while we inhabit this earth. To the church at Thessalonica and to us today as well, Paul warned that these times would come and admonished us to "encourage one another, and build up one another" in the last days (1 Thess. 5:11).

Tolerance and *compromise* have become words of great threat and ominous danger to our society. When we come to tolerate what God has already condemned, then we have lost sight of who holds the plumb line that we are to live by. There should be no compromise to moral absolutes, and there *are* absolutes laid down by our Creator. Even a pagan society should know right from wrong. When we accommodate those who tolerate sin and compromise our own beliefs, then we too fall into the trap of deception, dishonesty, and deceit.

Christian conduct and character are what God expects of His people. It takes a lifetime to build a good reputation and only one bad choice to destroy it. How we behave when no one is looking is a true test of our character.

**But examine everything carefully; hold fast to
that which is good. (1 Thess. 5:21)**

September 7
To carry care to bed is to sleep with a pack on your back. –Haliburton

God intended for those hours that we recline and rest at night to be hours of peace and total relaxation. Restful sleep can prepare us for a day of hard work, vigorous play, clear thinking, study, or service. It gives our bodies and minds an interim to revamp, to reprogram, and to rebuild. It is important when we lie down at night for the rejuvenation of the mind and body not to weigh down the mattress with the pressure of unnecessary worry and care. Such a burden hinders sleep, and rest is impossible.

Fear keeps many from restful sleep. Fear often stems from the unknown or unseen—bumps in the night or shadows that take on the likeness of things in our own imaginations. Then there is worry, which leads to anxiety, which leads to the inability to shut down the mind. Anger can also destroy rest. That is why Paul tells us in Ephesians 4:26, "Do not let the sun go down on your anger," warning us that carrying anger to bed gives the devil many opportunities. Perhaps you are burdened with concerns of a family member, a friend, or your church. Maybe it is the affairs of the nation and the world, a business decision, or just your long to-do list for tomorrow. Whatever your concern, whatever is keeping you from the rest that God desires for you, give it to Him. Jesus comforted His disciples with these words: "Peace I leave with you; My peace I give to you; not as the world gives, do I give to you. Let not your heart be troubled, nor let it be fearful" (John 14:27). This is one of the roles of the indwelling Spirit, day and night—to give us peace.

I came across this little poem that really spoke to me. I don't know who wrote it, but the author surely had a bird's-eye view on rest and trusting.
Said the robin to the sparrow,
"I should really like to know
why these anxious human beings rush about and worry so."
Said the sparrow to the robin,
"Friend, I think that it must be,
that they have no Heavenly Father such as cares for you and me."

**Come to Me, all who are weary and heavy-laden,
and I will give you rest. (Matt. 11:28)**

September 8
He conquers who endures. –Perseus

Keeping the faith is sometimes a challenge in our world today. We want to hold fast to the things that are godly, holy, and righteous, yet the pull to compromise values and faithfulness to what is right often clouds our judgment and causes us to stumble into doubt and skepticism.

In his letter to young Timothy, Paul stressed the importance of a pure heart, a good conscience, and a sincere faith. He warned that when we stray away from these things, we become fruitless and ineffective as believers, watering down the effectiveness of our witness. Paul went on to say that we must hold to the "mystery of the faith with a clear conscience" (1 Tim. 3:9). He challenged Timothy to discipline himself "for the purpose of godliness" (4:7). I believe that Paul was trying to tell Timothy that following Jesus is not a soft life and neither does Jesus portray it that way. To follow Jesus we must die to ourselves. It will cost you everything. Your life will change, old things will pass away, and all things will become new. But don't worry—it is a good change, a great change! And Paul knew that firsthand.

We don't understand all that God wants to do in and through us, and we never will. However, He showed mercy to us when He saved us "with the faith and love which are found in Christ Jesus" (1 Tim. 1:14). Paul recognized this grace shown to him as he testified to Timothy and to us "that Christ Jesus came into the world to save sinners, among whom I am foremost of all" (v. 15). Endurance takes courage and strength. That is why our heavenly Father tells us over and over again to call on Him. Jeremiah 33:3 is often called our telephone call to God: "Call to Me, and I will answer you, and I will tell you great and mighty things, which you do not know." Then and only then can we conquer, if we listen.

In order to be effective, fruitful Christians, we must live effective, faithful lives.

Godliness is profitable for all things, since it holds promise for the present life and also for the life to come. (1Tim. 4:8)

September 9
Love your enemies. (It will drive them nuts.)

We will have enemies no matter how hard we try not to simply because of the conflict of natures. If we are in Christ, His Spirit is in us and our nature should be godly. If we are of the world, our nature is sinful and Satan rules. Sadly, we are all born with an old sin nature handed down through our ancestor, Adam. Even when we are born again into the kingdom of God, we still possess that old nature. However, the Spirit of God that takes up residence within us at salvation gives us the power to control that sinful nature and to live as children of God.

Jesus was perfect and holy. His Father is God. He was without sin, yet He had many enemies. His greatest persecution came when He began His ministry of helping and healing those who came to Him. He was constantly ridiculed and scorned by the religious establishment of the day. Many people loved Him, but many more hated and mocked at Him. Why? we ask. What did they see in Jesus that made Him their enemy? Jesus confronted their sin, and that is all that it takes for some to become hostile toward you. Some listened to Jesus and were delivered from their sinful lifestyles, and salvation was their reward. Others resented his teaching concerning their sin and His reproof. When a person has no desire to change from their evil ways, the one who tries to help and rescue them becomes the enemy.

There is a battle raging between God and Satan. We must know that if Jesus had enemies, we certainly will too. The battle is for dominion in the hearts of humankind. Who reigns supreme in your heart today? If it is Christ, then reach out to your enemies with loving-kindness. It will blow them away, and your Holy God will be glorified. Jesus said, "Blessed are you when men cast insults at you, and persecute you, and say all kinds of evil against you falsely, on account of Me. Rejoice, and be glad, for your reward in heaven is great" (Matt. 5:11–12a).

But I say to you, love your enemies, and pray for those who persecute you in order that you may be sons of your Father who is in Heaven. (Matt. 5:44–45a)

September 10
The flowers of all tomorrows are in the seeds of today. –Chinese proverb

When our daughter was on staff with a Christian ministry, we talked a lot about seed planting, sowing, and harvesting. She realized that she would never know the fruition of her efforts or see the full harvesting of the seeds planted, nurtured, and watered by the faithful group of laborers with whom she worked. However, as God allowed them to have a part in the process, she was always confident that He would give an abundant increase.

After his conversion, Paul was probably one of the most dynamic and outspoken witnesses of the gospel in the New Testament. He had a passion for spreading the message of Christ to the lost world. His boldness in ministry and his fervent desire to establish churches among the early Christians was unsurpassed. Paul felt totally called of Christ. He suffered much hardship for the cause of Christ, but he never wavered from his "goal for the prize of the upward call of God in Christ Jesus" (Phil. 3:14). That goal was to plant seeds of faith in the hearts of humankind and to rescue the perishing. Paul was convinced that God had set him apart, even from his mother's womb, to preach Jesus to the Gentiles (Gal. 1:15–16).

God has chosen each of us for that very purpose, to rescue those who are dying without Christ. Like Paul and like our daughter Tessa and her young group of missionaries, all Christians, all who have named the name of Jesus, are called to be seed-bearers, laborers in the fields that are white unto harvest. We possess the keys to the kingdom, if we have chosen to follow King Jesus, and therefore have a responsibility to scatter the seeds of righteousness and the knowledge of the One who can save the lost from destruction and eternal doom. Many flower bulbs have to be planted in the winter in order to bloom in the spring. It is never too late or too early to sow a word of witness to those around us.

Now He who supplies seed to the sower and bread for food, will supply and multiply your seed for sowing and increase the harvest of your righteousness. (2 Cor. 9:10)

September 11
The fear of the Lord is to hate evil; Pride and arrogance and the evil way ... (Prov. 8:13a)

The anniversary of 9/11 is again upon us. Our hearts are still heavy with the memory and horror of such a horrific act. The grief of a nation so blessed and yet so violated by an act of evil men cannot be suppressed or forgotten.

"And so we have the prophetic word made more sure, to which you do well to pay attention as to a lamp shining in a dark place" (2 Peter 1:19a). America would do well to heed the warning signs of a God who loves us. He loves all humankind, but He does not tolerate evil brought against those who love Him. The question is, do we love Him? Do the people who are called by His name love Him? When a nation founded on Christian principles allows all of His ways to be compromised and all of His truths to be watered down, what more can we expect than to see humankind desperate for answers and hope?

Franklin Graham says, "The Bible identifies man's trouble from the beginning to end—the fall of the human race—and lays out what is to come. We do not have to ask what in the world is going on. God has already told us what is going on in the world. His Word radiates with answers. God is speaking but few are listening."

Signs of the times are definitely everywhere. Jesus said, "But when these things begin to take place, straighten up and lift up your heads, because your redemption is drawing near" (Luke 21:28). Signs are given to us so that we might heed the danger ahead. For the saved person, there is rejoicing, but for lost humankind, there is eternal separation from God. Now is the time for salvation.

We can't afford to miss the warning signs, the harbingers, that God's Word said would come. Jesus said, "I am the way, and the truth, and the life; no one comes to the Father but through Me" (John 14:6). Jesus is the answer for the world today. Let us pray today that we will see no more evil such as was revealed on September 11, 2001.

Blessed is the nation whose God is the Lord. (Ps. 33:12a)

September 12
God hath not promised us a quiet journey, only a safe arrival.

God's promises are real, and they are never broken . His Word is filled with more than two thousand promises, and each one carries with it a guarantee of God's faithfulness to carry them out.

When we look at life with all of its bumpy roads and hard knocks, we can be confident that He knows. His provisions for our journey through time and space are quite adequate, and we are limited only by our own inability to trust Him through it all.

Joshua was God's man to lead the Israelite people into the promised land after Moses's death. Just as God had been with Moses, He would be with Joshua. God's promise to Joshua was, "No man will be able to stand before you all the days of your life. Just as I have been with Moses, I will be with you; I will not fail you or forsake you" (Joshua 1:5). Three times God instructed Joshua to be strong and courageous. He also told him to remember and do all that Moses had commanded him (v. 7). God reminded Joshua to meditate on the book of the law day and night and not to let it depart from his mouth, to "do according to all that is written in it" (v. 8). Like Joshua, God has given us all the promises of His Word, but He expects us to remember them, abide by them, and heed their instruction, "then you will have success." As the Lord finished his word to the new leader of His people, He again gave Him those most encouraging words: "for the Lord your God is with you wherever you go" (v. 9). As we read through the journey of Joshua and the Israelite people, we know that it was not an easy one, but God never wavered on his promises and He never will on His promises to us.

The greatest of all of God's promises was the promise of His Son, Jesus. With that promise came the assurance of life everlasting and a safe arrival in our eternal home if we trust Him. "I go to prepare a place for you. And if I go and prepare a place for you, I will come again, and receive you to Myself; that where I am, there you may be also" (John 14:2–3).

**And lo, I am with you always, even to the
end of the age. (Matt. 28:20b)**

September 13
Dost thou love life? Then do not squander time, for that is the stuff life is made of. –Franklin

The older a person gets, the more valuable time becomes. As children, we never thought about having enough time to complete a project or allowing enough time to play here or walk there. There were no schedules or time frames to bind us and no deadlines to meet. My childhood was spent in the 1940s and 1950s. That was a great time to live and enjoy life. Things were slow and easy. My life was simple and relaxed, uncomplicated. I reflect often on those times.

Jesus lived a similar life. He probably spent His early days playing around His earthly father's carpentry shop. He had siblings with whom He must have enjoyed playing games and having fun. Life was uncomplicated for Him at that point, and we are told that "Jesus kept increasing in wisdom and stature, and in favor with God and men" (Luke 2:51). People loved Jesus, and at the age of thirty He began the ministry for which He had been born. He was baptized by his cousin John, and the Holy Spirit descended on Him like a dove. He then set out to do the will of His heavenly Father. God even gave Satan permission to tempt His Son, and Jesus passed the test by defeating the devil with scripture. Jesus went about doing good and healing the sick. He performed many miracles, and many followed Him. It was not long, however, before things changed. Although He came to bring peace to the earth, humankind caused Him much pain and grief. You see, when Jesus confronted sin, even the religious leaders of the day turned on Him. Although His ministry was powerful, He became unpopular with those who opposed His teachings of truth, obedience, and forgiveness. Jesus tried to tell them that He came that they might have life and have it abundantly (John 10:10), but many did not believe. He was crucified after three years of ministry. Living only to age thirty-three, his life was short but amazing, powerful, and effective. What an impact He made on this world! He squandered no time but did the will of the One who sent Him. Are you living a life for others as Jesus lived? When we do, our lives are not wasted!

Remember that my life is but breath. (Job 7:7)

September 14
I believe the promises of God enough to venture an eternity on them. –Isaac Watts

When Jesus comes again, the consummation of all of His promises and prophesies will come to fulfillment. Most have been fulfilled already, but there are more to come, including the rapture and His glorious return for His church. *Consummatio*n is to make complete. He promised that He would come again, and He will. In 1 Thessalonians 4, Paul tells us about the rapture of the church and how those who have chosen Christ in this lifetime will suddenly be taken up to meet Him in the air. We can read about the tribulation that will take place on earth after the church has been taken out in Matthew 24. Then in Revelation 20 we see Satan bound and thrown into the abyss, where he will be shut up, and the abyss will be sealed for one thousand years. These things and much more will come to pass. I am not able to comprehend many of these, but I rejoice that I know the One who holds the keys to the kingdom and I put my trust in Him.

When, in the end times, God consummates the final promises and prophesies that He has made to us and shown us in His Word, the world can look back (if that is possible from eternity) and see nothing but truth—no lies, no broken promises, no unfulfilled prophesies. God's promises are sure, and we can count on them as done. We have only to look back through Bible history from where we are to see the faithfulness of our sovereign God and how He has fulfilled all the promises He has made.

Darkness is closing in on the world as sin and hopelessness seek to cover the hearts of humankind. Satan seeks to blind the eyes of those who will not see. Oh, God, open up the shutters to dispel the darkness. Remove the scales from the eyes of the unbelieving. Let your glorious light shine through your people that we might reveal the hope that is in us—the hope that we have in Jesus Christ our Lord, Creator of the universe, and Savior for all who will trust in Him. Pray with me today.

**For our citizenship is in heaven; from which also we eagerly
wait for a Savior, the Lord Jesus Christ. (Phil. 3:20)**

September 15
He who buys what he does not want, will soon want what he cannot buy.

Compulsive spending is at epidemic proportions in our society today. Retail businesses feed on the sickness of a society that has lost all sense of controlled spending. Retailers are trained in the art of placing pick-up items in easy view of compulsive customers so that on impulse they will indulge and go beyond their planned spending. It's a game of enticement that preys on the human weakness of greed.

Bankruptcy is a national problem as well. Not only are individuals from every walk of life falling into the trap of "easy credit," but our nation is so broke that it will take an act of God for us to ever overcome the debt. People or nations that try to live beyond their means are sacrificing peace of mind and security in order to hoard frivolous things that have little earthly worth and no eternal value.

God calls us to invest in heavenly things, the riches that will not burn up at the judgment. If we could only be enticed to indulge in the lasting things of life like compassion, love, kindness, generosity, patience, faithfulness, and especially salvation, in the end our means would have been well spent. Jesus has paid the price, but are we willing to take freely what He has already purchased for us? He says in the book of Matthew, "The kingdom of heaven is like a treasure hidden in the field, which a man found and hid; and from joy over it he goes and sells all that he has, and buys that field. Again, the kingdom of heaven is like a merchant seeking fine pearls, and upon finding one pearl of great value, he went and sold all that he had, and bought it" (13:44–46).

We have the riches of the kingdom at our fingertips, yet many pass by and never acknowledge the greatest of all gifts, salvation, bought and paid for by God's own Son, the pearl of great price. Do not buy into the world's way. There will come a time when you will want what God has to offer, and it will be too late.

For you have been bought with a price: therefore glorify God in your body. (1 Cor. 6:20)

September 16
Willful waste makes woeful want.

Americans are renowned for their wasteful and extravagant lifestyles. We slave each day to accumulate more and more things, then in senseless flamboyance, we throw to the wind the excess or unwanted. Most times our wants outweigh our needs, and we become bound by the insatiable desire for more.

God intends for us to be good stewards of our worldly goods, just as He expects faithfulness over spiritual things. I believe we all desire to hear the Master say to us, "Well done, good and faithful servant; you were faithful with a few things, I will put you in charge of many things; enter into the joy of your master" (Matt. 25:23).

God desires to bless His children. There is nothing wrong with having the good things of this life. The danger comes when *they have us* and we are not faithful in our handling of the excess. If we are wasteful, we might one day find ourselves wanting.

Time is another commodity that is often wasted. It can never be regained. We can't see time as it passes; only the clock and the calendar give us a reading of time as it moves forward. The older we get, the swifter time flies by. I know that I am getting older when I hear my children saying that time is moving by so quickly. God gave to each of us the same number of hours in a day, days in a week, weeks in a month, and months in a year. What we accomplish is up to each of us. He, after all, does have a plan for our lives (Jer. 29:11), and He expects us to invite Him into our lives so that He can show us that plan.

Being wasteful with our precious life span is not what He had in mind. He even inspired Solomon to tell us, "There is an appointed time for everything. And there is a time for every event under heaven" (Eccles. 3:1). We honor our Maker when we value the time He has allotted us.

Fill your day this day with worthwhile things. Start out by asking the One with the plan to move you in the right direction. He is waiting for you to ask!

And the Lord said, who then is that faithful
and wise steward ...? (Luke 12:42)

September 17
If you enjoy your job, you never have to go to work.

Life is short at its very best. Enjoy what you do, or rather do what you enjoy! It is very important when you choose a job, profession, or career to help supply the needs of this life to embark on an occupation that offers you not only a living but a life. I have encountered people, some professional people, who have spent their entire lives at jobs that they really didn't like. They felt that they had too much invested—education, money, time, and so on—to change, so they endured the drudgery, going to work each day with a half-hearted effort to see each day through. Sometimes making do with fewer material things and working at something that you like doing might be a better plan.

I was always blessed to be able to fulfill my dream to be a housewife and a mother. I went to college and loved it, but lofty ambitions were not ever my desire. My husband has always made a comfortable living for us and, though we were never wealthy, we had all we needed. He loved my being at home, so it was a good plan for us. After our children were grown, I was able to pursue some dreams in business, but my heart was and is at home.

Whatever you pursue in life, make sure that you pray about it. Seek God first. Know what His plan is for you. Then you will not waste valuable time and effort trying to find it.

If you are in a job or occupation today that you feel bound to, ask God what you need to do to make a change. You might have to alter your lifestyle, but your life might be richer in the long run.

Many times God calls us to do things that we don't want to do. Jonah was one of those people who ran from God and tried to avoid the mission that God had for him. We often set out to do what we want to do but find that the blessings are in what God has for us to do. Spending three days in the belly of a large fish would make you rethink things in a hurry. May we all do life God's way!

But we urge you, brethren, to excel still more, and to make it your ambition to lead a quiet life and attend to your own business and work with your hands. (1 Thess. 4:11)

September 18
Don't criticize what you don't understand, son. You never walked in that man's shoes. —Elvis Presley

A critical nature is not of God. If you are a person who criticizes everything, just know that God frowns on such actions and does not want us to have a critical, negative attitude.

People who condemn and comment in a critical way about things around them actually think that by condemning or criticizing, they look like an authority on the subject. In reality it only shows their ignorance and insensitivity. To openly embarrass someone cuts deeply and leaves scars. Someone once said that when we judge and criticize another person, it says nothing about that person; it merely says something about our own need to be critical.

We are to be encouragers! There is much insecurity in our fellow humans today, and it is not hard to see that there is a definite need to lift self-esteem in many with whom we come in contact each day. Who doesn't need a boost in self-esteem every now and then!

Be aware of that this day and set out to find the good in those around you. Pass out sincere compliments, give a pat on the back or a little hug, write a thank you note, make a happy phone call, or tell someone what a good job he or she is doing. Encouragement goes a long way, and it usually boomerangs right back to you. William Arthur Ward said it like this: "Flatter me, and I may not believe you. Criticize me, and I may not like you. Ignore me, and I may not forgive you. Encourage me, and I will not forget you. Love me, and I may be forced to love you."

Many criticized Jesus when He walked on this earth, but He never retaliated. I have often said that I wish I had the wisdom to handle situations like Jesus did. Psalm 12:6 says, "The words of the Lord are pure words; as silver tried in a furnace on the earth, refined seven times." Lord, help us to refine our words before we speak them.

Let the words of my mouth and the meditation of my heart be acceptable in Thy sight, O Lord, my rock and my Redeemer.

(Ps. 19:14)

September 19
Life's roughest storms prove the strength of our anchors.

It is very important when you are fishing to have a steadfast anchor that will hold your boat in place so that you can fish in your chosen spot without being shifted around. My daddy, being the fisherman he was, taught me that. If he found a good fishing hole, he would drop his anchor, and then he was able to throw his baited hook right into the spot where he just knew he would catch a big one. If a boat is not properly anchored, it can suddenly shift from the wind or the waves of a passing boat. Chances are you could be tossed into the water or thrown into the bottom of the boat. A good anchor holds a boat securely in place.

Our lives need an anchor. If we don't have one, we will be cast about by every wind of doctrine and swallow every lie that Satan throws our way. The storms of life will toss us so that we will be washed onto the shores of despair and hopelessness. Without an anchor, our lives will be wrecked and blown apart. We will sink and be lost forever. Hebrews tells us that we can be encouraged because our God is unchangeable and does not lie (6:18). "This hope we have as an anchor of the soul, a hope both sure and steadfast" (v. 19).

Prepare for the storms; they will come. Get ready for the turbulence; it is inevitable. Corrie ten Boom, who faced the worst of storms in life as she endured the tortures of the Holocaust, put it like this: "In order to realize the worth of the anchor we need to feel the stress of the storm." Corrie's anchor was Jesus, and she trusted Him to the end.

Jesus wants to be your anchor. He is steadfast and sure. He never changes. You can trust in that and secure your life to the immovable anchor that will never shift or turn loose His hold on you. When the storms of life come crashing down, He holds fast to give us security and hope. He will never let go, and His grasp on you will never give way.

Those who still reject Me are like the restless sea.... There is no peace, says my God, for them! (Isa. 57:20, 21 TLB)

September 20
The way of the wicked is an abomination to the Lord, but He loves him who pursues righteousness. —Prov. 15:9

God loves the sinner, always, but He hates the sin. Like a loving father, He disciplines His children to bring them to repentance. If sin continues, He punishes in order to deter sinful behavior from persisting. If we ignore His effort to gently turn us from a destructive, sinful lifestyle, then He calls us home. Death is our deliverance from sin and its destructive influence when we deliberately choose to disregard His way. Let me stop here to say, as Hebrews 12:8 makes so clear, "If you are without discipline, of which all have become partakers, then you are illegitimate children and not sons." Strong words? Yes! If you are living a lifestyle contrary to God's Word and are experiencing no conviction or discipline and have no remorse or sorrow, God wants you to realize that you are not His child. The Holy Spirit, who indwells Christians at salvation, convicts of sin. The same Holy Spirit draws lost people to be saved. No one can be satisfied to live a lifestyle of sin and be comfortable in it without conviction if he or she is a child of God.

Do we think that God is not paying attention? Do we, even as Christians, think we can go about our own selfish ways with no regard for those God has called us to influence and win to the cause of salvation in Christ Jesus? It cannot happen. God paid a great price for our sins to be forgiven, and He expects us to feel the pain of our sinfulness, repent, and turn from it. "It is for discipline that you endure; God deals with you as sons; for what son is there whom his father does not discipline?"(Heb. 12:7). It would be like requiring one of your children to live justly while allowing another to live unjustly without correction or punishment. God is a just and fair Father.

We are all chosen to be God's children, whoever will come; however, some choose to accept Jesus and be saved while some reject Him and are lost. "All discipline ... yields the peaceful fruit of righteousness" (Heb.12:11).

Therefore, to one who knows the right thing to do, and does not do it, to him it is sin. (James 4:17)

September 21
Thought is the soul of the act. —Robert Browning

Sin is conceived through the mind. It travels to the heart and will of a being and manifests itself in the flesh through the actions of its prey. For this reason, we are to set our minds on the things that are honorable, right, pure, lovely, of good repute, excellent, and worthy of praise (Phil. 4:8). Paul says that if we do this, then God will guard our hearts and minds and give us peace. That is a promise that I want to claim!

It is important that Christians always stay on alert. Satan is like a prowling lion sneaking up on his prey. He loves it when he can bring down a person who names the name of Jesus and destroy his or her witness.

LSD is a deadly drug that hit the streets years ago and has destroyed the lives of many people as they have chosen to indulge. The effects of this horrific drug have destroyed lives, homes, minds, and careers and stolen the futures of many a young person. I am not sure what these initials stand for, but James makes it clear in the Bible. He reminded us of this deadly LSD long before our time. As we look all the way back to Genesis, we find its beginning. In the Garden of Eden, when the first humans chose to lust after something that was forbidden and to listen to their own voices rather than the voice of God, that is when sin was born.

When we allow ourselves to be carried away and enticed by our own lust (James 1:14), we fall into the trap of LSD: lust, sin, and death. "Then when *lust* has conceived, it gives birth to *sin*; and when sin is accomplished, it brings forth *death*" (v. 15, emphasis added). This LSD that James addresses is as deadly as any drug and equally as destructive. Just as the drug brings down its victims, lust, sin, and spiritual death confiscate joy, peace, love, goodness, and all the things that people long for out of life. They replace them with heartache, sadness, hate, discord, and the list goes on. God provided us a better way. Stay on alert and focus on Him.

Submit therefore to God. Resist the devil and
he will flee from you. (James 4:7)

September 22
The trouble with speaking one's mind
is that it limits conversation.

How do you pray? Are you in a one-way conversation with God? Do you tell God what you want, need, and desire, or do you ask Him to supply your needs according to His will for your life? Do you refuse to change, so you call on God to get on board with you? So often we pray with never a thought of God's will. Our conversation is one-sided as we cry for our way. God does not work according to our agendas. He has a much greater vision. Bargaining with Him is not on the radar; neither is He happy when we go ahead with our own way and call on Him to rescue us from the effects and consequences of our disobedience. He always supplies grace and our needs but not all our desires and wants.

Moses had been a faithful and obedient leader when God called him from tending his father-in-law's sheep to lead the Israelite people out of Egyptian bondage. Moses never wavered in his obedience, even though at times he was uncertain about his own ability. Moses listened to God and trusted Him. He did all that God required of him. From the ten plagues to the crossing of the Red Sea, to receiving the Ten Commandments, Moses listened to God. Even as God put the Israelites in time-out for forty years, Moses was faithful to rely on God, reminding the people always of God's faithfulness. Sadly, as we look toward the end of his life of 120 years, we see that Moses was not permitted to enter the promised land. But God let him see it from afar. His life had been spent with people who would not listen, people who grumbled and listened only to their own selfish hearts for their own selfish desires. Maybe Moses got impatient and frustrated with them as he had been many times before. Nevertheless, he failed to really listen and obey God's instructions at the end. Instead of speaking to the rock as God had told him to in order to bring forth water before the congregation, Moses struck the rock. "You rebelled against My command to treat Me as holy before their eyes" (Num. 27:14). In other words, he chose to do it his way.

**Therefore you shall not bring this assembly into the
land which I have given them. (Num. 20:12b)**

September 23
No noise is so emphatic as one you are trying not to listen to.

Try to mentally tune out the TV if you are talking on the telephone. Try to ignore the conversation behind you as you wait in line at the grocery store. Try to shut out a crying baby as the sermon goes on in spite of that sweet sound. Try to sleep with noise in the other room. The outside noise becomes the extreme and seems the loudest.

In our world today, where we as Christians are trying to walk to the drumbeat of our living Savior, the noises of the world clang louder and louder. It is so easy to get distracted by the things of this world that pull for our attention and allegiance. As the newspapers and television blare out the sounds of the world around us, we often get discouraged, discontented, distracted, and dismayed.

The Pharisees of Jesus's day were totally distracted by the things of the world. They dwelled on the minor while missing the major. Their emphasis was on being sure that their hands were washed before eating bread, that they cleansed themselves before eating after coming from the marketplace, and that they were constantly washing their cups, pitchers, and copper pots (Mark 7:4). Jesus confronted them about this, calling them hypocrites, and repeated the words of the Lord from Isaiah that said that they were honoring God with their lips but not their hearts. He went on to say that they worshipped Him but taught as truth the precepts of the world (Isa. 29:13) and neglecting the commandments of God. The Pharisees were marching to the emphatic sounds of the world and missing the still, small voice of God.

Look around you today and see what is distracting you. What outside noises, voices, conversations, and even sweet sounds are stealing your allegiance to God and hindering your walk with Him? Are you trying hard not to listen, or are you tuning the world in with one ear and the things of God with the other? Have social media, television, and the computer become more important than reading God's Word? God loves our time with Him.

Do not love the world, nor the things in the world. If anyone loves the world, the love of the Father is not in him. (1 John 2:15)

September 24
Nobody ever forgets where he buried the hatchet. –Kin Hubbard

To forgive and forget as our heavenly Father forgives and forgets our sin is not an impossible task. It is, however, perhaps the one thing we humans fall furthest short of. We love to remember the hurts done to us and recall the wrongs against us. We often hear it said, "I forgive you, but I'll never forget it." Is that forgiveness? When we ask God to forgive our sins, He says that He puts them in the past and remembers them no more (Isa. 43:25). "As far as the east is from the west, so far has He removed our transgressions from us" (Ps. 103:12). Do we think that God requires any less from us?

When our grandson, Wesley, was a little thing, he would cross his little arms over his chest, pooch out his lips, and drop his head in a pout when he was disciplined. Then with puddles in those big brown eyes, he would say, "You're not my best friend anymore!" Only moments later, with a hug that melted this grandmother's heart, he would say, "I sorry" and accept his discipline, and all was well. Correction builds character in us, but we must first acknowledge that we are wrong and say with all sincerity, "I sorry."

Let past hurts die and be put away. Bury them and do not remember them again. When they show their ugly heads, say a prayer for the ones you have chosen to forgive.

Every time God forgives one of your sins, he buries the hatchet. He buried each of our ugly sins—past, present, and future—when he shed His blood on that merciless and agonizing cross. As they lay His lifeless body in the empty tomb that day, those sins were buried as well. The beauty is that they remained buried and He was raised that we might have new life in Him. Praise God for His mercy and all-sufficient grace.

Today is a good day to share the truth of God's forgiveness and remember no more the hurt that was done to you. Forget it!

If we confess our sins, He is faithful and just to forgive our sins, and to cleanse us from all unrighteousness. (1 John 1:9)

September 25
A nickel goes a long way now. You can carry it around for days without finding a thing it will buy.

Money cannot buy true happiness, but it is not wrong to possess riches or the things riches can buy. God wants His children to enjoy all the good things in this life. The problem comes when we allow material riches to replace spiritual riches. There is no substitute for what God can bring into a life. Money cannot buy peace in your soul, comfort in your heart, and certainly not entrance into the kingdom of heaven. When money and the things it can buy become a substitute for God's riches, then we have put the cart before the horse. I love the way Mignon McLaughlin put it. She said, "'Your money or your life.' We know what to do when a burglar makes this demand of us, but not when God does."

A rich young ruler came to Jesus with the desire to follow Him and asked Jesus what he needed to do to obtain eternal life. Jesus told him that he needed to keep the commandments, and the young man expressed to Jesus that he already does that. He went on to ask, "What am I lacking?" (Matt. 19:20). Jesus then struck a nerve when He said, "Go and sell your possessions and give to the poor, and you shall have treasures in heaven; and come, follow Me" (v. 21). The young man was sad because he owned a lot of property and he did not want to part with it.

How often we want to hang onto earthly possessions and sacrifice the abundant life that only Christ can give. God's riches, whether spiritual or material, need to glorify the Father. We must dedicate all we have to Him, and He will direct us in our stewardship. It all belongs to Him anyway, and He keeps better records than the IRS. John Wesley said, "When I have money, I get rid of it quickly, lest it find a way into my heart." Jesus said, "For where your treasure is, there will your heart be also" (Matt. 6:21)

Thou shalt rejoice in every good thing which the Lord thy God hath given unto Thee. (Deut. 26:11)

September 26
A good marriage is the union of two good forgivers. —Ruth Bell Graham

I am a pro at emotional manipulation. Ask my husband. I am not proud of it, but when he says something hurtful to me or when we disagree and it gets ugly, I tend to withdraw, to pull away as if that is going to solve something. I don't pout; I just don't want to talk to him. I can't say that my silence is golden because I am sure it is very frustrating to him, which is the whole point since it is my way of retaliating. After all, Ecclesiastes says, "There is a time to be silent and a time to speak" (1:7). Right? For some reason, I am always the one who feels worse when I take this approach. The battle continues to rage, and no one wins.

There is only one way to settle your differences, and I am still learning. God calls us to live peacefully. I am sure that if I stopped to pray before activating my retaliation plan, maybe even count to ten, I would not handle things the way I do. Let me stop here and say that I don't always react with the silent treatment, but when I do, it is not good for either of us. Silence is golden only when it keeps the two parties from saying things that would drive the argument deeper.

In marriage it is very important for each partner to give his and her all to the other. There is always a lot of give and take, forgiveness, and compromise. Anything less is holding back and robbing the relationship of total commitment. The scriptures compare the marriage relationship with God's relationship to the church. Can we imagine God withholding anything from His people? Never would He. His only Son, Jesus, was the ultimate sacrifice for us. "No good thing does He withhold from those who walk uprightly" (Ps. 84:11b).

I hope you are more mature than I am when you are pushed into a corner and you want to come out fighting. Life is too short to let someone else's words cause distress or make or break your day. Step back and look at the big picture. Is the stress worth it? Does bitterness solve anything? I don't think so. Have a peaceful day. God is good!

Walk in love, just as Christ also loved you. (Eph. 5:2)

September 27
Some people look for divine guidance in the Ten Commandments, but most are looking for loopholes.

On the Israelites' journey to the promised land, God made a spectacular visit to His chosen people. As He descended in fire and smoke onto Mount Sinai, He called Moses to come up to the top of the mountain so that He could give to him the laws that He intended the people to live by. God reminded Moses of who He was and how He had brought them out of the bondage of the Egyptians. Then He proceeded to write in stone the Ten Commandments that we know and are called to live by even today. Exodus 20 lists them just as God gave them. They are clear and precise—clearly not suggestions, but commands. We are all sinners and in need of direction and guidance. God knew this and made a way for us by giving us clear instructions. These very laws were given to point us to the Lamb of God, Jesus, who would take away the sins of the world.

Obedience is very important to God. There is no place for loopholes in His commands to us. His holiness was never more evident than it was that day on Mount Sinai. And He made sure that the people knew that they were to worship Him and Him alone. "You shall have no other gods before Me" (v. 3). As His finger wrote all of His laws in stone for the saints of old, He writes them on the hearts of those of us today who choose to put our trust in Him. Their faith was based on the promise made in Genesis 3:15 of the seed that would come from the woman. That seed was Jesus Christ. They saw Him from afar, whereas we look back and see His finished work on the cross and place our faith in Him and what He has accomplished for us. "Therefore the Law has become our tutor to lead us to Christ, that we may be justified by faith" (Gal. 3:24). With His laws written on the hearts of those who call Him Lord, our desire should be to cherish His divine guidance.

**I will put My laws upon their heart, and upon
their mind I will write them. (Heb. 10:16)**

September 28
Anticipating is even more fun than recollecting.

Gather the family around to plan a vacation and just watch the excitement and enthusiasm burst forth. The anticipation of the fun and relaxation, just the idea of getting away for a few days with a change of scenery and schedule, brings an atmosphere of pleasure and expectation. Packing and planning and mapping the travel route all bring on pleasurable hours of family fun. After the trip is all over, recollecting the memories made is fun but not nearly as exhilarating as the planning.

Just the thought of heaven and eternity with Christ brings a feeling of anticipation to Christians. Reading God's Word and getting little tidbits here and there about heaven should make us start to get our bags packed and our hearts in order! Eternity with our Creator is beyond any vacation that we could ever imagine. As we think of those we love who have gone before us, it is with anticipation that we long for the time that we will again see them and know them as they were known. Picture no more suffering or heartache and our bodies transformed and made perfect. There will be praising and singing on the streets of gold, and there will be no need of sun, moon, or stars for the Lamb of God will be the light that illuminates the Holy City. Eternity will be a glorious time that never ends. We will not return to this old world to reminisce, recall, or recollect for all things for the saved will be new.

There is no paradise that we could book, no reservation available to take us to a place that begins to compare with what God has planned for those who love Him and have chosen to give their lives to Him. When we say yes to Jesus, our names are immediately written in the Book of Life and our confirmations are secure.

Got your bags packed? Made your reservations? Read all you can in preparation for an eternity that is indescribable. The Bible gives good directions on how to get there!

Things which eye has not seen, and ear has not heard, and which have not entered into the heart of man, all that God hath prepared for those who love Him. (1 Cor. 2:9)

September 29
The entire sum of existence is the magic of being needed by just one person.

Sometimes we forget just how much we need one another. Oftentimes we get so busy or self-absorbed that we forget how much a kind word, a sincere smile, or a reassuring pat on the shoulder means. The human touch gives encouragement and comfort.

As my mother lay so desperately sick on her bed in her last days, she made known to me on numerous occasions how much she wanted me at her side. I made every effort to be there for her. Many times as I sat by her bed, I thought back on all the times that I had reached out to her, and she was always there for me.

I recall how, as a child, I feared going to the dentist. I remember on one occasion that I ran down the street in front of our house to avoid going to a dreaded appointment. After some gentle persuasion, Mother convinced me that it would be all right and that she would be by my side. My only consolation was that my mother could go in with me. She stood by me the entire time, holding my hand to comfort and console me. I can remember to this day how that made it all bearable and gave me peace. My hand in hers was all I needed. She never let me down, and I knew that I would never let her down.

God is real, and He wants to be our comfort and peace at all times. He promised that He would never leave or forsake us (Heb. 13:5). It is reassuring to have a God who makes a promise like that. Many times I feel His presence and know that He is beside me to help and comfort me. One such time was when my precious mother slipped into eternity. I sat alone beside her in the wee hours of the night, holding her hand as she had held mine. What a gift God gave me, to be with her as she gently moved into the arms of her Savior.

Who needs you today? Let them know that you are there for them. Like a boomerang, love and caring always come back to you.

Draw near to God and He will draw near to you. (James 4:8)

September 30
The trouble with making mental notes
is that the ink fades so fast.

Alzheimer's disease is one of the dreaded diseases of our time. It seems that more and more people from as young as forty-five years of age and older are affected by this monster that robs the brain of memory and the ability to think and reason. The mind seems to disintegrate, leaving the person functional for a while and gradually robbing them of all control. There seems to be no rhyme or reason to the onset of Alzheimer's disease. Its subtle symptoms just creep up like a hidden thief and rob its victims of life and living, placing them in mere existence.

A wonderful, aging preacher, Reverend Waldo Woodcock, visited our church one Sunday and spoke to our senior adults. I recorded the following "do's" in my notes and believe them to be good advice to us all, old or young.

1. Read some every day.
2. Think positive thoughts.
3. Work some.
4. Rest some.
5. Play some.
6. Laugh some (medicine for the soul).
7. Exercise some.
8. Develop a hobby.
9. Do at least one good thing that's unexpected every day.
10. Try giving yourself away.
11. Don't be afraid of anything.
12. Pray some every day. (God wants fellowship with you).

I don't like to admit it, but I have gotten to that stage myself—you know, going into a room to get something and forgetting what you went to get. I just stand there until it comes to me or go back and trace my steps in hopes it will jar my memory. The mind is one of God's most complex creations. We think the computer is amazing, but it does not compare to the complexity of the human brain. When God created man in His own image, He gave him the ability to think as God thinks. We have the capacity to do more than our time on this earth will ever allow us to do. That is why it is important for us not to waste time with trivial things but to focus on the things of God.

Make your own list of do's today that will stimulate your mind and get you to thinking.

For who has known the mind of the Lord, that he should instruct him? But we have the mind of Christ. (1 Cor. 2:16)

October

"For I know the plans that I have for you," declares the Lord, "plans for welfare and not for calamity to give you a future and a hope. Then you will call upon Me and come and pray to me, and I will listen to you. And you will seek Me and find *Me*, when you search for me with all your heart." (Jer. 29:11–13)

October 1
How wise are Thy commandments, O Lord. Each one of them applies to somebody I know. —Sam Levenson

How obvious are the sins of others! Are we blinded to our own faults and downfalls, or do we just choose to ignore or excuse them? When the world around us is doing what is right in their own eyes, do you find yourself trying to fit into their mold or holding fast to the teachings of God's Word that tell us that if we belong to Him, we are to be different from the world? It doesn't take much to justify your sin by the world's standards if everybody's doing it. When we get away from God's plan for our lives, we are chasing a lost cause.

Sin shows its ugly head in many areas of our lives. The choices we make are not always the right choices, even as Christians. The people we associate with do not always reflect Christ's way. Our actions are not always God-centered. However, we are each accountable to God for our own choices, thoughts, and actions. When the time comes for us to give an account of how we have lived this earthly life, God will not call on our friends to testify on our behalf, nor will He ask for our input at the judgment seat. Each person will stand before Him alone. Our lives will be an open book with no pages hidden or torn out.

God knows every man's and woman's heart and desires for each of us to walk steadfastly before Him so that, in the end, eternity with Him will be ours. The story of the rich man and Lazarus in Luke16 gives us a vivid picture of why we don't procrastinate when it comes to giving our lives to Jesus. The rich man in his fine purple clothing walked by the beggar, Lazarus, day in and day out with never a thought of helping him. When they both died, the rich man found himself being tormented by the flames of hell. He begged Abraham to send Lazarus to dip his finger in water and cool his tongue for he was in agony. When that was not possible, he begged Abraham to send him to warn his five brothers so that they would not come there. Abraham said to him, "If they do not listen to Moses and the prophets, neither will they be persuaded if someone rises from the dead" (v. 31). Let's be ready!

Let us search and try our ways, and turn again to the Lord. (Lam. 3:40)

October 2
Worry is a thin stream of fear which, if encouraged, becomes a wide channel into which all other thoughts flow. –Unknown

What do you fear the most? Is it death? Is it the hidden things that darkness hides, or is it the unknown tomorrow? Do you fear loneliness, pain, or suffering? Maybe it is other nations or their leaders. One of the greatest bonuses of being a Christian is knowing that whatever we face, Christ our Lord is with us. We will never face anything that He will not be there for us to give us the peace and courage we need to sustain us.

There is no assurance offered to us anywhere like the promises we have in God's Word. Our steadfast hope is that God never fails and His grace is sufficient for all our needs. His loving-kindness comforts our sorrows and calms our fears. His strength becomes our strength when we lean on Him. Our Savior is more than adequate to meet all of our needs.

I have yet to find a place in the Bible where God called someone to do a job for which He did not empower them. Over and over again, He called ordinary people to do extraordinary things. His promise to each of them was the assurance that He would strengthen and help them. From Adam in the book of Genesis to John in the book of Revelation and all in between, God's miraculous plan will be fulfilled. We need not worry or fear, for just as the promises made to the great cloud of witnesses who have gone before us have been kept by the Great I Am, so will His faithfulness be to you and me.

Through the prophet Isaiah, God spoke a great promise to the Israelite people that resonates with us today as well:

Do not fear, for I am with you; do not anxiously look about you, for I am your God. I will strengthen you, surely I will help you, surely I will uphold you with My righteous right hand. Behold, all those who are angered at you will be shamed and dishonored; those who contend with you will be as nothing, and will perish. You will seek those who quarrel with you, but will not find them. Those who war with you will be as nothing, and nonexistent. For I am the Lord your God, who upholds your right hand. (Isa. 41:10–13).

America has this promise as well if we put our trust in Him!

God is our refuge and strength, a present help in trouble. Therefore, we will not fear. (Ps. 46:1–2a)

October 3
Happiness depends on circumstances; joy does not.

David asked God to restore to him the joy of his salvation (Ps. 51:12). He had known the joy of fellowship with God and service to his king but had forfeited it for sins of the flesh. He lost his joy through the guilt of sin and separation from Holy God. David disobeyed God. He committed adultery, murdered, lied, and coveted. God loved David still, but David lost his peace with God and God waited for his repentance.

Sin separates us from the joy that we have in Christ. It destroys our peace and fills us with guilt. We can fill our lives with all sorts of activities and distractions, some very entertaining, that make us happy for a time to try to dispel the dark shadows of sinfulness in our lives, but joy does not come again until we receive God's cleansing through *our* repentance and *His* forgiveness. His cleansing purifies us and restores us to a right relationship with Him. His forgiveness was made possible for us when He shed his precious blood on the cross to cover our sins. No more sacrificing rams and goats—Jesus, the perfect Lamb of God, became our perfect sacrifice. Only He can take away our sins and restore our joy.

Like David, we need deliverance from our sins in order to enjoy living. David also asked God for a "willing spirit to sustain me." He desired not to fall away again. "Create in me a clean heart, O God, and renew a steadfast spirit within me" (Ps. 51:10).

God's Word tells us that we can have joy in the midst of hardship and suffering. I have watched many who have walked through trials, pain, grief, and struggles and glorified God through their hard times. Nehemiah's words come to my mind as he encouraged God's people with the words, "The joy of the Lord is your strength" (Neh. 8:10). David came to realize that the joy of the Lord far outweighs the short-lived pleasure of sin.

In Thy presence is fullness of joy; in Thy right hand there are pleasures forever. (Ps. 16:11b)

October 4
Some people make the world a better place just by being in it.

I found this little saying on a poster and taped it to the back of the door by my mother's bed. Each time her caregiver shut the door to her room, the words flashed before her eyes. Mother spent many solitary hours on her bed in her last days. Many times she questioned why God was keeping her here when "I am no good for anything," she would say. We would all assure her that she was a blessing to everyone because she was showing us how to handle trials with grace and trusting God for whatever each day would bring. She encouraged and inspired us all.

The author of this little saying must have known my mother. Her very existence was an inspiration to all who knew her. From the age of forty she suffered from the crippling pain of rheumatoid arthritis. In her later years, osteoporosis set in also and brought on additional pain and suffering as the vertebrae in her back began to collapse. The combination of the two debilitating diseases brought her low, and eventually she got to a bedridden state. Many times I saw her face almost chalky with pain, but amazingly, she never complained. My sweet daddy never left her side. A devoted husband, he loved and encouraged her, exercising her limbs in hopes that one day she would walk again.

None of us knows where life will lead us or the challenges we will face as we walk this earthly journey. There is one thing we can know, and that is that our God will never leave us or forsake us (Heb. 13:5).

He is faithful, and He calls us to that as well. It is easy to be light and shine brightly for Him when all is going well with our health, circumstances, and future. The hard part comes when we have to look past the difficult things and trust the One who can walk us through them. For some that is perplexing. Maybe that is why we admire those who seem to handle trials with so much grace.

The assurance of our loving heavenly Father enables His children to trust Him in good times and hard times. Like Job of old and like my mother, let us hold fast to His path and "come forth as gold" (Job 23:10).

**My grace is sufficient for you, for power is
perfected in weakness. (2 Cor. 12:9)**

October 5
Great are the works of the Lord. —Ps. 111:2

Grandchildren are such a blessing, and they enlighten us in our later years to all the wonders around us that we would miss if not for their little insights and imaginations. They have a way of seeing things that we sometimes don't.

When one of our grandsons was about two years old, he begged to go for a golf cart ride like we always had to do when they were visiting. It is always a thrill for all of them to ride to the back of the field in hopes of seeing a deer or to pet the horses in the back pasture. As we rode along, the sun was just beginning to go down, creating a beautiful sunset. It moved behind a rather large, dense cloud but shone brightly all around the edges of the cloud. I pointed out to him the beauty of the scene. Immediately he pointed out a little boy's view of the whole picture. "It's a tractor, Gran-Gran!" he shouted with excitement. Then he looked at me as seriously as a two-year-old can and said, "It's probably God's tractor." What a thrilling revelation for a child and an even greater one for a grandmother—for my grandchild, that God is real, and for me, the assurance that he knows that at such a young age.

The handiwork of our God is all around us. Sometimes we get so familiar with its beauty that we take it for granted. The changing seasons, the sunsets, the amazing differences in the animals, the sun by day and moon and stars by night, the vastness of deserts and the rolling oceans, the freshly plowed fields and the growing crops, the flowers and the trees—God wants us to enjoy his beautiful creation and stand in awe of all that He has made for our good pleasure. He also expects us to be good stewards of all that He has blessed and entrusted to our care. We are to tend and preserve it so that all generations can enjoy what He has made.

The most awesome of all his creation is humankind. We are called to worship the Creator while finding pleasure in the creation. It's a win-win!

**And God saw all that He had made, and
behold, it was very good. (Gen. 1:31)**

October 6
There are two ways of spreading light: to be the candle or the mirror that reflects it. –Edith Wharton

We definitely have a moral crisis going on in America and, for that matter, all over the world. America, supposedly being a Christian nation founded on Christian principles, makes our downfall more obvious than that of other nations. The willing deaths of millions of innocent, unborn babies and the sanctioning of partial-birth abortion sends shivers down the spines of those of us who see the handwriting on the wall. God does not tolerate such actions and, I fear, will judge America as He did the Israelites in Jeremiah's day. They were sacrificing their young to idols, and God gave them a word through the prophet Jeremiah, but they remained stiff-necked and did not obey His voice (7:23). "Yet they did not obey or incline their ear, but walked in their own counsels and in the stubbornness of their evil heart, and went backward and not forward" (7:24). He went on to say that they were not ashamed of their abomination, nor did they blush (8:12). God's judgment was swift.

God loves America just as He loves Israel. But He is a Holy God and abhors evil and disobedience. He will not stand for it, nor will He overlook it. His judgment will fall on us as it did Israel if we do not repent and turn from our wicked ways. God desires to show mercy, but there is no mercy without repentance. Moral decay brings with it a stench that is unbearable to those striving to live like Jesus. Sexual immorality and self-inflicted physical abuse from drugs, alcohol, suicide, and pornography, all of which poison the very soul of a being, further substantiate our obvious crisis and grieve the heart of God.

God does not tolerate sin. He expects moral purity and holiness from His chosen ones. We are to be the light that exposes sin and dispels the darkness of worldliness. Christians are to shine out like beacons to lead the lost to the safe harbor that is found in Jesus Christ our Lord. Do your part today to brighten the corner where you are!

Then the righteous will shine forth as the sun in the kingdom of their Father. He who has ears, let him hear. (Matt. 13:43)

October 7
Excellence is to do a common thing in an uncommon way.

"Finally, brethren, whatever is true, whatever is honorable, whatever is right, whatever is pure, whatever is lovely, whatever is of good repute, if there is any excellence and if anything worthy of praise, let your mind dwell on these things" (Phil. 4:8). Paul was an encourager. He never stopped visiting and writing to the churches that he established in order to give them guidance and encouragement. There were times, however, when instruction and reprimand were needed to keep a church on the right track. Paul longed for the early Christians to excel in the cause of Christ. Many times he was writing to them from a prison cell, but he never wanted them to become pessimistic, discouraged, or disheartened as a result of his struggles and sufferings in sharing the gospel.

In today's world we are finding it more and more challenging to reach the lost world. Christians seek to be creative as we search for ways to fulfill the Great Commission found in Matthew 28:19–20, which God calls us to when we become His disciples. His desire is that "every creature" will hear and come to know Him before it is too late. God's commission to us definitely is not a common thing, but we must creatively implement uncommon ways to reach those who run from the truth. Realizing that we cannot save anyone on our own, we still are responsible for offering the lost world the truth that comes only from God, pointing them to Him so that His Holy Spirit will draw them as we pray to the Father that they will hear His voice, repent, and be saved.

Is your challenge today a simple one that seems common and unpretentious? Will your modest efforts go unnoticed and unrewarded? Maybe they will, but God's excellent way calls us to "press on toward the goal for the prize of the upward call of God in Christ Jesus" (Phil. 3:14). Little becomes much when we place it in His hands.

I can do all things through Christ who strengthens me. (Phil. 4:13)

October 8
Don't find fault. Find a remedy.

I have a wonderful friend who lives elsewhere, and we don't get to see each other often. But when we are able to get together, we pick up right where we left off. She is the kind of person who is the same every time you see her. She radiates with Christian love and never criticizes or finds fault with anyone. I commented to her one day, "Janie, you are so positive and never critical. That is such a wonderful attribute." She said, "My mother was my best example. She never had time for that. In fact, I'm not sure she ever even thought a bad thought. If she did, she never said it." I thought, *What a legacy to pass on!*

Finding fault is such a waste of time. Like gossip, it is powerfully destructive. We cannot be good or right or a good example to anyone apart from the power of Christ and the Holy Spirit in us. My, how we limit God when we fail to allow His power to dwell in us and control us.

Our old sinful nature shows its ugly head every time and reveals the secret places of a desperate heart in need of the Savior's grace and direction. Apart from Him, we can do nothing that is noble or significant toward solving differences.

What kind of remedy suffices when we are tempted to retaliate or criticize? How do we handle a difficult situation when we find ourselves up against the wall and having feelings of hatred or oppression? Maybe we could stop and ask ourselves, "What would Jesus do? How would Jesus handle a situation like this one?" A quick prayer always works for me. God is right there all the time and ready to offer us all of the help that we need. Many times we read in the Psalms where David said, "I call upon the Lord." David knew where his help came from. Do you? Are we capable of always seeing the best in people like Janie and her mother? If we know the One from whom our help comes, we too can find ourselves being free from fault-finding and criticism and resort to a better way of settling our differences.

**And call upon me in the day of trouble; I shall rescue
you, and you will honor Me. (Ps. 50:15)**

October 9
Early to bed, early to rise, makes a man healthy, wealthy, and wise.

My daddy was a farmer, so he got up before daylight every morning. Mother was right there with him, making sure that she prepared him a good breakfast before he started his busy day. They recalled many times how they always enjoyed that early morning time together. With four children, I am sure that those quiet moments before we all got up were precious and memorable to their relationship. It was a quiet time when they could share their hearts with each other about their day-to-day concerns, their finances, their plans for the future, and any issues that they might have been facing. I remember well rising to the smell of coffee and homemade biscuits.

Good habits are very important to living a successful and fruitful life. God desires for each of His children to have good health, prosperity, and good judgment. Choosing to live according to His guidance helps us to succeed and progress toward abundant living.

Just as we enjoy time alone with a spouse, a child, or a friend, time alone with our Creator God is a treasure that is beyond measure. Seeking Him in the early morning hours before the world begins to awaken helps you to examine your own heart and hear His voice in the quietness before a busy day begins. We must know stillness and solitude in order to hear the voice of God calling, beckoning, or drawing us. The prophets of old must have been attuned to God's call in order to follow His instructions and hear the utterances of His heart as He directed them. Until we make an intentional effort to hear Him, we will fail in our effort to follow as He leads.

My husband and I, too, have an early morning time together as my parents did. Coffee and conversation get any day off to a good start. I treasure that time. It is always followed by my quiet time alone with God, and I know that I am healthier, wealthier, and wiser for it.

In the morning, O Lord, Thou wilt hear my voice; in the morning I will order my prayer to Thee and eagerly watch. (Ps. 5:3)

October 10
Love is a fabric which never fades, no matter how often it is washed in the water of adversity and grief. —E. C. McKenzie

One of my most treasured belongings is an old quilt that was given to me by a dear lady in Tennessee. For many years my husband and I would go to Shelbyville to the Tennessee Walking Horse National Celebration, and we would stay with this precious lady. In our room was an old quilt that I admired on each visit. She knew that I loved old things, and on one occasion she handed me the lovely old quilt and told me that she wanted me to have it as a gift from her. I was delighted. It is obviously very old and was, without a doubt, used regularly for it is worn and tattered. The condition of the old quilt makes it even more meaningful and appealing to me because many have been warmed by it. The main thing that drew me to that old quilt, however, was the still-brilliant yellow color. Years of use had frayed the threads that bound it and even worn many of the pieces, but the color was faded very little. The beautiful yellow gave warmth and strength to a lovely antique that I still treasure today.

Paul expressed the excellence of love in his letter to the Corinthian church. He told them that all of their spiritual gifts and good deeds meant nothing if they did not have love. Then he told them what true love for one another looked like. "Love is patient, love is kind, and not jealous; love does not brag and is not arrogant, does not act unbecomingly; it does not seek its own, is not provoked, does not take into account a wrong suffered, does not rejoice in unrighteousness, but rejoices with the truth; bears all things, believes all things, hopes all things, endures all things" (1 Cor. 13:4–7). Like the brightness of that old quilt, love should not fade.

Pain and suffering often test love. They can fray us and wear us down, making us tattered and worn, but love can be strengthened through struggles and hardship. Love grows stronger as it is practiced and perfected. The old quilt was given to me in love, and love for one another is only made brighter the more it is given away.

Love never fails. (1 Cor. 13:8)

October 11
Even though we can't have all we want, we ought to be thankful we don't get what we deserve.

The depths of my very soul are not deep enough to go when I am seeking an answer from my God. There are times when I yearn to hear from Him, but silence is evident. I cry out, and in frustration, I wrestle with my own lack of faith, ashamed that I can't trust Him and wait. God is willing, but my spirit is not always ready to accept the

answers that He has before me. He never deliberately conceals anything from me, and I know that, but at times I cannot hear for the noise of my own conflict and impatience.

As I write this, I feel myself identifying with the psalmist as many times he cried out in despair but could not hear from God. His heart was willing to receive, but the deliverer was not ready. Many times sin clouds our thinking, and many times worldly distractions do the same. David begged God to examine him and try him, to test his mind and his heart (Ps. 26:2). "Hear, O Lord, when I cry with my voice, and be gracious to me and answer me" (Ps. 27:7). I feel those yearnings myself.

Like David, we know that God is there. He promises that He hears us when we call to Him with a repentant spirit and with a pure heart. Our cries never escape His ears. We are to "rest in the Lord and wait patiently for Him" (Ps. 37:7). Our hope is in the Lord, and we must wait for Him even though we do not deserve His answer.

When we seek the face of Holy God with our whole heart through prayer and the Word, He *will* show us the way that we should go. I am confident of that. His promises never fail. We can be certain of it. Even though my soul waits for the Lord, even now, His eye is on me and He has never forsaken me. My hope rests in Him. He is always faithful.

What is your cry today? Maybe it is a cry for an answer to something for which you have been praying for a long time. God told Paul that His grace was sufficient for him (2 Cor. 12:9). I am satisfied with His grace, if that is His answer to me. I certainly don't deserve that unmerited favor!

**I waited patiently for the Lord; and He inclined
to me and heard my cry. (Ps. 40:1)**

October 12
Change your life, improve the world. Improve the world, change many lives.

God has called on His chosen ones, those who have chosen for Him to reign supreme in their lives, to be salt and light in this world in which we live. Salt adds flavor and also preserves. Light dispels darkness and brightens the gloom. Light also exposes those things hidden in order that truth might be seen.

We each start out as a sinful human being, born with a sinful nature passed down from Adam, who chose to disobey God rather than to obey Him. As a result, sin entered into the world, causing havoc from the beginning. Sin always produces chaos and confusion. Disorder immediately followed the sin of Adam and Eve. One sin led to another sin and even flowed over to their offspring as one son killed the other.

Only God can change a life that has taken a wrong turn and followed the road to destruction. We are made in His image, but we do not have His heart until we allow the Holy Spirit to indwell us. Our born-again nature comes when we choose Jesus over the world and invite Him in. Jesus changed the world in the three short years that He ministered on this earth. Our light and salt influence only comes when we give ourselves to the One who can show us how it is done. With Christ in us, we have the power to live victorious lives and illuminate the darkness around us. Christ's followers add flavor to the world. Anything without salt is tasteless and bland. A joyful Christian radiates with peace, hope, love, confidence, and on and on, adding flavor and quality to life.

I really enjoy the show *Fixer Upper* on HGTV. Chip and Joanna Gaines take a house that has lost its zeal and transform it into a beautiful home for a family that is waiting to see the transformation. God does that for us if we allow that change in our life. Just as a fixer-upper house is changed and improves the entire neighborhood, so can we change the world and many lives if we let Christ rule. Are you ready to see your fixer-upper?

You are the salt of the earth.... You are the
light of the world. (Matt. 5:13, 14)

October 13
Any man who is good for anything, if he is always thinking about himself, will come to think himself good for nothing very soon. —Phillips Brooks

It is hard for us to see ourselves as God sees us. The world and all those around us see us one way, we picture ourselves another way, and our heavenly Father sees us in still another way. God sees what He knows we can become and what we are in Him. He sees us precious yet not perfect, sinful yet forgiven, human yet sanctified. He promises that He will continue His good work in us until the day that He comes to take us to be with Him. What a promise! Our vision could never be capable of such projection or insight.

How could we not all love and admire America's preacher, Billy Graham. Although we claimed him as our preacher, his mission and ministry reached out to the entire world. He never lost sight of God's calling on his life. A man of true integrity and humility, he never wavered from the gospel that He proclaimed, that good news to people that offers hope and the promise of eternal life with Holy God. His children said of him that the Billy Graham that the world saw was the same Billy Graham that they saw at home. There were not two Billy Grahams. "A righteous man who walks in his integrity— how blessed are his sons after him" (Prov. 20:7).

Glory be to God that He can see anything of worth in sinful people, but He does. He has provided a way in which we can be righteous, not perfect but in right standing with He who will give us the power to walk as sons of God. Billy Graham was not perfect; in fact, in many of his sermons he stated that Jesus was the only perfect man. However, he set out to do the will of his heavenly Father, and God blessed him with the power to walk in the footsteps of Jesus. By following Jesus we can all live lives of integrity and humility, fixing our eyes on Him, the author and perfecter of our faith (Heb. 12:2). By His blood at Calvary, we are made righteous, holy, sanctified, and redeemed. Praise God!

For God *sees* not as man sees, for man looks at the outward appearance, but the Lord looks at the heart. (1 Sam. 16:7b, emphasis added)

October 14

I believe the Bible is the best gift God has ever given to man. All the good from the Savior of the world is communicated to us through this book. —President Abraham Lincoln

"Despise God's Word and find yourself in trouble. Obey it and succeed" (Prov. 13:13 TLB). The Bible is our direction giver, our compass that navigates us through this life. Every word is true. There are no errors, no mistakes, and no flaws—mysteries, yes. God tells us that (Matt. 13:11). By faith we accept the revealed truths of His hand.

I am the Bible, God's wonderful library.

I am always, and above all the truth.

To the weary pilgrim, I am a strong staff.

To the one who sits in darkness, I am glorious light.

To those who stumble beneath heavy burdens, I am sweet rest.

To him who has lost his way, I am a safe guide.

To those who are sick in sin, I am healing, strength, and forgiveness.

To the discouraged, I am a glad message of hope.

(Author unknown)

"In the beginning was the Word, and the Word was with God, and the Word was God. He was in the beginning with God" (John 1:1–2). The Bible is God the Father, God the Son, and God the Holy Spirit. Everything God said in the scripture was culminated in Jesus. "And the Word became flesh, and dwelt among us, and we beheld His glory, glory as of the only begotten from the Father, full of grace and truth" (John 1:14). God's Word to us is the Sword of the Spirit that cuts deep and convicts us; it's truth is the bread of life that sustains us.

If you abide in my word, then you are truly disciples of mine; and you shall know the truth and the truth shall make you free. (John 8:31–32)

October 15
We will not waver; we will not tire; we will not falter, and we will not fail. Peace and freedom will prevail. –George W. Bush

We have all heard the saying, "Freedom is not free." Ronald Reagan put it this way: "Freedom is never more than one generation away from extinction. We didn't pass it to our children in the bloodstream. It must be fought for, protected, and handed on for them to do the same."

Tolerance has gotten to be the word for this generation. According to Webster's dictionary, to tolerate is "to allow to be, or to be done, without hindrance; to allow or permit by not preventing. To put up with or endure." The path of tolerance is chosen for different reasons. It can be through complacency or being content with the way things are. Or perhaps, people just don't want to get involved. Maybe it's chosen by people who lack the knowledge of absolute truth, who listen to those around them rather than seeking God's absolute standards for living from the Bible. Then there is compromise, to go along with something that is not right just to get it settled. Somebody once said, "If it is wrong, fight against it. If it is right, fight for it." There are a lot of ways to be wrong but only one way to be right. Abraham Lincoln once said to a man, "Sir, my concern is not whether God is on our side; my greatest concern is to be on God's side, for God is always right." He got that right!

The responsibility to pass God's ways on to the next generation is in the hands of the previous generation. Moses wrote God's words to us in Deuteronomy 11:18–20: "You shall therefore impress these words of mine on your heart and on your soul.... And you shall teach them to your sons, talking of them when you sit in your house and when you walk along the road and when you lie down and when you rise up. And you shall write them on the doorposts of your house and on your gates." What is God calling us to pass on to the generations? "To love the Lord your God and to serve Him with all your heart and all your soul" (v. 13). That must be our cry!

Thank God for the men and women who guard the freedom of our country. May we join them to preserve this one nation under God. May we never forget to stop and thank God for all the ways He has blessed us.

Blessed is the nation whose God is the Lord. (Ps. 33:12)

October 16
There is just one way to bring up a child in the way that he should go, and that is to travel that way yourself. —Abraham Lincoln

I have heard it said, "If only youth knew how to live and old age could." It seems by the time we have figured it all out, life is over. That is why it is so important to give God our young days, and then we don't have to live with so many regrets.

Josiah was eight years old when he became king of Judah. For thirty-one years he reigned and was a good and honorable king. His father, Amon, and his grandfather, Manasseh, before him had not served as righteous kings. They worshipped idols and did evil in the sight of the Lord. Josiah did not have godly examples to follow; however, we see in Josiah's heart the desire even at a young age to do right and follow God's ways. Josiah made a covenant before the Lord "to walk after the Lord, and to keep His commandments and His testimonies and His statutes with all his heart and all his soul" (2 Kings 23:3). He also inspired the people to enter into the covenant with him. The scripture goes on to tell us that there had been no king before him, nor did one come after him, whose heart, soul, and might were totally the Lord's (v. 25). We find in Matthew 1:10 that Josiah was an ancestor of Jesus Christ. Unfortunately, Josiah's sons did not follow in the footsteps of their father.

As much as we want our children and grandchildren to love God and serve Him, it ultimately has to be their choice. We should never, by any means, stop trying to influence and direct them toward the ways of God, always teaching them and living the right example before them. Because each of us has free volition, a right to choose our path in life, we can choose God or reject Him. He did not make us puppets but allows us to make our own choices. Sadly, many fall into the world's way rather than the way that God has for all those who love him. We are to live before our children as if we are the only Bible they will ever read. Jesus is our example.

Teach me good discernment and knowledge, for I believe in Thy commandments. Ps. 119:66

October 17
God never closes a door when He doesn't open a window.

In the late 1960s we bought a one-hundred-year-old, two-story, fixer-upper farmhouse at the edge of town. Our old house has added warmth and comfort to our lives. Through the years of raising three children, we have made improvements not only to keep it up but to create lovable, livable areas that add life and charm.

One of the best things we have done was to open up the kitchen onto the small back porch and glass in the porch to make a sitting area with a wood-burning stove and comfortable chairs. During the summer and winter, this small area affords us the comfort of indoors with the openness of outdoors. My husband and I have enjoyed many hours in this space with our cups of coffee. We can look out over the open pasture at the horses, see deer walking by the back fence, enjoy birds at the feeders, and spot friends and family as they drive up to the back door. Because our back door is also glass, we can see out of it with no problem.

I am so glad that God does not need a glass door to be able to see what is on the other side. Our lives are full of choices that we have to make. Many times those choices are hard and we need the help of wise counsel in order to discern what is best. When we call on God for His wisdom and insight, we can know without a doubt that His judgment will be in our best interest if we leave the choices with Him. God sees the big picture. He knows what lies on the other side. He sees our heart and knows our thoughts.

Have you ever wanted something so bad yet your plans fell through? Many times God's answers to our prayers depend on our motives. Jabez of Old Testament history came boldly before God and asked Him to enlarge his territory (1 Chron. 4:10). Why did God honor Jabez's request? Because he came with the right motives. He wanted (1) God to enlarge his territory, (2) God's hand to be on him, and (3) God to keep Him from evil. He acknowledged that He needed God. We may not get what we ask for because God may close the door, but you can be sure that when you can't see His plan, you can trust His hand to guide you to a better way.

And again, "I will put my trust in Him." (Heb. 2:13a)

October 18
Heaven is full of answers to prayers for which no one ever bothered to ask. —Billy Graham

How can we know God unless we spend time with Him? How can the Holy Spirit, who in His fullness indwells us at the point that we are born again of the Spirit, intercede for us if we do not first utter our prayers either in the quietness of our spirits or verbally? The Holy Spirit is aware of our needs, and even when we don't know how to pray, "the Spirit Himself intercedes for us with groanings too deep for words" (Rom. 8:26).

God sits on His throne waiting for us to bring our prayers, petitions, and intercessions to Him. God inhabits the prayers of His people just as He inhabits the praise of His people. He answers according to His will and in His timing. When we pray, we have the whole Trinity interposing for us. As the Holy Spirit hears our utterances, Jesus sits at the right hand of the Father making intercession for us. We can be confident that our prayers are adequately heard and will be diligently answered.

Why then do we wait? Why then are we so slow to ask and so reluctant to request an answer from Holy God? Why, sometimes, is that the last resort? We miss many blessings by not spending time in God's presence. He desires our fellowship and the time we can spend with Him. Like our earthly fathers, He knows what we need before we ask Him. But just as we enjoy hearing from our children, so our heavenly Father rejoices in our presence before His throne.

Daniel was a man of prayer. He knew the ways of God because he spent many hours seeking God and His answers. Three times a day Daniel would retreat to his roof prayer chamber where the windows were open toward Jerusalem. He would kneel, thanking God for His blessings before bringing his petitions before Him. From the time of his youth, God granted Daniel favor. From rejecting the king's rich food to trusting in his God when thrown into the lions' den and interpreting dreams and the handwriting on the wall, Daniel always called on his God for answers and direction. Have you bothered to call on God today?

And all things you ask in prayer, believing, you shall receive.
(Matt. 21:22)

October 19
Every limitation I have is an invitation by God to do for me what I cannot do for myself. —Stephen F. Arterburn

God is mighty and greatly to be praised. He calls us to deny ourselves, take up our cross daily, and follow Him (Matt. 16:24). He wants to be our strength. He desires our weakness so that His workmanship might be illuminated and His name glorified as He perfects us. Our limitations are human-made. God tells me that "I can do all things through Him who strengthens me" (Phil. 4:13). We are limited only by our own inability to give Him control. He wants us whole or the broken pieces.

Thus says the Lord, "Let not a wise man boast of his wisdom, and let not the mighty man boast of his might, let not a rich man boast of his riches; but let him who boasts boast of this, that he understands and knows Me, that I am the Lord who exercises lovingkindness, justice, and righteousness on earth; for I delight in these things," declares the Lord. (Jer. 9:23–24)

Jeremiah was a priest and a prophet sent by God during the reign of Josiah. Josiah had been a good king. He rid Judah of idol worship and saw revival among the people. However, when things began to deteriorate again, God sent Jeremiah to preach judgment, but Israel would not listen. Jeremiah was persecuted for his stand and his message of God's truth that he was called to deliver to the people, but he never wavered. He gave them words straight from God, and they could accept them or reject them. Jeremiah trusted God.

We can be inspired by the prophets of old to do as God calls each of us to do today, as well. The apostle Peter reminds us,

But even if you should suffer for the sake of righteousness, you are blessed. And do not fear their intimidation, and do not be troubled, but sanctify Christ as Lord in your hearts, always being ready to make a defense to everyone who asks you to give an account for the hope that is in you, yet with gentleness and reverence. (1 Peter 3:14–15)

The word for today is *trust*.

Do not fear, for I am with you; do not anxiously look about you, for I am your God. I will strengthen you, surely I will help you, surely I will uphold you with My righteous right hand. (Isa. 41:10)

October 20
Parents are embarrassed when their children tell lies, but sometimes it's worse when they tell the truth. –Elton Trueblood

Setting the right example for our children is a responsibility that Jesus was very serious about. He said in Luke 17:2 that it would be better if a millstone were hung around your neck and you be thrown into the ocean than for you to cause even one of His little ones to stumble. In other words, it would be better if we died and had no influence on them than to live and set the wrong example. These are pretty strong words, and Jesus used imagery to illustrate His point so that we would not miss this lesson.

Jesus was not only speaking to parents but to Christians as we live our lives before new Christians, babes in Christ, and also the lost world. To be a stumbling block can hinder spiritual growth of the believer and prevent the lost man or woman from coming to Christ for salvation.

The scribes and the Pharisees in Jesus's day were diligent to keep the Mosaic law to the fullest but seemed to be blind to spiritual things. They were the Jewish sect that was considered to be the religious leaders of their day, yet in their strict regard to go by the letter of the law, they missed the truth of it. Jesus strongly condemned them with seven woes in Matthew 23 for their hypocritical ways. Outwardly, they were pretending to be spiritual with all their rituals and public displays. They were making a show of righteousness before others to be noticed, yet their hearts were wicked. Jesus told his disciples, "Let them alone; they are blind guides of the blind. And if a blind man guides a blind man, both will fall into a pit" (Matt. 15:14). Causing others to stumble is serious. They were guilty of twisting the scriptures and often sought to trap Jesus as He taught.

Can we wear two faces and be effective as Christ's followers? Jesus says no. Causing anyone to be led away from the gospel is blasphemy.

God, help us to live like Christ before our children and our fellow people.

Pay close attention to yourself and to your teaching; persevere in these things; for as you do this you will insure salvation both for yourself and for those who hear you. (1 Tim. 4:16)

October 21
God takes life's broken pieces and gives us unbroken peace. —Wilbert Donald Gough

To be spiritually lost is one thing, but to be lost and broken is painful hopelessness. A broken condition is not terminal, even though it fills that way. A Christian as well as a lost person can experience brokenness. The difference is hope. The Christian comes through brokenness better and refined, whereas a lost person generally becomes bitter with no certainty of the future unless he or she turns to Christ. Hope is found in Jesus Christ.

Oftentimes our heavenly Father allows us to be broken for different reasons. His love is real for the lost sheep just as it is real for His sheep who have found the way. Job was a man who was "blameless, upright, fearing God and turning away from evil" (Job 1:1). He is perhaps our greatest hero of suffering and brokenness in the Bible. His suffering was so great that He called out to God to kill Him. In all of his anguish and despair, he never turned his back on his sovereign Lord, and his peace came in the end.

God is your peace in the midst of the storms of life. Are you placing a spiritual marker on the places where you have seen the hand of God in your life? Many times in scripture, God reminded His people to place a stone, an altar, or a marker, as a reminder of His faithfulness. He instructed them to tell their children so that they would know and pass it on to the next generation. What an important lesson for us. How often we forget how God brought us through a trial, delivered us from danger, healed our broken hearts, or carried us when we could not move another inch.

At one time I kept a journal with a list of times I obviously saw God in my life. Whether it was His protection, answered prayers, His working in the life of my children, or whatever I saw Him doing, I would record it. God's faithfulness is so far ahead of my record keeping that I can't keep up. Let the God of peace take your broken pieces today and give you the peace that surpasses all understanding.

Peace I leave with you, My peace I give to you; not as the world gives, do I give to you. Let not your heart be troubled. (John 14:27)

October 22
The deepest truth blooms only from the deepest love. –Heinrick Hiene

I have many times had the chilling thought of what my choice would be standing before evil men who would make me choose between my child and denying Jesus. I shudder to think that I would ever be put to the test, but God was put in that position. God turned His back on Jesus and sacrificed His only Son for you and for me. That is the truth. Evil humankind took an innocent, sinless man and nailed him to a cross in merciless slaughter. What is so amazing is that Jesus went willingly. He did what He came to earth to do. Jesus became the perfect sacrifice to atone for the sins of humankind—past, present, and future. Only God through Jesus could accomplish this most perfect act of love and redemption. Jesus, the Way, is the truth that sets us free and gives us life. His death on that cruel cross rendered powerless the forces of sin, giving us freedom not to sin.

The kind of love that God showed us that day over two thousand years ago is almost inconceivable. Shouldn't that make us want to love Him more? On the cross Jesus cried, "Father, forgive them for they know not what they do" (Luke 23:34 KJV). I am sure that Jesus knew that they *did* know what they were doing, but He forgave them anyway. Oswald Chambers said, "If human love does not carry a man beyond himself, it is not love." Humans can know the kind of love that Jesus portrayed that day. They can possess the indwelling Spirit of God by submitting to His calling to walk with Him in spirit and in truth, making possible a divine love. Rejecting the very presence of God in your life places you in the crowd that chose to shout, "Crucify Him!"

The arms of Jesus are open wide. He will turn no one away. Thanks be to God for His indescribable gift of love. Thank you, God, that you broke the shackles that bind and freed us to walk with you. Today we pray for all those who do not know you as their personal Savior. Let this be the day of their salvation. Teach us all to love as you loved.

Simon, son of John, do you love Me more than these? (John 21:15)

October 23
The world is a better place each time one more comes to know Jesus.

"But we urge you, brethren, to excel still more, and to make it your ambition to lead a quiet life and attend to your own business and work with your hands" (1 Thess. 4:10b–11). Paul wrote this to the church at Thessalonica in the context of purity and sanctification. But as I read it today, it gives me so much peace and so much assurance that I have not totally let God down.

Maybe you are like me and struggle with the question, "What can I do to make the world a better place?" I believe we all set out in life feeling we need to accomplish something of significance, value, and importance to the world. We ask ourselves, "What have I ever done to make God proud of me? Anything that would cause Him to say when I get to heaven, 'Well done, good and faithful servant'?" My life seems so humdrum compared to many who have preached to millions or taught the multitudes. Many talents have gone far beyond the local church and blessed audiences, inspiring and influencing others to follow Christ.

So what does God expect of those of us who live quiet lives, who tend to our own business and work with our hands? Paul says that we "make it our ambition" to do these things. In other words, we are to be content in the place God has given us to serve. God does not want us to feel inadequate and certainly not unworthy. Jesus said as He spoke to the multitudes in His Sermon on the Mount, "Let your light shine before men in such a way that they may see your good works, and glorify your Father who is in heaven" (Matt. 5:16).

Whether we reach one or millions for Christ, may His name be glorified. When we place our efforts in His hands, big or small, they become much if they are done in His name and glorify the Creator of all good and perfect gifts.

Through Him then, let us continually offer up a sacrifice of praise to God, that is, the fruit of lips that give thanks to His name. And do not neglect doing good and sharing; for with such sacrifices God is pleased. (Heb. 13:15–16)

October 24
The world, after all our science and sciences, is still a miracle, wonderful, inscrutable, magical and more, to whosoever will think of it. —Thomas Carlyle

Who made you? Who created you in His own image? Who ordained your life with purpose? Yes, you got it! God. "But now, O Lord, Thou art our Father, we are the clay, and Thou our potter; and all of us are the work of Thy hand" (Isa. 64:8). Look all around you at this gorgeous universe. When we think about the One who spoke it all into being, the One who has continued to keep everything in motion, we should never doubt the infinite ability of the Creator to direct, sustain, and fulfill a purpose for each of our lives.

Humans reach even beyond the world we live in to find answers to their questions about the creation and the universe. Where humans fail, however, is when he neglects to live with faith in the Creator. Jesus said, "For what is a man profited if he gains the whole world and loses or forfeits himself?" (Luke 9:25).

As humankind explores new horizons, they only create for themselves more questions about all that God has created. The awesomeness of a magnificent universe is evident as space travel brings it home to our finite minds. Research and science unfold miraculous findings only to reveal to us even more the magnitude of God's creation. In only six days Creator God spoke it all into being— yes, spoke it into being.

We will never know all the mysteries of this vast universe that we live in for this short life span. No matter how great the discovery or how vast the exploration, humans need most to believe in the Creator of it all, not the Creation. As marvelous as it is, the One who blessed us with life to live and enjoy the beauty and awesomeness of it all is the One to whom we give all worship and praise. From our biggest questions to our greatest needs, God has the answers. He spoke it all into His Word!

In the beginning God created the heavens and the earth.
And the earth was formless and void, and darkness was
over the surface of the deep; and the Spirit of God was
moving over the surface of the waters. (Gen. 1:1–2)

October 25
Miracles are of all sizes. And if you start believing in little miracles, you can work up to the bigger ones. –Norman Vincent Peale

Seen any miracles lately? It would do us all good to begin recording all the little miracles we encounter on a daily basis. Sometimes we take them so lightly, it's a wonder God even shows us another one.

The miracles around us—like the beauty of the world and the changing seasons, the birth of a baby, a changed heart, the rising and setting of the sun, just to name a few—often go unnoticed as we busily pass through this life. God is rich in His blessings and shows Himself to us in miraculous ways, but we don't always take notice. God does not change, and neither does His power diminish. His miraculous ways just get better and better the more we entrust our faith to Him.

In Matthew 11:20–24, Jesus spoke harshly to the people in the three cities of Chorazin, Bethsaida, and Capernaum. Most of His miracles to this point had been done in these cities, yet the people had not repented of their sin. Seemingly in disgust, Jesus spoke woes to them, saying that if cities like Tyre, Sidon, and Sodom had seen the miracles that these other cities had seen, they would have repented and not had judgment placed on them. When God reveals Himself to us in a real and miraculous way and we ignore it or pass it off as insignificant, He is offended. As a result, many times we miss His blessings.

Often miracles are done in order to bring about repentance, as Jesus stated in this case. Other times it is to bring glory to God. When Jesus performed His miracles as He walked on this earth, no one doubted that they were divine acts. Yes, there were some skeptics, but they could not deny that the acts were from God. Can we deny the hand of God in any of the miracles that we see every day in His Creation? Can you ignore the new creation that you are since your born-again experience?

As you experience miracles from God, acknowledge them, record them, and share them. Give God the glory He deserves.

Many, O Lord my God, are the wonders which Thou hast done.... There is none to compare with Thee. (Ps. 40:5a)

October 26
If God is your copilot, trade places. –Unknown

Who is in the driver's seat of your life? Do you make all of your decisions and choices on your own, or do you consult with the One who made you for guidance and discernment? Like a loving Father, God desires to lead us, to go before us, to protect us, and to guide us. His place is not alongside us or hovering over us. His place is at the controls of our lives through our own submission.

By faith we trust God to take control of our lives when we, in humble submission, die to ourselves and invite Christ into our hearts. Hebrews 11 references saints of old who triumphed in faith. We can learn from many like Abraham, Isaac, Jacob, Moses, Sara, Noah, David, Samuel, the prophets, and many others who looked to God for direction and followed through as they "conquered kingdoms, performed acts of righteousness, obtained promises, shut the mouths of lions, quenched the power of fire, escaped the edge of the sword, from weakness were made strong, became mighty in war, put foreign armies to flight" (vv. 33–34).

May we never forget or diminish the power and wisdom of Holy God as He leads those who will follow. Those who will allow His grace to reign in their lives and seek His truths are like "a tree firmly planted by streams water" (Ps. 1:3a). Giving God control is what we should submit to at salvation. He then is our rock, our anchor, our pilot. "He will not allow your foot to slip; He who keeps you will not slumber" (Ps. 121:3).

Is Jesus the Lord of your life? If yes, then your license has expired. He is in control, and you are safe. He wants first place in your life so that you will stay on the straight and narrow path. The way that is wide leads to destruction, and many go that way. Leave the driving to the One who knows the way and *is* the Way, the Truth, and the Life—Jesus the Christ!

For the love of Christ controls us … (2 Cor. 5:14a)

October 27
You don't get good to get God, you get God to get good. —Jentezen Franklin

*Outreac*h is a common word in our churches today. We use it as a term related to sharing Christ and seeking to bring lost souls into the fold. Our desire as Christians should always be to reach out beyond the walls of the church to those around us who do not know of our Savior and His power to save them. Many don't believe that they need to be saved. My experience has been, when asking the question, "What do you think it takes to be saved?" most think that you just have to be a good person. A good person? Yes, but one can be a good person and still be lost. Without Christ, we are doomed for eternal separation from God. No one wants to go to hell, but hell is a real place and those who are not saved are choosing that destination rather than eternal life in heaven. We cannot be saved until we realize we are lost.

More than a friend or any earthly being, Jesus offers us a friendship that is true and lasting. He "sticks closer than a brother" (Prov. 18:24). He leads us down the path of righteousness. Jesus gives us light for the path during the darkest times, and He guards our steps on the slippery slopes. His saving grace leads us to eternity, where we will dwell in His presence forever. That is just a taste of what children of God inherit when we come to Christ and grow in our relationship with Him. Did you just ask Jesus to come visit one day but not ask Him to stay? Jesus wants to dwell in us in the person of the Holy Spirit when we invite Him in. To have a relationship with someone means we are committed to them and we spend time with them. As our love grows for them, we want to serve them and we value their counsel.

If you are a child of the King, do not neglect to reach out to a lost person at every opportunity. Reach out with what you know—your testimony of what Christ has done in you. If you have not chosen Christ, now is the time to give your heart to Him. Jesus saves.

Therefore if any man is in Christ, he is a new creature; the old things passed away; behold, new things have come. (2 Cor. 5:17)

October 28
Get the last word—apologize.

Forgiveness is a welcome cleansing and brings with it a peace that unburdens a person who is being held hostage by the heaviness of unforgiveness. Whether friend or foe, companion or stranger, no one wants to carry around the burden of a guilty conscience that is at odds with another. Have you ever had an argument with your spouse, one of your children, a friend, or even your boss? There is no peace in your life until the conflict is resolved and you are on good terms again.

Somebody once said, "Forgiveness is not always easy. At times, it feels more painful than the wound we suffered, to forgive the one that inflicted it. And yet, there is no peace without forgiveness."

For the mature person, and especially the mature Christian person, having the last word is irrelevant. It is of far greater importance to be open to forgiveness and love than to demand the last word or an apology. I wonder sometimes if God ever gets tired of His children crying out to Him for forgiveness. It seems that I am constantly crying out in my spirit for Him to forgive a bad thought, a quick not-so-sweet response, or a prideful deed. God is so faithful to hear my prayer as I trust Him to do as John says He will do in 1 John 1:9: "If we confess our sins, He is faithful and righteous to forgive us of our sins and to cleanse us from all unrighteousness." Jesus is the child of God's advocate. He pleads our case before the Father.

God's forgiveness for our sins should always be our example. While we were yet sinners, Christ died for us (Rom. 5:8) He went to the cross, sinless as He was, to be the propitiation for you and for me.

We can pout, we can hold grudges, and we can turn our backs on the ones that hurt us, but nothing is ever settled that way. Forgiveness should be the badge of the Christian as we follow the One who showed us how it is done. Grace is undeserved favor from God. Grace received should be grace shared!

But Thy art a God of forgiveness, gracious and compassionate, slow to anger and abounding in lovingkindness. (Neh. 9:17b)

October 29
My worth is a gift of God. I do not have to earn it or prove it, just enjoy it.

People can be placed into three categories; spiritual, carnal, and natural. The spiritual person is saved and controlled or led by the Holy Spirit. The carnal person is saved but ruled by his or her own emotions. The natural person is spiritually lost and controlled by Satan and the world. Because of our fallen nature that entered the world after the fall of Adam and Eve in the Garden of Eden, we are creatures of sin and separated from Holy God. God cannot look on sin—He hates sin—but because He loves His creation, you and me, so much, He gave us another chance. God sent Jesus to be the propitiation, the sin-bearer, the One who delivers us from the wages of sin and death if we will grasp it and ask Him to come into our hearts. The Bible says, "For the wages of sin is death, but the free gift of God is eternal life in Christ Jesus our Lord" (Rom. 6:23).

Jesus's death on the cross was dreadful and ugly. It was a horrible display of sacrifice, as He willingly took the burden of sin that we should have paid and placed it on Himself as redemption for all of the sins of humankind—past, present and future. An ugly scene was made beautiful by the washing away of sin by the blood of the perfect Lamb. Darkness turned to day and mourning turned to joy as the Savior of all humankind arose from the grave that morning. We can celebrate the resurrection with humble hearts for the grace and mercy that was shown to us.

Celebrate Easter every day of the year as you remember the cross and all that was accomplished there. Living on this side of the cross, you have never had to take a perfect animal to the altar to be sacrificed for your sins. Jesus was our sacrifice once and for all. You never had to let a priest go into the Holy of Holies to ask for forgiveness for your sins. You have direct access to the Father through prayer. We on this side of the cross can live with the hope that, because of Jesus, abundant life here and eternal life in heaven is ours if we accept all that He did for us that extraordinary day.

Blessed are those whose lawless deeds have been forgiven, and whose sins have been covered. (Rom. 4:7)

October 30
Speaking out of turn often puts you at the back of the line.

We have all heard the old saying, "Open mouth, insert foot." Perhaps you have felt these words firsthand as you suddenly spoke out of turn or embarrassingly said the wrong words at the wrong time. You suddenly felt the insatiable urge to withdraw and disappear into a hole, pulling the dirt over on top of you. Life's embarrassing moments can often prove to be just that, or they can be areas of growth and maturity where we learn to think before we speak.

One of my dearest friends has the rare distinction of owning the OMIF award. Several friends have told her that they were going to write a book with all of her untimely comments. She so innocently speaks her heart only to end up red-faced and fanning.

Jesus's beloved disciple Peter could have received the same award for his impulsive personality. Among the disciples, he seemed to be the one who always spoke out first and boldly. When Jesus told of the suffering that He was facing before He went to the cross, Peter spoke out strongly to Jesus, saying, "This shall never happen to You" (Matt. 16:22). Jesus called him Satan and called him a stumbling block (v. 23) because Jesus knew that even though He was dreading the day, it was for this purpose that He had come to earth. Another time Jesus commended Peter as He asked the disciples, "Who do you say that I am?" Peter answered, "Thou art the Christ, the Son of the living God" (Matt. 16:15, 16). Jesus blessed Peter for this correct answer.

Not all of our words come out as we intend them. Sometimes words spoken in haste come back to haunt us. Weigh your words today. Let them be words of encouragement. Speak love. "The one who guards his mouth preserves his life; The one who opens wide his lips comes to ruin" (Prov. 13:3). By the way, my precious friend speaks more healing than blunder!

Let your speech always be with grace, seasoned, as it were with salt, so that you may know how you should respond to each person. (Col. 4:6)

October 31
All things are created twice; first in your mind, and then in your life.

Perhaps you have witnessed or even been the recipient of harsh, hurtful words that cut deeply and leave scars. Many times harmful words bring on actions that make matters even worse. On the other hand, a kind word can turn an entire situation around and melt a heart of stone.

Recently, I was listening as a talk show host questioned a young high school student. It seems the young girl was involved with a gang, and the host sought to find out exactly what they did at school. As the girl continued to talk, it was apparent that all the young people were concerned about was fitting in or being accepted by certain groups. The girl stated that they sit around and "hate each other." My heart broke to hear such a remark from this child. The hopelessness that she and obviously many of her friends were living with was distressing.

How have we failed this generation? Why have so many missed out on the truth of the One who keeps them from such despair? A heart filled with Jesus leaves no room for such feelings. We have fallen short as a people when we separate generations of people from the hope that comes only in Jesus Christ.

Evil is first conceived in a person's mind and then in the heart. It is lived out through our words and actions if not squelched. Young people are especially vulnerable to peer pressure. Many times they hear the one who speaks the loudest, the one who appears to have all the answers. Oftentimes, those are the wrong voices, and they find themselves caught in a web of deceitfulness and hate. They find themselves doing the very things that they despise in others.

We are all acceptable to God, no matter where we have been or where we are headed. It is never too late to surrender our broken pieces to the healer. He makes all things new in His time. He heals the brokenhearted and sets our feet on a new path. Speak truth to a young person today.

If any man is in Christ, he is a new creature; the old things passed away; behold, new things have come. (1 Cor. 5:17)

November

If you then being raised up with Christ, keep seeking the things above, where Christ is, seated at the right hand of God.... When Christ, who is our life, is revealed, then you also will be revealed with Him in glory. (Col. 3:1, 4)

November 1
God plus one is always a majority.

Do you ever feel as if you are standing alone? Your convictions might bring you to that place one day if they haven't already. It is not always easy to stand for right when all others around you are going with the flow. We see so much compromise in our world today, so much humanism, that it utterly sickens the body and discourages the soul of one seeking to do God's will. The creeping effect of sinful compromise and tolerance makes even the strongest Christians fearful for their own ability to remain steadfast and unwavering.

How can we stand when all around us is crumbling and succumbing to the world's way? God does not intend for us to go it alone! Noah stood alone with God while the world laughed. Moses was called to a greater ministry because he was willing to stand alone with God. Mary, the mother of Jesus, was willing to take insult from a skeptical world in order to fulfill God's plan. Paul and Silas preached boldly and were imprisoned many times for standing firmly for the gospel's sake.

The Bible tells us that the time will come when sound doctrine will not be tolerated, "but wanting to have their ears tickled, they will accumulate for themselves teachers in accordance to their own desires; and will turn away their ears from the truth, and will turn aside to myths" (2 Tim. 4:3–4). This tells me that it is even more important than ever to stand, speak truth, and testify to the grace of God. Paul commissions us to "be ready in season and out of season; reprove, rebuke, exhort with great patience and instruction" (v. 2).

The world around us is moaning for a savior, and we know the Savior. He loves all humankind and desires that we all come to Him and know Him in His fullness. He, too, knows what it is like to be hated, rejected, despised, and forsaken. He hung alone on that horrible cross for each of us, but He arose from death. We serve a Savior who is alive, and you are never alone when He is by your side! If God is for us, who is against us? (Rom. 8:31).

But in all these things we overwhelmingly conquer through Him who loved us. (Rom. 8:37)

November 2
Carelessness of speech comes across as ignorance.

Much wisdom comes from the psalmist. Often he targets the tongue as a vessel of good or evil. The Bible tells us that our speech can be as sharp as a sword, as deadly as a serpent, or as consuming as a fire.

Then again, it reminds us that the tongue can bring healing to the listener, offer encouragement, ignite praise, and turn away wrath. "The lips of the righteous feed many, but fools die for lack of understanding" (Prov. 10:21). If you have ever been the victim of a sharp tongue, spewing hurtful words in a careless burst of anger, then you know the truth of God's Word. I have, and it is hard to get over. What is the antidote for that kind of behavior? The psalmist tells us that "a gentle answer turns away wrath, but a harsh word stirs up anger" (15:1). In other words, never retaliate with the anger that is thrown out at you. Let your answer be gentle and nonthreatening. When we return harsh words with more harsh words, we are putting ourselves on the same level as our foolish attacker.

May we always ask God to give us the wisdom of Jesus. In every situation His words were profound. They were never careless or impulsive. His words were powerful and convincing. Even in His anger as the people were disrespecting the temple in a worldly manner, Jesus approached them not in condemnation but in discipline, reminding them that His house was not to be a house of thieves, buying and selling, but a house of prayer and of worship.

As Paul ministered to his fellow workers at the church in Colossae, his word to them was, "Let your speech always be with grace, seasoned, as it were, with salt, so that you may know how you should respond to each person" (Col. 4:6). Paul knew that words could either heal or hurt. Harsh words could deter a lost person from hearing the very heart of the gospel that believers are called to share with the lost world. As Paul taught his listeners, we too should "make the most of the opportunity" to witness (v. 5).

And I say to you, every careless word that men shall speak, they shall render account for it in the day of judgment. (Matt. 12:36)

November 3
Never pass up a chance to pass off a smile. —Author

The countenance speaks clearly the heart of a man, woman or child, or does it? Many a hurting heart masquerades behind a smile, a laugh, or a joke. Maybe you have been there. Maybe your heart was broken, burdened, or hurting and because you wanted no one to know, you smiled through it all. We all do it. "How are you?" "Fine, how are you?" We feel that no one wants to hear our woes, so we pretend all is well.

There is much pain in our world today. Many live daily with physical pain. There is much mental anguish and emotional suffering. Spiritual emptiness brings on a burden of hopelessness and guilt. Stress, brought on by fast-paced living and pressure, causes a breakdown of the human spirit. Our soldiers are coming home from war with posttraumatic stress syndrome.

How do we deal with all this? Does God want this? Did He send Jesus to earth to suffer, die, and rise again in victory to see His children live a defeated life? No, I don't think so. That is why we all call out to the One we know can help us—God. He is our help in times of need. "But Thou, O Lord art a shield about me, my glory, and the One who lifts my head. I was crying to the Lord with my voice, and He answered me from His holy mountain" (Ps. 3:3–4). Who do you cry out to when you are in need of comfort, strength, or a shield around you? He is there at all times, receiving us with open arms to comfort, heal, and sustain us.

Many are hurting out there, so don't pass up a chance to smile at those you meet, encourage them, help them, listen to them, comfort them, and most of all give them Jesus. He is the One who will lift them out of the darkest place and set their feet on solid ground. Jesus said, "Come to Me all who are weary and heavy-laden, and I will give you rest. Take My yoke upon you, and learn from Me, for I am gentle and humble in heart; and you shall find rest for your souls" (Matt. 11:28–29). Put on your best smile today for all you see and share your own needs with the One who loves you more than you will ever know!

Lift up the light of Thy countenance upon us, O Lord! (Ps. 4:66)

November 4
What goes around comes around.

In the book of Ecclesiastes we are told in chapter three, "There is an appointed time for everything." I realize that now, since I have lived long enough to testify to the fact. God's miraculous ways are so vast and His wisdom so extreme that we cannot fathom the degree of it. We can only know and believe that what He says is true and what He does is right.

Styles, fads, colors, and ideas all mimic pastimes, if we live long enough to see the full circle. You have heard it said, "Hold onto that long enough and it will come back in style," "Everything old becomes new again," or as Solomon declared, "So, there is nothing new under the sun" (Eccles. 1:9)

The same thing applies to good and bad deeds. The good seeds we sow in this life will be a blessing to us, to our children, and to our children's children. The bad seeds will be realized as well and will come back to haunt us, and our sins will be visited on our children (Exo. 20:5). We love it when the good things come back to us, but we do not want to believe that there are consequences to our bad deeds. Perhaps we should believe the scriptures when they tell us that bad choices not only affect us but also affect others. When we see that our sins or iniquities will be visited on our children, that should make us stop and think twice before we step out of God's will. "Visited" does not necessarily mean that our children or grandchildren will commit the sins that we committed but that they will feel the effects in a hurtful way, directly or indirectly. God does not cause this; it is just the effects of sin and how it trickles down to hurt even the innocent, generations later.

Solomon, who wrote the book of Ecclesiastes, learned many things in life the hard way. Even though God had blessed him with much wisdom and many riches, his book is often called the Book of Regrets. Why? Because he sought earthly things rather than godly things. His confession was, "Vanity of vanities! All is vanity" (Eccles. 1:2).

That which has been is that which will be, and that which has been done is that which will be done. (Eccles. 1:9)

November 5
If God called you, He is always with you. If He didn't call you, go and resign today!

Being wise enough to discern God's will enables us to make the right choices. But how do we acquire that kind of wisdom? How can we know His will for our lives? One way is to ask. James tells us that if we lack wisdom, we should ask God for it and it will be given "generously and without reproach" (1:5). We cannot expect to know God's will if we are not first seeking to live for Him. Proverbs 1:7 tells us that "fools despise wisdom and instruction." Unless we know Jesus, we cannot know wisdom.

I am afraid that there are many people in our world today who are standing at pulpits in our churches who have not been called by God to preach His Word. Unfortunately, it is just a job that they thought they could do, and they took it on without asking or hearing from God. That is a dangerous place to be and is outside of the will of God. All people, no matter your color or creed, are called to be children of God. "For God so loved the world, that He gave His only begotten Son, that *whoever believes in Him* should not perish, but have eternal life" (John 3:16, emphasis added). However, not all are called to pastor a flock. Paul challenged his listeners at Ephesus "to walk in a manner worthy of the calling with which you have been called" (Ephesians 4:1). He went on to say, "And He gave some as apostles, and some as prophets, and some as evangelists, and some as pastors and teachers, for the equipping of the saints for the work of service, to the building up of the body of Christ" (vv. 11–12). Only a God-called pastor will be effective as the overseer of His church. On the other hand, there are also those who have been called by God yet have never surrendered. Testimonies of such people reveals the regret of not following God's path for their lives.

We can and will live a wretched existence outside of God's will. We can be wealthy, popular, healthy, and educated yet be perfectly miserable apart from God's abiding fellowship. Trusting His plan for our lives is the better way. Seek Him first.

For it is God who is at work in you, both to will and to work for His good pleasure. (Phil. 2:13)

November 6
Laziness and failure are brothers. —Author

To be slothful most certainly leads to failure to be productive or successful, no matter what the challenge. To show up late for work, to goof off at any opportunity, to act uninterested or complacent, or to halfway do your job are all signs of a lazy attitude toward work and will accomplish nothing. Such conduct will surely lead to ineffectiveness and failure. Failure often leads to disappointment and disappointment to despair.

The right attitude toward work is a blessing. Work brings about achievement, with achievement comes pride, with pride comes respect, and with respect comes peace and sweet rest. As we learn to perform all of our labor "as unto the Lord," we certainly should be able to develop the right attitude toward work. The rewards of a job well done are numerous and satisfying.

In the parable of the talents, Jesus taught that the master of the three slaves spoke harshly to the slave who hid his talent in the ground. While the other slaves took the talents their master had given them and multiplied them, this one slave buried his where it was of no use to anyone. You see, Jesus taught that the master did not give the slaves more than they could handle. Matthew 25:15 tells us that each slave was given "according to his own ability." God expects from us only what we are capable of doing, what He has given us the ability or talent to do. Anything above that is a gift to Him and a reward to yourself. Little becomes much when we give it to God.

What has God, our Master, given you to do today? Will His response to you be, "Well done, good and faithful servant" (Matt. 25:21, 23) or "You wicked, lazy slave" (v. 26)? Jesus teaches this parable to convey the importance of what we do with our lives as we live them here on earth. "Whatever you do, do your work heartily, as for the Lord rather than for men; knowing that from the Lord you will receive the reward of the inheritance. It is the Lord Jesus Christ whom you serve" (Col. 3:23–24).

He also who is slothful in his work is brother
to him who destroys. (Prov. 18:9)

November 7
Fear defeats trust. –Author

When we come to Christ, we are to die to ourselves that Christ might live through us and be glorified in us. This is the opposite approach from the world's theory. The world shouts on every hand that we are to look after number one first. Television ads scream, "You are worth it!" and encourage self-gratification and selfishness.

How can we fight our old sin nature that tells us to be self-centered? A God-centered life is a God-controlled life. When we put our trust in Him as Lord and Savior, we are moved to let go and let God have the reins of our lives. Trust is simply relinquishing all authority over our lives to God's authority, surrendering our all to Him. Is that easy? No, it is not easy. It calls for a renewing of the mind, a steadfast trust in One who holds us more dearly than even we hold ourselves.

Fretting is the opposite of trusting God. Our worrying limits His working and hinders our spiritual growth. Is your trust deep enough that He can fulfill Himself through you? Is it fear of letting go that hinders your faith to trust the One who wants us to lay our burdens on Him? Somebody once said, "Worry does not take away tomorrow's troubles; it takes away today's peace." Fear grips like a vise and holds us captive to its grip, robbing us of God's wonderful power in our lives.

Jesus is our greatest picture of trust and obedience in the Bible. His life was in the hands of an angry mob, but His heart was in the hands of His Father, God. He prayed in the Garden of Gethsemane that if there was any other way, God would spare Him from what was coming, the cross. However, He never let His fear defeat the trust He had in His Father's plan for humankind. "He learned obedience from the things which He suffered" (Heb. 5:8). Yes, He was fully God, but He was also fully man. He had to press through His fear to obedience. We can rejoice that He did because, through His Holy Spirit, He gives us power to defeat fear and trust the risen One!

Rest in the Lord and wait patiently for Him; Do not fret. (Ps. 37:7)

November 8
The easiest thing to choke on is your own words. —Author

How many do you suppose were in the mob that day when they cried out for Jesus to be crucified? Were they later sorrowful and wishing that they could take their words back? Every Easter we are reminded of those haunting word of the hungry crowd: "Crucify Him! Crucify Him!"

Barabbas was a sinful man—a murderer and a sinner. We can look on that day of Barabbas as our day of hope and freedom. As the crowd shouted for Barabbas to be freed and Jesus to die, we look back on a picture of atonement. Jesus was innocent yet condemned, while Barabbas was guilty yet redeemed. Jesus took his place. Jesus took our place.

Calvary is a picture of God's amazing love for all humankind as He offered up Himself, Jesus, God incarnate, to be the perfect sacrifice for the sins of all humankind. Yes, for all who would walk free from the dark cell of sin and would repent, He made a way. We can be free indeed as Barabbas was that day because Jesus took our place, "being justified as a gift by His grace through the redemption which is in Christ Jesus" (Rom. 3:24).

Have you realized your freedom yet? Have you walked out of the world's darkness into God's glorious light? Do you know the One who offers you true freedom, releases your shackles, and gives you life abundant? It was not by accident that Barabbas was chosen by the crowd that day to go free. Jesus came to die for you and for me. His whole purpose for coming to earth was happening as the crowd turned on Jesus and chose Barabbas to be freed. We are Barabbas, in need of a Savior.

We were in that crowd that day, but because of God's mercy and grace He made a way for us to be redeemed. Jesus was the perfect sacrifice for our filthiness. Grace—God's *R*iches *A*t *C*hrist's *E*xpense— happened that day, and grace happens every day a lost soul is freed from the bondage of sin and death, eternal death. Jesus paid the price for Barabbas, and Jesus paid the price for you and me.

For while we were still helpless, at the right time
Christ died for the ungodly. (Rom. 5:6)

November 9
When broken and spilled out, we can see
all the stones in the puddle clearer.

Brokenness is not something we desire. However, it is an inevitable condition if we fail to trust God with our daily living. God wants total control of the lives of His children—not in a sense that He dictates our every move or invades the intimate process of choices, but rather His desire is for us to make heartrending decisions of surrender and dying to ourselves so that He can have first place. His precise reason is to keep us focused and on the right track for the abundant life that He has promised all those who trust Him. Such a process grows, strengthens, and enables us to walk the straight and narrow path. Vance Havner, in *By the Still Waters*, puts it this way: "It takes broken soil to produce a crop, broken clouds to give rain, broken grain to give bread, broken bread to give strength. It is the broken alabaster box that gives forth perfume—it is Peter, weeping bitterly, who returns to greater power than ever."

In today's world we see very little brokenness over sin. David, a man after God's own heart, committed adultery and murder. His fellowship with God was broken and his peace gone from him. Many of the psalms show us his cries of anguish and despair as he lamented in repentance before God, begging Him to restore to him the joy of His salvation. Repentance is necessary for remission of sin. Repentance is not sorrow that you got caught but truly being sorry for your sin, turning away from it, and going in the opposite direction. It is realizing that only God can forgive you and set you on the right path again.

Sin shatters a life quicker than anything else. Sin has tentacles that reach out far beyond oneself, destroying and demolishing everyone in its path. Sin's effects are far-reaching and devastating. God's Word tells us that "all have sinned and fall short of the glory of God," but we have been " justified as a gift by His grace through the redemption which is in Christ Jesus" (Rom. 3:23–24). When we fail to repent, we are saying that Jesus died in vain. For our own healing and to restore our relationship with God, we must be broken and spilled out.

Create in me a clean heart, O God. (Ps. 51:10a)

November 10
True charity is helping those you have every reason to believe would not help you.

"Do unto others as you would have them do unto you." This has come to be known as the Golden Rule, and golden it is. Twice in the New Testament gospels we see it repeated as Jesus said it, once in Matthew 7:12 and again in Luke 6:31. Different Bible interpretations say it a different way, but all have the same meaning. Jesus calls on us to treat everyone like we ourselves want to be treated. Knowing that God's way is always best, why then do we so often strike out and retaliate when insult or injury is hurled our way? Indignation mounts, and before you know it we are acting the same way that our offender is acting. We are so inclined as sinners to face off and fight rather than turn the other cheek.

God calls Christians to be different, to be set apart. We are not to behave as our old sinful nature begs but instead to control ourselves in a way that we think before we speak and stop before we react. It takes practice, but the Holy Spirit is our helper and is always in the believer to be called on. We can ask ourselves, "How would Jesus handle this?" or "What would Jesus do?" Paul instructs us in Romans 14:19, "So then let us pursue the things which make for peace and the building up of one another."

Growing up in small-town America, I thought everybody loved me. I knew my family loved me, my church family all seemed to love me, and those I met in our little town were very congenial and friendly. It didn't take long after leaving home and getting into the "big world" to realize that everybody did *not* love me. Such is life. Everyone did not love Jesus either. Jesus said that loving those who love us is easy; the challenge comes when we are called to love our enemies. Today, concentrate on sweetening your speech and seasoning it with love and kindness. Be considerate, tactful, and complimentary. We are called to be encouragers and esteem highly our fellow humans even if our grace given is not returned.

Give, and it will be given to you; good measure, pressed down, shaken together, running over. (Luke 6:38)

November 11
Your life is God's gift to you. What you do with it is your gift to God.

We don't touch the tip of the iceberg of our potential in this life. The average life expectancy has stretched to include even more years of life. With new medical breakthroughs and health-conscious seniors, longevity is not a rare occurrence anymore. Still, we don't learn, experience, or accomplish a fraction of what is out there for us to take in.

God's world is not only beautiful and wonderfully made, it is also exciting, challenging, and forever affording opportunity for new and different adventures and learning. Take a look around you. The scientific world is unveiling the unheard of; artists are creating masterpieces of art, music, dance, and so on; sports figures are breaking records before the old ones get on the books; and technology surpasses our comprehension. God has gifted humans with the knowledge and desire to create and expand.

God chose Solomon to follow his father, David, as king of Israel. Solomon loved the Lord as his father did. In his prayer to God, he asked for wisdom and understanding to lead his people, the ability to discern good from evil. God was pleased with Solomon's request. Because Solomon's priorities were right, God gave him wisdom that surpassed any that had been before him or would come after him. He also gave him great riches and honor and promised him a long life if he walked in God's ways (1 Kings 3:10–14). The Proverbs are filled with the wisdom of Solomon. Unfortunately, Solomon often failed to heed his own advice, and in his book of Ecclesiastes he reveals to us that his shortcomings caused him to squander much time and energy on things of the world. He testifies to all generations that his worldly living was all vanity, causing him to miss out on many of God's blessings.

Because all wisdom and knowledge are found in Christ, let us not live our lives without Him in first place. May we realize our shortcomings and repent before we squander our lives on things that don't matter.

As you therefore have received Christ Jesus
the Lord, so walk in Him. (Col. 2:6)

November 12
Difficulties in your life don't come to destroy you but to help you realize your hidden potential.

Years after the old two-story farmhouse was abandoned, left in ill repair, and dilapidated, it was in dire need of some TLC from someone who would see its potential and take on the project. That would be my husband and me. Even though he was very skeptical, my husband listened to my heart's cry and we purchased the old house for a song and set out to make this humble place livable and our home.

Because we were young and money was short in those days, we borrowed seven thousand dollars to make repairs and improvements. With careful planning, stretching our dollars, and doing some of the work ourselves, in no time we moved into our partially renovated home.

For almost fifty years, the old farmhouse has taken on new life and been our comfortable refuge. We have knocked out walls, sanded floors, painted and papered walls, made window treatments, and done anything else to bring out the beauty of the once-forsaken old house. Our before-and-after pictures show the transformation of much love and hard work. We have raised three wonderful children in this old place along with every pet imaginable. We have enjoyed many family gatherings, wedding receptions, grandchildren camps, and even our fiftieth wedding anniversary celebration. This old house has been a blessing to us for many years. It was difficult at times to get it all done, but it was worth it. It is home.

God is in the transformation business. He takes these old bodies, riddled with sin, and changes them into new creations. "Therefore if any man be in Christ, he is a new creature; the old things passed away; behold, new things have come" (2 Cor. 5:17). The only thing it costs us is our hearts. When we give our hearts to Jesus, we are born again by the Spirit and the renovation begins. Old habits are torn away, everything takes on a fresher look, and our eternal home with Jesus is certain after He takes up residence. God sees your potential. Do you?

For our citizenship is in heaven, from which also we eagerly wait for a Savior, the Lord Jesus Christ; who will transform the body of our humble state. (Phil. 3:20–21)

November 13
Days spent well are lives spent well. –Author

Life at its best is short. We laugh sometimes at how fast Friday seems to come around again. The older we get, the shorter the days, weeks, months, and years become, it seems. Every birthday is an occasion to be thankful for, and good health becomes more of a realized blessing. How swiftly our days on this earth do fly by! God told us that, but when we are young we miss the reality of it. The psalmist states, "Man is like a mere breath; his days are like a passing shadow" (144:4).

God has allotted to each of us a lifetime. For some it is only a few short years, while for others a lifetime is one hundred plus years. It is not how many years we live but what we do with those years that counts. Let's look for a moment at life as a roll of paper towels. The full roll is long and continuous, clean and useful when we get it. As it rolls out and we use it up in many different ways, it gradually has fewer and fewer sheets, and in no time, it is gone. As we absorb all that life has to offer, we often run into many spills and messes that need to be cleaned up. Family and friends need us, and we are there to help. Then there is window washing and polishing. How often we must wash away grime in order to see more clearly what life has to offer or how best to make a decision or polish away our rough edges in order that our lives will shine out for Jesus. Much on the roll is wasted on useless projects, while most is used up on necessary labor. Soon, it is gone, used up. Another roll is put in its place, and the process begins again. Such is life. "You are just a vapor that appears for a little while and then vanishes away" (James 4:14b).

How are you using the roll of life allotted to you? When you get to the end of the roll, will you be able to look back and say you were useful to God and to your fellow people? Will the One who gave you life be able to say, "Well done"?

**So teach us to number our days, that we may present
to Thee a heart of wisdom. (Ps. 90:12)**

November 14
Love what you do and do what you love. –Ray Bradbury

It is very important to be excited about the things we do. Enthusiasm and enjoyment in what we are doing plays a big part in what is accomplished there. To be locked into a job that you dislike, are not skilled at, or have no knowledge of is a precarious position. Each day can be a dread when there is a lack of passion for where you spend so much of your time. Apathy will often set in where there is no zeal for what you do with your time, causing depression and unrest.

Life can be interesting and exciting as we live each day to the fullest. Humdrum living is not God's plan for His children. Jesus said, "The thief comes only to steal, and kill, and destroy; I came that they might have life, and might have it abundantly" (John 10:10).

Whether it be work, play, or worship, enthusiasm and enjoyment in what we do are contagious. Fun things are not fun if there is a lack of excitement. Try worshipping when there is indifference or dissension among the members or even working day by day at an occupation where coworkers are negative or uncooperative. The atmosphere is stifling.

In ministry, it is very important to have a passion, even a calling, for what you do. If we are doing something in our churches just because a position needs to be filled and no one else will step up to the plate, then we might be out of God's will and possibly hindering someone more gifted or qualified from taking that position because we rushed ahead of God. Prayer is our best option before we leap out on our own.

When Jesus offered the call to his disciples, they immediately dropped all that they were doing and followed Him. The call to follow was already in their hearts. They had a desire, an aspiration to heed His invitation to be part of what He was doing. Their eagerness was evident as some dropped their nets and others left their families to minister and serve with Jesus. Oswald Chambers says, "The call of God is the expression of God's nature, not of our nature." He wants us to love what we do, especially when we are doing His work.

Let your light shine before men in such a way that they may see your good works and glorify your Father who is in heaven. (Matt. 5:16)

November 15
Give thanks with a grateful heart.

God expects gratitude from those He helps. His loving-kindness and tender mercy are poured out to His children over and over again, and we should respond with a thankful heart.

Luke tells the story of the lepers who were healed by Jesus. Leprosy was a dreaded disease in Jesus's day and very painful not only physically but emotionally. Lepers were outcasts and were required to cry out "Unclean!" when anyone came near them. They usually had to live in dark places and completely cover their diseased bodies. It was a horrible existence. Jesus was traveling between Samaria and Galilee when ten lepers approached Him. "They stood at a distance and called out" to Him (Luke 17:12). They asked Jesus to have pity on them. The scripture goes on to tell us that "as they were going, they were cleansed" (v. 14). Jesus healed the poor, pitiful men. You would think that they would all turn and shout with joy and thanksgiving to God for their healed bodies, bowing down to Jesus in humility and gratitude. Not so. Only one of them came back to thank Jesus.

So many times, like the lepers, we take the good things God has to offer and reject the giver of them all. Often we pray and when that prayer is answered, we never go back and thank Him for His willingness to hear our prayers and acknowledge Him as the one who answered them. Like selfish children, our prayers are usually self-centered. What happens to us matters to God. We are His children. Just as we like for our own children to appreciate the things that we do for them, so our heavenly Father wants to know that we are grateful for the things that He works out in our lives. Prayer is an amazing avenue to God. Christians have direct access to Him, and Jesus sits at His right hand, making intercession for us. "And whatever you do in word or deed, do all in the name of the Lord Jesus, giving thanks through Him to God the Father" (Col. 3:17). God is good all the time. Thank Him!

Every good thing bestowed and every perfect gift is from above, coming down from the Father of lights, with whom there is no variation, or shifting shadow. (James 1:17)

November 16
When it controls your actions, you can say you have it–faith.

Sometimes our greatest faith is exercised when God says, "Wait." At no other time in our Christian lives are we more helpless and hopeful at the same time. Often when we wait we call for a sign from God or even the smallest act to show us that He is working all things out for our good (Rom. 8:28). His Word tells us that He does that, but why do we doubt? It would not be faith if the end were visible. Faith is trusting when we can see no evidence of His working, but we trust anyway. To the world that might seem strange, but we either believe God or we don't. However, if you know His Word and have observed His faithfulness to all generations, you will see that God has His best for those who wait on Him and for those who leave the choices with Him.

Prophesy has come to be an intriguing study to me. Everything that God has prophesied to this point in history has been fulfilled. God has never broken a covenant, nor has He wavered in any way from His plan. Humankind has faltered in many ways—we can see it all throughout the scriptures—but God's perfect plan for His people never changes. God Himself never changes. "For I, the Lord, do not change" (Mal. 3:6). Because God is trustworthy, we can have the faith that we need to rely on Him in every situation that we will ever face. So where does our faith come from? It comes from believing His Word. "So faith comes from hearing and hearing by the word of Christ" (Rom. 10:17). If God said it in His Word, you can believe it and trust it!

Fully trusting God's promises enables us to move past our own doubts and rely on God's unwavering promises to us. Taking Him at His word is faith. Moving past our doubts and acting on what He calls us to do is faith. "Without faith it is impossible to please Him, for he who comes to God must believe that He is, and that He is a rewarder of those who seek Him" (Heb. 11:6). You might be like me and have been praying for something for years and years. At this time I have not seen my prayer answered. But one thing I am certain of: in God's timing, it will be answered. I might not be here to see it, but He is faithful and will answer according to His will. You can trust Him too!

**Lead me in Thy truth and teach me. For Thou art the God
of my salvation; For Thee I wait all the day. (Ps. 25:5)**

November 17
The important thing about a choice is
what you choose. –Author

I heard this little illustration on the radio one day, and it really caught my attention and drove a most significant point home. A man and his wife went to a restaurant to dine. On the menu were the words "choice of vegetable." As the man gave his dinner order to the waitress, he asked, "What is the choice of vegetables?" She replied, "Green beans." He replied, "The menu says you have a choice of vegetables." Her response was, "Do you want it or not?" Sometimes the choice is not always what we expect. In this lifetime we will have many choices to make, some significant and some not so significant.

As Moses came to the end of his life, God chose Joshua to lead the children of Israel into the promised land. God commissioned Joshua to be strong and courageous and promised him that He would "be with you; I will not fail you or forsake you" (Joshua 1:5). Toward the end of Joshua's life, as he had been faithful to lead as God had commanded, he called the people together and told them that they had a choice to make.

Joshua reviewed their history of God's faithfulness to them. He reminded them that God is a holy and jealous God and would not tolerate their worshipping foreign gods (24:19–20). He told them to "choose for yourselves today whom you will serve" (v. 15). Joshua had already made his choice for himself and his family: "But as for me and my house, we will serve the Lord." Verse 24 tells us that the people made the right choice as well. "And the people said to Joshua, 'We will serve the Lord our God and we will obey His voice.'"

Whether you choose beans or beans is not a big choice in this life, but who you will serve is. God wants our whole heart. He abhors fence straddlers. Being a gray-area Christian makes Him sick. Jesus Himself said to the church in Laodicea, "I know your deeds that you are neither cold nor hot, so because you are lukewarm, and neither hot nor cold, I will spit you out of My mouth" (Rev. 3:15–16). God, help us to make good choices as You did when you chose us!

**But you are a chosen race, a royal priesthood, a holy nation,
a people for God's own possession. (1 Peter 2:9a)**

November 18
Brag on yourself and watch the crowd disappear. –Author

Insecurity sometimes makes people feel that they have to boast about their own accomplishments. It is really a sad display of effort because bragging is unappealing and unavailing. Such a futile effort only repels those around them and leads the listeners to feel such a person is conceited and self-centered. In most cases, however, the braggart is most likely starving for attention and acceptance.

Many times in the New Testament, Jesus exposed the scribes and the Pharisees for who they were. Being the "religious leaders" of the day, they should have been the ones teaching truth, but instead they were putting heavy loads on the people to keep the letter of the law. They flaunted their deeds so that they would be noticed, and they loved "the place of honor at banquets and the chief seats in the synagogues, and respectful greetings in the market places, and being called by men, Rabbi" (Matt. 23:5–7). Jesus knew their hearts, and He called them hypocrites, vipers, blind guides. They wanted to be seen by men, appearing noble on the outside, "but inside they are full of dead men's bones and all uncleanness" (v. 27). It sounds as if Jesus was being hard on them, but when people are being a stumbling block to others, it is our responsibility to remind them of that and offer correction.

Maybe you know someone with the tell-tale signs of a lack of self-confidence. Maybe they come across as a bigot. Often the obvious is not the true person. There can be a deeper need that is crying out. You might be God's instrument in the life of emotionally starved people if you reach out to them. Perhaps they need a friend who will encourage them, love them, and offer a genuine compliment when needed. Even gentle correction can be given at the right time. Insecurity can be masked as confidence.

Do nothing from selfishness or empty conceit, but with humility of mind let each of you regard one another as more important than himself. (Phil. 2:3)

November 19
Peer pressure is when we march to someone else's drumbeat rather than our own. –Author

Peer pressure is evident from the very youngest child to the very oldest adult. Nothing has more influence on the life of a human being than another human being. Everything we do and say influences someone in one way or another. For this reason, our responsibility to our fellow humans is great. Jesus talked about it in His sermon to His disciples when He told them, "It is inevitable that stumbling blocks should come, but woe to him through whom they come! It would be better for him if a millstone were hung around his neck and he were thrown into the sea, than that he should cause one of these little ones to stumble" (Luke 17:1–2). Our behavior and speech can easily lead someone astray.

The list of sinful choices is endless. On the other hand, the good choices far outnumber those. God's desire for us is abundant living. Disobeying His plan for our lives leads us off the righteous path and onto the destructive path. Jesus warns us, "Enter by the narrow gate; for the gate is wide, and the way is broad that leads to destruction, and many are those who enter it. For the gate is small, and the way is narrow that leads to life, and few are those who find it" (Matt. 7:13–14).

When we step out into a sinful world, its influence is all around. Young adults, teens, and even young children are faced with choices we never even dreamed of as children in our day. Conforming to another person's way of thinking rather than making our own decisions and choices can be detrimental to our well-being. That is why seeking God first in all that we do is our best option. He will never lead us astray.

When Rehoboam was made king, the people came to him and asked him to lift the burden from the people that his father, King Solomon, had placed on them. Rehoboam chose not to listen to the elders who advised him to do just that but instead chose to go to his peers, "the young men who grew up with him," who advised him to make their burden heavier. He acted foolishly and listened to them. As a result, the nation divided, and "Israel has been in rebellion against the house of David to this day" (1 Kings 12:19).

We must obey God rather than men. (Acts 5:29)

November 20
Nobody gets lost on the straight road.

Have you ever wondered why rivers are crooked, flowing haphazardly downward and forking off to make creeks and streams? They follow the path of least resistance.

It's not always easy to follow Christ. However, if we will keep our eyes fixed on Him, He stands waiting for us at the end of that straight and narrow road. Like the waters of the flowing river, we are rushing along through life's daily living, not always looking or caring where we are going. Sometimes when choices get hard, we tend to take the easy solution or perhaps make a wrong decision by not thinking things out or giving the matter up to prayer. Subsequently, we venture off and find ourselves drifting along with the crowd and going with the flow of the world. Because we know that Jesus is the Way, we hear Him calling us back to the path that He would have us to walk on.

I had never read *Pilgrim's Progress* until a few years ago. What a vivid picture of the Christian life and the hurdles one crosses to get to the end of this life. When we come to Christ, the battle begins, but the irony is that there is no life apart from a life with Christ. There is no value to life apart from a relationship with God through Jesus Christ. The Way is by no means hidden, but Jesus warned us that "few are those who find it" (Matt. 7:14). We must listen in order to hear!

Why do you think many don't find it? Because they are following the path of least resistance. We must listen when He calls and enter by the narrow gate to follow the road that is laid out for those who choose to walk God's way. Satan is on that road with his temptations and distractions. He seeks to discourage and lure us with his deceitful and cunning ways. But once we belong to Jesus, nothing can snatch us out of His hand (John 10:28). He is our defender on that narrow road. There will be many side trails and pathways that lure us, but we must keep our eyes on the One who made the Way for us and sealed us until the day when He will take us to be with Him for eternity.

I am the light of the world; he who follows Me shall not walk in the darkness, but shall have the light of life. (John 8:12)

November 21
My home is in heaven. I'm just passing through this world. —Billy Graham

Because God created us in His own image, we have within us the desire and hunger for fellowship with other believers. In John 13:35, Jesus told His disciples that their love for one another was one way that the world could know that they loved Him. From the Garden of Eden, when God saw the need for Adam to have human companionship, to our present time, it is still so evident that people need the love and acceptance of other people. Christ's body, the church, is a retreat like none other. God always intended for it to be a place where we could find love, acceptance, forgiveness, brotherhood, friendship, and fellowship that surpasses any other place.

Ask anyone on the street where they want to go when they die, and most likely you will get the same answer, heaven. Ask them where they attend church, and many will confess that they don't have a church home, that they do not attend anywhere. Why would anybody want to go to heaven when they don't want to go to church? If you don't want to spend time with Christians on earth, why would you want to spend eternity, forever and ever, with them?

Paul's mission after his conversion was to be an instrument of Jesus Christ, "to bear His name before the Gentiles and kings and the sons of Israel" (Acts 9:15). Jesus called out this tentmaker, persecutor of Christians, and very strict Jewish Pharisee; changed his heart; and sent him out "in order that the manifold wisdom of God might now be made known through the church to the rulers and authorities in the heavenly places" (Eph. 3:10). With boldness and confidence, Paul preached salvation to the Gentiles and established churches because he knew that it would bring glory to God for God's people to worship together.

You can meet Jesus today as you fellowship in His church with His people. One day He will return for His bride, the church. Be ready!

To Him be the glory in the church and in Christ Jesus to all generations forever and ever. Amen. (Eph. 3:21)

November 22
If the Kingdom of God is not first, it doesn't matter what's second. —Neal A. Maxwell

What God thinks about you is much more important than what people think. To please God should be our aim as Christians. He tells us that if we trust Him, we will "not be disappointed" (1 Peter 2:6). Should He expect any less of us? Perhaps we should try a little harder not to disappoint Him. Our human nature seeks the approval of people, as we often wonder what others think of us. How am I being perceived? Am I coming across to others as I feel in my heart? Am I being a stumbling block, or am I being a building block? Paul challenges us in the book of Romans to be transformed by the renewing of our minds and not to think more highly of ourselves than we ought to because it is by God's grace that we have been given faith (12:2, 3). With Christ in us, we have the gifts that He gives us and are only responsible for using the resources that He has gifted us with. We should never allow the world around us to squeeze us into its mold. To consume ourselves with what others think is to lessen what God thinks of us. He is the only one that we have to please.

How can we be the best servants to our God whom we desire to serve? How can we bring a pure heart before Him as we seek Him? How can we surrender all to the One who wants to be the Master of our lives? We must stand in His presence unhindered! Transparent! We must first love God enough to surrender all. We must die to ourselves and become transparent before Him. He sees all and knows all anyway, but He desires that we submit, give up our filthy pride, and willingly expose those things that hinder our honesty and transparency before Him. We must ask God to cleanse our hearts, replacing our pride with His truth. Clean vessels unto honor are usable in His kingdom. He is a jealous God. He gives us His best, and He wants us to give Him our best!

**For am I now seeking the favor of men, or of God? Or am I
striving to please men? If I were still trying to please men,
I would not be a bond-servant of Christ. (Gal. 1:10)**

November 23
People do not go to the church to play golf, and people do not go to the golf course to worship.

It is amazing how we human beings can rationalize our own desires. It is almost a laughing matter to hear people striving to convince themselves and others that some of their greatest spiritual moments occur within the beauty of the golf course on Sunday morning or while appreciating the peacefulness of the water and the beauty of nature as they fish their Sunday morning away at the lake. God must get amused at the excuses His people use to satisfy their desires to do as they please. As we justify our means for self-gratification, His law to "remember the Sabbath Day to keep it holy" never changes. He still calls us to remember to "forsake not the assembling of yourselves" (Heb. 10:25). It is something about being in God's house with God's people on the day that He has set aside for rest that blesses and inspires us throughout the next week.

Not only is the Sabbath a day set aside to worship, but from the beginning of time humankind was commanded by our Creator to rest on the seventh day of the week. Genesis 2:3 tells us that "God blessed the seventh day and sanctified it." Webster's Dictionary states that *sanctify* means to "set apart as holy." God's commandment given through Moses is that we are to "remember the Sabbath day to keep it holy" (Exo. 20:8). If the God of the universe needed rest, is it possible that we too might need a day of rest? He thought so.

God rewards obedience. In Isaiah 56, the Lord expresses His desire for obedience in many areas of our lives. Keeping from profaning the Sabbath is foremost. He longs for His house to be a house of prayer (v. 7) and worship. Disobedience is harmful, and He warns us about turning to our own way.

In today's world we can observe those who consider the Sabbath to be a day of rest and worship and see how God has blessed them. Businesses like Chick-fil-a and Hobby Lobby have made a statement in their stand not to open their businesses on Sunday. This gives their managers and employees a day to rest, worship, and spend time with their families. In return, their businesses are thriving. When we honor God's laws, we will see the blessings.

And by the seventh day God completed His work ... and He rested on the seventh day from all His work which He had done. (Gen. 2:2)

November 24
The Gospel has two sides—the believing side and the behaving side.

If we believe God, we want to keep His commandments. If we believe God, we want to live our lives to please Him. Sin disappoints God and grieves His Holy Spirit. How then do we focus on obedience rather than rebellion? How then can I be holy? How can I be godly? In order to master life, we must be willing to put God first and think on things that are good and proper. Our priorities must be such that we organize our lives so that we dwell on kingdom building and diminish our earthly thoughts and desires. Our actions often speak louder than our words, and those around us can't hear what we say for seeing what we do. How a person behaves is a good indicator of the heart.

In today's world, tolerance has come to supersede common sense and moral laws. I developed this little acrostic of the word *tolerance* that helps us to see exactly how far we have delved into and away from what God expects.

T: taking things as they are
O: overlooking sin
L: losing sight of God's standards
E: evolving into the world's way
R: rejecting truth
A: accepting by silence
N: neutral thinking
C: conforming to the world
E: evolution into moral decay

Many Christians have gone the way of the world, excusing what is going on around us by saying, "Well, that is how they see it," or "Everybody has an opinion. Let them express theirs." No. If we believe the Gospel that we embraced at salvation, then we are to behave as God has instructed us to in the Bible. Also, to love others is to give them truth and correction, not to go along with them when they are in direct conflict with what God teaches.

If we are not careful, we will be like the frog that let the heat slip up on him. I am sure you have heard the story that is sad but true. If you throw a frog into a pot of boiling water, he will jump right out. But if you put the frog in a pot of cold water on the stove and gradually heat the pot up, he will stay there and slowly cook to death. Tolerance brings slow death to a person, a church, and a nation. Tolerating sin and sinful behavior brings decline to any people. If we believe God, we need to behave like we do!

Let us hold fast the confession of our hope without wavering for He who promised is faithful. (Heb. 10:23)

November 25
You don't have any guarantees for tomorrow. You can't do anything about yesterday. But you have today.

I love it when I can have my grandchildren at my house and I have nothing pressing to do. That way we can spend quality time together. I can give them my undivided attention and really enjoy our time together. Recently, they came to spend two days and a night. I laid aside everything, and we had a ball. "Papa" and I took them out to eat and then off to play putt-putt golf. I had planned all their favorite snacks, and we played games together inside and spent a lot of time outside. I was theirs for that time. They loved it, and so did I. Do you need to give others time today? Maybe you neglected them yesterday and before you knew it, it was today. Today is a good time to invest yourself into the life of others. They will love you for it, and you will be better for tomorrow. Today is the only day we are promised.

Regret is one thing that we don't ever want to experience. So many times when people lose a loved one, the first thing they express is, "Why didn't I spend more time with them? Why was I always so busy with other things and neglectful about taking time with them?" There is no need to go there. If we knew that someone was going into eternity tomorrow, we would probably smother that person today, and that is not a good plan either.

Seek God first today and ask Him to lead you. When Jesus came to earth, He was about His Father's business. Jesus's life was short, only thirty-three years. His ministry years were even shorter, only three years. But what an impact He made on this world in a short time. We have been promised the same power that Jesus had when we come yielded to Him in total submission. Jesus faced many hardships and afflictions and much adversity. As children of God we can live without regret. We can boldly profess Jesus to the lost world in the time that we have been given. Oh, that we can each reach some in order that no one will perish. True, there are no guarantees for tomorrow in this world, but Jesus has made certain that we have a guarantee for eternity. Secure your place today by making time for Him. Jesus Christ is the same yesterday, today—*yes,* and forever (Heb. 13:8).

And do not neglect doing good and sharing; for with such sacrifices God is pleased. (Heb. 13:16)

November 26
The praying saint cannot keep from worship. The prayerless saint cannot rise to worship.

When we come to the story of the cross, we sometimes miss the dynamics of how Jesus wants us to pray. Before Jesus ever went to the cross, even though He knew that was His purpose, He asked His disciples to join Him in prayer. His own strength and consolation came from spending time with His Father. He wanted His disciples to know that. As He hung in agony on the cross, suffering for the very ones who put Him there, Jesus cried out not for himself but for those who ridiculed and spit on Him, those who beat and tortured Him, those who despised and rebuked Him. His prayer was, "Father, forgive them." What a picture for us. What a reminder for us that even in suffering, we can and should pray for our accusers, our enemies, and those who despitefully use us.

The prayers of a righteous one put that one in the very presence of the living God. When we come to His throne of grace, we stand in the presence of the Holy One. Worship is ours. In God's presence is fullness of joy (Ps. 16:11). As we exalt Him and lift up our prayers and petitions before Him, we worship. The joy is inexpressible as we stand before Him, laying down all of our burdens before Him and listening to that still, small voice as He answers. God is real, and He is ever faithful.

Jesus's first words from the cross were a prayer. Why then do we ever forfeit our time alone with Holy God? Do we not want to be renewed, strengthened, and satisfied? Isaiah said, "They that wait upon the Lord shall renew their strength; they shall mount up with wings like eagles, they shall run, and not be weary; and they shall walk, and not faint" (40:31). Prayer and time alone with the Father will help you soar to mountainous plateaus and plant your feet on higher ground, where worship is inevitable!

Hearts had to be changed that day on Golgotha as the crowd heard Jesus pray for them. We know that the thief on the cross was convicted, and we know of one Roman soldier who realized that Jesus was the Son of God. Do your prayers bring you or someone else to worship?

O Lord, I beseech Thee, may Thine ear be attentive to the prayer of Thy servant and the prayer of Thy servants who delight to revere Thy name. (Neh. 1:11a)

November 27
Be wise enough to trust the wisdom of God.

Have you ever thought about what causes a person's eyes to be opened to the things of God? A heart hardened to God is a thing to be reckoned with. Atheist, agnostics, Satanists, false teachers, or even good people who think their goodness and works will get them to heaven often do not want to hear anything about God, Jesus, the Holy Spirit, or truth, which is the Word of God. In Paul's letter to Timothy, he warns him of days to come when

men will be lovers of self, lovers of money, boastful, arrogant revilers, disobedient to parents, ungrateful, unholy, unloving, irreconcilable, malicious gossips, without self-control, brutal, haters of good, treacherous, reckless, conceited, lovers of pleasure rather than lovers of God; holding to a form of Godliness, although they have denied its power. (2 Tim. 3:2–5)

Paul goes on to say that we should avoid these people.

As we step back and take a look at modern society, we are constantly reminded that people without God, who seeks their own way, miss the mark completely. Education is a wonderful tool but should never be mistaken for the wisdom that God can give. There is nothing more dangerous than an educated fool. Science, with all of its wonders and discoveries, can never exceed the miraculous understanding and divine wisdom that is from God. The human mind can desire to know all but can never acquire true wisdom apart from knowing the God of the universe through His Son, Jesus Christ. Only He can give us "full understanding of the truth" (1 Cor. 1:5). Truth is what God says. In Christ and His Word, the Bible, we have all the wisdom of God. "But by His doing you are in Christ Jesus, who became to us wisdom from God, and righteousness and sanctification, and redemption, that, just as it is written, 'Let him who boast, boast in the Lord'" (1 Cor. 1:30–31). Only God in Christ Jesus can give us the divine wisdom and guidance that all humankind craves.

If any of you lack wisdom, let him ask God who gives to all men ... and it shall be given him. (James 1:5)

November 28
FAITH–Forsaking All I Trust Him

As Peter stepped out of the boat and walked on the water, his dependence was on Jesus. Jesus had said, "Come," and without hesitation, Peter stepped over the side of the boat, into the night, and onto the open sea, where he began to walk toward Jesus (Matt. 14:28–33). Such faith challenges us to widen our perspective of trust in Jesus as Lord and Savior.

Christians are called to walk in the Spirit. Then and only then can we know the empowered fulfillment of faith-walking. Walking indicates moving, not standing still. Movement means we have stepped out, and in stepping out we are progressing. Like Peter we will move closer to the Father as long as we keep our eyes and hearts on Him. Peter began to sink into the black, raging sea when He started to focus on the things around him that so easily grabbed his attention and took his focus away from the object of his faith. The wind frightened Peter, and he cried out in despair and fear. Jesus immediately "stretched out His hand and took hold of him" (Matt. 14:31).

Like Peter, we too long to have faith, to believe and trust in the One who is faithful whether we fail or not. Faith is knowing where to go when we need help and believing that He will be there for us, no matter what. Jesus's question to Peter was, "Why did you doubt?" Have you ever felt that God was asking you that question? We see that even when Peter doubted, Jesus rescued him. God is faithful even when we are not.

If you are a child of God, you need not doubt. He is always there to rescue you and set your feet on solid ground. There are times that our faith will be tested. There will be trials and hardships. But James tells us that "the testing of your faith produces endurance" (1:3). If you know Peter, he had a lot of growing to do, just as I do and probably you as well. But God is patient. Salvation is the very act of faith. It is forsaking all and trusting Christ. I pray you have taken that step of faith.

Therefore having been justified by faith, we have peace with God through our Lord Jesus Christ through whom we have obtained our introduction by faith into this grace in which we stand. (Rom. 5:1–2)

November 29
Forgiveness—God's prescription for our anger.

Many things can provoke a person to anger. We have only to go to the Old Testament to see how God's anger burned toward those who chose idol worship and disobedience over His faithfulness, protection, mercy, and patience. God's discipline usually brought them to a place of repentance where He forgave them and offered them another opportunity to get it right.

Has someone wronged you? Have you been dealt a blow that created within you feelings of exasperation? How can we deal with anger when it festers and fumes within us? How do we put aside this most harmful emotion that can turn quickly into an ugly monster? It is very important to get a handle on anger before it takes hold and causes you to get out of control, giving the devil an opportunity for a heyday.

In order to *deal* with anger, we must first realize the wrath that we feel and acknowledge it. Then we must stop and ask ourselves, "Why am I angry?" Many times we harbor our anger and resentment so long that we forget what we are mad about and what or who is the source of these ill feelings. Third, we must refuse to submit to retaliation or revenge.

God gives us the power to forgive and also to forget. We struggle with it in ourselves and He knows that, so when we call on the Holy Spirit to help us forgive, we can feel the emotions of bitterness, anger, resentment, and revenge all begin to diminish. Forgiveness should be our trademark as Christians, demonstrating loudly the reality of Christ in our lives. Jesus paid a horrific price so that we could be forgiven of our sins, so why shouldn't we be open to forgiving others? The Bible says that before coming to Christ, we "were by nature children of wrath" (Eph. 2:3). But His work on the cross delivered us from that. The Holy Spirit is our helper in times of need. Call on Him when you are in the midst of a situation that frustrates and blinds you. "Do not let the sun go down on your anger" (Eph. 4:26).

And be kind to one another, tender hearted, forgiving each other, just as God in Christ has forgiven you. (Eph. 4:32)

November 30
You don't even have to be smart to be a critic.

Criticism is a sign of ignorance and selfishness. If you notice, those who criticize the most and the loudest are those who do the least. Critical people have the idea that their criticism portray them as authorities.

Unjust criticism is also a sign of insecurity. People who are always seeking out the negative or dwelling on the weaknesses of others feel that in tearing other people down, they look bigger themselves. Such sad reasoning is destructive not only to the victims but also to the villains with the critical spirit. Criticism comes so easily to the human spirit. The old sin nature that we inherited from Adam manifests itself in a life that separates or withdraws from the Holy Spirit's influence. Christ in us projects encouragement, not critical or divisive words. He calls us to be promoters of His ways, encouragers to those who need encouragement, and supporters to those put on our path.

Criticism can bring on division and disunion. We see it all through the Bible. In Jesus's day, men questioned all that He did. He was ridiculed and scorned by the governmental authorities and by the scribes and the Pharisees. As a result, the people were divided and turned on Him. We are seeing it more and more today as Christians struggle to stand for what is right. In a nation that was founded on Christian principles, who would ever think that there would be an outcry to remove any and all things that speak to God and Christianity yet allow things of worldly influence and foreign worship to stand? Many times the voice of one critical person is heard above all the many voices of the masses. However, after the dust settles, it is the Word of God that speaks.

When we look back today at the life of Jesus, whose voice speaks loudest? It is not the scribes, the Pharisees, or the ones who shouted to crucify Him. It is not the government and its leaders. It is Jesus, the Word made flesh, and His Word will last forever. God has the last word. The Lord says in Isaiah 29:24, "And those who err in mind will know the truth, and those who criticize will accept instruction." Salvation changes the heart. Think before you speak! Critics quickly show their ignorance.

But avoid worldly and empty chatter for it will lead to further ungodliness and their talk will spread like gangrene. (2 Tim. 2:16–17)

December

Seek the Lord while He may be found; Call upon Him while He is near. (Isa. 55:6)

December 1
Truth is what God says.

Jesus said in John 8:31–32, "If you abide in My word then you are truly disciples of mine; and you shall know the truth, and the truth shall make you free." Our world today searches for truth. Our courts search for truth. Parents want truth from their children and employers from their employees. Why are we failing as a people in our search for truth? Because we are looking in all the wrong places. Truth is ours only when we look to God and His inspired Word for our answers. He promises that His truth "shall make you free."

Free from what? you might ask. Abraham's offspring questioned Jesus, saying that they had never been "enslaved to anyone." They obviously did not know the history of their ancestors, as the Jews were enslaved to the Egyptians for years before God called Moses to lead them out of bondage. However, Jesus was not talking about that kind of enslavement at all. Jesus went on to tell them that "anyone who commits sin is the slave of sin" (John 8:34), and only knowing the truth that comes from knowing Him can give them the freedom not to sin and the peace that comes with forgiveness. Jesus assured them that He recognized that they were slaves to sin because "My word has no place in you" (v. 37). They had not realized that Jesus was the Word made flesh, the truth that was dwelling among them; therefore, they were still looking back to Abraham and the prophets. The truth is that they must acknowledge Jesus as Lord in order to be free indeed.

Yes, truth is what God says! And what God says is truth. The Word was in the beginning and the Word is truth. When we fail to abide in His written Word, the Bible, we miss His instructions to us of how to walk in His ways and how to keep His statutes, His commandments, His ordinances, His testimonies, and His precepts. Joshua, David, the disciples, and many heroes of the faith exhorted those who followed after them to abide in the truth of what God said. We can know the truth that frees us from the bondage of sin if we too will abide in Christ Jesus as Savior, the Word made flesh, and His written Word, the Bible, that is so accessible to everyone.

The sum of Thy word is truth, and every one of Thy righteous ordinances is everlasting. (Ps. 119:160)

December 2
The true measure of loving God is to love Him without measure. –Bernard of Clairvaux, Guideposts

Can we ever love God as He loves us? Are we capable of such love? I often question my own heart to know the depth of such a love that would send His only son to a cruel cross before angry, selfish, and sinful humanity to die a horrible death and take on the sins of an entire world in order to deliver us from sin's deadly grip. The question haunts me: Could I offer up my son? I have two sons whom I love with all my heart. I would gladly die for them, but the thought of willingly giving their lives over in exchange for even a righteous person would be unthinkable, much less a sinful person. Yet God in all of His mercy sacrificed His perfect son for wicked and sinful me. I know no greater love .

Because God loves us without measure, we are expected to love Him without measure. How can we do that? By first inviting Him to indwell our hearts. With His indwelling Holy Spirit in us, we have the ability to abide in Him. "For the love of Christ controls us, having concluded this, that one died for all, therefore all died; and He died for all, that they who live should no longer live for themselves, but for Him who died and rose again on their behalf" (1 Cor. 5:14–15). Because of His righteousness, we too can be righteous (v. 21). To love without measure is to abide in Him and live by His ordinances.

With the completion of the world and all that is in it, on the sixth day, God created man in His own image. "Let Us make man in Our image" (Gen. 1:26). Because they (the Trinity) loved man, they saw that he needed a companion to complete him, so the woman was created. From the beginning, God the Father, Son, and Holy Spirit loved their mankind creation so much that immediately they sought to complete him.

I am not sure that we can ever love our Creator as deeply as He loves us, but it is our responsibility to offer Him our hearts that we might satisfy His desire to love us even more. Let your love be without limit!

Therefore be imitators of God, as beloved children; and walk in love, just as Christ also loved you, and gave Himself up for us, an offering and a sacrifice to God as a fragrant aroma. (Eph. 5:1–2)

December 3
It is not the temptations that cause you to stumble but the choices you make about them that makes the difference.

There is no sin in temptation. It is the yielding that gets us in trouble. Simply *choosing* to cross over the line is where we stumble and ultimately fall headlong into sin. When we take a long, hard look at Adam and Eve and that first original step into sin, we see how easily and how quickly sin's grasp can entangle us. All was well in the Garden of Eden. Adam and Eve's perfect world had been perfectly made and labeled "very good" by their Creator. They were in paradise. They tended the garden, and work was a pleasure. They walked with God in the cool of the day. They enjoyed all the animals that Adam himself had named. All was well until their big mistake. They chose to go against God's one restriction: "But from the fruit of the tree which is in the middle of the garden, God has said, 'you shall not eat from it or touch it'" (Gen. 3:2–3). With a little coaxing from Satan, they crossed over the line from unadulterated pleasure to disobedience. They chose to listen to Satan and to doubt God. The world would be void of sin had they chosen obedience over disobedience.

The Israelite people made many mistakes in spite of God's constant pleading to seek Him and to serve Him above all others (1 Cor. 10). Especially in the Old Testament, we can follow God's chosen people as He sent prophet after prophet to warn them of their impending doom if they did not turn from worshipping idols, acting immorally, grumbling, and trying His patience. They were to live by the commandments that He had handed down to them through Moses. However, temptation usually came when they mixed with other cultures and chose the worship of their false gods and turning away from the one true God.

Crossing over the line and getting off the narrow path can get us into lots of trouble. Satan is alive and well. He is constantly seeking whom he may devour and cause to fall into sin. Call on the Holy Spirit to help you today to avoid the pitfalls that lead to sin and disobedience.

No temptation has overtaken you but such as is common to man; and God is faithful, who will not allow you to be tempted beyond what you are able, but with the temptation will provide the way of escape also, that you may be able to endure it. (1 Cor. 10:13)

December 4
"If you see God in each other you will love each other as God loves you." Mother Teresa

Has anyone ever paid you a compliment that just made your day? A kind word, an encouraging remark, a pat on the shoulder, a hug, and even a smile are all like warm fuzzies that carry endless echoes that ring on and on after the fact.

This time of the year people begin to get the holiday spirit as the blessed Christmas season approaches and love abounds in the hearts of most people. Kindness and goodwill flow, outpouring from every hand. Even Scrooges muster up a little love for their fellow people.

Genuine, divine love, however, is not turned on like a faucet of hot and cold running water. True love that in turn produces kindness and all the other fruits of the spirit comes from a pure heart that is born of God. A true measure of our love for God is the way we love and treat people every day. Kind words and kind deeds exemplify a heart that is truly His.

I keep a little porcelain plaque in my kitchen window that reads, "Sow seeds of kindness and reap a crop of friends." Showing genuine kindness to others can't help but be a magnet that draws others to us. We all need to show kindness if we want kindness in return.

We find in the Bible the story of two young Moabite women who married brothers from Bethlehem in Judah. Their names were Ruth and Orpah. They were both very kind women and loved their mother-in-law, Naomi, very much. Sadly, Naomi's husband, Elimelech, died, leaving Naomi a widow. About ten years later both Ruth's and Orpah's husbands died. Naomi encouraged her daughters-in-law to return to their people. However, Ruth refused, vowing that wherever Naomi went, she too would go; where her mother-in-law lodged, she too would lodge. "Your people shall be my people, and your God, my God" (Ruth 1:16). Ruth spoke words of kindness and encouragement to Naomi as her loyalty revealed her love. God honored Ruth's kindness; she married Boaz and through his line became an ancestor of Jesus Christ. Kindness never goes unrewarded!

Little children, let us not love with word or with tongue, but in deed and truth. (1 John 3:18)

December 5
A free ride is usually on the wrong road.

The lottery has become big business in our state, and the deceptive success of gambling games has caused one state after another to take it on as a money-making machine for state revenue. Oh, how blinded humankind can be! Nothing wrong ever becomes right. People can be so easily deceived when it comes to a dollar bill. Just the fact that it says to our children that gambling is okay should be enough to deter lawmakers and voters from endorsing such a lie. However, we are saying by accepting such a thing that sin is all right if it pays for itself.

How ironic that education has been the focus of funding from the lottery, allowing our children to believe that it is a good thing because it pays for computers, books, teachers' raises, and scholarships. Everything that glitters is not gold. We find ourselves reaping bad seeds of such ignorant and worldly choices. Crime, poverty, gambling addictions, family problems, and the creation of more legalized gambling, just to name a few, are all the result of taking sinful hypocrisy into our states and involving innocent people in a lie. Wrong cannot be right, bad cannot be good, darkness cannot be light, and a lie cannot be truth.

God spoke harshly to the Israelites as they continuously chose evil over good. Rather than doing things God's way, they "did what was right in their own eyes" (Judges 17:6). God warned them about worshipping false gods, exchanging the truth for a lie, and being stiff-necked and disobedient. They might listen for a while, but then they fell back into their old ways of rebellion and disregard for the truth. God promises good to those who walk with Him. Do we not believe Him? Are there more blessings in sin? Of course not! Sin brings destruction and more sin. "The anger of the Lord burned against Israel and He gave them into the hands of plunderers" (2:14). Verse 19 says, "They did not abandon their practices or their stubborn ways." Have we become a stiff-necked nation, sending the wrong message to this generation and the next? There are no free rides. The lottery is sinful and is costly.

Do not be deceived, God is not mocked, for whatever a man sows, this he will also reap. (Gal. 6:7)

December 6
I will do the best I can, with what I have, when I can, for Jesus's sake.

Does your "fruit bowl" hold desirable fruit like love, joy, peace, patience, kindness, goodness, faithfulness, gentleness, and self-control? Or is it filled with the rotten, fermented fruits of hatred, envy, jealousy, anger, bitterness, and self-centeredness?

One of my most favorite decorations in my kitchen area is a huge bowl of fresh fruit. Not only is it homey, appealing to the eye, and fragrant, but those fresh, shiny pieces of fruit seem to say, "Welcome, come in, and help yourself." Oftentimes, however, time slips away and the uneaten fruit eventually begins to develop bruises and rotten spots. If they are not noticeable to the eye, I can certainly smell the difference and know that it is time to examine the fruit bowl and discard the bad or salvage it for fruit salad or such. It amazes me how fast one rotten piece of fruit can contaminate another and then another if not pulled from the bowl. A deteriorating bowl of fruit is anything but appealing and smells up the entire house.

We are called as Christians to be huge fruit bowls overflowing with the fruit of the Holy Spirit who lives inside of us and bursting with the sweet aroma of Christ to God. "For we are a fragrance of Christ to God among those who are being saved and among those who are perishing" (2 Cor. 2:15). Many are perishing, rotting away as the decaying fruit in the bowl. Without Christ in our lives and the Holy Spirit to guide us, we all possess the qualities of stinky fruit and are a foul aroma to God, who desires that none should perish.

Are you doing the best you can with what you have been given, when you can, for Jesus's sake? My fruit bowl is a reminder to me each time I take a fresh piece of fruit from it. I also recall my fleshly spirit when I see the bad spots and bruises and am reminded that my flesh has been crucified with Jesus Christ, giving me the power to overcome my sinful nature. Thank you, Jesus, for perishing so that I can live for you.

You lived out all the fruit of the Spirit as you walked among us.

If we live by the Spirit, let us also walk by the Spirit. (Gal. 5:25)

December 7
It is hard to fail, but it is worse never to have tried to succeed. –Theodore Roosevelt

Have you ever gone blackberry picking? Somehow the biggest, juiciest blackberries are always farther out into the patch. I find myself getting deeper and deeper into the briars to retrieve those luscious little nuggets. It takes a while to fill the bucket, but when it is full, I head home to make a pie or blackberry jelly. With the first taste of either, I know it was all worth the stickers and scratches.

Life is kind of like a berry patch. The good things in life are for the picking but not always easy to reach. There are goals and challenges along the way. Bumps, bruises, scrapes, and scratches are eminent. But when we set out on our journeys with less-than-lofty goals and succeed at nothing, what have we gained?

We must seek God to know His plans for our lives, "plans for welfare and not calamity to give you a future and a hope" (Jer. 29:11). Thus says the Lord as He sent out His message to the Israelite people through His prophet Jeremiah. The message is for us today, as well. He goes on to tell them that when they call on Him "and come and pray to Me, and I will listen to you and you will seek Me and find Me, when you search for Me with all your heart" (vv. 12–13). Their disobedience continued, but He never ceased to warn them before His judgment came.

Something good is always waiting at the end of our journey if our God is the director of our path and we are willing to seek Him first and listen to His instructions. I left a lot of blackberries in the middle of that patch for which I was just not willing to suffer another sticky step. We won't always succeed at everything we attempt, but those are the times when God might be building character and perseverance in us or sending us in another direction.

Never give up, and never give in. Remember, God plus one is a majority. You are in good hands!

**In all your ways acknowledge Him and He will
make your path straight. (Prov. 3:6)**

December 8
Work is the cheapest way to escape boredom.

These are not days in which Christians should be bored and apathetic. To be complacent in times like these is sinful because there is so much to be done for the kingdom. Will Christ's return find us indifferent to the woes of this world and the fate of those who are lost without Him? Will we be caught sleeping as the fields lay white unto harvest? God's call to His laborers is to be diligent about His work, going onto the highways and hedges to proclaim the good news.

In His Sermon on the Mount in Matthew, Jesus explained to the multitudes and to the disciples what He expected of those who follow Him. He used the images of salt and light. His followers are to be the "salt of the earth" and the "light of the world" (5:13, 14). He stated that when salt loses its saltiness, it is tasteless and might as well be thrown out and trampled by men. When those who name the name of Jesus no longer serve as light in a dark world, then darkness consumes the world and pointing the lost to Jesus becomes harder and harder. That has become evident in our world today. I never thought I would live to see people blatantly defiant of God, Christians, and religion in general. We may not realize it and they may not realize it, but the world is screaming for what we have. God wants us to share the good news, adding so much flavor in the world that they cannot refuse our Jesus. When we hide our light under a bushel, quietly delighting in the things of the Lord, we become hoarders of our faith. Not sharing is called selfishness.

The Great Commission found in Matthew 28:19–20 is Jesus's command to us to go and light the world: "Go therefore and make disciples of all the nations, baptizing them in the name of the Father and the Son and the Holy Spirit, teaching them to observe all that I commanded you; and lo, I am with you always, even to the end of the age." Our work is cut out for us. We must not delay for many are perishing while we are enjoying the blessings of salvation.

We must work the works of Him who sent Me, as long as it is day; night is coming, when no man can work. (John 9:4)

December 9
Love spoken in a whisper can be heard.

Our facial expressions can send a message before we ever open our mouths to speak. Our deeds can offer loving support or negative resistance. Our actions can speak louder than any word we say, and our tongues can trip us into hurtful speech or angry outbursts.

In the still of the night, a young boy named Samuel received a prophetic call from God. The scripture tells us that "word from the Lord was rare in those days, visions were infrequent" (1 Sam. 3:1). Samuel was living with Eli the priest and "ministering before the Lord." On this particular night when the voice of the Lord came to him, he thought it was Eli. Three times he ran to Eli. The third time, Eli told him that it was the Lord calling him. He said to answer Him with the words, "Speak, Lord, for thy servant is listening" (v. 9). Samuel spoke these words and received an important prophetic message from the Lord that night. "Thus Samuel grew and the Lord was with him, and let none of his words fail" (v. 19). Love in a whisper can be heard.

Maybe your whisper of love is in your smile. Share it with someone today whom you don't even know. Speak a kind word to someone in the mall or in the checkout line at the grocery store. As the day at work progresses, encourage a fellow worker with a compliment or a pat on the back. God put us all here for one another. His intent was not that we be enemies but that we love our neighbors as we love ourselves. As we seek Him first, we find in ourselves the desire to love others.

Just as God's love and His promise to be with Samuel came to him in a whisper, He speaks to us through His Holy Spirit with the same promise. Listen. You will hear Him whisper your name. "Call to Me, and I will answer you, and I will tell you great and mighty things, which you do not know" (Jer. 33:3). Some call this our telephone call to God, and you can be sure that you will never get a busy signal.

Let no unwholesome word proceed from your mouth, but only such a word as is good for edification according to the need of the moment, that it may give grace to those who hear. (Eph. 4:29)

December 10
A chip on the shoulder is the heaviest load one can carry.

My mother used to tell us not to ever carry a chip on our shoulders because there is always someone around ready to knock it off. It is funny that I knew what she was trying to say and the meaning behind it even at an early age. Maybe it was because she said it at the time that I was in the middle of a sensitive situation. I don't know, but I knew what she meant. Funnier still is that when I hear this expression, I always envision a potato chip on my shoulder.

A sensitive person is fair game to those who are out to make life miserable for those around them. People who are easily offended are not pleasant to be around because you never know what will set them off. The slightest little breeze in a conversation can shake their emotional sensitivity and send that chip flying. They are like a time bomb, and you never know what will set them off or when. Such a personality will wear you out, and most people avoid them. There is an anonymous quote that seems to speak to this: "Two natures beat within my breast; the one is foul, the other blessed. The one I love, the other I hate; the one I feed will dominate."

An irritable spirit is not of God. He calls us to peace and not pride, to humility and not haughtiness, to serenity and not sensitivity. Because our two natures are constantly battling against each other, we find ourselves in conflict. If we allow our foul flesh to control our actions, we react contrary to God's desire and His nature that indwells those who have chosen to walk with Him. "Walk by the Spirit, and you will not carry out the desire of the flesh" (Gal. 5:16). A battle rages between the two natures when we allow the flesh to dominate. Jesus has overcome and set us free from our passion to do wrong, so carrying a chip on our shoulders is not of Him but of our own choosing when we allow that "self" nature to dominate. The transformation of our fleshly nature comes only when we allow Christ to have control.

Cast your burden upon the Lord, and He will sustain you. (Ps. 55:22)

December 11
Reach for perfection. It may never be reached, but it is worth reaching for.

As we live and walk in this world, most people are consumed with staying well and healthy physically, yet many never give a thought to their spiritual health. Ironically, what does it profit a person to try to cling to a long life without Christ with no hope for eternity? Life is not over when we die. We will spend eternity in a real place, either heaven or hell. We make our choice in this life.

Truly healthy people are the ones who choose to walk through their lifetimes with the One who created them, the One who in all wisdom and knowledge knows the very heart and soul of all His creation.

Jesus was the only man who ever walked on this earth who was perfect. Because His Father, God, was without sin, He had no old sin nature. We, however, are born with an old sin nature passed down from Adam through our earthly father. Not only are we naturally sinful, but we begin dying from the time we are born. "Therefore, we do not lose heart, but though our outer man is decaying, yet our inner man is being renewed day by day" (2 Cor. 4:16). We are not to disregard the effort to become perfect as Christ was perfect. Paul explains that "He made Him who knew no sin to be sin on our behalf, that we might become the righteousness of God in Him" (5:21). We are set free from the power of sin because of the atoning provision made through Jesus when we accept Him as Savior.

The human body can be cared for, nurtured, and healed by the greatest physicians of our day. We can even live long lives, but eventually we will die and leave this world. Jesus said, "For what will a man be profited, if he gains the whole world, and forfeits his soul?" (Matt. 16:26). The little dash between our birth dates and our death dates is the only time we have to decide where we will spend eternity. Perfection comes when we make the right choice, heaven, where our perfect bodies await us. Choose Jesus. He honors our every effort to be more like Him.

Therefore you are to be perfect, as your heavenly Father is perfect. (Matt. 5:48)

December 12
A gift is not a gift unless you accept it. A giver is not a giver unless you release it.

"He who did not spare His own Son, but delivered Him up for us all, how will He not also with Him freely give us all things?" (Rom. 8:32)/

All the riches of God manifest themselves in God's greatest gift to the world, Jesus. How can we know the full meaning of such a gift, and how can it become real and personal? God did not just decide one day that He Himself should go to earth in the form of a man; His plan was in place from the beginning of time. In the Garden of Eden, we get our first clue of God's plan of redemption for humankind after sin entered the world as a result of His first children's disobedience (Gen. 3:15). As time progressed, God gave many more foreshadowings of the Christ to come through the pages of His Word. His plan was one of perfection and was carried out as He came to earth through the virgin birth of a baby, Jesus, who was conceived by the Holy Spirit. Everything that God spoke through the Scriptures was culminated in Jesus. "And the Word became flesh, and dwelt among us, and we beheld His glory, glory as of the only begotten from the Father, full of grace and truth" (John 1:14).

As this miraculous promised Messiah grew, He revealed to humankind God's plan for individual lives. He taught and preached with boldness and lived an exemplary life for all to follow. God's ultimate plan led to the cross, where God placed His perfect Lamb to suffer, bleed, and die for the sins of the entire world. What a gift! What a sacrifice! It was here that the gift of redemption was made available for all who would receive it—a perfect sacrifice. No more would the blood of perfect animals have to be sacrificed for sin. Jesus paid the price for sins—past, present, and future. That is Christmas!

But it didn't stop there. The gift goes on! On the third day, Jesus arose from the grave as God said He would, and He sits at the right hand of His Father, always making intercession for those who call on Him. That is Easter!

For God so loved the world, that He gave His only begotten Son, that whoever believes in Him should not perish, but have eternal life. (John 3:16)

December 13
Expect resistance, but pray for miracles! –Corrie ten Boom

Miracles come when we abide in the One who performs miracles. Without Him, we are merciless to accomplish anything, much less supernatural acts of faith and prayer. Jesus went about healing the sick and raising the dead. He instructed His disciples to do the same. Until they learned to abide in Him and pray for power from on high, they were ineffective and incapable of doing the miracles that Jesus desired of them.

In Mark 9, we find one particular miracle that Jesus did. A father brought his son to Jesus explaining that the boy was possessed with a spirit. Whenever it seized him, it would dash him to the ground, sometimes throwing him into the fire or the water. The boy would foam at the mouth and grind his teeth, and his body would stiffen. The unclean spirit was torturing this young man and had been doing so since childhood. The man had taken the boy to Jesus's disciples, but they had been unable to heal him. When Jesus heard this, He scolded his disciples, calling them "unbelieving." The father of the boy, too, was skeptical, saying to Jesus, "If you can do anything, take pity on us and help us!" (v. 22). "Jesus said to him, 'If you can!' All things are possible to him who believes" (v. 23). The anxious father cried out to Jesus, "I do believe; help my unbelief" (v. 24). Jesus then commanded the spirit, and it came out of the boy and He raised him up.

Why did the disciples meet resistance when they tried to heal this young boy? The scripture tells us that they questioned Jesus about it, wanting to know why they could not cast it out. I am sure that they must have been perplexed as any of us would be. Jesus answered them, "This kind cannot come out by anything but prayer" (Mark 9:29). The beginning of abiding is believing and trusting that through Christ we can do all things. Jesus said in John 15:4, "As the branch cannot bear fruit of itself, unless it abides in the vine, so neither can you, unless you abide in Me." Power for all that God calls us to do comes by abiding in Him. Prayer is our direct access to the power source.

Whoever confesses that Jesus is the Son of God, God abides in him, and he in God. (1 John 4:15)

December 14
Love looks through a telescope; envy through a microscope. —Josh Billings

Love is a feeling we cannot explain.
Its focus goes farther than a telescope's frame.
It mirrors the heart and projects joy within,
Love grows more deeply when to others we send. (Author)

Love is one emotion that has no limits. It goes the distance. As stated by the apostle Paul in 1 Corinthians 13:7, love "bears all things, believes all things, hopes all things, and endures all things."

Envy, on the other hand, is an emotion to avoid. Envy dissects another, often taking apart and destroying without pretense a person's character because of jealousy and covetousness. God calls us to love one another in such a way that we are happy for one another and rejoice at the accomplishments of our fellow people. When we love others as Christ loves us, we will be encouragers and not destroyers.

Let's think today of God's amazing love for us and the assurance we have of His peace, His provision, and His promise. As Jesus sat around the table with His disciples for the last time before His departure toward the cross, He sought to comfort them with these words: "Let not your heart be troubled; believe in God, believe also in Me. In My Father's house are many dwelling places; if it were not so, I would have told you; for I go to prepare a place for you. And if I go and prepare a place for you, I will come again, and receive you to Myself; that where I am, there you may be also" (John 14:1–3). Jesus's message to his disciples is His message to us today. He loved us so much that He was willing to die for us so that one day we would spend eternity with Him. That is love!

To love without hypocrisy is God's way. Unless we love God first with all our hearts, minds, and souls, it is impossible to love others with a genuine love as Paul describes.

Let love be without hypocrisy. Abhor what is evil; cling to what is good. Be devoted to one another in brotherly love. (Rom. 12:9–10)

December 15
If you want enemies, excel others; if friends, let others excel you. —Colton, A Dictionary of Thoughts, p. 174

People were comfortable with Jesus when He walked on this earth as long as He kept a low profile and didn't draw any attention to Himself. He grew up humbly in Nazareth, the son of a carpenter, known only as Joseph's son. However, when the word spread that He professed to be God, saying, "He who has seen Me has seen the Father" (John 14:9), He was immediately condemned by those who had set themselves up as the righteous and holy of the day. The scribes and the Pharisees set out to prove Jesus wrong and to discredit His every move. If Jesus had wanted to be popular with all the people, He could have gone along with their teachings and abandoned God's plan for His life. But Jesus *is* God, and He was on earth to honor His Father and to do His will. Jesus knew His Father's plan for His life. He knew that the fulfillment of that plan depended on His obedience. He knew that His Father's plan was for all those who were against Him to be saved from the wrath to come. He never diverged from that plan in order to satisfy His own ego or to play petty games to gain friendship or acceptance from the world or a certain group. He was on a mission from heaven to do His Father's will.

Are you an enemy of God today? The world, meaning those who have not accepted Christ as Savior and Lord of their lives, continues to try to destroy confidence in God's Holy Word, placing doubt and disbelief in the hearts of those who are seeking hope and truth. Jesus said, "He who is not with Me is against Me; and he who does not gather with Me scatters" (Matt. 12:30). As sad as it is, many are enemies of God and do not hold to His truths. Let us seek today not to be friends with the world but instead to embrace the truth that we have in the Bible, God's inspired Word. Abraham was called a friend of God (2 Chron. 20:7). How close are you to the Creator? To be called His friend would certainly be the greatest honor. His name is above every name. He excels all!

Beloved, do not imitate what is evil, but what is good. The one who does good is of God; the one who does evil has not seen God. (3 John 11)

December 16
God believes in me, therefore my situation is never hopeless. –A. Philip Parham, Letting God

A human without Christ is a superficial being. We can dust off, scrub clean, polish up, dress to perfection, smell pleasant, go to the finest places, keep the best company, drive the latest car, say all the right things, and yet still be wretched, poor, and blind. Only the living God can change the inner person. Billy Graham once noted that a communist in Hyde Park, London, pointed to a tramp, and said, "Communism will put a new suit on that man." A Christian standing nearby said, "Yes, but Christ will put a new man in that suit!" (Taken from *Day by Day with Billy Graha*m). "Therefore if any man is in Christ, he is a new creature; the old things passed away; behold new things have come" (2 Cor. 5:17).

Humankind without Christ is hopeless. Don't be satisfied to live your life in armor that cannot be penetrated, concerning yourself with only what is apparent. God wants to penetrate your heart so that the abundant life is yours. "Man looks at the outward appearance, but God looks at the heart" (1 Sam. 16:7). He desires that our hearts be totally His. Then and only then can we know the full and meaningful life that He planned for us. God believes in you. Do you believe in Him?

Today is my mother's birthday. She went to heaven many years ago now, and I still miss her so much. Every once in a while, though, God will give me a little visit with her in a dream. That happened just a few nights ago. It was not a long visit, with not even many words, but I did get a hug. My mother was my best cheerleader. She always made me feel like I made good decisions and brought out the best in me. Like Jesus, she believed in me! We all need that, and we miss it when it is gone. One day I will see her again, and I will tell her what her encouragement meant to me.

The beauty in having a living Savior is that He is always with us. One day we will see Him face to face as I will Mother, but today we can rejoice in the hope that He gives us to live by.

And now Lord, for what do I wait? My hope is in Thee. (Ps. 39:7)

December 17
Do small things with great love. –Mother Teresa

There lived in this century a great servant of the Most High God. She was small in stature, humble in spirit, and poor by earthly standards but tall, mighty, and rich in the eyes of the One who knew her best. Mother Teresa was a servant, a beautiful lady with an endless desire to give of herself to the glory of God. Her greatest work was done in Calcutta, but the impact of her life was felt all over the world. Even those of us who never knew her personally, revered and admired her for her selfless love and devotion to others and her unwavering trust and faith in God.

The world needs the impact of Christians today who love selflessly. As many believers shrink into the mold of the world, it is hard to tell the difference between those who are called to be light and salt and those who live in darkness. Jesus said that the world would come to know Him by the way believers "have love for one another" (John 13:35). In the Song of Solomon we see a picture of God's love for His chosen people, the Israelites, and also the love Christ has for His church. As we feast with Him at His banquet table, His banner over us is love (2:4). There is nowhere that we can go to escape God's love. The psalmist, David, makes us aware of it as he expresses God's omnipresence in Psalm 139. Wherever we are, His love is present. It is constant, it is perfect, it is far-reaching, and it is forgiving. He is Jehovah-Shammah, "the Lord is with us ... Immanuel" (Isa. 7:14). His love for us never fails, and ours for Him and others should not either.

How did a little woman in India impact a world? She never intentionally drew attention to herself or sought the praise of people, yet God used her in a mighty way. Mother Teresa's business card might display her own words: "The fruit of silence is prayer. The fruit of prayer is faith. The fruit of faith is love. The fruit of love is service. The fruit of service is peace." God uses ordinary people to do His greatest work.

Love one another as I have loved you. (John 15:12)

December 18
I never knew how to worship until I knew how to love. –Henry Ward Beecher

I don't know about you, but when I truly worship it brings tears to my eyes. It is overwhelming when you feel the presence of the Holy God and know His awesome love surrounds you. The humility I feel engulfs me, and I feel so unworthy of even His presence.

Possibly this is how the woman at the well felt. In John 4, we see Jesus alone at the well in Samaria. A Samaritan woman comes to the well to draw water, and Jesus asks her for a drink. She questions why Jesus, being a Jew, would ask her for water since Jews had little to do with Samaritans. Jesus proceeds to tell her of her sin and offers to her the living water that He gives so that she would never thirst again. She then requests of the Savior the living water. Before she departs, Jesus reveals to this woman that "true worshipers shall worship the Father in spirit and truth; for such people the Father seeks to be His worshipers" (v. 23). She left Jesus and went to the city, where she invited those in the city to "come, see a man who told me all the things I have ever done" (v. 29). We cannot truly worship Him until we truly know Him.

God's abiding love has no boundaries or limits. It has no height or depth. It goes beyond our imagination and exceeds our greatest expectation. To worship Him is a privilege and an honor reserved for those who abide in Him.

We cannot know true, abiding love and worship until we know the One who gives the living water. In order to love our families, our fellow people, and our brothers and sisters in Christ as we should, we must first love God with our hearts, minds, souls, and strength. Only then can we give Him the true worship that He deserves. And only then will sinners recognize that we have been with Jesus.

The wonders of God are many. His call is to all. We can worship His holiness only when we know His love. His love abounds in all-sufficient grace for His children.

Yea, I have loved thee with an everlasting love. (Jer. 31:3)

December 19
Education is not the filling of a pail, but the lighting of a fire. –William B. Yeats, Guidepost

Humankind's desire to know more about life and the world around us spurs on the inevitable pursuit for higher learning. I once heard it said that we learn something new every day. However, Solomon in the book of Ecclesiastes states, "There is nothing new under the sun" (1:9). Things that are old hat to one might, perhaps, be a revelation to others. Each person learns as it is entrusted or revealed to him or her.

Education opens many doors. In our world, as we know it, an educational degree often means a better job and higher pay. There are many whose education is earned simply from knowledge and ability incurred from time invested in a trade or experience in a workplace. To whatever degree your education has developed, God will overflow and multiply all knowledge and understanding to better the world around you, if you do your part. His purpose in our knowing is that we might share ideas, develop new interests, prosper humankind, and glorify Him.

Solomon was made king over all Israel after his father's death. Solomon loved the Lord and in his prayer asked God to give him "an understanding heart to judge Thy people to discern between good and evil" (1 Kings 3:9). Because of this unselfish prayer, God gave him what he asked for with a few more blessings besides. God blessed him with "both riches and honor" and the promise of longevity if he walked in His ways and kept His commandments (vv. 13,14). Solomon obviously knew that true wisdom comes from God. We can know what is in every book in every library in the world, but if we don't know God personally through His Son, Jesus, then all we have is head knowledge without wisdom. Wise men still seek Him today! "The fool has said in his heart, 'There is no God'" (Ps. 14:1). Unfortunately, Solomon let his old sinful nature take him down the wrong path, and God judged his sin and disobedience. His kingdom was divided, and generations suffered. Wisdom and knowledge are both a blessing if we seek God first and follow His ways.

Let not a wise man boast of his wisdom, and let not the mighty man boast of his might, let not a rich man boast of his riches; but let him who boasts boast of this, that he understands and knows Me. (Jer. 9:23–24)

December 20
A prayerless Christian is a powerless Christian. –Billy Graham

Life would be futile, fruitless, fearful, and frustrating without communion with the living God. Prayer is an open line of communication that allows direct access to the Father. We would not have very successful marriages or lasting friendships if we failed to spend time daily with those we love. Our children would feel unloved and neglected if we never took time to talk and listen to them. God loves each of us so much that He made a way that we can have fellowship with Him, and that is through prayer. It is amazing that we can communicate with Him with a thought, a whisper, groanings too deep for words, or cries of repentance, petition, or praise. However we choose to engage our time alone with Him, He welcomes us. Because in this life we always need a refuge, a safe place to go, He makes Himself constantly available.

Who do you run to in times of trouble? Who is your source of strength in your weakest hours? When trouble, disappointments, heartache, or doubt confronts you, where do you go? "Trust in Him at all times, O people; Pour out your heart before Him; God is a refuge for us" (Ps. 62:8). Many in the Old Testament, like the psalmist, knew where to find comfort and direction. In the New Testament, many followed Jesus, God incarnate, because they knew that He was the refuge that they were seeking. A refuge is a place we look for when we are lost, lonely, heartsick, or desperate. God gave us Jesus so that we could see Him (God) and know that He is real and always ready to help us. He wanted us to know that by surrendering to Jesus, we are never alone. As His Spirit indwells us, the whisper of our prayer invites Him to respond to our needs, and He offers us that refuge that we seek.

We can never have the close relationship with our Maker that we desire until we learn to spend time alone with Him. Daily fellowship with Him through prayer develops a closeness that grows even the weakest vessel and strengthens our awareness of our dependency on Jehovah. We are nothing without Him. Draw near to His throne today and receive strength, healing, purpose, direction, and peace, always remembering praise and thanksgiving! Prayer links the Father to His children, releasing the power of the Holy Spirit.

Pray without ceasing. (1 Thess. 5:17)

December 21
Christmas is the day that holds all time together. –Alexander Smith, Guidepost

Ask any child what his or her favorite holiday is, and most likely the response will be Christmas. Ask any adult the same question, and you will probably get the same answer. Christmas, with all the lights, presents, and excitement, brings out the child in all of us, and our spirits soar with goodwill and generosity. All of these things are wonderful but are far from the real meaning of Christmas.

Christmas holds all time together because of Jesus. Without Jesus's birth, there would be no need to celebrate. There would be no exchanging of gifts, no shining stars on the Christmas tree, and no carols to sing. Jesus is the bridge from the old to the new. He is the light that dispels all darkness. He is the hope for all generations. He is the gift of eternal life. Jesus is the Way, the Truth, and the Life. He is the promised One. Jesus is God incarnate.

From Genesis to Matthew, and the birth of the promised Savior, we are given foreshadowings and promises of the One who would come. He was seen as the One who would crush the head of Satan in Genesis. Noah's ark is a picture of the One who would rescue those who trust in Him, and the Abrahamic covenant is God's covenant with Abraham concerning land (Israel) and many descendants, blessings, and redemption as passed down through Isaac, Jacob, and their descendants. Then there is the Davidic covenant, which points to Jesus as coming through the line of David from the tribe of Judah. In each Old Testament book we get a glimpse of the promised Messiah as God inspired the writers to remind us of His promise. It is an amazing journey to go through the Bible and see the hand of God as He prepared to come to earth from the beginning to establish a new covenant.

Why would God's people not get excited about their promised One coming into the world? It is truly a time to celebrate and thank our Savior for redeeming us. Yes, Jesus is God incarnate, the Word made flesh. We rejoice in His birth and celebrate the world's greatest gift.

And the angel said to them, "Do not be afraid; for behold, I bring you good news of a great joy which shall be for all the people; for today in the city of David there has been born for you a Savior, who is Christ the Lord. (Luke 2:10–11.

December 22
The Spirit of God passes self-sufficiency.

The basic problem of the human race is not lack of education, nor is it the horrible diseases that still plague humankind. Our problems aren't rooted in government or law enforcement, in welfare or a rebellious generation. Our world's woes are symptoms of a deeper problem. What is it? A lack of commitment to, a lack of fear of, and a lack of reverence for Holy God, Jehovah.

When sin entered the world, humans took on the knowledge of good and evil. God tried to spare us of sin and give us all the good that He had created for us, but we chose our way over His way. The consequences of sin are always less gratifying than the moment of pleasure that sin brings. One bite of a piece of forbidden fruit could not have been worth what it cost the generations that have had to suffer because of that one taste. Regret means it is too late.

We don't know why people still feel that they have all the answers even when time and experience have proven time and again, over and over that God's way is the only way. It is a mystery beyond mysteries. The Holy Spirit's power is available to all who will acknowledge and accept it. Jesus makes it clear to us as He did to Paul that His grace is sufficient for us and that His power is made perfect in our weakness (2 Cor. 12:9). What more could we ask for? Forgiveness? He made that possible as well.

Only when we die to ourselves and let Christ live in us can we desire to be committed to His church, His mission, and our Christian walk. When people are born again by the Spirit, they have a reverential fear and awe of the One who made a new creation out of them (2 Cor. 5:17). It is impossible not to worship the One who makes all things new and gives the power to live in this world with a "peace that passes all understanding" (Phil. 4:7). We can claim victory over sin and death.

Let your confidence be in the all-knowing, sufficient God rather than in the human frailty of self. Come to Jesus.

Out of His glorious, unlimited resources He will give you the mighty inner strength of His Holy Spirit. (Eph. 3:16 TLB)

December 23
If God can be fully proved by the human mind, then He is no greater than the mind that proves Him. —Billy Graham

God is greater than humankind can ever imagine or comprehend. From the beginning of the time of humans' existence, they have marveled at the wonders of God and His creation. There are so many attributes of God that it is impossible to list them all in this small space.

I teach an adult Sunday school class, and we are in the fifth year of the three-year *Answers Bible Curriculum: Answers in Genesis* study by Ken Ham. After completing it, we elected to start over and do it again. Hence, we are two years into the second time around. What a blessing and a definite answer to prayer for me personally. In my prayers prior to finding out about this study, I had prayed to God that I wanted to know how the Bible flowed to know Him better and more completely. My answer came through this study, and my class has been just as enthusiastic as I have been, as it has led us through the entire Bible. By cross-referencing the scriptures, we have been able to walk with the prophets as God led them. We have been able to see the hand of God in ways that we had never seen before. This beautiful tapestry of God-inspired scripture, called His Word, is woven together in its entirety to show His amazing greatness and unfathomable deeds. It is totally inspiring, with clarity and truth. From the Creation to the cross, beyond to Revelation, and all in between, we have seen that He is eternal, omnipresent, omnipotent, omniscient, and much, much more. He alone is the Great I Am, the Beginning and the End, the only God, and worthy to be worshipped. God's Word to us is without error.

Through prophets, priests, and kings and through ordinary men and women like you and me, our amazing God has so controlled the universe that He made and yet allowed each person to be the individual he or she was created to be. We were not created to be puppets but living beings made in the image of our Creator (Gen. 1:26). Will our finite minds ever be able to perceive His miraculous ways? Not in this life but in eternity if we choose Him now.

**For since the creation of the world His invisible attributes,
His eternal power and divine nature, have been clearly
seen, being understood through what has been made,
so that they are without excuse. (Rom. 1:20)**

December 24
Jesus is the reason for the season!

As we come to the eve of Christmas day, let us reflect on the greatest of all gifts. Jesus was God's gift to a world that needed a Savior. He was perfect, without sin or blemish. His purpose was redemption, and His mission was salvation for all who would receive it. His message brought hope and He was love incarnate, for God is love.

Christmas is Jesus. He is the reason that we celebrate. His birth, life, death, and resurrection were all offered as the ultimate gift to an undeserving world. For centuries, God had pointed humankind to the day of Christ's birth. Isaiah and the prophet Micah proclaimed His coming. Seven hundred years after Micah's announcement that the Messiah would be born in Bethlehem, we know that it did come to pass just as he said it would. Only God, who knows all, could give that revelation, that prophesy to a man seven hundred years before it happened. "But as for you, Bethlehem Ephrathah, too little to be among the clans of Judah, from you One will go forth for Me to be ruler in Israel. His goings forth are from long ago, from the days of eternity" (Micah 5:2). The Old Testament saints looked for His coming, and we are blessed to look back and see the fulfillment of that prophesy. In the fullness of time, a tiny baby from the tribe of Judah was born in Bethlehem just as God said He would be. And they called His name Jesus (Luke 2:21).

As we look back each year on the events of that amazing first Christmas, we are reminded of the impact that His birth made on this world. Jesus *is* our hope and our greatest gift. He is our confidence.

What will you do with your gift? Will you reject it, pushing it away as if to say you don't need it? Will you take it, set it on a shelf, and never unwrap it to enjoy the freedom of knowing Him? Perhaps you will accept your gift and use it but never give back anything in return. Jesus gave His life, and He wants your heart. As God willingly gave His Son for us, we are called to surrender our all to Him that we might live the abundant life on earth and spend eternity with Him in heaven. His promise is our gift.

And this One will be our peace. (Micah 5:5)

December 25
Trust and obey for there's no other way.

Have you ever thought about why Mary, of all the women of her day, was chosen to be the mother of the Savior of the world? Here was a young peasant girl, a virgin, engaged to be married. I can only imagine that her reputation was impeccable for God to have "found favor" with her (Luke 1:30). But why Mary?

The angel Gabriel was sent from God to a small town in Galilee called Nazareth. His mission was to inform Mary that she had been chosen to conceive by the Holy Spirit and bear a son who would be the Savior of the world. Such an announcement would startle even the most mature young lady. Appalled, she got out the words, "How can it be?" (Luke 1:34). Many thoughts must have been racing through her mind. She was a young Jewish girl; she had heard the prophesy of the promised One. She must have wondered what God could have possibly seen in her for such an honor. Then, too, she must have been somewhat baffled to imagine such a miracle as conception by the Holy Spirit.

Gabriel wasted no time explaining to Mary how God would perform such a miracle, explaining that "nothing will be impossible with God" (v. 37). Immediately Mary totally surrendered to God's plan, saying, "Behold, the bond-slave of the Lord; be it done to me according to your word" (v. 38).

The first Christmas story is filled with total surrender to God's plan. Jesus, Mary, Joseph, Zacharias, Elizabeth, John the Baptist, the innkeeper, the shepherds, the wise men, Gabriel, and a host of angels all bowed before their God to bring about the birth of the new covenant One. God's plan was fulfilled. The long-awaited One was in sight.

Why Mary and all the others? Elizabeth nailed it! "And blessed is she who believed that there would be a fulfillment of what had been spoken to her by the Lord" (Luke 1:45). Mary *believed* God, and so did all the rest. And blessed are we, as well, if we believe that God will do what He says He will do. That is faith.

Jesus said to him, "Because you have seen Me, have you believed? Blessed are they who did not see, and yet believed." (John 20:29)

December 26
Wise men still seek Him today.

It took the wise men a long time to get to Jesus. They kept their eyes on the star that led them to where the young child was. God made the path bright and the road signs clear. The magi were detained by Herod as he picked them to determine the whereabouts of Jesus. They heard the king out but continued on their way, following the star that went before them. God's bright, shining star led them to the very feet of the Savior. They rejoiced, fell down, and worshipped Him. They brought amazing gifts and presented them to the young king. When the time came for them to return to their country, God warned them not to return to Herod but to go home another way. Herod's motives were evil. Again their wisdom was profound. They listened to God and obeyed Him rather than a man.

How wise are you? Do you seek your answers and make your decisions based on human findings or on God's truths? Do your choices depend on what the crowd is doing—the world's way? God sees the big picture, and we need to be wise enough to listen and go where He leads. He has our best interest at heart, and His plan is the best plan. We must seek Him first before the fact, not after the fact.

Our world is filled with smart, intelligent people. Many have come and gone who knew how to invent things, operate things, perform surgeries, analyze the stars and planets, build massive skyscrapers, rule nations, and on and on. God gives people the ability to do many things. However, humans cannot have wisdom apart from God. "The fear of the Lord is the beginning of wisdom, and the knowledge of the Holy One is understanding" (Prov. 9:10). Yes, wise people still seek Him today. They are those who fear Him and desire to follow His ways. May we come to Him, receive the gift of wisdom, and worship Him.

Jesus came to be the light of the world. Be wise and follow the light. He will never lead you astray, nor will He leave you or forsake you.

Where is He who has been born King of the Jews? For we saw His star in the east, and have come to worship Him. (Matt. 2:2)

December 27
Get off your blessed assurance and go to work for the Lord! —Harris Malcolm

We can thank God for giving us a full picture of His plan through His Word, the Bible. Our confidence lies not in the predictions of humankind but in the prophesies of Almighty God.

Isaiah was prophesying in the days of King Hezekiah. He was a trusted adviser to this king, who was a good king and one who received godly counsel well, unlike his father, Ahaz, before him. When Ahaz died and Hezekiah became king, Hezekiah tried to turn things around in Judah, getting rid of idol worship and helping the people to listen to God's message from the prophets. Isaiah and Micah were given valuable prophetic messages, not only for the people of Judah and Israel but for each of us today. Seven hundred years before Jesus was born, these prophets were talking and telling about His birth. Isaiah gives us a picture of Jesus's birth and also a clear prophesy of the cross where Jesus, the Suffering Servant, would die for the sins of all humankind. Isaiah's prophesy even gives us the name of Jesus, Immanuel, which means "God with us" (Isa. 7:14).

Prophets of old worked hard and suffered much for God's work to be carried on. We are blessed to be able to look back over more than six thousand years of history, from the beginning of time until now, and see how our amazing God accomplished all things from Creation to our present time. This is real history that we can believe in. All of God's prophetic announcements have been delivered in His timing. Imagine, seven hundred years before the birth of Jesus, God again gave a prophetic word pointing the world toward the coming of the Messiah. God in human form came to dwell among us, Immanuel. His presence with us would bring redemption for all who would trust in Him, as His obedience to His Father unfolded. Jesus was 100 percent God and 100 percent man. He was perfect and without sin. He met all of the qualifications for the perfect sacrifice for the redemption of humankind. He willingly surrendered to the Father's plan and became our sin bearer.

Thank you, Jesus, for coming to earth that first Christmas and for your finished work on the cross.

**For you have been called for this purpose, since
Christ also suffered for you, leaving you an example
for you to follow in His steps. (1 Peter 2:21)**

December 28
God has given us two hands—one to receive with and the other to give with. —Billy Graham

Being a good receiver is just as important as being a good giver. Step back today and see how you have received your blessings. Are you grateful, or do you take things for granted? Are you a tither or a hoarder of God's tithe? Do you glorify God with your spiritual gifts, or do you use them everywhere but in His kingdom's work? Do you bless others or expect to be blessed? Do you acknowledge God as the giver of all good things, or do you pat yourself on the back for all *you* have accomplished?

I don't know too much about football, but when our grandson, Reese, was playing on his high school team, I tried to learn a little more about the game. His dad had been a center in his day, so I was not totally ignorant of the game. As quarterback, Reese had a great responsibility to be the giver of the ball to the running back who was most open or nearest the goal. His receivers were very important to him as he shifted around after the snap to get his throw off to avoid getting sacked. Giving it to the right player at the right time could mean yards gained or even a touchdown. His accuracy in throwing meant a lot in terms of whether his receivers were able to catch the football. Both positions were important in order to move the ball down the field. Of course, those who guarded and protected them from the opposing team's players were extremely valuable, as well. I guess what I am trying to say is that even in this scenario, giving and receiving are both essential. Our grandson always knew how relevant his players were to his position and he appreciated them, but he knew the ultimate responsibility fell on him.

God wants to bless His children and will as long as we have a thankful heart and are good stewards, receivers, of all He gives. If we are in churches that are not faithful over monetary gifts, buildings, properties, and so on that were given to them for ministry, choosing instead to squander, tear down, or use them for lesser things, then we are not being good receivers. God wants His children to be good givers *and* good receivers.

Every good thing bestowed and every perfect gift is from above, coming down from the Father of lights. (James 1:17)

December 29
Make all you can; keep all you can; and give all you can. –John Wesley

What can a Christian theologian tell us about money? Apparently, a great deal. John Wesley was a leader in the Methodist movement in the 1700s. According to his biography, he not only taught his financial principles but lived by them, as well.

God desires for us to be prosperous if we go by the rules of good stewardship. Being prosperous also carries with it many responsibilities.

I recently read in the newspaper of a man who started out with modest means and went on to build his company into a multimillion-dollar business. When he sold his business for millions, he set out to divide half of the profits of the sale among his five hundred–plus employees. He expressed that his generosity stemmed from the fact that his employees had been faithful to the company over the years, and he credited them with helping him to make it the successful business it had become. Many wrote in to tell him how they admired his kindness and humanity.

All that we have is God's anyway. Many would like to take credit for their success, but all of our blessings come from the giver of all things. "He owns the cattle on a thousand hills, the wealth in every mine. He owns the rivers and the rocks and reels, the sun and moon that shine," as the little song I learned in my primary Sunday school class says (Ps. 50:10).

Whatever God blesses us with, may we always remember to give back a portion to His kingdom's work through our churches. The scripture teaches us that we are to pay our taxes and give back to God. "And Jesus said to them, 'Render to Caesar the things that are Caesar's, and to God the things that are God's'" (Mark 12:17). That is our first obligation. After that it is wise to be frugal, saving and giving. God generously gives, but He expects us to be good stewards of all that we acquire while on this earth. Adrian Rogers said, "It's about time we stopped buying things we don't need with money we don't have to impress people we don't like." These are wise words from another man who lived well.

Do not lay up for yourselves treasures upon earth, where moth and rust destroy, and where thieves break in and steal. But lay up for yourselves treasures in heaven, where neither moth nor rust destroys, and where thieves do not break in or steal; for where your treasure is, there will your heart be also. (Matt. 6:19–21)

December 30
Be killing sin or it will be killing you. –John Owen

In 2 Samuel 12, God sent His prophet Nathan on a mission. Nathan was to expose David's sin by telling him a parable that would lead him toward repentance.

If Nathan had not confronted David about his sin, would he have ever turned, or would he have continued on the wrong course, believing no one would know or that he could live as he wanted? We don't know. But God loved David just as he loves each of us. God sent the prophet to confront David concerning his affair with Bathsheba. "The thing that David had done was evil in the sight of the Lord" (2 Sam. 11:27). God knew that unless David could see his sin as it was and repent, he would never be useful in God's kingdom. Jesus would come from the house and lineage of David, fulfilling the covenant God had made with David (7:12–16). It was important that David get back on track.

Who is God laying on your heart today that is living a sinful lifestyle? So many times we listen to the world's way concerning confronting sin. We hear the words, "You are judging." No. We are not judging people when they are openly and blatantly living in sin. Condoning by our silence what God has already condemned is what we do when we ignore sinful lifestyles and actions. Even David tried to hide his sinful acts. When sin is displayed like a badge, people have judged themselves already. Ignoring and turning our backs on sin makes us a party to sin. Being an accomplice to sinful behavior and disobedience is certainly not God's way.

God calls us to care about the souls of others enough to approach them in love and lead the wayward sheep back to the fold. If they are lost and without Christ, then we have the opportunity to point them to the Good Shepherd. "My brethren, if any among you strays from the truth, and one turns him back, let him know that he who turns a sinner from the error of his way will save his soul from death, and will cover a multitude of sins" (James 5:19). Is loving others worth the risk?

**Therefore, to one who knows the right thing to do,
and does not do it, to him it is sin. (James 4:17)**

December 31
But seek ye first the kingdom of God and His righteousness; and all these things shall be added unto you. —Matt. 6:33 KJV

As you pass into another year, I leave you with these words from Jesus Himself. As we have sought Him and His righteousness first throughout this year, my prayer is that your desire to know Him better and seek Him out in the beauty of His holiness will persist into yet another year. May you study His Word with the zeal of a hungry beast, discovering the truths of God like never before. As the prophet Jeremiah lamented in his prayer to God, "Thy words were found and I ate them, and Thy words came for me a joy and the delight of my heart" (15:16). So may you clothe yourself in His righteousness and learn from Him. In Him is found all peace, hope, security, blessings, faithfulness, joy, encouragement, love, and all else that is good and right. His longing is that we feed on His Word as we walk by the Spirit, and in doing so, we will not desire the things of the flesh. The saved and unsaved alike struggle with the influence of evil in this world. God is our strength to ward off the strongholds that pull and tug at those with the best intentions.

I hope that these words from Jesus will be your theme for the New Year. Matthew 6:33 comes as a promise from Jesus, and we can stand on His promises because they never fail. He is Jehovah-Shammah, the Lord is with us.

Maybe you are reading this today and you have not made the choice to follow Him. Maybe you do not know what it means to seek Him first, His kingdom, and His righteousness. In order for us to dwell in His kingdom, whether while on earth or in heaven, we must be in right standing with Jesus. Jesus is all the words of God made flesh (John 1:14). The culmination of all the law, all the promises, all grace, and all truth came together in the person of God in the flesh, Jesus. We cannot get to God unless we accept Jesus as our Savior. He made the way for us to be saved when He went to the cross, died, and rose again. Jesus said, "Unless one is born again he cannot see the kingdom of God" (John 3:3). The new birth invites the Spirit to indwell us, and then we "may in Him have eternal life" (v. 15). Jehovah-Tsidkenu, the Lord is our righteousness (Jer. 23:6).

For God so loved the world, that He gave His only begotten Son, that whoever believes in Him should not perish, but have eternal life. (John 3:16)

This I Pray

Thank you, God, for a new day and for that day when we will see You and dwell in Your presence. May we seek You *today* so that we may see You on *that* day. There is no greater hope than to know that You wait for me and look forward to my dwelling with You forever. My prayer today is that all may know that You wait for them, as well, and anticipate a reunion of the saints as we come together on high. As You have gone to prepare our place, let us too prepare to meet You by *seeking you first* above all others. Hear us as we come to You first in the morning to receive Your mercies and Your instructions for each new day as we dwell in our earthly tents. As we shut down at nighttime, let us rest in Your loving arms for peaceful restoration. You only are our peace.

The Lord is my strength and my shield. My heart trusts in Him, and I am helped; Therefore my soul exults, and with my song I shall thank Him. (Ps. 28:7)

I love you, Gail

About the Author

Gail Gleaton Bell is the wife of David and the mother of three adult children, Todd (Kim), Tessa (Patrick), and Shane (Tara). She loves spending time with her ten grandchildren, Hillary (J.B.), Wesley, Carson (Savannah), Reese, Wesley, Lanier, Molly, Annie, Rhett, and Patrick, and two great-grandchildren, Jubilee and Benson. Serving God through her church, Dawson First Baptist Church, is a privilege that she does not take lightly. She serves as an adult Sunday School teacher, chairman of the prayer ministry team, soloist and member of the adult choir and delights in mission work through WMU. Gail enjoys cooking for family and friends, managing her rental property and selling Mary Kay Cosmetics. Life is busy and God is good!

Thus says the Lord, "Let not a wise man boast of his wisdom, and let not the mighty man boast of his might, let not a rich man boast of his riches; but let him who boasts boast of this, that he understands and knows Me, that I am the Lord who exercises lovingkindness, justice, and righteousness on earth; for I delight in these things," declares the Lord. (Jer. 9:23–24)

Printed in the United States
By Bookmasters